CENSORED

25TH ANNIVERSARY EDITION

CENSORED 2001

25 Years of Censored News

and the Top Censored Stories of the Year

PETER PHILLIPS & PROJECT CENSORED

INTRODUCTION BY NOAM CHOMSKY
CARTOONS BY TOM TOMORROW

SEVEN STORIES PRESS
New York / London / Sydney / Toronto

A Seven Stories Press First Edition

Seven Stories Press
140 Watts Street
New York, NY 10013
http://www.sevenstories.com

In Canada:
Hushion House, 36 Northline Road, Toronto, Ontario M4B 3E2

In the U.K.:
Turnaround Publisher Services Ltd., Unit 3, Olympia Trading Estate,
Coburg Road, Wood Green, London N22 6TZ

In Australia:
Tower Books, 9/19 Rodborough Road, Frenchs Forest NSW 2086

College professors may order examination copies of
Seven Stories Press titles for a free six-month trial period.
To order, visit www.sevenstories.com/textbook,
or fax on school letterhead to (212) 226-1411.

ISSN 1074-5998

9 8 7 6 5 4 3 2 1

Book design by Cindy LaBreacht

Printed in the U.S.A.

Dedication

MARY LIA-PHILLIPS

A dark haired beauty sitting among the fifty
Near the window, quiet and reserved
Evidence of wise maturity
As windows offer options to dull lectures
Each wondering about the other
But respecting the formality of professor and student.
Three years and two books,
the dark haired beauty reappears.
Nice to see you again, let's coffee and chat,
Sandpiper dinners, beach walks, midnight hikes,
introductions to chickens and former selves,
we find love.
Joining forever, our families merging,
Lives intertwined, and expanded,
Symphonies of caring and commitment.

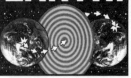

Contents

THIS MODERN WORLD

by TOM TOMORROW

IN A SECRET D.N.C. LAB, ADJUSTMENTS ARE MADE TO THE *GOREBOT 2000* ...

ALL RIGHT, LET'S TEST THE NEW SOFTWARE.

CLICK--WHIRR--AND SO, MY FEL-LOW AMERICANS, IT IS CLEAR THAT THE DEATH PENALTY IS *MORALLY ABHORRENT!* THE POTENTIAL FOR A MISCARRIAGE OF JUSTICE IS SIM-PLY *TOO GREAT!*

?

MY OPPONENT CLAIMS TO BE CERTAIN THAT AN IN-NOCENT PERSON HAS NEVER BEEN EXECUTED IN TEXAS--BUT DEFENSE LAWYERS THERE HAVE *SLEPT* THROUGH DEATH PENALTY TRIALS! OTHERS HAVE BEEN *DRUNK* OR HIGH ON *COCAINE!* ONE THIRD OF THEM WERE EVENTUALLY *DISBARRED!*

WHAT THE--

SOMEBODY *DO* SOMETHING!

ONE WITNESS WAS RELEASED FROM A *PSYCHIATRIC WARD* TO TESTIFY! ANOTHER WAS A PATHOLOGIST WHO *ADMITTED* FAKING AUTOPSY REPORTS! MY FRIENDS, WE CANNOT GRANT SUCH AN INCOMPETENT AND CORRUPT JUDICIAL SYSTEM THE POWER OF LIFE AND DEATH! WE *MUST* ABOLISH THE DEATH PENAL-TY ONCE AND FOR--*CLICK--WHIRRR*--

HERE--I THINK I'VE GOT IT--

FOR THE LOVE OF GOD, *HURRY!*

CLICK! THE DEATH PENALTY IS AN *EFFECTIVE DE-TERRENT!* THE SYSTEM *WORKS!* CLICK! THE SYS-TEM *WORKS!* CLICK! THE SYSTEM *WORKS!*

THAT'S MORE LIKE IT.

LET'S BE A LITTLE MORE *CAREFUL* NEXT TIME, GENTLEMEN! THIS IS THE *GOREBOT,* FOR CHRISSAKES-- NOT THE *NADERBOT!*

Preface

By ignoring critical social issues, mainstream corporate media dismisses democratic values in the United States.

Since the fall of 1999 there have been four major political demonstrations in the United States. The cities of Seattle, Washington, D.C., Philadelphia, and Los Angeles each hosted either a major political party convention or global economic institution meetings where thousands of activists protested, engaged in nonviolent civil disobedience, and in rare, often provoked cases, caused superficial damage to public and private property.

Corporate media has labeled the protesters as unorganized groups of radical environmentalists, single-issue extremists, and anarchists bent on disrupting social order. The extensive involvement of unions and labor in Seattle has generally been explained as a one-time aberration, and the global trade issues focusing on NAFTA and the WTO have been mostly forgotten.

The corporate media was particularly vehement in its denigration of the demonstrations at the Democratic and Republican conventions, presenting the demonstrators as acting out radical fantasies in a desperate attempt to sustain the momentum of Seattle.

At first glance it may seem that Mumia rallies, anti-water-fluoridation teach-ins, marches against Occidental Oil's threats to the U'wa tribe, police brutality demonstrations, and black-clad anarchists have little in common and no centralized leadership. But a deeper analysis will determine that each of the protesting individuals and social action groups share a common disdain for institutionalized power structures that service the corporate elites of the world at the expense of working people and the environment.

The demonstrators represent millions of us who recognize that the New World Order does not allow for grassroots democratic processes, so we had better create our own. The New World Order preaches globalization, corporate growth, and individual belt tightening, while proceeding with building institutions for top-down, public-private partnerships to control and regulate the behaviors of the global masses. But we aren't buying what they're selling.

Fifty-five million nonvoters in the U.S. already recognize that our corporate-dominated two-party system has been corrupted by money and have opted out of the charade. They recognize that our collective ability to participate has been structured out of the political decision-making process. They want to take that power back.

The activists in Philadelphia and Los Angeles speak for the millions of us who had to work overtime to make ends meet in our bifurcating economy. We silently cheer the demonstrators and daily resist bureaucratic rules and top-down management in our own ways. Overt resistance to national and global power structures is a manifestation of the deep mistrust working people feel toward governments and their mega-corporation partners.

The activists are a new progressive movement focusing on globalization. They represent a vanguard of political actors emerging from the grassroots of hometown USA. They share a spirit of resistance that is manifesting itself in every country in the world. They have successfully used the Internet and satellite links to stream e-mail, radio, and TV images globally and continue to work toward building real news systems independent of corporate media.

It is in the spirit of resistance that Project Censored presents it 25th anniversary edition and the Top Censored Stories of 2001. Corporate and governmental abuses of power are a dominant theme in the news stories that continue to not be covered by our ten huge media conglomerates in the United States. The usual culprits are present in this year's list of the top 25 most censored news stories. Reading them reminds us that corporate media fails to keep the American public informed of important issues in our society.

Noam Chomsky does an outstanding job in his introduction, putting into context the macrosociopolitical issues the corporate media likes to ignore, and Ed Herman in Chapter 6 adds to this theme by giving specific comparative examples that demonstrate media bias in framing the news. Chapter 7, by Norman Solomon, focuses on the danger that continued corporate media domination poses to our withering democracy. And we are very pleased to include a never-before published interview with Walter Cronkite on the crisis in corporate media.

The antiglobalization demonstrations this past year are such an important underreported news story that we have included three chapters that address various aspects of these events. Chapter 8, by Marrianne Manilov, covers media's continuing dismissal of the important issues in the antiglobalization movement, and in Chapter 11 Eric Galatas briefs us on the success of independent media centers all over the world as alternatives to the corporate media. Robert Hackett, from MediaWatch Canada, describes in Chapter 9 the emerging media democratization movement and its links to antiglobalization resistance worldwide.

We are also very pleased to include, in Chapter 3, original articles from independent scholars on former Censored stories. Michael Parenti provides an update on the children of Iraq. Michel Chossudovsky writes on HAARP, and how USAID's promotions of genetically modified seeds are creating famine in Ethiopia. Sam Epstein and Barbara Seaman both review the issues of cancer-causing substances in our environment, and Larry Shaw presents an update on media coverage of the WTO.

The 2000 presidential election exposed the serious failures of this process in our country. A continuing undercovered story from the election is that of African-American disenfranchisement in Florida. Chapter 2, Democracy in Chains, is the Director's Choice for the most important undercovered story in the last ten weeks of 2000.

We are pleased to include in this 25th anniversary edition a review of all of Project Censored's stories since 1976. We have also compiled a full update on the history of Junk Food News, a feature that was started by Carl Jensen in 1984.

Project Censored, all 175 of us, are proud to present you with this volume dedicated to motivating social action and freedom of information. The top award-winning publications are listed in Appendix A, and we encourage you to subscribe to as many of them as you can afford. You can become a freedom of information/First Amendment activist by joining one or several of the media activist groups listed in Appendix B. Also visit Project Censored's web site at www.projectcensored.org for weekly updates on censored news.

Peter Phillips
Director Project Censored
Sonoma State University

THIS MODERN WORLD

by TOM TOMORROW

A LOT OF AMERICANS ARE PRETTY DARNED SUSPICIOUS ABOUT THIS WHOLE *CENSUS* THING--AND IT'S *NO WONDER!*

HAH! THEY WANT TO KNOW HOW MUCH *MONEY* I MAKE! ANYONE WHO WOULD WILLINGLY HAND OVER *THAT* KIND OF PERSONAL INFORMATION TO THE GOVERNMENT WOULD HAVE TO BE SOME KIND OF--

--TAXPAYER?

OH, WHO ASKED *YOU*?

CITIZENS WHO RECEIVED THE *LONG FORM* HAVE *PARTICULAR* CAUSE FOR CONCERN!

OH SURE, THEY *SAY* THEY WANT TO KNOW WHEN WE GO TO WORK SO THEY CAN BETTER MANAGE THE FLOW OF RUSH HOUR *TRAFFIC*--

--BUT WHAT IF THEY JUST WANT TO KNOW WHEN THEY CAN *BREAK INTO OUR HOUSES* AND *ROB US BLIND*?

DIDJA EVER THINK OF *THAT*?

WHY--WHO *KNOWS* HOW THE INFORMATION THEY WANT COULD BE USED AGAINST US?

YEAH--WHY WOULD THEY CARE IF WE LIVE IN A *MOBILE HOME* OR NOT--

--UNLESS THEY WANT TO KNOW WHERE THEIR SECRET *WEATHER CONTROL MACHINES* SHOULD SEND THE *TORNADOES*?

SO FOR GOD'S SAKE, PEOPLE--THROW THOSE CENSUS FORMS *AWAY*--BEFORE IT'S *TOO LATE!*

TOM TOMORROW SAYS HE RENTS AN APARTMENT WITH *COMPLETE* PLUMBING FACILITIES-- AND HAS A TELEPHONE CAPABLE OF MAKING *AND* RECEIVING CALLS!*

AND THE FOOL GAVE US THIS INFORMATION *VOLUNTARILY*? WELL, HE'LL CERTAINLY REGRET *THAT* SOON ENOUGH!

BWAH HA HA HA!

CENSUS DEPARTMENT
DIVISION OF GLOBAL DOMINATION

* ACTUAL LONG FORM QUESTIONS.

Acknowledgments

Project Censored is managed through the department of sociology in the School of Social Sciences at Sonoma State University. We are an investigative sociology project dedicated to freedom of information thoughout the United States.

More than 175 people were directly involved in the production of this year's *Censored 2001: The 25th Anniversary Edition.* University and program staff, students, faculty, community experts, research interns, funders, and our distinguished national judges all contributed time, energy, and money to make this year's book an important resource for the promotion of freedom of information in the United States.

I want to personally thank those close friends and intimates who have counseled and supported me through another year of Project Censored. Most important, my wife Mary Lia-Phillips, who as my lover, friend, and companion lives with Project Censored on a daily basis. The men in the Green Oaks breakfast group, Noel Byrnes, Bob Butler, Rick Williams, Colin Godwin, and Bill Simon are personal advisors and confidants who help with the difficult decisions. Thanks go also to Carl Jensen, founder of Project Censored, and director for 20 years. His continued advice and support are very important to me and our work. Trish Boreta, Project Development Officer, is an important daily associate administrator of the Project. Her dedication and enthusiasm is greatly appreciated. Katie Sims, supervisor of our story management team, deserves a special thank-you; despite my tendency toward total disorganization, she is ever vigilant influence in the other direction.

A huge thanks goes to the people at Seven Stories Press. They are more than a publishing house, but rather close friends, who help edit our annual book in record time, and serve as advisors in the annual release process of the "Most *Censored* Stories." Publisher Dan Simon is an understanding good friend, and deserves full credit for assembling an excellent suppport crew including operations director Jon Gilbert, editors M. Astella Saw and Greg Ruggiero, associate editor Lazar Bloch, and book designer Cindy LaBreacht. Thanks also to the great sales staff at Publishers Group West, who see to it that every independent bookstore, chain store, and wholesaler in the U.S. are aware of *Censored* each year. Thanks to Hushion House, our distributors in Canada, as well as Turnaround Publishers Services Ltd. in Great Britain.

Thank you to Noam Chomsky, who wrote the introduction this 25th anniversary edition. He served as a national judge for close to two decades and is a long time supporter of the Project.

Thanks also to the authors of the most *Censored* stories for 2001, for without their often unsupported efforts as investigative news reporters and writers the stories presented in *Censored* would not be possible.

Our guest writers this year are Ed Herman, Norman Solomon, Sam Epstein, Michael Parenti, Larry Shaw, Barbara Seaman, Michel Chossudovsky, Robert Hackett, Eric Galatas, and Marrianne Manilov. They each wrote an original article on an important contemporary media issue or an important update on a prior censored story.

This year's book again features the cartoons of Tom Tomorrow. "This Modern World" appears in more than 90 newspapers across the country. We are extremely pleased to use Tom Tomorrow's wit and humor throughout the book.

Our national judges, some of whom have been involved with the Project for 25 years, are among the top experts in the country concerned with First Amendment freedoms and media. We are honored to have them as the final voice in ranking the top 25 most *Censored* Stories.

An important thanks goes to our major donors and funders, including: Anita Roddick and The Body Shop International, Working Assets, Office of the President & Office of the Provost at Sonoma State University, School of Social Sciences at Sonoma State University, and several hundred donors from throughout the United States. Without their core financial support Project Censored simply could not continue.

Members of the Organization of News Ombudsmen deserves a thank you for their continuing assistance with identifying the most superfluous stories published in our Junk Food News chapter.

This year we had 89 faculty/community evaluators assisting with our story assessment process. These expert volunteers read and rated the nominated stories for national importance, accuracy, and credibility. In November, they participated with the students in selecting the final top 25 stories for 2000.

Most of all, we need to recognize the Sonoma State University students in the Media Censorship, Sociology 435 class who worked long hours in the library conducting coverage reports on more than 200 underpublished stories. Each has become an expert in library database research. Student education is the most important aspect of Project Censored, and we could not do this work without their dedication and effort.

Patrick Kelleher is our webmaster and an excellent computer problem solver. The Project Censored web site at www.projectcensored.org has just boomed under his supervision.

Lastly, I want to thank our readers, and supporters from all over the United States and the world. Hundreds of you nominated stories for consideration as the most *Censored* news story of the year. Thank you very much!

PROJECT CENSORED STAFF AND STUDENT INTERNS 2001

Peter Phillips, Ph.D.	Director
Carl Jensen, Ph.D.	Director Emeritus and Project Advisor
Trish Boreta	Development Officer
Victoria Calkins	Writing Team Coordinator
Pat Thurston	Radio Team Coordinator: Host of *For the Record*
Laurel Holmstrum	Fiscal Planning
Kimberly Lyman	Bookkeeping
Katie Sims	Story Management Team Leader
Patrick Kelleher	Webmaster
Crystal Edney	Adminstrative Support
Julieta Mancilla	Student Assistant

COMMUNITY VOLUNTEERS: Dennis Bernstein, Paul Strurud, Bonnie Faulkner, Mary Lia-Phillips, Ron Liskey, Naomi Igra

TEACHING ASSISTANTS: Victoria Calkins, Katie Anderson, Jeremiah Price

FALL 2000 INTERNS: Katie Anderson, Amy Bonczenwski, Patrick Cadell, Heidi Chesney, Andrew Cochrane, Bonnie Faulkner, Michelle Fleming, Gabriel Frobs, Sharone Goldman, Kathy McMills, Scott Newhall, Michael Oliva, Christine Palella, Karen Parlette, Steve Quartz, Lynn Ritzman, Zach Sartin, Ben Siino, Jeffifer Swift, Jeff Vandevoir, Jaleah Winn

SUT JHALLY, Professor of communications, and executive director of The Media Education Foundation, University of Massachusetts

NICHOLAS JOHNSON,* Professor, College of Law, University of Iowa; former FCC Commissioner (1966–1973); author of *How To Talk Back To Your Television Set*

RHODA H. KARPATKIN, president of Consumers Union, nonprofit publisher of *Consumer Reports*

CHARLES L. KLOTZER, editor and publisher emeritus, *St. Louis Journalism Review*

NANCY KRANICH, Associate Dean of the New York University Libraries, and president-elect of the American Library Association

JUDITH KRUG, director of the Office for Intellectual Freedom, American Library Association; editor, *Newsletter on Intellectual Freedom; Freedom to Read Foundation News;* and the *Intellectual Freedom Action News*

ROBERT McCHESNEY, research Associate Professor in the Institute of Communications Research and the Graduate School of Library and Information Science at the University of Illinois at Urbana-Champaign; author of *Rich Media Poor Democracy, Telecommunications, Mass Media, and Democracy: The Battle for the Control of U.S. Broadcasting 1928–35,* and other books on media

WILLIAM LUTZ, Professor of English, Rutgers University; former editor of *The Quarterly Review of Doublespeak;* author of *The New Doublespeak: Why No One Knows What Anyone's Saying Anymore* (1966)

JULIANNE MALVEAUX, PH.D., economist and columnist, King Features, and Pacifica radio talk show host

JACK L. NELSON,* Professor, Graduate School of Education, Rutgers University; author of 16 books and over 150 articles including *Critical Issues in Education* (1996)

MICHAEL PARENTI, political analyst, lecturer, and author of several books including *Inventing Reality; The Politics of News Media; Make Believe Media; The Politics of Entertainment;* and numerous other works

DAN PERKINS, political cartoonist, creator of Tom Tomorrow

BARBARA SEAMAN, lecturer; author of *The Doctors' Case Against the Pill, Free and Female, Women and the Crisis in Sex Hormones,* and others; cofounder of the National Women's Health Network.

ERNA SMITH, Chair of the journalism department at San Francisco State University, author of several studies on mainstream news coverage on people of color

SHEILA RABB WEIDENFELD, * President of D.C. Productions, Ltd.; former press secretary to Betty Ford

HOWARD ZINN, Professor Emeritus of political sicience at Boston University, author of *A People's History of the United States; You Can't be Neutral on a Moving Train: A Personal History of Our Times;* and *The Zinn Reader: Writings on Disobedience and Democracy*

* Indicates having been a Project Censored Judge since its founding in 1976

PROJECT CENSORED 2000 FACULTY, STAFF, AND COMMUNITY EVALUATORS

Julie Allen, Ph.D.	English
Milinda Barnard, Ph.D.	Communication Studies
Philip Beard, Ph.D.	German Studies
Marty Bennett, M.A.	Santa Rosa Community College, Labor History
Barbara Bloom, Ph.D.	Criminal Justice Administration
Andrew Botterell, Ph.D.	Philosophy
Maureen Buckley	Counseling
Elizabeth Burch, Ph.D.	Communications Studies
Jim Burkland	Community Expert, Geology
Noel Byrnes, Ph.D.	Sociology
Barbara Butler, MLIS, MBA	Acting Director of Library
James R. Carr, Ph.D.	University of Nevada, Geology
Ray Castro, Ph.D.	Social Policy
Liz Close, Ph.D.	Nursing
Lynn Cominsky, Ph.D.	Physics, Astronomy
Steven Coombs, Ph.D.	Education
Bill Crowley, Ph.D.	Geography
Victor Daniels, Ph.D.	Psychology
Laurie Dawson	Labor & Education

Randy Dodgen, Ph.D.	History, Asia
Peter Duffy, J.D.	Community Expert, Politics & Law
Fred Fletcher	Community Expert, Labor Issues
Dorothy Friedel, Ph.D.	Geography
Richard Gale, Ph.D.	Hutchins School
Susan Garfin, Ph.D.	Sociology
Patricia Lee Gibbs, Ph.D.	Sociology, Foothill College
Robert Girling, Ph.D.	Business, Economics
Mary Gomes, Ph.D.	Psychology
Myrna Goodman, Ph.D. Candidate	Sociology/Gender Studies
Scott Gordon, Ph.D.	Computer Science
Diana Grant, Ph.D.	Criminal Justice Administration
Velma Guillory-Taylor, Ed.D.	Women and Gender Studies
Debra Hammond, Ph.D.	History of Science
Dan Haytin, Ph.D.	Sociology
Laurel Holmstrom	Sociology Department
Sally Hurtado, M.S.	Education
Pat Jackson, Ph.D.	Criminal Justice Administration
Thomas Jacobson, J.D.	Environmental Studies and Planning
Sherril Jaffe, M.A.	English
Mary King, M.D.	Community Volunteer
Jeanette Koshar, Ph.D.	Nursing
John Kramer, Ph.D.	Political Science
Virginia Lea, Ph.D.	Education
Benet Leigh, M.A.	Communication Studies
Wingham Liddell, Ph.D.	Business/Economics
Tom Lough, Ph.D.	Sociology
John Lund	Community Expert, Politics, Stock Market
Rick Luttmann, Ph.D./CFP	Economics/Budgets
Robert Manning	Community Expert, Peace and Justice
Kenneth Marcus, Ph.D.	Criminal Justice
Perry Marker, Ph.D.	Education
Dan Markwyn, Ph.D.	History
Doug Martin, Ph.D.	Chemistry
Elizabeth Martinez, Ph.D.	Foreign Languages
Phil McGough, Ph.D.	Business
Eric McGuckin, Ph.D.	Anthropology
Robert McNamara, Ph.D.	Political Science

Andy Merrifield, Ph.D.	Public Administration
Catherine Nelson, Ph.D.	Political Science
Robert Lee Nichols	Lt. General United States Marine Corps (Retired)
Leilani Nishime, Ph.D.	American Multicultural Studies
Linda Nowak, Ph.D.	Business/Marketing
Tim Ogburn	Community Expert, International Trade
Tom Ormond, Ph.D.	Kinesiology
Wendy Ostroff, Ph.D.	Cultural Studies
Ervand Peterson, Ph.D.	Enviornmental Studies
Jorge E. Porras, Ph.D.	Sociolinguistics
Arthur Ramirez, Ph.D.	Mexican American Studies
Jeffrey Reeder, Ph.D.	Foreign Languages
Rabbi Michael Robinson	Community Expert, Social Justice
R. Thomas Rosin, Ph.D.	Anthropology
Gardner Rust, Ph.D.	Music
Richard Senghas, Ph.D.	Anthropology
Cindy Stearns, Ph.D.	Women's Studies
John Steiner, Ph.D.	Sociology
Elaine Sundberg, M.A.	Education
Velma Taylor, Ed.D.	Sociology/Women & Gender Studies
Bob Tellander, M.A.	Sociology
Laxmi G. Tewari, Ph.D.	Ethnomusicology
Suzanne Toczyski, Ph.D.	Foreign Languages
Carol Tremmel	Extended Education
David Van Nuys, Ph.D.	Psychology
Francisco H. Vazquez, Ph.D.	Hutchins, Liberal Studies
Greta Vollmer, Ph.D.	English
Albert Wahrhaftig, Ph.D.	Anthropology
Sandra Walton, MLIS	Archival management
Tim Wandling, Ph.D.	English
D. Anthony White, Ph.D.	History
R.Richard Williams, J.D.	Community Volunteer, Politics & Law
Richard Zimmer, Ph.D.	History

SONOMA STATE UNIVERSITY SUPPORTING STAFF AND OFFICES

Ruben Armiñana: President and Staff in the Office of the President
Bernard Goldstein: Chief Academic Officer and Staff
Robert Karlsrud: Dean of School of Social Sciences and Staff
William Babula: Dean of School of Arts and Humanities
Larry Furukawa-Schlereth: Chief Financial Officer and Staff
Jim Myers: Vice-President for Development and Staff
Barbara Butler and the SSU Library Staff
Tony Apolloni and the Staff in Sponsored Programs
Paula Hammett: Social Sciences Library Resources
Steve Wilson and the Staff at the SSU Academic Foundation
Jonah Raskin and Faculty in Communications Studies
Susan Kashack and Staff in SSU Public Relations Office
Colleagues in the Sociology Department: Noel Byrne, Kathy Charmaz, Susan Garfin, Dan Haytin, Robert Tellander, David Walls, and Department Secretary Laurel Holmstrom

The Project Censored crew (SSU Faculty, students, and PC staff), Fall 2000.

THIS MODERN WORLD
by TOM TOMORROW

Project Censored 25th Anniversary

BY NOAM CHOMSKY

A review of the stories that have been selected by Project Censored over 25 years reveals several clear patterns. The stories are of considerable interest to the media constituencies: the corporate sector, the state authorities, and the general public. They fall in a domain in which corporate–state interests are rather different from those of the public. That such stories would tend to be downplayed, reshaped, and obscured—"censored," in the terminology of the project—is only to be expected on the basis of even the most rudimentary inspection of the institutional structure of the media and their place in the broader society.

Media service to the corporate sector is reflexive: the media are major corporations. Like others, they sell a product to a market: the product is audiences and the market is other businesses (advertisers). It would be surprising indeed if the choice and shaping of media content did not reflect the interests and preferences of the sellers and buyers, and the business world generally. Even apart from the natural tendency to support state power, the linkage of the corporate sector and the state is so close that convergence of interests on major issues is the norm. The status of audiences is more ambiguous. The product must be available for sale; people must be induced to look at the advertisements. But beyond this common ground, divisions arise.

We can make a rough distinction between the managerial class and the rest. The managers take part in decision-making in the state, the private economy, and the doctrinal institutions. The rest are to cede authority to state and private elites, to accept what they are told, and to occupy themselves elsewhere. There is a corresponding rough distinction between elite and mass media, the former aiming to be instructive, though in ways that reflect dominant interests; the latter primarily to shape attitudes and beliefs, and to divert "the great beast," as Alexander Hamilton termed the annoying public.

The managers must have a tolerably realistic picture of the world if they are to advance "the permanent interests of the country," to borrow the phrase of James Madison, the leading framer of the constitutional order, referring to the rights of men of property. The world view of planners and decision makers should conform to the permanent interests, not just parochially but more broadly. The great beast, in contrast, must be caged. The public must have faith in the leaders who pursue what is commonly called "America's mission," perhaps subject to personal flaws, or making errors in an excess of good will or naivete, but dedicated to the path of righteousness. Firm in this conviction, the public is to keep to pursuits that do not interfere with the permanent interests. It must accept subordination as normal and proper; better still, it should be invisible, the way life is and must be.

The political order is largely an expression of these goals, and the doctrinal institutions—the media prominent among them—serve to reinforce and legitimate them. These are tendencies that one would be inclined to expect on elementary assumptions, and there is ample evidence to support such natural conjectures.

The realities are commonly revealed during the electoral extravaganzas. The year 2000 was no exception. As usual, almost half the electorate did not participate and voting correlated with income. Voter turnout remained "among the lowest and most decisively class-skewed in the industrial world."[1] This feature of so-called "American exceptionalism," reflecting the unusual dominance and class consciousness of concentrated private power, has been plausibly attributed to "the total absence of a socialist or laborite mass party as an organized competitor in the electoral market."[2] The same is true of the "media market": it is virtually 100 percent corporate, with a "total absence of socialist or laborite" mass media. In both respects, the system works.

Control of the media market by private capital is no more a law of nature than its control of the electoral market. In earlier days, there was a vibrant labor-based and popular press that reached a mass audience of concerned

[1] Thomas Ferguson and Joel Rogers, *Right Turn* (Hill & Wang, 1986).
[2] Walter Dean Burnham, "The 1980 Earthquake," in T. Ferguson and J. Rogers, eds., *The Hidden Election* (Pantheon, 1981).

and committed readers, on the scale of the commercial press. As in England, it was undermined by concentration of capital and advertiser funding; one should not succumb to myths about markets fostering competition. Unlike in most of the world, business interests are so powerful in the United States that they quickly took control of radio and television, and are now seeking to do the same with the new electronic media that were developed primarily in the state sector over many years—a terrain of struggle today with considerable long-term implications.

Most of the population did not take the year 2000 presidential elections very seriously. Three-fourths of the population regarded the process as a game played by large contributors (overwhelmingly corporations), party leaders, and the PR industry, which crafted candidates to say "almost anything to get themselves elected," so that one could believe little that they said even when their stand on issues was intelligible. On most issues citizens could not identify the stands of the candidates—not because of ignorance or lack of concern; again, the system is working. Public opinion studies found that among voters concerned more with policy issues than "qualities," the Democrats won handily. But issues were displaced in the political–media system in favor of style, personality, and other marginalia that are of little concern to the concentrated private power centers that largely finance campaigns and run the government. Their shared interests remained safely off the agenda, independently of the public will.[1]

Crucially, questions of economic policy must be deflected. These are of great concern both to the general population and to private power and its political representatives, but commonly with opposing preferences. The business world and its media overwhelmingly support "neoliberal reforms": corporate-led versions of globalization, the investor-rights agreements called "free trade agreements," and other devices that concentrate wealth and power. The public tends to oppose these measures, despite near-uniform media celebration. And unless care is taken, people might find ways to articulate and even implement their concerns. Opponents of the international economic arrangements favored by the business-government-media complex have an "ultimate weapon," the *Wall Street Journal* observed ruefully: the general public, which must therefore be marginalized.[2]

---

[1]For data on the elections, here and below, see Ruy Teixeira, *American Prospect*, December 18; Thomas Patterson, head of the Harvard University Vanishing Voter Project, op-eds, *New York Times*, November 8, *Boston Globe*, December 15, 2000.

[2]Glenn Burkins, "Labor Fights Against Fast-Track Trade Measure," *Wall Street Journal*, September 16, 1997.

For the public, the trade deficit had become the most important economic issue facing the country by 1998, outranking taxes or the budget deficit—the latter a concern for business, but not the public, so that lack of public interest must be portrayed as the public's "balanced-budget obsession."[1] People understand that the trade deficit translates into loss of jobs; for example, when U.S. corporations establish plants abroad that export to the domestic market. But free capital mobility is a high priority for the business world: it increases profit and also provides a powerful weapon to undermine labor organizing by threat of job transfer—technically illegal, but highly effective, as labor historian Kate Bronfenbrenner has demonstrated in important work.[2] Such threats contribute to the "growing worker insecurity" that has been hailed by Alan Greenspan and others as a significant factor in creating a "fairy-tale economy" by limiting wages and benefits, thus increasing profit and reducing inflationary pressures that would be unwelcome to financial interests. Another useful effect of these measures is to undermine democracy. Unions have traditionally offered people ways to pool limited resources, to think through problems that concern them collectively, to struggle for their rights, and to challenge the monopoly of the electoral and media markets. Capital mobility provides a new way to avert these threats, one of several that are cleaner than the resort to violence to crush working people that was another feature of "American exceptionalism" over a long period.

No such matters are to intrude into the electoral process: the general population is induced to vote (if at all) on the basis of peripheral concerns.

Higher income voters favor Republicans, so that the class-skewed voting pattern benefits the more openly pro-business party. But more revealing than the abstention of those who are left effectively voiceless is the way they vote when they do participate. The voting bloc that provided Bush with his greatest electoral success was middle-to-lower income white working-class voters, particularly men, but women as well. By large margins they favored Gore on major policy issues, insofar as these arose in some meaningful way during the campaign. But they were diverted to safer preoccupations.

The public is well aware of its marginalization. In the early years of Project Censored, about half the population felt that the government is run by "a few big interests looking out for themselves." During the Reagan years,

---

[1]On how the feat was accomplished, see my "Consent without Consent," *Cleveland State Law Review*, 44.4 (1996).

[2]*Uneasy Terrain: The Impact of Capital Mobility on Workers, Wages, and Union Organizing* (Cornell 2000), updating her earlier studies.

as "neoliberal reforms" were more firmly instituted, the figure rose to over 80 percent. In 2000, the director of Harvard's Vanishing Voter Project reported that "Americans' feeling of powerlessness has reached an alarming high," with 53 percent responding "only a little" or "none" to the question: "How much influence do you think people like you have on what government does?" The previous peak, 30 years ago, was 41 percent. During the campaign, over 60 percent of regular voters regarded politics in America as "generally pretty disgusting." In each weekly survey, more people found the campaign boring than exciting, by a margin of 5 to 3 in the final week.

The election was a virtual statistical tie, with estimated differences within the expected error range. A victor had to be chosen, and a great deal of attention was devoted to the process and what it revealed about the state of American democracy. But the major and most revealing issues were largely ignored in favor of dimpled chads and other technicalities. Among the crucial issues sidelined was the fact that most of the population felt that no election took place in any serious sense, at least as far as their interests were concerned.

A leading theme of modern history is the conflict between elite sectors, who are dedicated to securing "the permanent interests," and the unwashed masses, who have a different conception of their role in determining their fate and the course of public affairs. Over the centuries, rights have been won by constant and often bitter popular struggle, including rights of workers, women, and victims of a variety of other forms of discrimination and oppression; and the rights of future generations, the core concern of the environmental movements. The last 40 years have seen notable advances in this regard. But progress is by no means uniform. New mechanisms are constantly devised to restrict the rights that have been gained to formal exercises with little content.

The political order was consciously designed to defend the "permanent interests" against the "levelling spirit" of the growing masses of people who will "labor under all the hardships of life, and secretly sigh for a more equal distribution of its blessings," Madison feared, and may seek to improve their conditions by such measures as agrarian reform (and today, far more). The political system must "protect the minority of the opulent against the majority," Madison advised his colleagues at the Constitutional Convention. Forty years later, reflecting on the course and prospects of the system of which he was the most influential designer, Madison observed that power was to be in the hands of "the wealth of the nation," not the great masses of people "without property, or the hope of acquiring it," who "cannot be expected to sympathize sufficiently with [the rights of the propertied minority or] to be safe depositories of power" over these rights.

The problems and conflicts persist, though their nature has radically changed over time. A particularly important shift took place with the "corporatization of America" a century ago, which sharply concentrated power and create a new and different America" in which "most men are servants of corporations," Woodrow Wilson observed. This different America was "no longer a scene of individual enterprise,... individual opportunity and individual achievement," he continued, but a society in which "small groups of men in control of great corporations wield a power and control over the wealth and business opportunities of the country," administering markets and becoming "rivals of the government itself"—more accurately, becoming barely distinguishable from government. Wilsonian progressivism also gave a new cast to the traditional vision of the political order. In his so-called "progressive essays on democracy," Walter Lippmann, the most influential figure in American journalism in the twentieth century, described the public as "ignorant and meddlesome outsiders" who should be mere "spectators of action" instead of participants, their role limited to periodic choice among the "responsible men" who are to function in "technocratic insulation," in World Bank lingo.

The doctrine, labelled "polyarchy" by democratic political theorist Robert Dahl, is conventional in elite opinion. It has been given still firmer institutional grounds by the reduction of the public arena under the "neoliberal reforms" of the past 20 years, which shift authority even more than before to unaccountable private concentrations of power, under the cynical slogan "trust the people." Democracy is to be construed as the right to choose among commodities. Business leaders explain the need to impose on the population a "philosophy of futility" and "lack of purpose in life," to "concentrate human attention on the more superficial things that comprise much of fashionable consumption."[1] People may then accept and even welcome their meaningless and subordinate lives, and forget ridiculous ideas about managing their own affairs. They will abandon their fate to the responsible men, the self-described "intelligent minorities" who serve and administer power—which lies elsewhere, a hidden but crucial premise. It is within this general framework that the media function.

----

[1] For sources, see Stuart Ewen, *Captains of Consciousness: Advertising and the Social Roots of the Consumer Culture* (McGraw-Hill, 1976).

Like other major sectors of the economy, the corporate media are tending toward oligopoly. The process reduces still more the limited possibility that public concerns might come to the fore when they interfere with state–corporate interests, or that state policies might be seriously challenged.

On loyalty to state power, the common understanding is sometimes articulated with refreshing candor. For example, the leading political commentator of the *New York Times* opened the new year by hailing Clinton's "creative compromise" for the Middle East. Since the President has spoken, we "now know what the only realistic final deal looks like," and "now that we know what the deal looks like, the only question left is: Will either side be able to take it?"[1] How could there be a different question?

Not appropriate for discussion, and kept in the shadows, are the terms of the President's statesmanlike plan. Anyone with access to the Israeli press and a map, or the alternative media here, could have discovered throughout the recent negotiations and the seven-year "peace process" that Clinton's "creative compromise," like its predecessors, is designed to imprison the Palestinian population in isolated enclaves in the territories that Israel conquered in 1967—separated from one another, and from the vastly expanded region called "Jerusalem," by Israeli settlements and infrastructure projects, and also separated from the Arab world. One well-known Middle East specialist estimates that "25 percent of West Bank territory has been arbitrarily absorbed into Jerusalem" alone, with U.S. authorization and support.[2] In Jerusalem, we learn from the press, Arab neighborhoods are to be administered by Arabs and Jewish neighborhoods by Jews. What could be more fair? At least, until we look a little further and find that the Arab neighborhoods are isolated sections of the tiny former East Jerusalem, while the Jewish "neighborhoods" that are to be integrated within Israel include "settlements like Ma'ale Adumim"[3]—a city that was established well to the east in order to bisect the West Bank—along with other "neighborhoods" extending far to the north and south. Like other major settlement projects of the Oslo period, Ma'ale Adumim has flourished thanks to the Labor doves whose magnanimity we are called upon to admire for their "concessions" in the territories they conquered in 1967. Another part of the "compromise" is an Israeli salient that partially bisects the remaining territories to the north,

---

[1]Thomas Friedman, *New York Times*, January 2, 2001.

[2]Augustus Richard Norton, *Current History*, January 2001.

[3]Jane Perlez, "Clinton Presents a Broad New Plan for Mideast Peace," *New York Times*, December 26, 2000.

and other mechanisms to ensure that the resources and usable land of the occupied territories will be in the hands of the leading U.S. client state, long a pillar of U.S. policy in the strategic Middle East region.[1]

Without proceeding, the outcome conforms very well to the rejectionist stand that the United States has upheld in international isolation for more than 25 years, effectively denying the national rights of one of the two contending parties in the former Palestine. The record has been dispatched to the depths of the memory hole with a degree of efficiency and uniformity that is rather impressive in a free society. Without substantial independent research, readers of the U.S. media could scarcely have even a limited grasp of one of the major stories of the year 2000.

Even the most elementary facts are not proper media fare if they interfere with the image of impartial benevolence. Consider just a single illustration: the role of U.S. helicopters, very important to the Israeli army because "it is impractical to think that we can manufacture helicopters or major weapons systems of this type in Israel," the Ministry of Defense director-general General Amos Yaron reported. The late 2000 confrontations began on September 29, when Israeli troops killed several people and wounded over 100 as they left the al-Aqsa Mosque in Jerusalem after Friday prayers. On October 1, U.S. helicopters with Israeli pilots killed two Palestinians. The next day, helicopters killed 10 and wounded 35 at Netzarim, the scene of a great deal of fighting: the small Israeli settlement there is hardly more than an excuse for a military base and roads that cut the Gaza Strip in two, isolating Gaza City and separating it from Egypt as well (with other barriers to the south). On October 3, the defense correspondent of Israel's leading journal, *Ha'aretz*, reported the largest purchase of U.S. military helicopters in a decade: Blackhawks and parts for Apache attack helicopters sent a few weeks earlier. On October 4, *Jane's Defence Weekly*, the world's most prominent military journal, reported that the Clinton Administration had approved a request for new Apache attack helicopters, the most advanced in the U.S. arsenal—having decided, apparently, that the upgrades were not sufficient for the current needs of attacking the civilian population. The same day, the U.S. press reported that Apaches were attacking apartment complexes with rockets at Netzarim. The German press agency quoted Pentagon officials who said that "U.S. weapons sales do not carry a stipulation that the weapons can't

---

[1] As the Clinton compromise faced collapse, it was finally recognized that the Palestinians object to the Bantustan-style enclave structure imposed by U.S.-Israeli diplomatic and development programs during the Clinton years. See Jane Perlez, Joel Greenberg, *New York Times*, January 3, 2001, citing Palestinian objections.

be used against civilians. We cannot second-guess an Israeli commander who calls in helicopter gunships." So matters continued. A few weeks later, the local Palestinian leader Hussein Abayat was killed (along with two women standing nearby) by a missile launched from an Apache helicopter, as the assassination campaign against the indigenous leadership was initiated.[1]

Rushing new military helicopters under these circumstances was surely newsworthy, and it was reported: in an opinion piece in Raleigh, North Carolina, on October 12. An Amnesty International condemnation of the sale of U.S. helicopters on October 19 also passed in virtual silence.[2] Such facts will not do. Rather, we must join in praise for our leaders, recognizing that their words stipulate the "only realistic final deal," while we ponder the strange character flaws of the intended beneficiaries of their solicitude.

The examples are selected virtually at random. In fact, even the valuable record of 25 years provided by Project Censored can do no more than barely skim the surface. What it has been investigating is a major phenomenon of "really existing democracy," which we ignore at our peril.

---

[1] Yaron, Globes, *Journal of Israel's Business Arena*, December 21, 2000. October 1–2 attacks, Report on Israeli Settlement (Washington, D.C.), November–December 2000. Amnon Barzilai, "Israel Air Force closes largest helicopter deal of decade," *Ha'aretz*, October 3. Robin Hughes, "USA approves Israel's Apache Longbow request," *Jane's Defence Weekly*, October 4. Charles Sennott, *Boston Globe*, October 4. Dave McIntyre (Washington), *Deutsche Presse-Agentur*, October 3, 2000. Gideon Levy, *Ha'aretz*, December 24, and Graham Usher, *Middle East Report*, Winter 2000, on Abayat assassination in Beit Sahur on November 9.
[2] Ann Thompson Cary, "Arming Israel…," *News and Observer* (Raleigh, NC), October 12. "Amnesty International USA Calls for Cessation of all Attack Helicopter Transfers to Israel," Amnesty International release, October 19, 2000.

THIS MODERN WORLD

by TOM TOMORROW

Panel 1:
CONSERVATIVES HAVE BEEN BRINGING UP HILLARY CLINTON'S OLD CATCHPHRASE A LOT LATELY...HOSTS DERIDE IT ON *TALK RADIO*...

--SO I GUESS THAT MAKES ME PART OF THE *VAST RIGHT WING CONSPIRACY!* HA, HA!

YOU AN' ME *BOTH*, RUSH! HAW, HAW!

Panel 2:
...PUNDITS MOCK IT ON *CABLE NEWS SHOWS*...

--SPEAKING AS A CARD-CARRYING MEMBER OF THE *VAST RIGHT WING CONSPIRACY*--SNICKER, SNICKER--

Panel 3:
...AND REPUBLICAN POLITICIANS RIDICULE IT AT *EVERY OPPORTUNITY*...

WELCOME TO THE SHOW, SENATOR!

I'M PROUD TO BE HERE, LARRY--AS A REPRESENTATIVE OF THE *VAST RIGHT WING CONSPIRACY,* OF COURSE! *CHUCKLE!*

Panel 4:
...AND *RIGHTLY SO!* AFTER ALL, WHAT KIND OF PARANOID *LUNATIC* WOULD IMAGINE THAT REPUBLICANS MIGHT MEET BEHIND CLOSED DOORS AND--WELL--*COORDINATE* THEIR *EFFORTS*?

--SO YOU SEE, CONSTANT REPETITION OF THE PHRASE WILL REMIND VOTERS OF HER HUSBAND'S MISDEEDS--

--AND MAKE HER LOOK LIKE SHE'S GOT A *PERSECUTION COMPLEX!*

GENTLEMEN, START YOUR *FAXES!*

Panel 5:
SHEESH! I MEAN, IF YOU WERE *THAT* DELUSIONAL, YOU'D PROBABLY BELIEVE THE *DEMOCRATS* WERE DOING THE *SAME THING*...AND HOW LUDICROUS IS *THAT*?

THEY HAVE CONSPIRACIES--

--*WE* HAVE STRATEGY SESSIONS!

I'M HERE TO WORK ON OPERATION: *DESTROY LAZIO!*

NOT SO *FAST*, PAL! WHAT'S THE *SECRET PASSWORD*?

TOM TOMORROW © 6-14-00 ... tomorrow@well.com ... www.thismodernworld.com

How Project Censored Stories Are Selected

Sonoma State University Project Censored students and staff screen several thousand stories each year. About 700 of these are selected for evaluation by faculty and community evaluators. Our 89 faculty/community evaluators are experts in their individual fields and they rate the stories for credibility and national importance. Often more than one of our evaluators will examine and rate the same story. The top ranked 200 stories are then researched for national mainstream coverage by our upper division students in the annual Media Censorship class. The class examines the corporate media's coverage of the story and takes a second look at the credibility and accuracy of the story in relationship to other news articles on the topic. About 125 stories each year make the final voting level. A collective vote of all students, staff, and faculty narrows the stories down to 60 in early November. A second vote is taken a week later, after a short 300-word summary of each of the top 60 stories is prepared, and sent out with a voting sheet to all faculty/community evaluators, students, staff, and self-selected national judges. This Project-wide vote by some 150-plus people establishes which 25 stories will be listed in our annual book. The final ranking of stories is decided by our national judges, who receive a synopsis and full text copy of the top 25 stories.

While selection of these stories each year is a long, subjective process, we have grown to trust this collective effort as the best possible means of fairly selecting these important news stories. This process, we believe, gives us an annual summary list of the most important undercovered news stories in the United States.

PROJECT CENSORED MISSION STATEMENT Project Censored, founded in 1976, is a nonprofit project within the Sonoma State University Foundation, a 501(c)3 organization. Our principle objective is the advocacy for, and protection of, First Amendment rights and freedom of information in the United States. Through a faculty/student/community partnership, Project Censored serves as a national media ombudsman by identifying and researching important news stories that are underreported, ignored, misrepresented, or censored in the United States. We also encourage and support journalist, faculty, and student investigations into First Amendment and freedom of information issues. We are actively encouraging the development of a national interconnected, community-based media news service that will offer a diversity of news and information sources via print, radio, television, and internet to local mainstream audiences.

HOW TO INVEST IN FREEDOM OF INFORMATION Project Censored is a nonprofit tax-exempt organization. Funds for the Project are derived from sales of this book, and donations from hundreds of individuals. You can send a support gift to us through our website at www.projectcensored.org, or by mail to:

Project Censored
Sonoma State University
1810 East Cotati Avenue
Rohnert Park, CA 94931

CHAPTER 1

The Top 25 Censored Stories of 2000

BY PETER PHILLIPS AND PROJECT CENSORED

Media consolidation is creating a new form of censorship in the United States and undermining democracy in the process.

Since the passage of the Telecommunications Act of 1996, a gold rush of media mergers and takeovers has been occurring in the U.S. More than half of all radio stations have been sold in the past four years, and the merger upon merger that resulted in AOL–Time-Warner–CNN has created the largest media organization in the world. Less then ten major media corporations now dominate the U.S. news and information systems. Giant companies, such as Clear Channel, own more than 800 radio stations. Ninety-eight percent of all cities have only one daily newspaper, and these are increasingly controlled by huge chains like Gannett and Knight Ridder.

Censorship in the United States today is seldom deliberate. Instead it comes stealthily under the heading Missed Opportunities. Mega-merged corporate media are predominantly interested in the entertainment value of news and the maintenance of high audience viewing/reading levels that lead to profitable advertising sales. Nonsexy or complex stories tend to receive little attention within these corporate media systems.

A recent Pew Research Center poll showed more than 77 percent of all journalists admitted that news stories that were perceived as important but dull are sometimes ignored. More than a third polled stated that news stories that would hurt the financial interests of their news organization often or sometimes go unreported.

This structural arrangement is what censorship looks like in America today: not usually a deliberate killing of stories by official censors, but rather a subtle system of information suppression in the name of corporate profit and self interest. Corporate media censorship is an attack on democracy itself. It undermines the very fabric of our society by creating a highly entertained but poorly informed electorate.

Given that corporate media systemically censor important news stories, it is not hard to understand why more than 50 million eligible voters do not bother to vote. Without essential knowledge of important political issues, voter apathy is rampant, and political parties may tend to appear different, but act alike.

Recent efforts at national media reform through micro-power community radio and campaign finance changes that would mandate access for all candidates on national media have been strongly resisted by the National Association of Broadcasters (NAB). NAB, considered one of the most powerful corporate lobby groups in Washington, works hard to protect more than $200 billion dollars of annual advertising and the several hundred million dollars political candidates spend in each election cycle.

We now recognize that corporate media's political power, and its failure to meet its First Amendment obligation to keep us informed, leaves a huge task before us. We must mobilize our resources to redevelop news and information systems from the bottom up. We can expand our distribution of news via small independent newspapers, local magazines, independent radio, and cable access TV. Using the Internet we can interconnect with like-minded grassroots news organizations to share important stories globally.

This work has already started. Independent media centers have sprung up in more than thirty cities in the past year, and direct news from the front lines of the antiglobalization corporate power resistance movement is freely available. Thousands of alternative news organizations already exist. We just need to connect and put this news on the breakfast tables of millions of working people. We have the power to write, broadcast, and recreate news distribution in the U.S. and the world. By working together, we can bridge the Internet gap and refill the news wasteland so that every working person in the country knows the issues, recognizes the choices, and can make informed decisions about the future of our society.

The top 25 most censored stories for 2000 are the news that the corporate media refused to cover. If our 25-year average is correct, about one third of these stories will appear in the corporate press sometime in the next few years. While Project Censored is seldom acknowledged by the corporate media, we do shame them into covering these stories as if they discovered them themselves. Thousands of journalists working in the corporate media are dedicated believers in the First Amendment and the public's right to know. They are faced with the "daily grind"—as a close journalist friend of mine says— "of filling holes in the voids of newsland." Increasingly these "hole fillers" must have entertainment value or they will not be used.

The following stories may not be the most entertaining stories of the year, but they sure are important. Please give them the close attention they deserve and send encouragement to the authors and publications. Also write or call your local corporate media outlets to ask them why they didn't cover these real news stories in 2000. It is going to take a whole generation of persistence by grassroots media activists to turn this situation around. Together we can make it happen.

1 CENSORED

World Bank and Multinational Corporations Seek to Privatize Water

Sources:
INTERNATIONAL FORUM
ON GLOBALIZATION:
SPECIAL REPORT
June 1999 from PRIME July 10, 2000
Title: "The Global Water Crisis
and the Commodification
of the World's Water Supply"
Author: Maude Barlow
www.ifg.org/bgsummary.html

THIS
July/August 2000
Title: "Just Add Water"
Author: Jim Shultz

IN THESE TIMES
May 15, 2000
Title: "Water Fallout:
Bolivians Battle Globalization"
Author: Jim Shultz
www.inthesetimes.com

CANADIAN DIMENSION
February 2000
Title: "Monsanto's Billion-Dollar
Water Monopoly Plans"
Author: Vandana Shiva
www.purefood.org/Monsanto/
waterfish.cfm

CANADIAN DIMENSION
February 2000
Title: "Water Fallout"
Author: Jim Shultz

SAN FRANCISCO BAY GUARDIAN
May 31, 2000
Title: "Trouble on Tap"
Author: Daniel Zoll
www.sfbg.com/News/34/35/bech2.html

SAN FRANCISCO BAY GUARDIAN
May 31, 2000
Title: "The Earth Wrecker"
Author: Pratap Chatterjee
www.sfbg.com/News/34/35/bech1.html

Corporate News Coverage: *Toronto Globe and Mail*, May 11, 2000

Faculty Evaluators: Tom Jacobson Ph.D., Tom Lough Ph.D., Leilani Nishime Ph.D.
Student Researchers: Christina Van Straalen, Mike Graves, Kim Roberts

Global consumption of water is doubling every 20 years, more than twice the rate of human population growth. According to the United Nations, more than one billion people already lack access to fresh drinking water. If current trends persist, by 2025 the demand for fresh water is expected to rise by 56 percent more than the amount of water that is currently available.

Multinational corporations recognize these trends and are trying to monopolize water supplies around the world. Monsanto, Bechtel, and other global multinationals are seeking control of world water systems and supplies.

The World Bank recently adopted a policy of water privatization and full-cost water pricing. This policy is causing great distress in many Third World countries, which fear that their citizens will not be able to afford for-profit water. Grassroots resistance to the privatization of water emerges as companies expand profit taking. San Francisco's Bechtel Enterprises was contracted to manage the water system in Cochabamba, Bolivia, after the World Bank required Bolivia to privatize. When Bechtel pushed up the price of water, the entire city went on a general strike. The military killed a seventeen-year-old boy and arrested the water rights leaders. But after four months of unrest the Bolivian government forced Bechtel out of Cochabamba.

Bechtel Group Inc., a corporation with a long history of environmental abuses, now contracts with the city of San Francisco to upgrade the city's water system. Bechtel employees are working side by side with government workers in a privatization move that activists fear will lead to an eventual takeover of San Francisco's water system.

Maude Barlow, chair of the Council of Canadians, Canada's largest public advocacy group, states, "Governments around the world must act now to declare water a fundamental human right and prevent efforts to privatize, export, and sell for profit a substance essential to all life." Research has shown that selling water on the open market only delivers it to wealthy cities and individuals.

Governments are signing away their control over domestic water supplies by participating in trade treaties such as the North American Free Trade Agreement (NAFTA) and in institutions such as the World Trade Organization (WTO). These agreements give transnational corporations the unprecedented right to the water of signatory companies.

Water-related conflicts are springing up around the globe. Malaysia, for example, owns half of Singapore's water and, in 1997, threatened to cut off its water supply after Singapore criticized Malaysia's government policies.

Monsanto plans to earn revenues of $420 million and a net income of $63 million by 2008 from its water business in India and Mexico. Monsanto estimates that water will become a multi-billion-dollar market in the coming decades.

UPDATE BY MAUDE BARLOW This story is of vital importance to the earth and all humanity. The finite sources of freshwater (less than one half of one per cent of the world's total water stock) are being diverted, depleted, and polluted so fast that, by the year 2025, two-thirds of the world's population will be living in a state of serious water deprivation. Yet governments are handing responsibility of this precious resource over to giant transnational corporations who, in collusion with the World Bank and the World Trade Organization, seek to commodify and privatize the world's water and put it on the open market for sale to the highest bidder. Millions of the world's citizens are being deprived of this fundamental human right, and vast ecological damage is being wrought as massive industry claims water once used to sustain communities and replenish nature.

Recently, a civil society movement has been created to wrest control of water back from profit-making forces and claim it for people and nature. Called the Blue Planet Project, this movement is an alliance of farmers, environmentalists, Indigenous Peoples, public sector workers, and urban activists who forced the issue of water as a human right at the March 2000 World Water Forum in the Hague. The Project is holding the first global citizens' summit on water in Vancouver in July 2001. One major project has been support of the water activists in Cochabamba, Bolivia, who, led by union leader Oscar Olivera, forced the giant engineering company Bechtel to leave the country and stopped a World Bank–imposed privatization scheme that more than doubled the price of water to the local people.

The mainstream press has been reluctant to tell this story. Our fight in Canada started with concern over the potential of bulk water exports sought by some politicians and corporations. Water is included in both NAFTA and the WTO as a tradable good; once the tap is turned on, corporate rights to water are immediately established. But our mainstream press generally supports economic globalization and these trade agreements and will permit only selective reporting on opposition positions. *Blue Gold*, my paper on the commodification of water published by the IFG in 1999, has been printed in several languages and sold all over the world but has been ignored by the North American media.

The story of the destruction of the world's remaining freshwater sources is one of the most pressing of our time; there is simply no way to overstate the nature of this crisis. And yet when the mainstream media report on it—which is not nearly often enough or in sufficient depth—they seldom ask the most crucial question of all: Who owns water? We say the earth, all species and all future generations. Many in power have another answer. It is time for this debate.

For more information on this story and the Blue Planet Project, please contact The Council of Canadians: phone (613) 233-2773; fax (613) 233-6776; address, 502-151 Slater Street, Ottawa, ON, Canada, K1P 5H3; website, www.canadians.org.

Maude Barlow is the National Chairperson of the Council of Canadians and a director with the International Forum on Globalization.

UPDATE BY JIM SHULTZ Eight months have passed since the people of Cochabamba forced the departure of a subsidiary of the Bechtel Corporation and restored control of the region's water supply into public hands. The story has brought unprecedented attention to the issue of water privatization and important events continue to unfold, both locally and internationally.

Locally, Cochabamba's residents are working closely with the newly reconstituted water company, SEMAPA, to extend water service to more families. In Alto Cochabamba, one of the city's poorest neighborhoods, a community water tank had remained uncompleted for years and became a local trash dump. Today the tank is in full operation,

bringing public water into the neighborhood for the first time. Civic leaders say they are building a utility that is run by the people rather than by corrupt politicians or an overcharging corporation beyond local democratic reach.

As a direct result of the Democracy Center's reporting, Cochabamba's water rebellion is also drawing substantial world attention and solidarity. In December, a delegation of leading citizen action and labor groups from the U.S. and Canada came to Cochabamba for an international conference on water privatization. These groups and others have also pledged their support against Bechtel's latest attack, a lawsuit for as much as $20 million—compensation for losing their lucrative Cochabamba contract. It is an action that pits one of the world's wealthiest corporations against the people of South America's poorest nation.

Bechtel has been actively shopping for the friendliest international forum possible and apparently has decided its best chances lie in a suit under a Bilateral Investment Treaty (BIT) signed previously between Bolivia and Holland. Late last year Bechtel quietly reshuffled corporate papers to place its subsidiary under Dutch registration, in preparation for such action. International groups are gearing up to help Cochabamba leaders fight Bechtel's lawsuit. "This is going to be the first major international civil society fight against a corporate legal action under such a treaty," says Antonia Juhasz of San Francisco-based International Forum on Globalization.

The Democracy Center's articles, which ran primarily in the progressive press and were distributed widely via the Internet, also attracted publication in some dedicated city dailies such as the *San Jose Mercury News, San Francisco Examiner,* and *Toronto Star* (thanks to distribution by the Pacific News Service). Most mainstream coverage of the story, however, was limited to the dispatches of the Associated Press Bolivian correspondent. AP correspondent Peter McFarren came under fire for stories that eagerly repeated the Bolivian government's and Bechtel's public line, falsely blaming the water uprising on "narcotraffickers." One reader of the Democracy Center's articles noted the difference in the reporting and uncovered that McFarren was, at the same time, actively lobbying the Bolivian Congress to approve a controversial project to ship Bolivian water to Chile. When that conflict of interest was reported to AP, McFarren suddenly submitted his resignation.

More information on the story, including subscription to the free e-mail newsletter in which the stories originated, is available at www.democracyctr.org.

Jim Shultz: JShultz@democracyctr.org

UPDATE BY PRATAP CHATTERJEE *Engineering News-Record* magazine ranks Bechtel as the biggest construction company in the United States; it is also the biggest private company in northern California. It has built mega-projects from the Alaska pipeline and the Hoover dam to the San Francisco Bay Bridge, from natural gas pipelines in Algeria to refineries in Zambia. Hardly a day passes without the company signing a new contract somewhere in the world; all told it has worked on 19,000 contracts in 140 countries in the past century, many of them with taxpayer money. Yet an extensive review of Bechtel contracts over the last 100 years shows that time and again the company has been found guilty of sleazy political connections. In fact, if there's a pattern to Bechtel's public works projects, it's this: The company works under cover of the utmost secrecy and routinely jacks up the cost of projects far beyond the original bid, sticking taxpayers with huge, often unexpected bills.

If these cost overruns do generate some headlines, the environmental and social impacts of the company's construction activities rarely get a mention: managing bombsites for nuclear testing in Nevada, helping hack off the top of a sacred mountain on the Pacific island of New Guinea to build the world's largest gold mine, planning pipelines for Saddam Hussein in Iraq, drawing up development plans for a man accused of killing half a million Hutu refugees in the Democratic Republic of the Congo (former Zaire), building toxic refineries for Chevron in Richmond that destroy the San Francisco Bay.

Bechtel's management and spin doctors went into overdrive when staff at headquarters read the *San Francisco Bay Guardian* story and started to ask hard questions. We obtained an internal memo that explained why they had decided not to respond to the story:

"We're not currently considering legal recourse (for) a number of reasons:

➤To win a libel or defamation lawsuit, Bechtel would have to show that the journalists, activists, or politicians in question either knew that such statements were false or entertained serious doubts about their accuracy. This could be very difficult to prove.

➤A lawsuit would give Bechtel's most vocal critics another public forum in which to reprise their claims. Defense attorneys would be permitted to engage in wide-ranging discovery into Bechtel's nonpublic business affairs—including making substantial document requests and taking depositions from Bechtel employees—to probe whether or not the critical claims were true.

➤Bechtel would have to prove the amount of damages suffered as a result of the alleged defamation. Bechtel would have to demonstrate some monetary loss, which might be difficult (and would, again, open us up to discovery of data)."

The mainstream press regularly writes about the contracts that Bechtel wins and completes but they rarely ever dig deeper to find out about the impact of these projects. No mainstream press has ever looked at a broad overview of the company's history or been able to probe into the company's inner workings: this is partly because the company refuses to give the media access to the company staff and management.

Pratap Chatterjee: pchatterjee@igc.org

2 CENSORED
OSHA Fails to Protect U.S. Workers

Source:
THE PROGRESSIVE
February 2000
Title: "Losing Life and Limb on the Job"
Author: Christopher D. Cook
www.progressive.org/cook0200.htm

Faculty and Community Evaluators:
Fred Fletcher, Virginia Lea, Ph.D.
Student Researchers: Mike Graves, Ambrosia Crumley, Dana Balicki

United States labor laws are poorly enforced and fail to meet the basic human rights of U.S. workers. Each year, about 6,000 workers die on the job from accidents and another 50,000 to 70,000 workers die annually from "occupationally acquired diseases." The Occupational Safety and Health Administration (OSHA) is not capable of effectively overseeing U.S. workplaces.

The entire federal and state worker health and safety apparatus involves just 2,300 inspectors, who must cover America's 102 million workers in 6.7 million workplaces. That comes to one inspector for every 44,348 workers. Theoretically, it would take OSHA 110 years to inspect each workplace under its jurisdiction just once.

Needed by labor and despised by business, OSHA may be a worker's best friend in government, but critics say OSHA has never been weaker or less worker-friendly. Recent studies show that United States labor laws have loopholes, are poorly enforced, and fail to meet human rights standards that our nation requires of other countries.

Titan International, an Illinois-based company, has been under fire lately at its plant and at other subsidiary locations. Despite a lengthy recent record of safety violations and injuries (including two deaths), Titan's Des Moines plant has stymied five attempts by Iowa OSHA to inspect some twenty-three complaints lodged by workers. Titan Tire refused entry to OSHA even with an inspection warrant—a violation of law and a direct assault on the integrity of the Occupational Safety and Health Act. Titan was held responsible by the Polk County District Court in Des Moines and was fined Iowa's maximum civil-contempt penalty—just $500— which Titan is appealing.

Titan workers are being maimed across the country. Workers say it is usually the result of decrepit machines, minimal training, and punishing hours. Since May 1999, the United Steelworkers of America (USWA) has been challenging Titan with a slew of unfair labor practice charges. These include, but are not limited to, illegally moving jobs and equipment to avoid a union contract, refusing to bargain in good faith, discriminating against union members, and trying to permanently replace striking workers. Union officials say that fines are too low and that companies, even in worker death cases, are only getting slapped on the wrist.

In Titan's Des Moines plant on March 20, 1997, Don Baysinger, a tire builder with 27 years of experience, was pinned between two tire-tread machines for more than twenty minutes. Baysinger died two days later of asphyxia-related symptoms. Titan paid only a $10,000 OSHA fine for failure to have emergency stops on the equipment and for being inadequately guarded.

Another death occurred at the Des Moines plant in November 1999. Nearly 2,000 gallons of highly flammable heptane poured unnoticed onto the ground and headed into the street. A passing car ignited the chemicals and set off a massive fire, killing Bulkamatic Transport Company's driver Donald Oswald.

Titan often develops close relationships with job-starved cities. In 1997 Brownsville, Texas gave Titan $6.5 million in free land, site improvements, and utility and wage subsidies. The state of Texas added $448,000 for job training for 168 workers. Titan received similar subsidies from the state of Virginia to the tune of $500,000.

In these times, it is hard to get the attention of an OSHA inspector as there are so few of them. Instead of addressing or attempting to alleviate an issue or complaints early on, inspectors seem to respond "only when there is a death or serious injury," says union official Tim Johnson. Regardless of who is to blame, OSHA is woefully ill-equipped to monitor the workplaces of America.

UPDATE BY CHRISTOPHER D. COOK On the surface this is a story about the untold daily horrors that still exist on today's assembly line. But this story is about more than a "bad apple," runaway company abusing its workers—though that, in and of itself, is a disturbingly commonplace scandal about which we hear little in the mainstream press. The broader significance is that firms like this can—and do—regularly get away with it, thanks to a remarkably anemic worker health and safety enforcement system. Companies can turn inspectors away and delay inspections for months. Fines are minimal and routinely reduced. And while business complains about government intervention in the workplace, the reality is that there are just 2,300 federal and state inspectors charged with monitoring 6.7 million work sites across the U.S.—so firms like Titan can endanger workers with impunity.

Regrettably little has changed since this story appeared. The United Steelworkers of America continues to battle Titan, which has attempted to replace striking U.S. workers with laid-off workers from a Titan spin-off in Uruguay. On November 22, 2000, the Detroit city council declared the motor city a "Titan-free zone" to express its support for the workers.

The mainstream press has shown little interest in this story. I promoted the story to the *Washington Post*—with local and national hooks—to no avail.

There is a distressing lack of national groups focusing on injured workers. I encourage people interested in learning more to contact the United Steelworkers of America, Public Citizen, and the AFL-CIO, which studies worker injuries and deaths on the job, as well as government inspector per worker ratios.

Christopher D. Cook: cdcook@igc. apc.org

3 CENSORED

U.S. Army's Psychological Operations Personnel Worked at CNN

Sources:
COUNTERPUNCH
February 16, March 1, 2000
Title: "CNN and PSYOPS"
Author: Alexander Cockburn
www.counterpunch.org/cnnpsyops.html

Foreign coverage: *Trouw* (Dutch daily newspaper) February 21, 2000; *Japan Economic Newswire*, April 5, 2000; *Le Monde Du Renseignement* February 17, 2000; *The Guardian* April 12, 2000 www.emperors-clothes.com/articles/devries/psyops2.htm

U.S. Coverage; National Public Radio, April 10, April 16, 2000; *Tampa Tribune* April 23, 2000, pg. 6; *TV Guide* April 2000

Faculty Evaluators: Andy Merrifield Ph.D., Elizabeth Burch Ph.D.
Student Researchers:
Molly Garrison, Bruce Harden

From June 1999 to March 2000, CNN employed military specialists in "psychological operations" (Psyops) in their Southeast TV bureau and CNN radio division.

"Psyops personnel, soldiers, and officers, have been working in CNN's headquarters in Atlanta through our program 'Training With Industry,'" Major Thomas Collins of the U.S. Army Information Service said in a telephone interview on February 18, 2000. Collins asserted, "They worked as regular employees of CNN. Conceivably, they would have worked on stories during the Kosovo war. They helped in the production of news."

CNN had hosted a total of five interns from U.S. Army Psyops, two in television, two in radio, and one in satellite operations. The military/CNN personnel belonged to the airmobile Fourth Psychological Operations Group stationed at Fort Bragg, North Carolina. One of the main tasks of this group of almost 1,200 soldiers and officers is to spread "selected information." The propaganda group was involved in the Gulf War, the war in Bosnia, and the crisis in Kosovo.

The military personnel stayed with CNN for at least two weeks "to get to know the company and to broaden their horizons." Collins maintains that "they didn't work under the control of the army." The temporary outplacement of U.S. Army Psyops personnel in various sectors of society began a couple of years ago. Contract periods vary from weeks to one year.

Colonel Christopher St. John is commander of the Fourth Psychological Operations Group. In a military symposium on special operations that was held behind closed doors in Arlington, Virginia, in early February, Col. St. John said the cooperation with CNN was a textbook example of the kind of ties the American army wants to have with the media. Still, the Psyops people in Arlington were not entirely satisfied with news handling during the war on Serbia. In their opinion, too much information about the results of the bombings came to the surface.

CNN and other media coverage of the war in Kosovo has attracted criticism for having been one-sided, overly emotional, overly simplified, and relying too heavily on NATO officials. On the other hand, journalists have complained about the lack of the reliable information from NATO; for almost all of them it was impossible to be on the battlefield and file first-hand reports. The question remains: Did the military learn from TV people how to hold viewers' attention? Or did the Psyops people teach CNN how to help the U.S. government garner political support?

TV Guide reported in April that Psyops also had team members working at National Public Radio (NPR). This prompted two NPR stories on the program *All Things Considered.* Jeffrey Dvorkin, NPR's vice president for news, stated: "We recruited from the army and got three interns, and that was a mistake. And when we discovered that they were from Psyops branch, we finished the arrangement, and it won't happen again."

4 CENSORED

Did the U.S. Deliberately Bomb the Chinese Embassy in Belgrade?

Sources:

IN THESE TIMES
December 12, 1999
Title: "A Tragic Mistake?"
Author: Joel Bleifuss
www.inthesetimes.com

IN THESE TIMES
June 26, 2000
Title: "Mission Implausible"
Author: Seth Ackerman
www.inthesetimes.com/acker-man2415.html

PACIFIC NEWS
October 20, 1999
Title: "Reports Showing U.S. Deliberately Bombed Chinese Embassy Deliberately Ignored by U.S. Media"
Author: Yoichi Shimatsu

FAIRNESS & ACCURACY IN REPORTING
February 9, 2000
Title: "NY Times on Chinese Embassy Bombing: Nothing to Report"
Action Alert (No author given)
www.fair.org/activism/china-response2.html

Foreign news coverage: *The Herald* (Glasgow), *The Politiken* (Copenhagen), *The Scotsman*, *The South China Morning Post*, *The Times* (London), *The London Observer*

Faculty/Community Evaluators: Philip Beard Ph.D., Robert Lee Nichols, Lt. General U.S. Marines (Retired)
Student Researchers: Stephen Hayth, Erich Sommer, Melanie Burton

Elements within the CIA may have deliberately targeted the Chinese embassy in Belgrade, without NATO approval, because it was serving as a rebroadcast station for the Yugoslavian army.

The London Observer and Copenhagen's *Politiken* reported that, according to senior U.S. and European military sources, NATO knew very well where the Chinese embassy was located and listed it as a "strictly prohibited target" at the beginning of the war. The *Observer* stated that the CIA and its British equivalent, M16, had been listening to communications from the Chinese embassy routinely since it moved to its new site in 1996. The Chinese embassy was taken off the prohibited target list after NATO detected it sending Yugoslavian army signals to forces in the field. "Nearly everyone involved in NATO air operations (radio) signals command knows that the bombing was deliberate," said Jens Holsoe of *Politiken*, lead investigative reporter on the news team reporting on the story.

President Clinton called the bombing a "tragic mistake" and said it was the result of a mix-up. NATO claimed that they were using old maps and got the address wrong. However, *Observer* reporters quoted a Naples-based flight controller who said the NATO maps that were used during the campaign had correctly identified the Chinese embassy. A French Ministry of Defense report stated that the flight that targeted the Chinese embassy was not under NATO command, but rather an independent U.S. bombing raid. In July 1999, CIA director George Tenet testified before Congress that of the 900 sites struck by NATO during the bombing campaign, the only one targeted by the CIA was the Chinese embassy.

In response to the claims by the *New York Times* and the *Washington Post* of having investigated this story and having found no substantiation, Seth Ackerman states that within the CIA there are strong anti-China elements. The Counter-Proliferation Division within the CIA is known for its opposition to Clinton's China policy. The CIA's regular targeting office, the Central Targeting Support Staff, was not consulted about the mission. Instead the Counter-Proliferation Division forwarded the target information to U.S. forces.

The CIA was outraged not only because the Chinese were helping the Serbs by serving as a rebroadcast station, but also because they believed that Yugoslavia had sold the wreckage of the downed U.S. F-117 stealth fighter to the Chinese, thereby improving China's ability to develop a stealth-proof radar system.

According to the *New York Times* April 17, 2000 edition, the CIA still claims that the bombing was an accident, but cannot explain "why so many mistakes occurred." The chairman of the House Intelligence Committee, Porter Goss, said he was confident that the strike was not deliberate, but added "unless some people are lying to me" to his statement.

The bombing of the Chinese embassy was described by Chinese Ambassador Li Zhaozing as "a horrifying atrocity, something rarely seen in the entire history of the worst of diplomacy."

UPDATE BY JOEL BLEIFUSS The information and evidence presented by the *Observer* in London and *Politiken* of Copenhagen, pointing to a deliberate U.S. decision to bomb the Chinese embassy in Belgrade, has been totally ignored by the mainstream press. Though some reporters, including Steven Lee Myers, the *New York Times'* Pentagon correspondent, raised doubts about the bombing, Myers has nonetheless concluded, with some skepticism, that the bombing was a mistake. FAIR, the media watch group, has further information on the bombing allegations at: www.fair. org/ activism/embassy-bombing.html, www. fair.org/activism/ china-response2. html, and www.fair.org/activism/embassy-update.html.

Joel Bleifuss: itt@inthesetimes.com

5 CENSORED

U.S. Taxpayers Underwrite Global Nuclear Power Plant Sales

Source:
THE PROGRESSIVE
March 2000
Title: "Pushing the Nuclear Plants: A U.S. Agency Hooks Foreign Clients"
Author: Ken Silverstein and Ian Urbina
www.progressive.org

Faculty Evaluator:
Wingham Liddell, Ph.D.
Student Researchers:
Ambrosia Crumley, Licia Marshall, Adam Sullens

The U.S. tax-supported Export-Import Bank (Ex-Im) is solidly backing major U.S. nuclear contractors such as Westinghouse, Bechtel, and General Electric in their efforts to seek foreign markets for nuclear reactors. Between 1959 and 1993 Ex-Im spent $7.7 billion to help sell American-made reactors abroad.

Most countries do not have the capital to buy nuclear power, so contractors, in order to be competitive, provide 100 percent of the financing. Ex-Im offers terms too good for Third World countries and Eastern European buyers to pass up. If the host country defaults on its loan, the Ex-Im steps in with American taxpayer dollars.

Westinghouse built the Bataan nuclear power facility in the Philippines in 1985 at a cost of $1.2 billion, 150 percent above their projections. However, the Bataan plant was never brought online due to the fact it was near an active volcano. Despite the fact that the plant never generated a single kilowatt of energy, the Philippines still pays about $300,000 a day in interest on the Ex-Im loan that funded the project. Should the Philippines default, U.S. taxpayers will pick up the tab.

In Turkey, the Ex-Im has approved a preliminary loan in support of a Westinghouse-led consortium's $3.2 billion bid to build the Akkuyu plant on the Mediterranean coast. The Akkuyu plant site is near an active fault line in a region that has experienced a number of strong earthquakes over the last 100 years. Despite safety and environmental concerns, Vice President Gore wrote to Turkish officials on behalf of Westinghouse. National security specialists believe that Turkey's nuclear energy program contains a military element. Several members of the U.S. Congress have accused Turkey of supplying Pakistan with uranium enrichment technology.

The Clinton administration has also allowed American contractors to sell reactors to China, claiming the nuclear energy market of China is vital to the U.S. nuclear supply industry. Ex-Im has guaranteed a $322 million loan for two Westinghouse nuclear deals in China. This approval comes despite Beijing's refusal to abide by nonproliferation rules established by the International Atomic Energy Act. The decision to allow the sales was reportedly made over the objections of national security advisor Sandy Berger, who cited Chinese exports of "dual-use" technology to Iran, Iraq, and Pakistan.

Estimates are that some 70 nuclear power plants will be built in Asia in the next 25 years. China will be one of the principal buyers. In 1997, President Clinton's Export council (headed at the time by the CEO of Westinghouse) declared, "The nuclear energy market of China is critical to the survival of the U.S. nuclear power supply industry."

"American contractors are selling a product that most people don't want," Dave Martin of the Toronto-based Nuclear Awareness campaign says. U.S. taxpayers are subsidizing this industry. Without Ex-Im, which offers terms just too good for Third World countries to pass up, American firms would not succeed in selling nuclear power plants worldwide.

UPDATE BY IAN URBINA Discussion of the perils of the nuclear industry is rare enough in the mainstream media. But even less attention is paid to the U.S. funding institutions that make many of these nuclear plants possible. With virtually no oversight or public accountability, the U.S. Export-Import Bank continues to direct huge sums of taxpayer dollars toward irresponsible and inefficient projects, few of which could ever pass domestic safety standards. At the same time that the U.S. government

has acquiesced to the need for cheaper, cleaner, and safer forms of energy at home, it unscrupulously peddles nuclear energy abroad to keep U.S. contractors afloat.

There have been some developments since our article originally ran. Nearly a billion dollars over budget, the Temelin plant in the Czech Republic went online on October 9, 2000. The reactor sparked massive international protests, which on several occasions forced the closing of the Austrian-Czech border. Protests are now turning to Temelin II, an unfinished second reactor at the same plant, which is scheduled for completion next year. Antinuclear activists and members of the Austrian and Bavarian governments are vowing to block it.

In Bulgaria, the Kozloduy reactors remain online. The European Union (EU) maintains that unless four of the six Kozloduy reactors are closed, Bulgaria will not be allowed entrance into the Union. The EU has also threatened to forbid Lithuania membership if it continues to postpone the shutdown of the Ignalina plant, which still operates partly because of Westinghouse work and Ex-Im backing.

In Turkey, the movement to block the Akkuyu project won a stunning victory in July 2000. Stating that the project was simply too expensive and too dangerous, the Turkish government finally agreed to cancel it. Turkish president Ecevit pointed out that "the world is abandoning nuclear energy," and said that the government would instead begin focusing on conservation, natural gas, and hydroelectric, solar, and wind energy.

China remains the grand prize for the U.S. nuclear industry. With U.S.–Chinese trade relations growing closer by the day, Ex-Im will face even less difficulty in opening this market to U.S. contractors.

To follow the activities of the lending agencies behind these projects, two important sources to check out are Bank Watch (www.bankwatch.org) and the Bank Information Center (www.bicusa.org). For general information on nuclear projects, the Nuclear Information and Resource Service & World Information Service on Energy (www.nirs.org) and the Campaign for Nuclear Phaseout (www.cnp.ca) are excellent.

Ian Urbina: iurbina2@aol.com

6 CENSORED

International Report Blames U.S. and Others for Genocide in Rwanda

Sources:
ALTERNET
July 25, 2000
Title: "Loyal Opposition: Clinton Allowed Genocide"
Author: David Corn
www.alternet.org/story.html?
StoryID=9494

COVERTACTION QUARTERLY
Spring/Summer 2000
Title: "The Role of the U.S. Military"
Author: Ellen Ray

Faculty Evaluator:
Peter Phillips, Ph.D.
Student Researchers:
Adam Sullens, Michael Runas

Bill Clinton and his administration allowed the genocide of 500,000 to 800,000 people in Rwanda in 1994. In a clear effort to avoid responsibility and embarrassment, the Clinton administration has refused to acknowledge its role in failing to prevent the genocide in Rwanda. This allegation comes from the recent report released in July by a panel affiliated with the Organization for African Unity (OAU).

OAU set up a panel comprised of two African heads of state, chairwomen of the Swedish Committee for UNICEF, a former chief justice to the Indian Supreme Court, and a former Canadian ambassador to the United Nations (UN). The panel was asked to review the 1994 genocide, the actions preceding the massacre, and the world's response to the killings.

The panel concluded that the nations and international bodies that should have attempted to stop the killing chose not to do so. The report, which received modest but insufficient media coverage, convincingly condemns the United Nations, Belgium (a former colonial occupier), France (which maintained close relations with Rwanda), and the United States. The report found that after the genocide began, the Clinton administration chose not to acknowledge that it was taking place. Under the 1948 UN Genocide Convention, once genocide is recognized the nations of the world are obligated to prevent the killings and to punish the murderers. But the Clinton administration did not want to become involved with Rwanda after 18 Americans were killed in Somalia six months before. The report says, "the Clinton administration held that there was no useful role for any peacekeeping operation under the prevailing circumstances."

According to the report, the killings could have been stopped before they began. The report refers to the well-known fax that Canadian Lieutenant-General Romeo Dallaire, commander of the UN peacekeeping troops in Rwanda, sent to the UN three months before the genocide began. In the fax, Dallaire warned that an extermination campaign was coming. In fact, three days before the genocide started, a Hutu leader told several high-ranking UN officials that "the only plausible solution for Rwanda would be the elimination of the Tutsi." While the report states that "there were a thousand early warnings that something appalling was about to occur in Rwanda," the Clinton administration took every step possible to avoid acknowledging that genocide was taking place.

Dallaire asked for an additional three thousand UN troops, which would have brought the total to 5,000, a number likely to have been able to prevent the genocide. However, Madeleine Albright played a key role in the Security Council of the UN in blocking the troop expansion. In fact Albright is cited by the report as "tossing up roadblocks... at every stage."

Perhaps even more disturbing are reports linking U.S. Special Forces to the training of Rwandan Patriotic Army (RPA) troops. The Special Forces Command Team known as Joint Combined Exchange Training (JCET) is a special foreign armed forces training unit. Since 1994, under the leadership of Paul Kagame, Green Berets were training the RPA. They have been trained in landmine detection and small unit movement. This training continues even though there is mounting evidence that the U.S.–trained Rwandan soldiers have been in the thick of the atrocities inflicted upon the Hutu refugees from before the genocide began up until the present.

UPDATE BY DAVID CORN There are several forms of censorship. In totalitarian societies, governments simply forbid journalists from publishing and disseminating embarrassing, inconvenient, or troubling information. But in supposedly open societies, where the cyber-fast flow of information creates a white noise that can drown out the trivial and the significant, there are more subtle and less conspiratorial acts of news suppression. Most notably, there is the question of triage. A tremendously important matter can receive but several inches of attention in the middle of a newspaper or a brief mention halfway through a news broadcast. (I. F. Stone used to say that the *Washington Post* was a great newspaper—you never knew where in it you would find a page-one story.) If a story is not deemed vital—if there is no page-one headline, no follow-up—the subject can fade quickly and be swept aside by other news. And—poof! —it's as if the story never appeared in the first place.

In the column that has been selected as the #6 Censored story of 2000, I attempted to rescue a crucial story from the disposal bin. When an Organization of African Unity panel last summer released a report on the Rwanda genocide of 1994, the *New York Times* published a news story on the study in the middle of its first section. The article noted that the OAU panel had been critical of Secretary of State Madeleine Albright and the United States—and that, predictably, the Clinton Administration had brushed aside the criticism. But the story did not go into details. And that was it. When I looked up the report on the OAU's Web site, I was astonished at how sharp a critique it was of the Clinton administration's response (or lack thereof) to the genocide, in which 500,000 to 800,000 Tutsi were massacred by the Hutu. Moreover, the report demolished the Clinton assertion that he had not been fully aware of the genocide when it had been under way. (The president had offered this excuse in 1998 while making an apology in Rwanda for his inaction.) That is, the report showed that the president had prevaricated when he had

issued his apology. The OAU study also put forward a convincing case that the Clinton administration had stood in the way of a swift and strong international response to the Rwanda genocide. It was a devastating piece of work. Yet as far as I could see, it had little impact on the Clinton administration and did not register with the American public. Clinton's lies about his personal sexual behavior seemed more important to the media than his lies about genocide.

My modest aim was to write a column that would inform people of the full breadth of the OAU report. In the same piece, I also referred to the plight of Canadian General Romeo Dallaire, who had been the commander of the UN forces in Rwanda. A few months before the OAU report came out, Dallaire retired early from the military for medical reasons. He had been suffering from post-traumatic stress disorder related to his service in Rwanda. For years he had been hounded by the belief that he could have prevented the genocide had the United States, the UN, and the international community decided to act more forcibly at the start of the massacre. A few weeks before the report was published, he had been found drunk, lying in a park in Canada. Afterward he revealed he had twice tried to commit suicide. His sad tale went unreported in the United States, except for one brief mention in a Baltimore newspaper that reprinted a *Toronto Star* article. Dallaire's personal story and the OAU's criticism of Clinton were important topics that warranted more than cursory coverage.

Sadly, not much additional information has developed since publication. The Rwanda genocide has receded further in time and memory. It has not been on the top of the list when journalists assess the Clinton presidency.

There was no mainstream press response to this article, as far as I could tell. But that was not surprising. My column was necessary only because the mainstream media had decided not to cover this subject.

To get more information, one can read the report at www.oau-oua.org/Document/ipep/ipep.htm.

For general information on human rights and genocide in Africa and elsewhere, visit the sites of Human Rights Watch (www.hrw.org) and Amnesty International (www.amnesty.org).

7 CENSORED

Independent Study Points to Dangers of Genetically Altered Foods (Dismissed by Media and Biotech Industry)

Sources:
IN THESE TIMES
January 10, 2000
Title: "No Small (Genetic) Potatoes"
Author: Joel Bleifuss
www.inthesetimes.com

EXTRA!
May/June 2000
Title: "Genetic Gambling"
Author: Karen Charman

MULTINATIONAL MONITOR
January/February 2000
Title: "Don't Ask, Don't Know"
Author: Ben Lilliston
www.essential.org/monitor/mm2000/mm0001.05.html

Corporate news coverage: Wide coverage in England including *The Independent*, *The Herald*, *Irish Times*, *The Guardian*, *The Times* (London); *The Washington Post*, October 15, 1999, p. A3 (negative review); *The Wall Street Journal* attempted to debunk the story with the headline "Attack of the Killer Potato," February 16, 1999

Faculty Evaluators: Lynn Cominsky, Myrna Goodman, Richard Senghas
Student Researchers: Katie Anderson, Kate Sims, Stephanie Garber

In 1998, Arpad Pusztai, a researcher at Rowett Research Institute in Aberdeen, Scotland, preformed the first independent non-industry sponsored study analyzing genetically engineered food and its effects on mammals. The study had been undertaken to determine whether or not the spliced genes themselves could be damaging to the mammal ingesting them. However, preliminary data from the study suggests something even more startling: The actual process of genetic alteration itself may cause damage to the mammalian digestive and immune systems.

Pusztai's study found that rats fed transgenic potatoes (artificially bio-engineered to include a gene from another species) showed evidence of organ damage, thickening of the small intestine, and poor brain development. The transgenic potatoes used in the study had been genetically engineered to contain lectin, a sugar-binding protein, to make the plants pest-resistant. The adverse reactions only occurred in the group that was fed the transgenic potatoes. The control group, fed plain potatoes mixed with lectin from the same source, were normal.

These results indicated that the adverse reactions were not caused by the added lectin, but by the process of genetic engineering itself. "All the presently used genetically modified material has been created using essentially the same technology," Pusztai told the *Sunday Herald* "If there really is a problem, it won't just apply to the potatoes, but probably to all other transgenics."

In August 1998 Pusztai appeared on the British television program *The World in Action* to report the findings of his study. In an attempt to quell the resulting public furor, Rowett Institute director Philip James (who had approved Pusztai's TV appearance) said the research didn't exist. He fired Pusztai, broke up his research team, seized the data, and halted six other similar projects. It came out later that Monsanto, a leading U.S. biotech firm, had given the Rowett Institute a $224,000 grant prior to Pusztai's interview and subsequent firing.

Evidence emerged to support the legitimacy of Pusztai's research. The research that James claimed did not exist showed up during an internal audit. Later, *Lancet*, the prestigious British medical journal, published a peer-reviewed paper Pusztai had coauthored supporting the research. Prince Charles began to question the safety of genetically engineered foods on his website and became allies with Pusztai. The Prince wrote an article in the *Daily Mail* expressing concerns over the lack of prerelease safety research on genetically engineered foods.

Back in 1992 the U.S. Food and Drug Administration had determined that genetically engineered foods were in most cases "the same as or substantially similar to substances commonly found in food" and thus are not required to undergo specific safety tests prior to entering the market. The FDA's policy was a dramatic shift away from the long-standing requirement that companies prove their products are safe. Says Rebecca Goldburg of the Environmental Defense Fund, "The FDA's policy strongly favors food manufacturers at the expense of consumer protection."

According to author Ben Lilliston, no independent or government-sponsored research into the effects of genetically engineered foods on mammals is now being carried out in either the United Kingdom or the United States. As Pusztai wrote in *Lancet*, "[These] experiments need to be repeated. We would be happy to oblige. It was not we who stopped the work."

UPDATE BY BEN LILLISTON "Genetically engineered crops have been introduced in the U.S. in a quiet, almost stealthy manner. Most Americans know little about this radically new way of producing food, and even less about what type of risks these foods pose. Traditionally, U.S. regulatory agencies are some of the toughest in the world in protecting human health and the environment. But, as the article points out, genetically engineered foods have entered the marketplace almost entirely unregulated.

The story was published at the beginning of a turbulent year for the biotech industry. For the first time since engineered crops have been introduced, we saw a decline in the overall planting of GE crops in the U.S. In response to growing domestic and international criticism, the Food and Drug Administration announced it was drafting new rules for regulating these crops. Perhaps the most important event in the last year was the contamination of the food supply with the unapproved genetically engineered Star-Link corn. The corn had been approved by the Environmental Protection Agency for consumption by animals but not humans, because of concerns that it may cause allergic reactions. The StarLink discovery by a coalition of advocacy groups has resulted in approximately 300 food products recalled, mass litigation within the agriculture community, and drops in exports to key markets including Japan. StarLink has also raised questions about the U.S. regulatory system, and, at the end of 2000, several bills in Congress were proposing major changes in the way U.S. agencies regulate these crops.

The last year has seen dramatic changes within the agriculture community regarding GE crops. Farmers are now having to worry about liability, markets, and cross pollination. Grain elevators are facing increased expenses associated with testing and segregating genetically engineered and non-GE crops. And even giant grain processors like Archer Daniels Midland are warning farmers about growing genetically engineered crops. The entire food sector is wary of the impacts these crops are having on our ability to export.

The mainstream media has been consistently behind the ball on the story of genetically engineered crops—particularly the regulatory angle. While they have been quick to cover the latest scientific breakthroughs by the industry, and report extensively on the promise of the technology, they have ignored the inability of U.S. regulatory agencies to keep up with the advances and unique risks of biotech foods. While the Star-Link debacle has received considerable coverage, few reporters have identified the underlying cause, which is the overwhelmed, antiquated system that allowed it to happen.

There are numerous resources on the web for more information on genetically engineered foods:

Institute for Agriculture and Trade Policy: www.sustain.org/biotech/

Greenpeace USA: www.greenpeace usa.org/ge/

Union of Concerned Scientists: www. ucsusa.org

Ag Biotech Info-Net: www.biotech-info.org

Ben Lilliston: blilliston@iatp.org

UPDATE BY KAREN CHARMAN Genetic technologies, like chemical and nuclear technologies before them, have the potential to alter in unforeseen and unwelcome ways all that we depend upon for our survival—our environment, our food, and our health. Like the products of chemical and nuclear technologies, biotechnology products are being ushered out into the environment and onto the market for people to consume without fully considering, let alone understanding, either their long- or short-term impacts.

Through intellectual property patents, biotechnology grants private corporations ownership to previously unowned living things. The economics behind biotechnology are the technology's driving force, but discussion of life patents and their implications are absent from most media accounts and, consequently, public debate.

My story on media coverage of biotechnology for *Extra!* pointed out that scientific understanding of how genes work in organisms is in its infancy. The same is true for scientific understanding of ecology. Yet without a thorough understanding of the web of life and how its different components interact with each other, it's impossible to know what the true impact of releasing these novel organisms will be or to assess whether we should be taking this genetic gamble.

Much less risky solutions exist to the problems biotech purports to solve. But they are not being presented in the mainstream media. Instead, most coverage continues to uncritically spread industry-promoted myths about biotechnology while failing to comprehensively and accurately report the technology's impacts, risks associated with biotechnology, and why it is being pushed so hard. Biotech food has become a flash point with consumers overseas and now that opposition is growing here on the home turf, biotech promoters are attempting to manage the public debate with sophisticated PR. Unfortunately, much of the PR continues to appear in the mainstream media.

A number of citizen groups are now doing excellent work on genetic engineering issues. The Organic Consumers Association (www.purefood.org) has a website with a tremendous amount of information and links to other sites covering genetic engineering. The Institute for Agriculture and Trade Policy (www.iatp.org) has in-depth information on economics and trade issues related to agricultural biotechnology. The Ag Bio-Tech InfoNet compiles scientific reports and technical analysis on biotechnology and genetic engineering in food production, processing, and marketing.

In addition to becoming informed about genetically engineered food, people can take simple action on their own by buying and requesting organic food.

Karen Charman: aurora@ulster.net

UPDATE BY JOEL BLEIFUSS The U.S. media has not covered the disturbing public health questions raised by Arpad Pusztai's research into genetically engineered potatoes. Genetic engineering continues to receive a clean bill of health by U.S. regulatory agencies despite the fact that no independent, government-supported research into the effects of genetically engineered foods on mammals has been or is being conducted. This is in large part because the biotech industry has a sophisticated PR apparatus in place that has so far successfully been able to spin the industry's line that genetically altered food is absolutely safe. Concerns raised by scientists like Pusztai or Michael Hansen at Consumers Union are all but ignored. As Hansen told me, "But for the folks that criticize it, Pusztai's study is still a much better-designed study than the industry-sponsored feeding studies I have seen in peer-reviewed literature. Pusztai's are the kinds of experiments that need to be done with engineered foods.

Joel Bleifuss: itt@inthesetimes.com

8 CENSORED

Drug Companies Influence Doctors and Health Organizations to Push Meds

Sources:
WASHINGTON MONTHLY
May 12, 2000
Title: "Drug Rush"
Author: Stephen Pomper

MOJO WIRE MAGAZINE
November/December 1999
Title: "Prozac.org"
Author: Ken Silverstein
www.motherjones.com/mother_jones/N
D99/nami.html

DENDRON #43
Spring 2000
Title: "NAMI:
The Story Behind the Story"
Author: David Oaks
www.MindFreedom.org/DENDRON/de
ndron43/namislush/namislush.html

NETWORKER
March/April 2000
Title: "Exposing the Mythmakers"
Authors: Barry Duncan, Scott Miller
Jacqueline Sparks
www.familytherapynetworker.com/

Faculty Evaluators:
Victor Daniels, Ph.D.,
Cindy Sterns, Ph.D.

Student Researchers:
Bruce Harden, Karen Parlette,
Licia Marshall, Steve Quartz

More than 130 million prescriptions were written in 1999 for depression and mental health related symptoms, at a cost of $8.58 billion. Physicians know that antidepressants are only part of the answer for mental health, but marketing by drug companies has created the mythology of pills as cure-alls. A 1999 federal research study found that the newer antidepressants were effective in only half of the cases and only outperformed placebos by 18 percent.

Drug companies spend $5 billion annually to send sales representatives to doctors' offices. Sales reps keep FBI-style dossiers on physicians that include information such as the names of family members, golf handicaps, and clothing preferences. Hard sales tactics and small gifts are part of the pitch. In addition, pharmaceutical companies provide perks (such as tickets to sporting events) and outright compensation to doctors for their participation in the prescribing of particular drugs to their mental health patients.

On another front, pharmaceutical companies are reaping big profits by promoting forced drug use through programs at the National Alliance for the Mentally Ill (NAMI). With drug company funding, NAMI promotes a program of in-home forced drug treatment, called the Program of Assertive Community Treatment (PACT). The money is funneled through a suborganization of NAMI called the NAMI Campaign to End Discrimination. While PACT has some features that clients like, it also puts an emphasis on "medication compliance." For instance, PACT at times includes daily psychiatric drug deliveries to people's doorsteps and living rooms, backed up by court orders. PACT enforces medication compliance by visiting clients' homes daily to stand and watch as clients take their medicine—involuntarily—in their own living rooms. There is a clear conflict of interest here since the pharmaceutical companies are reaping profits from the drugs the patients are forced to take.

The psychiatric drug industry is pouring millions into a NAMI-controlled slush fund, which is the monetary force behind one of NAMI's central goals: to get PACT into every state by 2002. NAMI leaders claim their hands are clean of drug money.

They bill NAMI as "a grassroots organization for individuals with brain disorders, and their family members." However, Janet Foner, a co-coordinator of Support Coalition International, an activist organization of "psychiatric survivors," says NAMI does a good job in some areas, but argues that the group's corporate sponsors help shape its agenda. "They appear to be a completely independent organization, but they parrot the line of the drug companies in saying that drugs are essential [in treating mental health disorders]."

NAMI has a policy of never disclosing its drug company funding. *Mother Jones* researchers used internal documents to prove that NAMI received $11.72 million from the psychiatric drug industry in just two and a half years. NAMI's leading donor is Eli Lilly and Company, which is the maker of Prozac.

UPDATE BY STEPHEN POMPER "Drug Rush" explores the lopsidedness in the FDA's regulation of new drugs. Over the last decade, AIDS activists seeking quicker access to breakthrough treatments and pharmaceutical companies eager to get their products on the shelves have successfully pressured Congress to ramp up the process for approving new drugs. But once drugs are on the market, the FDA has scant resources for monitoring their safety. The agency is short on medically trained epidemiologists to track the bad effects of new drugs. The nation's safety monitoring system relies on voluntary (and unreliable) reporting by private physicians. And at the same time, the pharmaceutical industry encourages the rapid uptake of new products through consumer advertising (including, thanks to newly relaxed regulations, television advertising) and physician-focused promotions ranging from free pens to complementary basketball tickets.

In the months since the article appeared, the FDA has been increasingly active in trying to bolster its safety monitoring programs. An internal report, released in November 2000, concluded that the FDA should do more to monitor drugs once they're approved. Officials within the FDA's Office of Post-Marketing Drug Risk Assessment have said that they'd like to see organizations like the Agency for Healthcare Research Quality receive more money to monitor prescription drugs once they are on the market. They have also called for funds collected under the Prescription Drug User Fee Act to be earmarked for safety monitoring. As FDA Commissioner Jane Henney wrote in a letter to the *Washington Monthly*: "Although [monitoring for drugs on the market] has been updated, the monitoring system requires a significant infusion of resources to make it stronger."

Readers interested in exploring the FDA's regulation of new drugs should begin with Public Citizen's website, David Willman's excellent coverage of the Rezulin crisis in the *L.A. Times*, and the *Washington Post's* recent six-part series on the conduct of U.S. drug testing in foreign countries.

Stephen Pomper: pomper_andersen@hotmail.com

UPDATE BY DAVID OAKS The guinea pigs are fighting back. You haven't heard much about this rebellion in the mainstream press, but there's a 30-year-old social change movement led by people who have experienced human rights violations in the mental health system. These are the activists who educated me about the issues described in my piece.

For centuries, the psychiatric industry has churned out new methods and models to profitably control people diagnosed with mental disabilities. The difference this time is that an increasingly sophisticated and united "mad movement" is resisting the latest corporate trend.

The involuntary psychiatric drugging of people living in their own homes, in their own neighborhoods, is an especially alarming phenomenon. Since my article was published, the use of coerced outpatient psychiatric drugging is accelerating. In the USA, psychiatric drug industry front groups have won increased federal support for this authoritarian approach. In Canada, the U.K., and Australia, similar front groups are making headway. We are witnessing the globalization of a new "chemical prison" industry.

The guinea pigs did win a major battle since my article was published. In July 2000, hundreds of mental health consumers and psychiatric survivors in California stopped a proposal in the State Assembly that would have legalized involuntary outpatient psychiatric drugging.

The mainstream press perspective on forced psychiatric drugging has almost always been from the wrong end of the needle. Corporate media typically ignore the marginalized individuals who feel violated by forced psychiatric procedures.

For example, the popular press is not reporting a related news story that has emerged in mainstream medical industry publications: Recent studies indicate that long-term use of the drugs most commonly administered during involuntary procedures has been linked to such extreme changes in the size and shape of the brain that these drug-induced brain alterations are visible under MRI and CT scans.

The dominant media tend to either glorify the drug industry's most recent magic pill, or vilify the supposedly dangerously mentally ill. While it is important to respect the many clients who willingly choose to take prescribed psychiatric drugs, the public deserves to hear more about holistic alternatives to the corporate biopsychiatric medical model.

Readers seeking more information about, or involvement in, the "guinea pig revolt" may contact these nonprofit groups:

Support Coalition International, which I direct, is open to the public, and is led by psychiatric survivors. Support Coalition unites nearly 100 grassroots groups in a dozen countries, and publishes *Dendron News*. Web site: www.MindFreedom.org. Phone (in the U.S.): (877) MAD-PRIDE.

National Association for Rights Protection & Advocacy (NARPA) holds an annual conference of advocates, attorneys, and activists working for the rights of people diagnosed with psychiatric disabilities. Web site: www.NARPA.org.

International Center for the Study of Psychiatry & Psychology (ICSPP) is a hub for psychiatrists, psychologists, and other mental health workers who are bravely challenging their own industry's ethics. Several of these mental health professionals have authored relevant books. I especially recommend recent books by Ty Colbert, Ph.D., Loren Mosher, M.D., and

ICSPP's director, Peter Breggin, M.D.
Website: www.icspp.org
David Oaks: dendron@efn.org

9 CENSORED

EPA Plans to Disburse Toxic/ Radioactive Wastes into Denver's Sewage System

Source:
THE PROGRESSIVE
May 2000
Title: "Plutonium Pancakes"
Author: Will Fantle
www.progressive.org

Faculty Evaluator: Randy Dodgen, Ph.D.
Student Researchers:
Kim Roberts and Mike Graves

The Environmental Protection Agency (EPA) plans to pump toxic waste water into Denver's sewer system in order to clean up a Superfund site at the Lowry landfill.

Between 1950 and 1980, at the Lowry landfill near Denver, millions of gallons of hazardous industrial wastes were dumped into shallow unlined pits. The EPA declared the 480-acre site a Superfund site in 1984. Now the EPA wants to treat the contaminated groundwater at the landfill and discharge it into the Denver metropolian area sewage system. The sewage system would then use the sludge from the treated water to fertilize Colorado farmlands.

Citizen groups say that the landfill is widely contaminated with highly radioactive plutonium and other deadly wastes. Adrienne Anderson, a lawyer and instructor at the University of Boulder, stated that EPA's plan is a way to "legally pump plutonium into the sewer line." Plutonium is widely considered one of the most deadly substances on the planet.

Anderson and her students have accrued some 200,000 files on the Lowry landfill. One document entitled "Preliminary Evaluation of Potential Department of Energy Radioactive Wastes," dated December 13, 1991, found that the levels of plutonium and radioactive americium detected at the Lowry landfill were 10 to 10,000 times greater than the average levels reported for a nuclear weapons plant in that area. The document had been released by the Lowry Coalition, a group of corporations and government agencies that dumped materials at the site. The polluters included Adolph Coors (who once produced nuclear fuel), Lockheed Martin, Rockwell (then-operator of the U.S. Department of Energy's Rocky Flats nuclear bomb plant), Hewlett Packard, IBM, Waste Management, and the *Denver Post*. The EPA itself also dumped pesticides and other lab wastes at the site.

In 1961 Colorado State Trooper Bill Wilson stopped a milk truck that was spraying liquid on the ground at Lowry. According to Wilson, the truck's operator told him he was dumping radioactive wastewater from the Rocky Flats plant and had the government's permission to do it. Wilson realized that he couldn't do anything about it, but he filed reports on identical activities he witnessed for several more years with the state's transportation regulator.

Gwen Hooten, at EPA's region 8 office in Denver, is in charge of the Lowry cleanup. She and other EPA officials deny that the site is poisoned by plutonium or any other nuclear wastes. Hooten dismisses the 1991 document as "invalidated data."

Critics are not buying it. Any plutonium, heavy metal, or other toxic wastes pumped through the sewage system will likely settle there for years. The problem will only become more widespread.

In 1993 the EPA classified municipal sludge as a fertilizer for farmers. Denver municipal sludge is already being spread on farmland as biosolids. Wheat grown on this land is sold for human consumption.

UPDATE BY WILL FANTLE The legacy of toxic waste left during last century's time of ignorance and uncontrolled disposal practices will likely vex our environment and children for decades to come. Beyond containment of the problem, there are no obvious answers.

Since the publication of "Plutonium Pancakes," the city of Denver began accepting the Lowry landfill's toxic liquid discharges. The EPA's solution to the headache—mostly relying upon diluting Lowry's toxins by flushing them into the city's wastewater stream—was halted after a couple of months, according to Steve Pearlman of the Wastewater Reclamation District.

The treated wastewater remained sufficiently poisonous to harm the growth and reproductive rates of microorganisms used to measure health and safety. Pearlman says the district has made some changes and will begin accepting the Lowry toxins again in the near future. The district has also eased its detection standards for certain contaminants (including some that are radioactive), a move Pearlman attributes to lab testing capabilities.

Adrienne Anderson, the outspoken opponent of the disposal plan, has been embroiled in a whistleblower case brought about by her testimony on behalf of the union representing the workers at the Wastewater District. Her comments at an EPA hearing were challenged, leading to a court trail.

During the course of the trial, Anderson discovered that she had been the subject of a coordinated PR campaign aimed at discrediting her. The attacks were part of an effort undertaken by the district to win public support and acceptance for the spreading of the district's sludge on Colorado farm fields.

The district even garnered an award from the national pro-sludge Water and Environment Federation for the PR campaign. The three-ring binder detailing the district's work (obtained by Anderson through a Freedom of Information Act request) contains an entire section describing how they labored to sabotage Anderson.

Anderson says union workers have also suffered under the Lowry waste treatment plan. Workers concerned with their health and safety have been forced out, with one employee even receiving an anonymous death threat.

Throughout, the region's most powerful media have largely remained silent. The state's two biggest newspapers, the *Denver Post* and the *Rocky Mountain News* (which merged in the last year), are among the many powerful corporations who had dumped toxic wastes into Lowry. Their hand in the mess may partly explain their silence, but e-mail messages reveal another story. As part of her digging into the smear campaign against her, Anderson says, she found an e-mail exchange between the district and a local reporter "cackling about the defamatory attacks on me."

While occasional reportage of the Lowry situation continues out of state and nationally (including a *Christian Science Monitor* update), Anderson says "no reporter in Denver will talk to me." News releases issued by her, the union, and others are routinely ignored. And the electronic media, she indicates, has been unwilling to commit investigative resources to the story.

Those seeking more information can contact Adrienne Anderson at (303) 492-2952 or via e-mail at: andersa @mho.com.

10 CENSORED

Silicon Valley Uses Immigrant Engineers to Keep Salaries Low

Sources:
LABOR NOTES
September 2000
Title: "Immigrants Find High-Tech Servitude in Silicon Valley"
Author: David Bacon

WASHINGTON FREE PRESS
July/August 2000
Title: "Silicon Valley Sweatshops"
Author: David Bacon

Corporate Media Coverage:
San Francisco Chronicle,
September 29, 2000, p. A29

Community Evaluators:
Fred Fletcher, Ervand Peterson
Student Researchers:
Ambrosia Crumley, Jennifer Swift,
Terrie Girdner, Naomi Igra

High-skilled immigrant workers in Silicon Valley are being exploited by employers. Existing immigration law sets a cap on the number the H1-B visas the industry can use to hire immigrant engineers, so this year Silicon Valley electronics giants have been pushing for more H1-B workers. While H1-B status laborers boost corporate bottom lines, there is a devastating effect on the workers themselves.

AFL-CIO vice president Linda Chavez-Thompson accuses the industry of using the H1-B visa program to keep their workers in a position of dependence. She points out that these workers are often hired under individual contracts, which by U.S. law means they don't have the right to organize. For the high-tech industry this protection against strikes and unions is a key attraction of the H1-B program, especially in the aftermath of the Boeing Corp. engineers who mounted one of the most successful strikes in recent history.

Like other contract labor programs for lower wage and factory laborers, the H1-B program gives employers the power not only to hire and fire workers, but to grant legal immigration status as well. If an employer does not like something a worker does—such as defending themselves by filing discrimination complaints—the employer has the power to deport the worker.

One contract worker from India, Kim Singh, says that an employer withheld 25 percent of his earnings, none of which was returned when his contract was up. Another employer had him working seven days a week with no overtime compensation.

High-tech companies claim that a domestic labor shortage justifies the use of immigrant contractors with H1-B visas. Labor advocates counter that the problem is not a labor shortage, but instead the industry's unwillingness to pay the salaries that American high-tech workers demand. Moreover, use of immigrant labor protects high-tech companies

from strikes and union demands. Civil rights groups add that if Silicon Valley companies were interested in increasing the domestic high-tech labor market, they could train American workers—an approach that could also increase minority representation in the high-tech sector. The industry's resistance to such alternatives indicates that its reliance on immigrant workers is not about a domestic labor shortage but about a desire for dependent employees and higher profits.

Both the Republicans and Democrats want the industry's substantial campaign contributions to continue. So while the two parties quarrel over the details, both support revamping of U.S. immigration law in order to supply more immigrant labor to U.S. industry. Yet if Silicon Valley would take the millions they are pouring into political contributions and raise salaries instead, they would find all the workers they need.

African-American and Latino engineers protest the increase in H1-B visas because they believe it will eliminate jobs for engineers of color in an industry where local minority representation is already very low.

The practice of recruiting highly skilled workers from developing countries, such as India and the Philippines, perpetuates the loss of skilled workers in those countries, a situation called "brain drain." Such workers end up subsidizing U.S. industry instead of contributing to industry in the native countries that paid to educate them.

Last February the AFL-CIO proposed a reform that would benefit workers instead of making them more vulnerable. The proposal includes a general amnesty for undocumented families already here. The proposal would also bring an end to employer sanctions and allow workers the right to organize to protest unfair and exploitative treatment.

UPDATE BY DAVID BACON "Immigrants Find High-Tech Servitude in Silicon Valley" exposed the impact of Silicon Valley's H1-B contract labor program on both contract workers themselves, and on other workers in high-tech and other industries. The media generally accept uncritically the idea that a legitimate purpose of immigration law is to supply labor to U.S. industry, and therefore saw little wrong with contract labor proposals.

Other proposals to institute and expand contract labor programs in agriculture, meatpacking, and other industries were made this year. If adopted, they will have a disastrous impact on immigrant workers, treating them as cheap, disposable labor instead of giving them legal status and protecting their rights. Efforts to organize unions by immigrants and nonimmigrants alike will be made much more difficult.

These consequences for workers were ignored by the generally supportive way the mainstream press covered Silicon Valley's effort to pass a bill expanding the H1-B program. A few articles covered fraud in the program's administration, but hardly any looked at the exploitation of the workers themselves, and none at the bill's potential impact on labor and union organizing.

This year immigrant rights groups were joined by the AFL-CIO in an historic call for a general immigration amnesty and the repeal of employer sanctions (the law which makes it a crime for an undocumented worker to hold a job). That received some press coverage, but the media then ignored the way those proposals fell victim to calls for contract labor.

In early October, Silicon Valley's proposal was adopted by a unanimous vote in the House, and only one dissent, Ernest Hollings, in the Senate. To ensure the right outcome, the vote was held late at night, after the Republican leadership had assured Democrats that no more significant votes would be taken.

Microsoft, Intel, and other high tech giants showed their gratitude by contributing hundreds of thousands of soft-money dollars, through the Michigan Chamber of Commerce, to the unsuccessful reelection campaign of Senator Spencer Abraham (R-MI), who shepherded the bill to passage.

The H-1B+ strategy, which tried to tie limited immigration reforms to the proposal, failed. Republican Congressional leaders passed the contract labor proposal without amendments. In an election year in which both parties were courting the votes of the powerful and wealthy high-tech industry, no one wanted to vote against it, with or without pro-immigrant reforms.

In subsequent weeks, the administration and Democratic leaders tried to tack the proposal, called the Latino Immigrant Fairness Act, onto other legislation. Through the November election, that effort was resisted by Republicans, and Democrats negotiated further and further concessions. In the closing days of Congress, an agreement was reached on legislation which contained almost none of the original proposals.

Meanwhile, the danger of contract labor actually increased. Agribusiness negotiated an expansion of the current "guestworker" law, which permits growers to import farm workers. In return, many undocumented farm workers would have been allowed to apply for visas. Although anti-immigrant Congress members defeated that proposal, it will be reintroduced next year.

In Nebraska, scene of the nation's largest workplace immigration raids two years ago (see "The INS Takes On Labor," *The Nation*, September 1999), the governor proposed a contract labor program to supply workers to the meatpacking industry. And as unions and community organizations geared up to organize workers in nonunion plants, the INS resumed wholesale deportations.

A new Republican administration will have an even more favorable attitude toward business proposals for contract worker programs. Divisions among Democrats will make it difficult to defeat them. At the same time, the anti-immigrant Right will oppose any broad amnesty for undocumented workers or effort to lift employer sanctions and end INS workplace raids.

The AFL-CIO, churches, and community organizations, however, remain committed to those pro-immigrant reforms. That promises a fight over these proposals in this year's Congress.

For more information, contact the Labor Immigrant Organizers Network— (510) 643-2355, the National Campaign for Dignity and Amnesty—(212) 473-3936, the AFL-CIO—(202) 637-5000, or the National Network for Immigrant and Refugee Rights—(510) 465-1984.

David Bacon: dbacon@igc.apc.org

11 CENSORED

United Nations Corporate Partnerships— A Human Rights Peril

Sources:
DOLLARS AND SENSE
July/August 2000
Title: "United McNations"
Author: Kenny Bruno

MULTINATIONAL MONITOR
March 2000
Title: "Perilous Partnerships"
Author: Danielle Knight
www.essential.org/monitor/mm2000/0
0march/economics1.html

Corporate News Coverage: *Toronto Star*, March 19, 1999; *Washington Post*, July 27, 2000, p. A6

Faculty Evaluators: Tim Wandling, Ph.D., Robert Tellander
Student Researchers: Cassandra Pojda, Bonnie Faulkner, Terrie Girdner

In a move to make the United Nations more corporate-friendly, officials are calling for UN-corporate partnerships. The UN's new partners include multinational giants like McDonald's, Disney, Dow, and Unocal.

A business-friendly ideology at the UN is based on a desire to gain favor with the United States, the UN's largest funder, and to raise money through private sources. The practice of the U.S. withholding dues from the UN for political purposes has jeopardized its operations. Now facing a funding crisis, the UN is turning to direct corporate aid on an unprecedented scale. UN officials are keenly aware that support from the United States is predicated upon a friendly stance toward business. U.S. business pressure led to the closure of the UN's Center on Transnational Corporations in the early 1990s.

UN agencies have entered into an array of partnerships with giant corporations, including many that citizen movements have denounced for violations of human and labor rights. Human rights groups around the world are increasingly challenging the new partnership arrangements for fear that these new relationships will undermine the UN's ability to serve as a counterbalance to global corporate power. Human rights groups fear that corporations will get a public boost by wrapping themselves in the UN flag while making no commitments to adjust their behavior to reflect the institution's principles. They are calling on the UN to pull back from the partnerships and set clear guidelines for any cooperative ventures with business enterprises. At stake are the core values of the UN itself as the partnerships undermine the primacy of human rights, health, labor rights and environmental protection to favor markets and profits.

Executive director of UNICEF Carol Bellamy warned in April 1999, "It is dangerous to assume that goals of the private sector are somehow synonymous with those of the United Nations." Ward Moorehouse of the Center for International and Public Affairs in New York stated that "the UN's job must be to monitor and hold corporations accountable, not to give out special favors."

General Kofi Annan set the stage for the partnership initiative by calling on CEOs to join a "Global Compact" with the UN. He also challenged business leaders to enact the nine principles derived from UN agreements on labor standards, human rights, and environmental protection.

One of the controversial partnerships is the Global Sustainable Development Facility (GSDF) set up to fund sustainable development projects worldwide. The GSDF is now headed by a steering committee that includes Dow Chemical, the world's largest producer of chlorine and pesticides, and Asea Brown and Bovari, one of the main suppliers for the controversial Three Gorges Dam in China.

The UN High Commissioner on Refugees, Sadako Ogata, is now co-chair of the Business Humanitarian Forum with Unocal President John Imle. Unocal is a business partner with Burma's murderous military regime. Unocal's gas pipeline project in Burma has generated thousands of refugees seeking to escape the militarized pipeline area.

UNESCO, the UN's educational arm, is teaming up with Disney and McDonald's to present "Millennium Dreamer" youth awards to two thousand kids. It "should have crossed UNESCO officials' minds that young people have more than enough exposure to these two brands already," said Beth Handman, a curriculum specialist in New York city schools.

UPDATE BY KENNY BRUNO The Battle in Seattle revealed the existence of a growing citizens' movement actively opposing corporate globalization and the international institutions that support it. Many in this movement see the United Nations, with its unique dedication to universal values of peace, human rights, environmental protection, and public health, as a potential counterbalance to the WTO and its pro-corporate agenda of free trade and investment. However, under financial pressure, due largely to the United States' refusal to pay its dues, and fearful of irrelevance in world affairs, the UN has turned toward "partnerships" with the private sector, including some of the same companies against which citizens' movements campaign. These include Nike, Shell, Rio Tinto, and many others. "Perilous Partnerships" revealed the trend toward partnerships with business at the UN.

The rhetoric around the partnerships reveals a tendency for the UN to endorse a view of corporate-led globalization supported by the WTO, World Bank, and IMF. This endorsement comes precisely at the time of a popular backlash against corporate globalization, and represents a betrayal of "we the peoples" the UN is supposed to represent. In addition, the partnerships have no monitoring or enforcement of corporate behavior; therefore companies can sign onto UN principles without having to adhere to them. For some of these companies, the partnerships amount to a slick PR initiative, a chance to "bluewash" their image by wrapping themselves in the blue flag of the United Nations while carrying on with business as usual.

After publication of "Perilous Partnerships," the International Forum on Globalization sponsored an all-day teach-in on the UN and corporate globalization. Later that week, the Alliance for a Corporate-free United Nations— a grouping of nongovernmental organizations from around the world—was born. UN officials have acknowledged some of our concerns, though the momentum toward partnerships has not been stopped. At the time of this writing, the General Assembly has been deadlocked since December 12, 2000, over a resolution that would encourage such partnerships.

Limited coverage of the story from the UN's point of view started in January 1999, with Kofi Annan's launch of the Global Compact with corporations. Coverage of our critique of the partnerships has been nonexistent on television, while radio coverage has been limited to local stations, with the exception of Pacifica. In print, the *New York Times* did one major piece, in the context of the Millennium Summit, while *Business Week* ran a short blurb. In Europe, there has been somewhat more print coverage, including an exchange of opinion pieces in the *International Herald Tribune* and a highly critical piece in the *Guardian*.

This coverage, along with exchanges of letters between our Alliance and UN officials, our report "Tangled Up In Blue," and a great deal of other information is available on this theme at www.corpwatch.org/un. We encourage you to visit the site and add your voice to those who believe the UN's role should be to monitor and hold accountable the global corporations, rather than to form partnerships with them.

Kenny Bruno: kbruno@verizon.net

12 CENSORED
Cuba Leads the World in Organic Farming

Sources:
THIRD WORLD RESURGENCE
Spring 2000 Issue #118/119
Title: "Cuba's Organic Revolution"
Author: Hugh Warwick

SUSTAINABLE TIMES
Fall 1999
Title: "Farming With Fidel"
Author: Alison Auld

DESIGNER/BUILDER
August 2000
Title: "Cuba's New Revolution"
Authors: Stephen Zunes

Corporate Media Coverage: Gannett, September 15, 1999; *Dallas Morning News*, January 25, 1998, p. 35A; *The Economist*, April 24, 1999; *Lewiston Morning Tribune*, January 27, 2000, p. 1A; Associated Press, June 5, 2000

Faculty Evaluators: Tony White, Ph.D., Albert Wahrhaftig, Ph.D.
Student Researchers, Bruce Harden, Dana Balicki

Cuba has developed one of the most efficient organic agriculture systems in the world, and organic farmers from other countries are visiting the island to learn the methods.

Due to the U.S. embargo and the collapse of the Soviet Union, Cuba was unable to import chemicals or modern farming machines to uphold a high-tech corporate farming culture. Cuba needed to find another way to feed its people. The lost buying power for agricultural imports led to a general diversification within farming on the island. Organic agriculture has become key to feeding the nation's growing urban populations.

Cuba's new revolution is founded upon the development of an organic agricultural system. Peter Rosset of the Institute for Food and Development Policy states that this is "the largest conversion from conventional agriculture to organic or semi-organic farming that the world has ever known." Not only has organic farming been prosperous, but the migration of small farms and gardens into densely populated urban areas has also played a crucial role in feeding citizens. State food rations were not enough for Cuban families, so farms began to spring up all over the country. Havana, home to nearly 20 percent of Cuba's population, is now also home to more than 8,000 officially recognized gardens, which are in turn cultivated by more than 30,000 people and cover nearly 30 percent of the available land. The growing number of gardens might seem to bring up the problem of space and price of land. However, "the local governments allocate land, which is handed over at no cost as long as it is used for cultivation," says S. Chaplowe in the *Newsletter of the World Sustainable Agriculture Association*.

The removal of the "chemical crutch" has been the most important factor to come out of the Soviet collapse, trade embargo, and subsequent organic revolution. Though Cuba is organic by default because it has no means of acquiring pesticides and herbicides, the quality and quantity of crop yields have increased. This increase is occurring at a lower cost and with fewer health and environmental side effects than ever. There are 173 established vermicompost centers across Cuba, which produce 93,000 tons of natural compost a year. The agricultural abundance that Cuba is beginning to experience is disproving the myth that organic farming on a grand scale is inefficient or impractical.

So far Cuba has been successful with its transformation from conventional, high input, mono-crop intensive agriculture to a more diverse and localized farming system that continues to grow. The country is rapidly moving away from a monoculture of tobacco and sugar. It now needs much more diversity of food crops as well as regular crop rotation and soil conservation efforts to continue to properly nourish millions of Cuban citizens.

In June 2000, a group of Iowa farmers, professors, and students traveled to Cuba to view the approach to sustainable agriculture. Rather than relying on chemical fertilizers, Cuba relies on

THIS MODERN WORLD
by TOM TOMORROW

organic farming, using compost and worms to fertilize soil. There are many differences between farming in the United States and Cuba, but "in many ways they're ahead of us," say Richard Wrage, of Boone County Iowa Extension Office. Lorna Michael Butler, Chair of Iowa State University's sustainable agriculture department, said that "more students should study Cuba's growing system."

NOTE: While two national wire services covered this story, very few newspapers actually picked it up. The *Washington Post* (November 2, 2000, p. A29), gave an anti-Castro spin to the story by focusing on community gardens as necessary to off set food shortages and nutritional problems. The gardens were depicted as contributing only "slightly" to food production in a socialist agriculture system with problems of "inefficiency and lack of individual incentives." Nothing was said about the successful transformation of Cuban agriculture to a mostly organic system.

13 CENSORED

The World Trade Organization is an Illegal Institution

Source:
COVERTACTION QUARTERLY
Spring/Summer 2000
Title: "Seattle and Beyond:
The Illegality of the WTO"
Author: Michel Chossudovsky
www.caq.com/

Faculty Evaluators: Richard Senghas, Ph.D., Andy Merrifield, Ph.D.
Student Researchers: Kate Sims, Dana Balicki, Brian Baptista

Something not mentioned by the corporate press or most of the 1,200 groups from 85 countries that opposed the World Trade Organization (WTO) policies during and after the Seattle demonstrations in 1999, is the fact that the WTO is actually an illegal institution.

The WTO was put in place in 1994 following the signing in Morocco of a "technical document" negotiated behind closed doors. Even the heads of the delegations involved in the agreement were not completely informed of the statutes it contained. The instatement of the WTO as a world body was done without the consultation of the citizens (or even their representatives) of the various nations. Following the Morocco meeting, the agreement was either rubber-stamped or never formally ratified by national governments, yet membership in the WTO requires acceptance of its precepts without exception.

The 1994 agreement has been casually embodied in international law, bypassing the democratic process in most all of the member countries. It blatantly overrides national laws and constitutions while providing extensive powers to global banks and multinational corporations. This totalitarian intergovernmental body has been empowered, under international law, to "police" economic and social policies at the country level, suppressing the rights of national governments. Also, the WTO neutralizes the authority of UN agencies such as the International Labor Organization, designed to oversee international trade conduct. It furthermore contradicts the Universal Declaration of Human Rights.

The deregulation of the U.S. banking system was approved by the U.S. Senate barely six weeks before the WTO convention in Seattle. With the stroke of a pen, most all international restraints on Wall Street's powerful banking con-glomerates were revoked. In the months since the Seattle protests, multinational banks and corporations have begun taking over whole countries, causing the collapse of national economies and looting the resources of the indigenous peoples.

The clauses of the defunct Multilateral Agreement on Investment (MAI) (Censored Story #1 of 1999), which was to provide "national treatment to foreign banks and MNCs," are also in the process of becoming a fait accompli through the WTO. U.S. bank deregulation has allowed speculative capital investments globally. U.S. and EU financial giants are moving toward global control of monetary policy and financial markets.

14 CENSORED

Europe Holds Companies Environmentally Responsible, Despite U.S. Opposition

Source:
IN THESE TIMES
April 17, 2000
Title: "The Big Stick Approach"
Author: Joel Bleifuss
www.inthesetimes.com

Faculty Evaluator: David Van Nuys, Ph.D., Peter Phillips, Ph.D.
Student Researchers: Michael Runas, Molly Garrison, Deanna Battaglia

In the near future, the European Union will hold any company that enters the European market responsible for the environmental impacts of its products. Known as Extended Producer Responsibility (EPR), the new regulations will make manufacturers change product design, the kinds of materials used in manufacturing, and the methods by which products are disposed to insure environmental integrity. American corporations have enlisted the aid of the Clinton administration to derail these proposals.

EPR regulations were hugely successful in Germany in the 1990s, requiring all manufacturers, both domestic and foreign, to recycle all product materials, shifting the costs of managing packaging waste from taxpayers to the waste producers. By 2006, vehicles sold in Europe must contain no heavy metals such as lead, mercury, or cadmium, and must be manufactured from recyclable materials. The EU plans to implement EPR regulations for all products that contain electrical circuits, phasing out the use of toxic metals in the production of consumer items like refrigerators and computers.

Joel Bleifuss writes, "the beauty of EPR is that by putting the financial burden on the companies for the environmentally responsible impacts of products throughout their life cycle, industry has a natural economic incentive to act in an environmentally responsible manner." Writing in *Beverage Industry* magazine, E. Gifford Stack of the National Soft Drink Association describes EPR as a "big stick approach." "Because the stick delivers a pretty good financial whack," he notes, "producers also have a financial incentive to design their products to make less waste."

The Clinton administration has done everything it can to block EPR. The President's Council on Sustainable Development, established in 1993 to examine ways to encourage environmentally sustainable growth, held heated discussions about EPR, but in its proposed program the council's industry-dominated task force concluded that users and disposers share equal responsibility with manufactures and suppliers for environmental effects—a position that puts the blame back on the consumer instead of the manufacturer.

Of course, U.S. corporations could take such responsibility, they just don't want to bear the cost. And the EPA and other branches of government are doing what they can to make sure that they won't have to. "We are not going to simply follow in the footsteps of Europe," stated Elizabeth Cotsworth, acting director of EPA's Office of Solid Waste.

Despite the best negative efforts of the Clinton administration, the concept of EPR is spreading. The Organization of Economic Cooperation and Development (OECD), an association of the world's most developed countries, is promoting ERP as a promising new public policy tool. Ignoring protests from the U.S., the OECD is drawing up guidelines on the best ways to implement the EPR program in other countries.

UPDATE BY JOEL BLEIFUSS Though it is a revolutionary—and at the same time entirely feasible—means of greatly reducing negative environmental effects of corporate manufacturing practices, the topic of extended producer responsibility (EPR) has not been touched by the U.S. media. Big business would heartily oppose EPR, since the only way it would work is through government regulation. Some environmental organizations are promoting the idea. The Environmental Defense Fund has information on EPR at: www.environmentaldefense.org/programs/PPA/vic/epr.html. Information on the waste generated by the electronics industry can be found on the Inform Inc. website: www.informinc.org/eprgate.htm

Joel Bleifuss: itt@inthesetimes.com

15 CENSORED

Gerber Uses the WTO to Suppress Laws that Promote Breastfeeding

Sources:
ENVIRONMENT AND
HEALTH WEEKLY
November 18, 1999
Title: "Corporate Rights
vs. Human Need"
Author: Peter Montague
www.rachel.org/bulletin/index.cfm
?St=4

MULTINATIONAL MONITOR
September 2000
Title: "Milking Profits in Pakistan"
Author: Robert Weissman

Faculty Evaluators: Suzanne Toczyski, Ph.D., Linda Novack, Ph.D.
Student Researchers: Deanna Battaglia, Nathalie Manneville

Gerber Baby Foods Corporation has used the World Trade Organization (WTO) to suppress a Guatemalan law that encouraged mothers to breast-feed their children.

For many years, the potential market for baby food corporations has deteriorated because of low birth rates in developing countries. In order to create demand for their products, Gerber Baby Foods has aggressively sought to expand their market in Third World countries, particularly Guatemala.

Under WTO rules, corporate intellectual property rights have higher priority than human health. Small, poor countries can be intimidated by transnational corporations into opening their markets to foreign corporations, and their governments cannot invoke their own domestic laws as a precondition of doing business. In effect, the WTO has given corporations a powerful new way to challenge the laws of any federal, state, or municipal government.

In 1983, the government of Guatemala passed a law and regulations with the goal to inspire new mothers to breast-feed their infants, and to fully understand the harm that could be done to their baby if they used breast-milk substitutes. The Guatemalan law prohibited the use of labels that associated infant formula with a healthy, chubby baby similar to those found on all Gerber packages. Manufacturers were prohibited from sending out free samples of their products because this encouraged mothers to stop breastfeeding and to become customers. The law required packaging labels to carry a statement that breastfeeding is nutritionally superior. The law also restricted baby food manufacturers from targeting young mothers in the hospital. All of these regulations went into effect in 1988, and all other domestic and foreign manufacturers of baby foods, with one exception, Gerber, came into compliance. Gerber, the U.S baby food manufacturer, objected to Guatemala's law. Gerber refused to remove its trademark picture of a smiling chubby baby from its product labels. Gerber also refused to add a phrase to the labels saying that breast milk is superior. Although the Guatemalan Ministry of Health made numerous attempts to negotiate with Gerber, the company reportedly continued to market its infant formulas and to give free samples to women and children.

In November 1993 Gerber lost its appeal but opened up a new line of attack on Guatemala stating that the law was a "expropriation of Gerber's trademark." In 1995, when the World Trade Organization came into being, Gerber dropped its claim regarding expropriation and began to challenge Guatemala before a WTO tribunal. Guatemala realized they were in battle with an immense power.

The government changed its law to concede to Gerber's marketing practices.

Heavy marketing by the baby food industry has contributed to a drop in breastfeeding rates in both the United States and Third World nations. Advertisers intend to convince women that breastfeeding their babies isn't modern, and that bottle-feeding is healthier. The premise of such advertising is medically false. Breastfeeding provides infants with significant immunity to disease, as well as creating an emotional bond between mother and child.

Baby formula leads to 1.5 million infant deaths each year in Third World countries, as mothers often unwittingly prepare the formula with contaminated water, causing fatal diarrhea. According to the United Nations Children's Fund (UNCF) only 44 percent of women in Third World countries currently breastfeed.

UPDATE BY PETER MONTAGUE During the last quarter of the twentieth century, the industrialized world was swept by a resurgence of "free trade" ideology that had its roots in late-nineteenth-century England. In his novels, Charles Dickens cataloged the frightful inequalities and widespread misery that free trade brought to the people of England, but, unfortunately, the modern resurgence of free trade has no Charles Dickens telling its story. Nevertheless, the inequalities and misery are spreading around the globe, largely unreported by the corporatized media. The main thrust of modern free trade ideology is to weaken national governments and give freedom to transnational corporations to do as they please. As a result, social safety nets, even in the advanced countries of northern Europe, are being dismantled. The forms of democratic self-governance at national, state, and local levels are losing substance as power shifts to the private sector. This long-term shift away from democracy, away from governmental control of corporate behavior, is the sweeping backdrop against which history is unfolding in our time. My story merely described a few details of this backdrop.

Of course the widely reported "Battle of Seattle" coincided with the ministerial meeting of the World Trade Organization (WTO) in late November 1999. For the first time since the Vietnam War, churches, labor unions, environmentalists, democracy activists, and students joined forces to assert their opposition, this time to the corporate agenda called "globalized free trade." Thus for the first time the battle lines were drawn: those favoring popular control of governments (and of democratically set standards for labor and environment) versus those favoring corporate control of such matters. As a result of the Battle of Seattle, a worldwide network of NGOs (non-governmental organizations) has developed, using the Internet for communication, aiming to reassert democratic controls over corporations, economies, and standards affecting workers and the environment. A titanic struggle is thus under way worldwide—the forces of popular democracy vs. the forces of corporate control, again largely unreported in the corporatized media.

The mainstream media largely ignored this story. As Ben Bagdikian has documented in the sixth edition of *Media Monopoly* (Boston: Beacon Press, 2000), the mainstream press in the U.S. is now controlled by just six corporations. It should come as no surprise that these six corporations report very little about the most important story of our time—free trade ideology undermining the role and power of national and subnational governments worldwide, giving corporations free rein to do as they please.

The organization Public Citizen, in Washington, D.C., has an excellent web site describing its Global Trade Watch campaign (and some of the best free trade publications available anywhere); go to www.citizen.org/pctrade /tradehome.html Many good listservs about globalization and free trade are also available free from the Institute for Agriculture and Trade Policy (IATP) at 208.141.36.73/listarchive/index.cfm?mt hd=sub

Peter Montague: peter@rachel.org

16 CENSORED

Human Genome Project Opens the Door to Ethnically Specific Bioweapens

Sources:
WASHINGTON FREE PRESS
January/February 2000
Titles: "Genetic Bullets,
Ethnically Specific Bioweapons"
Author: Roy Blake

KONFORMIST
March 2000
Title: "Ethnic Weapons
for Ethnic Cleansing"
Author Greg Bishop
www.konformist.com

NORTH COAST XPRESS
Fall 2000
Title: "The Human Genome
Project and Eugenics"
Author: Robert Lederman

Corporate news coverage:
Daily Telegraph (London),
July 7, 2000; Agence France Presse,
January 21, 1999; *The Gazette*
(Montreal), November 16, 1998,
p. A4; *Baltimore Sun*, January 22,
1999, p. A18; *Salt Lake City Tribune*,
January 27, 1999 p. A13;
Times Union (Albany), February 2,
1999, p. D2

Faculty/Community Evaluators:
Rabbi Michael Robinson,
Velma Guillory-Taylor, Ed.D.
Student Researchers: Terrie Girdner,
Karen Parlette, Jennifer Swift

The Human Genome Project may now open the door to the development and use of genetic weapons targeted at specific ethnic groups. This project is currently being conducted under the auspices of the U.S. Energy Department, which also oversees America's nuclear weapon arsenal.

In October 1997, Dr. Wayne Nathanson, chief of the Science and Ethics Department of the Medical Society of the United Kingdom, warned the annual meeting of the Society that gene therapy might possibly be turned into gene weapons which could potentially be used to target particular genes possessed by certain groups of people. These weapons, Nathanson warned, could be delivered not only in the forms already seen in warfare such as gas and aerosol, but could also be added to water supplies, causing not only death but sterility and birth defects in targeted groups.

Current estimates of the cost of developing a gene weapon have been placed at around $50 million—still quite a stretch for an isolated band of neo-Nazis, but well within the capabilities of covert government programs.

On November 15, 1998, the *London Times* reported that Israel claimed to have successfully developed a genetically specific "ethnic bullet" that targets Arabs. When an Israeli government spokesman was asked to confirm the existence of ethnic weapons, he did not deny that they had them, but rather said, "we have a basket full of serious surprises that we will not hesitate to use if we feel that the state of Israel is under serious threat."

Some scientists worry that the modified genes that corporations have spliced into fish, fowl, fruit, and vegetables have permanently altered the world's food supply. Some may be intended to reduce populations.

The U.S. has a long history of interest in such genetic research. The current home of the Human Genome Project is the Cold Springs Harbor laboratory on Long Island, New York—the exact site of the notorious Eugenics Research Office that was started in 1910 by the Harriman family. The project's 1910 agenda included governmental imposition of sanctions on such human rights as reproduction, and on U.S. immigration, based on the alleged inferiority of particular ethnic groups. The Eugenics Research Project established medical and psychological conditions that would qualify one for sterilization or euthanasia. Prominent advocates of the program such as the Rockefeller family, Henry Ford, and Margaret Sanger helped smooth the way for the passage of forcible sterilization laws in 25 states. These laws allowed the forcible sterilization of tens of thousands of people, mostly of minority status, during the first half of the twentieth century.

The November 1970 issue of the *Military Review* published an article entitled "Ethnic Weapons" for command-level military personnel. The author of the article was Dr. Carl Larson, head of the Department of Human Genetics at the Institute of Genetics in Lund, Sweden. Larson wrote of how genetic variations in races are concurrent with differences in tolerances for various substances. For instance, large segments of Southeast Asian populations display a lactose intolerance due to the absence of the enzyme lactase in the digestive system. A biological weapon could conceivably take advantage of this genetic variance and incapacitate or kill an entire population.

UPDATE BY GREG BISHOP The ubiquitous nature of racism and the ruling power structure's history of handling "undesirables," as well as dealing with an enemy (almost always of different racial stock than a dominant aggressor) virtually assures us that the more powerful countries and their allies are continuing to look into new and better ways of subduing and killing whole (or major parts of) foreign populations.

When the *London Times* broke the story of the Israeli bioweapons project and interest in the development of pathogens that would disable or kill by ethnicity, they quoted an unnamed British intelligence source that said that these sorts of weapons were "theoretically possible." They were not only theoretical but had been researched for nearly 50 years. The lynchpin of the *Times* article was the writer's reliance on a specifically genetic explanation for ethnic weapons.

Bioweapons have been used since at least the Roman Empire, when armies dumped dead animals into an enemy's water supply to spread disease. Research into ethnic-specific bioweapons was first broached publicly in 1970, when Dr. Carl Larson's article "Ethnic Weapons" appeared in the *Military Review*. Larson discussed the possibility of utilizing differing races' sensitivity or low resistance to specific compounds (such as lactose intolerance among Asians) as either a bioweapon in itself, or as a "vector" that would allow other poisons or microorganisms to more easily enter a human body when defenses were lowered or destroyed. This method was not as surgically accurate as the military might want it to be, since many populations are not completely homogenous. The strange thing about the *Times* coverage was that it completely ignored this history and the fact that any technology for killing more of the enemy than your own would most likely be (and has been) looked upon with interest by military strategists.

No updates have yet appeared (or I have been unable to locate any) on the subject of Israeli ethnic weapons. In this country, continuing a historic policy toward Native Americans, it has been revealed that the American Indian Health Service (HIS, funded by the federal government, who employ the doctors and nurses) coerced Native American men and women into forced sterilizations in the early to mid-1970s. The General Accounting Office (GAO) estimated that 3,400 people (mostly women) underwent the treatment, but their study only covered four of twelve IHS regions for four years. Activists put the estimate much higher, at 60,000 to 70,000. This, coupled with the suspicion raised by the hantavirus outbreak in the Four Corners region of Arizona/New Mexico/Colorado/Utah, keeps suspicion and fingers pointed at the federal government and at least some government policies toward the American Indian population. (Hantavirus is one of many "new" diseases that have come under suspicion of having their origins in genetic engineering or biowarfare labs.) As reported in a 1994 Project Censored update, Utah's Dugway Proving Grounds biowarfare research site was also reopened despite local residents' protests over fears that the facility was originally closed because of safety concerns. Fort Dietrick, the site of the most notorious CIA drug and army biowarfare research in the United States, now houses major research facilities of the National Cancer Institute, raising issues of conflict (or collusion) of interest.

No major press outlets were consulted about publication of the story. It was written to appear on the Konformist.com website. Public awareness spread from there. There appears to have been no followup in the mainstream media on the original 1998 *London Times* story.

For more information on this story:

Cole, Leonard A., *Clouds of Secrecy: The Amy's Germ Warfare Tests Over Populated Areas* (Rowman & Littlefield, Totowa, N.J.), 1988.

Hersh, Seymour M., *Chemical and Biological Warfare: America's Hidden*

Arsenal (Bobbs-Merrill, Indianapolis), 1968.

Murphy, Sean, *No Fire, No Thunder: The Threat of Chemical and Biological Weapons* (Monthly Review Press, New York), 1984.

Piller, Charles, *Gene Wars: Military Control Over the New Genetic Technologies* (Beech Tree Books, New York), 1988.

Spiers, Edward M., *Chemical and Biological Weapons: A Study in Proliferation* (St. Martin's Press, New York), 1994.

WEBSITES:

www.disinfo.com/pages/dossier/id293/pg1.html
Article by Preston Peet on U.S. biowarfare testing in Puerto Rico in the 1930s. Island population was deliberately infected with cancer in a program run by Dr. Cornelius Rhodes, who went on to win seats on the Atomic Energy Commission and the Rockefeller Institute, as well as running U.S. chemical warfare programs in WWII. Many useful links.

www.ratical.org/ratville/sterilize.html
Long and detailed article on the American Indian sterilization program.

cns.miis.edu/pubs/reports/zilin.htm
This Center for Nonproliferation Studies site features text of threat assessment presented to Congressional subcommittee in October 1999, by Dr. Raymond Zilinskas. Includes information on bioweapons and ethnic weapons.

www.gene.ch/gentech/1999/Jan-Feb/msg00070.html
Genetech discussion list featuring exchanges on ethnic weapons. Concentrates on possibility of genetically engineered versions.

UPDATE BY ROBERT STERLING, EDITOR OF THE KONFORMIST Let me add personal knowledge of response to the article of which the author Greg Bishop was unaware. While the media response was predictably nonexistent, I did receive numerous comments that spoke volumes. The main thrust of "Ethnic Weapons for Ethnic Cleansing" was reports of an Israeli biowarfare program targeting Arabs. One of the key groups of readers of the *Konformist* are Zionist Jews, courtesy of the promotion of the provocative writings of Israel's Barry Chamish, a dedicated Zionist who has done tremendous work investigating the Rabin assassination and the suppressions involved with it. What is interesting is that though I received quite a few e-mails from the Zionist community, none denied the accuracy of the story. Instead, they brashly admitted it was true, then added it was necessary because Israel needed to defend itself from its Arab neighbors. What is most telling is that many letters included references to Arabs that were derogatory and dehumanizing. That such a destructive philosophy is accepted by so many uncritically in Israel explains much of the vicious thuggery performed against the Palestinians over the last four months (not to mention the last 33 years). This is why I submitted the story, because it underscored an important point that no group has a monopoly of hatred and oppression, and that authoritarian values of all flavors must be rejected and battled with words.

UPDATE BY ROBERT LEDERMAN While the average person has no particular interest in nor any tangible use for the Human Genome Project, it, more than the economy or whichever political party is in power in Washington, will very significantly mold the future of human life on this planet. Like its origin, eugenics, the Human Genome Project (HGP) has been presented to the public as an effort by our government to help people live happier, healthier, and more productive lives. Nothing could be further from the truth.

When I first wrote the article "The Human Genome Project and Eugenics" I received a lot of correspondence from media people and scientists who felt I was unfairly associating the HGP with eugenics and its expression in Nazi Germany during the Holocaust. Since then I've found on the HGP's own website an introduction to the project that makes exactly the same connection in no uncertain terms.

From vector.cshl.org/eugenics.html: Although it is easy to conceive of the Human Genome Project and genetic engineering as an entirely new epoch in scientific history, this is not our first-scale involvement with human genetics. Our current rush into the "gene age" has striking parallels to the eugenics movement of the early decades of the 20th century. Eugenicists sought an exclusively genetic explanation of human development, neglecting the important contribution of the environment. Their flawed data were the basis for social legislation to separate racial and ethnic groups, restrict immigration from southern and eastern Europe, and sterilize people considered "genetically unfit." Elements of the American eugenics movement were models for the Nazis, whose radical adaptation of eugenics culminated in the Holocaust.

As of this writing, the human genomes of the populations of Estonia, Tonga, and Iceland have been bought and patented by private corporations with many more such corporatized human lineages to follow. James Watson, the discoverer of the structure of DNA and the project's first director, has spoken publicly of his enthusiasm for human germline engineering—making permanent inheritable changes in the human populations' DNA. In the brief time since I wrote the article, insurance companies have publicly admitted that they will use prospective clients' DNA in deciding whether to grant them health insurance. Mayors and governors across America are following New York City Mayor Rudolph Giuliani in demanding that DNA samples be taken from every person arrested regardless of how minor their crime. Man-made transgenic organisms are being introduced into the human food supply and environment under the guise of distributing vaccines and improving nutrition with what can only be described as either reckless enthusiasm or an intent to do harm. In short, we will soon be living in a society in which eugenics science applied by government may play a greater role in one's destiny than any other factor.

While all of this is happening the public is being misled into believing that the Project's main purpose is to cure diseases and extend human life. Once this genie is out of the bottle, it will never be put back in. While it may seem like science fiction to most people, the Human Genome Project represents the single biggest threat to human freedom that has ever been devised.

The following websites contain a great amount of scientific, historical, and propaganda material on eugenics and the Human Genome Project. Some of the sites are anti-eugenics and others, including a neo-Nazi site, are pro-eugenics and blatantly racist. My including them in this list should not be construed as an endorsement of any of the statements contained therein, other than those in my own articles.

Baltech.org/lederman/spray/
www.hli.org/issues/pp/bcreview/index.html
www.georgetown.edu/research/nrcbl/sco
  penotes/sn28.htm
www.biol.tsukuba.ac.jp/~macer/SG.html
www.notdeadyet.org/eughis.html
www.techreview.com/articles/as96/allen.html
www.hli.org/issues/pp/bcreview/index.html
www.csu.edu.au/learning/ncgr/gpi/grn/e
dures/scope.28.2.html
users.erols.com/straymond/EUGENICS2.htm
home.att.net/~eugenics/
www.sightings.com/general3/eugene.htm
www4.stormfront.org/posterity/

17 CENSORED

IMF and World Bank Staff Tightly Connected to New Yugoslav Government

Sources:
EMPEROR'S NEW CLOTHES
September 28, 2000
Title: "The International Monetary Fund and the Yugoslav Election"
Author: Michel Chossudovsky and Jared Israel
emperors-clothes.com/indexe.htm

SAN FRANCISCO BAY GUARDIAN
August 23, 2000"
Title: "Colony Kosovo
Author: Christian Parenti
www.sfbg.com/News/34/47/47wvkoso.html

Faculty Evaluator:
Peter Phillips, Ph.D.
Student Researchers:
Jaleah Winn, Katie Sims, Dana Balicki, Steve Quartz

The G-17 is a Yugoslav economist group that supported presidential candidate Vojislav Kostunica and wrote the policy statements for the post-election economic reform of Yugoslavia.

The impression the G-17 likes to give is that it is an independent and Yugoslav-oriented group. The reality is vastly different. It is actually funded through the Washington-based Center for International Private Enterprise (CIPE), a group set up through the National Endowment for Democracy, which is a CIA-related group created in 1983.

The G-17 group calls for Yugoslavia to work more closely with the International Monetary Fund (IMF) toward the development of a market economy. Former Eastern bloc neighboring countries that have followed this tack have had massive wage deflation and increased poverty for the bulk of their citizens.

One of the key participants in the G-17 group is Veselin Vukotic. It was Vukotic who in 1989–90 orchestrated the breakup of more than 50 percent of Yugoslavia's industry, some 1,100 firms, resulting in the layoff of more than 614,000 workers.

Three of the G-17 members, Dusan Vujovic, Zeliko Bogetic, and Branko Milanovic, are Washington-based staff members of the IMF and World Bank. Dusan Vujovic, a senior economist at the World Bank, is the key link between the G-17 and Western institutions. From 1994–96, Vujovic played a key role in forcing structural adjustments programs in Bulgaria. Social services, including price controls, subsidized food, housing, and medical care, were stripped away. The World Bank now admits that more than 90 percent of Bulgarians live below extreme poverty level.

On its website the G-17 states that its aim is to establish ...a network of experts in all Serbian towns able to create and practically implement necessary changes in all fields of social life." With Kostunica in power in Yugoslavia, the G-17 will try to implement market reforms. They are not simply a group of economists, but rather a network supported by the IMF and the World Bank.

Other former Socialist/Communist countries have followed IMF and World Bank recommendations. Their first activity is to do away with social service protections. Second, they use economic manipulation and new laws to force businesses—public and private—into bankruptcy. These businesses are then purchased at rock bottom prices by multinational corporations. In Hungary, market reforms led to the closing of the only light bulb manufacturing firm, forcing everyone in Hungary to buy lightbulbs manufactured by General Electric.

Ukraine signed an agreement with the IMF in 1994. They received a $360 million loan in exchange for "economic shock treatment" policies for their citizens. The price of bread shot up 300 percent, electricity 600 percent, and public transportation 900 percent, and Ukraine currency collapsed. People were forced to buy necessities at "dollarized" prices when they were earning, on average, $10 a month. The U.S. dumped grain surpluses on the Ukraine market, destroying the domestic agriculture market. Misery and poverty skyrocketed in Ukraine after IMF policies were implemented.

According to writer and IMF researcher Professor Chossudovsky, the G-17 paradigm economic program for Yugoslavia contains the same measures the IMF forced on Russia, Ukraine, Bulgaria, Peru, and many other nations. The results have been social and economic devastation. The same thing will happen in Yugoslavia if the G-17 is allowed to implement their policy recommendations.

UPDATE BY MICHEL CHOSSUDOVSKY AND JARED ISRAEL The Kostunica government has already started to implement deadly IMF "economic medicine." The first step consisted of lifting price controls on fuel, and basic consumer goods and services. Prices have increased, as much as three times, causing extreme hardship for Yugoslav people.

The country had been impoverished by years of economic sanctions, not to mention the IMF reforms applied in 1989–90, before the break-up of federal Yugoslavia. But a system of state subsidies and price controls nonetheless prevented a total collapse in the standard of living, as occurred in neighboring Bulgaria.

That system of price controls is now being disbanded by the Kostunica government on orders of the International Monetary Fund (IMF):

When Kostunica supporters forced out most managers in state-owned shops and factories and put their own people in charge, that system of controls collapsed and prices immediately shot up. The cost of cooking oil has more than tripled since last Friday, when Milosevic announced that he was stepping aside. The prices of sugar and cigarettes are about to jump again. After Kostunica's supporters forced out Milosevic-era factory directors, the new ones are moving quickly to make their plants more profitable. (*Los Angeles Times*, October 15, 2000)

To make sure the government could not finance subsidies, the G-17 economists forcefully took control of the Central Bank and immediately imposed a freeze on money creation ("printing of money"). This held up the outflow of cash, which the government needed to sustain price controls on basic consumer goods.

According to interviews conducted with Belgrade residents shortly after the election, the price of milk had already doubled from 8 to 14 dinars per liter, largely affecting children; the price of cooking oil had more than tripled, from 13.5 to 55 dinars; sugar had gone from 8 to 45 dinars. These interviews support the earlier *Los Angeles Times* report.

Shoppers are commenting, "Ah,

democratic prices!" The Serbian use of black humor masks rising anger among ordinary people. Faced with this simmering rebellion, the Kostunica government, advised by the G-17 economists, have performed a dazzling flip.

Prior to the October 5 coup d'état, the government made some attempt to protect domestic producers and ensure (under very difficult conditions) the distribution of essential food staples, fuel, and electricity at controlled prices. The Kostunica coalition abolished price controls, then seemed to be using the suffering it created to justify the dumping of low-priced (often inferior) food and products, thus destroying small producers.

The Western media, which just a few days earlier had congratulated Kostunica for removing price controls, now uncritically trumpets the line that it's all Milosevic's fault.

Concerning the rapid increase in prices, the program drafted by Dinkic's G-17 Plus is rather explicit:

> Immediately after taking the office, the new government shall abolish all types of subsidies. This measure must be implemented without regrets or hesitation, since it will be difficult if not impossible to apply later, in view of the fact that in the meantime strong lobbies may appear and do their best to block such measures.... This initial step in economic liberalization must be undertaken as a "shock therapy" as its radical nature does not leave space for gradualism of any kind. (From the G-17 'Program of Radical Economic Reform, www.g17.org.yu/english/programm/programr9.htm)

The G-17 program attacking Milosevic had stated in no uncertain terms that they would get rid of price controls. They have driven Milosevic out and begun to do it. Naturally if prices have spiraled, it is Milosevic's fault.

Michel Chossudovsky: chossudovsky @videotron.ca

Jared Israel: Emperors1000@aol.com

18 CENSORED
Indigenous People Challenge Private Ownership and Patenting of Life

Sources:
GENEWATCH
October 1999
Title: "Indigenous Peoples' Statement on the Trade Related Aspects of Intellectual Property Rights (TRIPS) and the WTO Agreement"
Author: Kimberly Wilson

THIRD WORLD RESURGENCE
#110–111
Fall 1999
Title: "A Call for Support for African Group Proposal on TRIPS Article 27.3(b) on Patenting of Life"

EARTH FIRST!
March/April 2000
Title: "Looting Indigenous Medicine in Chiapas"
Author: Rural Advancement Foundation International

Faculty Evaluator: Tom Lough, Ph.D.
Student Researchers:
Ambrosia Crumley, Karen Parlette, Adam Sullens

"We, indigenous peoples from around the world, believe that nobody can own what exists in nature except nature herself." This is the first line from the indigenous people's statement on intellectual property rights. There is a portion of the WTO agreement called the Trade-Related Aspects of Intellectual Property Rights (TRIPS) that will allow multinational corporations to apply for patents on living creatures and life processes. Indigenous peoples from around the world, however, believe that private ownership of life forms is unnatural and inappropriate.

On July 25, 1999, a gathering of indigenous peoples signed a document that called for an amendment to the TRIPS agreement that would be put as a priority item on the agenda at the WTO Ministerial Conference in Seattle. The document eloquently states that all life forms and the life-creating processes are sacred and should not be subject to proprietary ownership. Specifically targeted was article 27.3b of TRIPS, which will denigrate and undermine rights to culture and intellectual heritage; destroy plant, animal and genetic resources; and even discriminate against indigenous ways of thinking and behaving. Indigenous knowledge and cultural heritage collectively evolve through generations. This means that no single person can claim to have invented or discovered medicinal plants, seeds, or other living things.

The TRIPS agreement as it stands substantially weakens indigenous people's access to and control over genetic and biological resources, and contributes to the deterioration of their quality of life. The people are very specific about what should be amended to article 27.3b. Amendments should clearly prohibit the patenting of plants and animals. They aim to ensure that a system is created that will protect knowledge, innovations, and practices in farming, agriculture, health, and medical care, and conserve the biodiversity of indigenous peoples and farmers. Agreements are needed to prevent the piracy of seeds, medicinal plants, and the knowledge about their use; and prevent the destruction and conversion of indigenous people's land.

In Chiapas, Mexico, 11 indigenous people's organizations, known as the Council of Indigenous Traditional Midwives and Healers Chiapas, are demanding that a $2.5 million, U.S. government-funded bioprospecting program suspend its search for indigenous medicine in Chiapas, Mexico. The project is cited as robbery of traditional indigenous knowledge and resources, for the sole purpose of producing pharmaceuticals that will not benefit the communities that have managed and nurtured these resources for thousands of years. The companies involved include Glaxo-Wellcome, Bristol Myers Squibb, and Dow Elanco Agrosciences. The project claims that royalties will be sent back to the indigenous people, but the reality is that long-term benefits may never materialize. Many people reject both intellectual property and the process established for benefit sharing. The critical issue now is that the project is apparently proceeding not only without proper consultation with the affected communities but also against the express wishes of a very significant sector of the Chiapas community.

UPDATE BY KIMBERLY WILSON The United States remains one of the only countries in the world that recognizes patents on life forms. It would be unthinkable in Thailand, for example, to allow a private company to claim ownership of medicinal plants, animal cells, or human genes. The U.S. patent office has thrown open the doors to the biotechnology industry, allowing entire species of plants, transgenic animals, and over 500,000 whole or partial genes to be patented. Under the U.S. system, basic biological resources are privatized—accessible only to those willing and able to pay royalty fees for access or research. Questions about new genetic technologies in agricultural and human research go beyond social and environmental concerns, raising fundamental issues of power and control. Who should

be granted property rights over pieces of the natural world? Who should control common biological and genetic resources?

In the past year, the issues of life patenting received a considerable amount of media attention as scientists announced a draft map of the human genome. Some of the country's top geneticists have formed ties with private companies and are now luring investors with promises of strong patent portfolios based on human genetic information. President Clinton and Tony Blair took up the issue when they met in March 2000. Their joint statement, which seemed to criticize gene patents, led to the plummeting of biotech stocks worldwide. Sensing the vulnerability of the industry, critics grew quieter and the mainstream press has largely overlooked the issue. Within the scientific community, questions about patents on life continue to be controversial. A few monthly science journals report regularly on the issue.

The circle of knowledge about life patenting needs to widen. It is not necessary to be a geneticist or a lawyer to understand the basics of patent law, or to see the natural world becoming commodified via the patent system. Rather than insisting that other countries change their patent laws to accommodate U.S. life patents, citizens can insist that the U.S. change its laws to harmonize with the rest of the world. There are a handful of organizations that offer educational materials and activist resources for those interested in learning more.

Council for Responsible Genetics (CRG): www.gene-watch.org

Rural Advancement Foundation International (RAFI): www.rafi.org

Greenpeace International and Greenpeace Germany: www.greenpeace.org

Institute for Agriculture and Trade Policy (IATP): www.iatp.org

PUBLICATIONS FOR FURTHER READING:

Martin Teitel & Hope Shand, "*The Ownership of Life: When Patents and Values Clash,*" 1998.

Kristin Dawkins, *Gene Wars: The Politics of Biotechnology*, New York: Seven Stories Press, 1997.

Andrew Kimbrell, *The Human Body Shop: The Cloning, Engineering, and Marketing of Life*, Washington, D.C.: Regnery Publishing, 1998.

Kimberly Wilson: kimberly.wilson@sfo.greenpeace.org

UPDATE BY HOPE SHAND OF RAFI The vast majority of the world's biological diversity originates in the tropics and subtropics. The genes from plants, animals, and microorganisms, found primarily in the South, are the strategic raw materials for the development of new food, and pharmaceutical and industrial products. But genetic resources are seldom raw materials in the traditional sense, because they have been selected, nurtured, and improved upon by farmers and indigenous peoples over thousands of years. When scientists and researchers go searching for valuable genetic material and traditional knowledge about them,

it is often called "bioprospecting." But critics call it "biopiracy."

"Biopiracy" refers to the appropriation of the knowledge and genetic resources of farming and indigenous communities by individuals or institutions who seek exclusive monopoly control (patents or intellectual property) of these resources and knowledge.

Indigenous People Protest in Chiapas: The efforts of indigenous peoples in Chiapas, Mexico, to stop a U.S. government-funded bioprospecting project illustrates the larger struggles of communities and nations to control their sovereign genetic resources and knowledge in a world where biological products and processes are being privatized and patented.

In December 1999 Rural Advancement Foundation International first wrote about eleven indigenous people's organizations under the umbrella of the Council of Indigenous Doctors and Midwives from Chiapas (Consejo de Medicos y Parteras Indigenas Tradicionales de Chiapas), who were demanding the suspension of the International Collaborative Biodiversity Group–Maya (ICBG-Maya). The ICBG-Maya is a U.S. government-funded $2.5 million, 5-year project aimed at the bioprospecting of medicinal plants and traditional knowledge of the Mayan people. The project is led by the University of Georgia, in cooperation with a Mexican university research center, El Colegio de la Frontera Sur (ECOSUR) and Molecular Nature Ltd., a biotechnology company based in Wales. The ICBG's self-stated goal is to promote drug discovery from natural sources, biodiversity conservation, and sustainable economic growth in developing countries.

The council believes that the bioprospecting project and the pharmaceuticals they seek to discover will not ultimately benefit the communities that have managed and nurtured these resources for thousands of years. According to Sebastian Luna, a spokesperson for the council, "the project explicitly proposes to patent and privatize resources and knowledge that have always been collectively owned.... Besides being totally contradictory to our culture and traditions, the project creates conflict within our communities as some individuals, pressured by the grave economic situation, collaborate with the researchers for a few pesos or tools."

After one year of fruitless talks with the ICBG-Maya and Mexican government authorities, the council held a press conference on September 12, 2000, to again demand termination of the Chiapas project and all bioprospecting projects in Mexico. Shortly thereafter, the Mexican government denied the ICBG-Maya permission to conduct bio-assays (that is, analysis of bioactive compounds) on plants collected in Chiapas. While the ICBG project is not officially terminated, its activities have been temporarily suspended.

RAFI believes that biopiracy is the inevitable consequence of international agreements such as the Biodiversity Convention that have no real capacity to regulate bioprospecting or to ensure equitable benefit-sharing with local communities. Without agreed rules and monitoring mechanisms, all bioprospecting becomes biopiracy. RAFI's web site (www.rafi.org) provides regular updates on biopiracy worldwide. Together with partner civil society organizations, RAFI has produced the Captain Hook Awards 2000—a poster highlighting the most egregious cases of biopiracy as well as the most exemplary actions by civil society and governments to halt these practices.

19 CENSORED

U.S. Using Dangerous Fungus to Eradicate Coca Plants in Colombia

Sources:
CounterPunch, London Observer
June 1–15, 2000 and July 2, 2000
Title: "McCaffery's Plagues:
New Biowar on Drugs"
Authors: Alexander Cockburn
and Jeffrey St. Clair

LONDON OBSERVER
July 2, 2000
Title: "U.S. Prepares to Spray
Genetically-Modified Herbicides"
Author: Ed Vulliamy

Corporate Media Coverage:
Milwaukee Journal, December 23, 1999, p. A8; *Seattle Times*, July 2, 2000, p. C3; Minnesota Public Radio, "Marketplace," October 3, 2000

After the Project Censored Award's deadline the following story also appeared:

INTER-PRESSE
October 19, 2000
Title: "Plan Colombia's Herbicide Spraying Causing Health and Environmental Problems"
Author: Kintto Lucas

Faculty Evaluators: Tom Lough, Ph.D., Tom Ormond, Ph.D.
Student Researchers: Jennifer Swift, Katie Anderson

The United States plans to deploy, or may have already deployed, new biological weapons for the war on drugs that seriously threaten both humans and the environment. The bio-weapon is Fusarium EN-4, a plant fungus used in many chemical weapons developed by the United States in the 1950s and 1960s. Fusarium is being redesigned to attack coca, cannabis, and opium crops in producer countries in the Third World.

This work is proceeding despite evidence that the fusarium, if deployed, will have profound and disastrous impacts on the humans and ecologies of the countries in which they are used.

Pathogens developed long ago at Fort Detrick, Maryland, the center for the U.S. bio-war program, were frozen but not destroyed when the facility was closed by President Nixon in 1969. Veterans of the Soviet biological warfare effort are now working on this research with UN funding in order to shield the United States from charges of violating the internationally negotiated biological weapons convention.

Peru has already banned the testing and/or deployment of the fungi fusarium. Colombia, however, was forced to accept spraying as part of a $1.8 billion aid package that was approved in Congress in July 2000.

Mycotoxicologist Jeremy Bigwood, working with a fellowship grant to carry out research into fusarium derivatives used in biological warfare, states that the threat fusarium presents can not be fully defined because "it mutates into another organism capable of attacking many other plants." Bigwood also states that fusarium can mutate and lethally affect humans with immune deficiencies.

Eduardo Posada, president of the Colombian Center for International Physics, found fusarium to be "highly toxic." His data found that the mortality rate among hospital patients who were immune-deficient and infected by the fungus was 76 percent. "The mutated fungi can cause disease in a large number of crops, including tomatoes, peppers, flowers, corn and vines," he said. He added that the mutated genus could stay in the ground for 40 years. According to Bigwood, U.S. government researchers initially insisted that the EN-4 strain was "species specific." But, he says, there are 200 other plant species within the genus that don't contain coca that could be affected.

Kintto Lucas reports that the Colombian military is using U.S.–supplied planes to fumigate huge areas near the

Ecuador border. Border residents reported that last summer and autumn planes could be heard over Colombia, and that several people in the area have died from extensive fumigation. A Monsanto herbicide, glycophosphate, is reportedly being used, but there are fears that fusarium is, or will be used in the regional spraying as well.

20 CENSORED

Disabled Most Likely to be Victims of Serious Crime

Source:
TASH NEWSLETTER
March 2000
Title: "The Invisible Victims"
Author: Dan Sorensen
158.96.231.221/dmhsearch/dmh-query.asp

Faculty Evaluator: Julie Allen, Ph.D.
Student Researchers:
Jennifer Swift, Natalie Guilbault
Research consistently finds that people with substantial disabilities suffer from violent and other major crime at rates four to ten times higher than that of the general population. Estimates are that around 5 million disabled people are victims of serious crime annually in the United States.

People with substantial disabilities represent at least 10 percent of the population of our country (including, among others, 1.8 percent with developmental disabilities, 5 percent with adult onset brain impairment, and 2.8 percent with severe major mental disorders). An estimated 40 percent of all American families have loved ones or close friends with substantial disabilities. Being disabled is not just being a person with a physical handicap. It also includes people with developmental disabilities (such as mental retardation or epilepsy), traumatic brain injury, severe major mental disorders, degenerate brain diseases (such as Alzheimer's, Parkinson's, and Huntington's), permanent damage from a stroke, organic brain damage, and other substantial disabilities.

Disabilities often make people easy targets for crime and abuse. Dan Sorensen estimated that in California only 4.5 percent of these crimes are actually reported to authorities, compared to an average 44 percent report rate for the general population. Several studies suggest that 80 to 85 percent of criminal abuse of residents in institutions is never reported to authorities. Evidence also shows that when these crimes are reported, there are lower rates of police follow-up, prosecution, and conviction. Reasons include the difficulty in investigating cases, the lack of special skills and special training required for these cases among law enforcement, the isolation of and communication difficulties for some victims, and the negative stereotypes and prejudices that continue to contribute to discrimination against these victims.

Sexual abuse rates of disabled men

and women are also significantly higher than in the general population. Research shows, through structured interviews of 27 women and men with mild mental retardation in four San Francisco Bay Area counties, that just under 80 percent of the women and 54 percent of the men had been sexually abused at least one time. These rates compare to 13 percent of women in the general population who have been victims of at least one rape in their lifetimes.

A more recent study of 40,000 children in Omaha schools from 1995 to 1996 found that children with disabilities suffered a rate of abuse 3.44 times greater than children without disabilities, and children with behavior disorders suffered a relative rate of physical abuse 7.3 times that of nondisabled children. The relative rates for sexual assault was 5.5 times greater, for neglect 6.7 times higher, and for emotional abuse 7 times higher. These findings are consistent with other studies demonstrating that children and adults with psychiatric disabilities suffer some of the highest rates of crime and criminal abuse among people with disabilities.

High crime rate against the disabled is significant when compared to the 8,000 hate crimes, one million elder abuse victims, and one million spousal assault victims each year. This means that crimes against the disabled make them proportionately one of the highest victim populations in the country.

UPDATE BY DAN SORENSEN The epidemic of crime and violence against people with disabilities will not be adequately addressed if it remains largely unknown. The media must educate the public about this problem as it has done about child abuse, elder abuse, and domestic violence. Crime and violence against people with disabilities is most likely the largest, measured by the number of violent crimes, among these targets of violence in our society.

Additional evidence continues to be uncovered since the publication of "The Invisible Victims." A major epidemiological study of more than 40,000 school children found that the rate of violence against children with disabilities was 3.44 times greater than against children without disabilities and 5 to 7 times higher for some categories of children with disabilities. Dick Sobsey is studying homicides against people with developmental disabilities and is finding a pattern of sentencing discrimination with these murderers getting substantially lesser sentences. Several studies report very high rates (8.5 to over 20 times higher) of violent crime against people with psychiatric disabilities.

The Governor of California has established the first permanent comprehensive program that addresses crime and violence against people with disabilities, The Crime Victims with Disabilities Initiative. The Attorney General of California is committed to developing a training package on how to investigate and prosecute crimes against people with disabilities, how to interview the victims, and how to prepare for the related trials. Important work in this area is going on in Wisconsin, Pennsylvania, Texas, Vermont, and many other states.

The press and media continue to largely ignore this issue. I know of only three significant stories on this issue over the last ten years. Most reports describe isolated crimes with no hint that there is a large, serious, and persistent pattern of violence directed against people with disabilities.

Interested persons can contact Dan Sorensen at (916) 651-9906 or dsorense @dmhhq.state.ca.us. Another excellent source of information is from ICAD at www.quasar.ualberta.ca/ddc/ICAD/icad. html. Cavet also has good information at www.cavenet2.org.

21 CENSORED
U.S. Military Bombing Range Destroys Korean Village Life

Source:
FREESPEECH.ORG
September 1, 2000
Title: "U.S. Bombing Range in South Korea: 'Hell On Earth!'"
Author: Karen Talbot
www.freespeech.org

Corporate Media Coverage: *Christian Science Monitor*, June 2, 2000, p.8; *New York Times*, June 18, 2000, p.6; Associated Press, June 19, 2000

Faculty Evaluators: Robert Tellander, Peter Phillips, Ph.D.
Student Researchers:
Melanie Burton, Michael Runas

Every weekday for the past 50 years, from eight o'clock in the morning to eleven o'clock at night, U.S. fighter planes in Korea have dropped 400 to 700 bombs on the Koon-ni range, less than one mile from local villages. The targets for the bombs are islands in the beautiful Aia bay where the people derive their livelihoods by fishing. As the A10 and F-16 U.S. fighter aircrafts swoop over the countryside, they drop depleted uranium (DU) shells. The DU shells add radioactive contamination to the other toxic wastes and oil that have been accumulating near these villages for the last half century.

In July 2000, author Karen Talbot visited Maehyang-ri, a village eight miles from the bombing range, where low altitude planes fly directly overhead. She describes meeting an elderly woman who allowed them to visit her garage to see a hole in the roof and an unexploded bomb inside. Many bombs are found in the villages and there are thousands on the hillsides surrounding the area.

The constant bombardment, with its unbearable noise and pollution, has taken a great toll on the health of the villagers. Throughout the years, at least 12 people have been killed and numerous others have been wounded. The number of cancer cases is disproportionately large and growing, and women are increasingly experiencing miscarriages and birth defects. While U.S. military personnel are given earplugs, members of the South Korean police and military who stand guard inside the fences are not, nor are the villagers. Noise levels have been measured off the decibel scale. Mental health is a serious issue, with constant tension from noise and danger of accidents.

Lockheed-Martin now owns the Koon-ni range. This kind of privatization of the military comes as no surprise, because 50 years of dropping bombs and spraying bullets has been very lucrative for arms manufacturers.

For the good part of 50 years most Koreans knew nothing about this, but protests are growing. Hundreds of thousands of students, farmers, and workers are joining the protest. The popular demand "U.S. military out of Korea" has gained momentum in the wake of the recent highly successful summit between the leaders of North and South Korea. On December 12, 1998, more than 1,500 villagers occupied the bombing range, but were pushed off by Korean police. In June 2000, a huge demonstration took place in Maehyand-ri with thousands of people from all over Korea, including a large contingent of autoworkers for the Kia Motor Company. Five hundred people again stormed the fences and occupied the range.

Powerful protests against the U.S. bombing range in Vieques, Puerto Rico, have been widely covered in the world press, but the similar situation in Korea is not yet as well known.

22 CENSORED
U.S. Government Suppressed Marijuana–Tumor Research

Source:
ALTERNET
May 31, 2000
Title: "Pot Shrinks Tumors; Government Knew in '74"
Author: Raymond Cushing
www.alternet.org/print.html?
StoryID= 9257

THIS MODERN WORLD   by TOM TOMORROW

Corporate Media Coverage: Associated Press and United Press International news wires, February 29, 2000

Faculty Evaluator: Mary King, M.D.

Student Researchers:
Jennifer Swift, Licia Marshall

A Spanish medical team's study released in Madrid in February 2000 has shown that tetrahydrocannabinol (THC), the active chemical in marijuana, destroys tumors in lab rats. These findings, however, are not news to the U.S. government. A study in Virginia in 1974 yielded similar results but was suppressed by the DEA, and in 1983 the Reagan/Bush administration tried to persuade U.S. universities and researchers to destroy all cannabis research work done between 1966 and 1976, including compendiums in libraries.

The research was conducted by a medical team led by Dr. Manuel Guzman of Complutence University in Madrid. In the study, brains of 45 lab rats were injected with a cancer cell, which produced tumors. On the twelfth day of the experiment, 15 of the rats were injected with THC and 15 with Win-55, 212-2, a synthetic compound similar to THC. The untreated rats died 12–18 days after the development of the tumors. THC treated rats lived significantly longer than the control group. Although three were unaffected by the THC, nine lived 19–35 days, while tumors were completely eradicated in three others. The rats treated with Win-55, 212-2 showed similar results.

In an e-mail interview for this story, the Madrid researcher said he had heard of the Virginia study, but had never been able to locate literature on it. "I am aware of the existence of that research. In fact I have attempted many times to obtain the journal article on the original investigation by theses people, but it has proven impossible," Guzman said. His response wasn't surprising, considering that in 1983 the Reagan/Bush administration tried to persuade American universities and researchers to destroy all 1966–76 cannabis research work, including compendiums in libraries,

reports Jack Herer. "We know that large amounts of information have since disappeared," he says.

Guzman provided the title of the work—"Antineoplastic Activity of Cannabinoids," an article in a 1975 *Journal of the National Cancer Institute*—and author Raymond Cushing obtained a copy at the UC Medical School Library in Davis, California, and faxed it to Madrid. The 1975 article does not mention breast cancer tumors, which were featured in the only newspaper story ever to appear about the 1974 study in the local section of the *Washington Post* on August 18, 1974. The headline read, "Cancer Curb Is Studied," and was followed in part by, "The active chemical agent in marijuana curbs the growth of three kinds of cancer in mice and may also suppress the immunity reaction that causes rejection of organ transplants, a Medical College of Virginia team has discovered. The researchers found that THC slowed the growth of lung cancers, breast cancers, and a virus-induced leukemia in laboratory mice, and prolonged their lives by as much as 36 percent."

Drug Enforcement Agency officials shut down the Virginia study and all further cannabis research, according to Jack Herer, who reports on these events in his book, *The Emperor Wears No Clothes*. In 1976, President Gerald Ford put an end to all public cannabis research and granted exclusive research rights to major pharmaceutical companies. These companies set out—unsuccessfully—to develop synthetic forms of THC that would deliver all the medical benefits without the "high."

UPDATE BY RAYMOND CUSHING When I was a cub reporter twenty-eight years ago at the daily *Advocate* in Stamford, Connecticut, my first city editor—a white-haired veteran of the *International Herald Tribune* named Marian Campbell—told me that the cure for cancer was the holy grail of all news stories.

"Unless they discover the cure for cancer," she would say over the clackety-clack of the manual typewriters, "this paper goes to press on time."

What I found out a quarter-century later is that not even the cure for cancer is a big enough story to crack the Berlin Wall of media censorship in this country. Toss in the facts that the cure appears to be a benign substance that has been illegal for 63 years, and that the government has knowingly suppressed evidence of its curative powers for 25 years, and you get twice the storyæand twice the censorship.

I won't name the "investigative journalists" who didn't respond when I sent them this story. I won't list the numerous "progressive" publications that ignored it. I won't describe the forbidding sense of professional isolation I endured in the months I tried to place the story.

Suffice it to say that it's what one would expect in a society that has criminalized its own young for two generations around the cannabis issue simply because we were told to do so.

Thousands of innocent people who

are in U.S. prisons for possessing or selling "the cure for cancer" await liberation and reparations. Someday our grandchildren will look back and ask, "What did you do to set the cannabis prisoners free?"

Here's what any responsible journalist should be doing:

Go to primary sources when evaluating cannabis research. The AP and other news organizations love to elevate "bad science" and suppress "good science" when it comes to cannabis. You have to read the original research articles yourself and make your own judgments.

Investigate and report on the war on children that is a major component of the war on drugs. The marijuana laws are the main tool the police use to persecute minors. No other policy affects more families in more insidious and devastating ways than cannabis prohibition.

Learn about the history of cannabis prohibition and about the pharmaceutical, liquor, and tobacco giants that are behind it. If you don't know the history of cannabis and hemp prohibition, you're too ignorant to justifiably call yourself a journalist.

If it turns out—as my story would seem to indicate—that cannabis is the cure for cancer and the government suppressed this information for 25 years (and continues to suppress it), then the body count alone will make this the biggest holocaust in recorded history. Virtually all federal drug policy makers of both parties since 1975—including legislators, presidents, and the DEA—will be complicit and criminally liable.

That's why they don't want this story covered.

To learn the history of cannabis prohibition, read www.jackherer.com. To read my story, type in the address at the beginning of this segment.

Raymond Cushing: raymondcushing@ireland.com

23 CENSORED

Very Small Levels of Chemical Exposures Can Be Dangerous

Sources:
EVERYONE'S BACKYARD
Summer 2000
Title: "Understanding 'Low Level' Chemical Exposures"
Author: Stephen Lester

IN THESE TIMES
August 21, 2000
Title: "What's In Your Green Tea?"
Author: Frances Cerra Whittelsey
www.inthesetimes.com/whittelsey2419.html

Corporate Media Coverage:
Chicago Tribune, December 26, 2000, Section 1, p. 10

Faculty Evaluator: Suzanne Toczyski, Ph.D., Lynn Cominsky, Ph.D.

Student Researchers: Stephen Hayth, Stephanie Garber, Adam Sullens, Nathalie Manneville

For years the public has been told that a low level of chemical exposure holds no significant risk to humans. The results of recent studies, however, show that even small amounts of chemicals (in drinking water, in foods) may in fact be very damaging.

One of the most important areas of research is the field of endocrine disrupters. New research in this area has shown that chemicals like dioxin, PCBs, and DDT act at very low levels to interfere with normal hormone functions of the body. Very low levels of these chemicals have been linked to a wide variety of health problems such as neurological and developmental problems, immune system disruption, learning disabilities, birth defects, and other reproductive anomalies.

The truth is that scientists know very little about how the body responds to small amounts of numerous chemicals. In the recent endocrine studies, health effects are being reported at levels of exposure not anticipated by our current understanding of how chemicals operate in the human body. The implication is that the standard methods for assessing chemical risks may not work for many low-level chemical exposures.

One proponent of the new thinking about how chemicals impact the human body is Dr. Pete Myers, one of the coauthors of *Our Stolen Future*. This book explores the threat contamination poses to fetal development, and the potentially wide-ranging impacts of chemicals on human potential. According to Myers, chemical attacks against fetal development work because some chemicals act as imposters, insinuating themselves in the body's natural hormone system that normally directs fetal development. These natural hormone signals work at very low concentrations. When traditional methods for measuring toxic effects and assessing risks are relied on solely, the impacts of low levels of chemicals that disrupt hormone signals will not be understood. As a result, risk factors for these low-level chemical exposures will be underestimated and established improperly.

Frances Cerra Whittelsey reports that seven out of ten green tea samples tested from New York store shelves showed DDT or Dursban contamination. Both are cancer-causing chemicals banned by the EPA in food products for the United States. Dangerous pesticides are still being used in countries all over the world and U.S. consumers have no assurance that green tea is free of pesticide contamination.

What is becoming apparent is that important low-level effects, such as disruption of a hormone signaling system, may be hidden by higher levels of chemical exposure, which cause more obvious impacts that are easier to measure. The full impact of low-level exposure may not be visible for years, perhaps decades, until the infant has grown into an adult. This time lag means that evidence linking cause and effect may no longer be available when the effect becomes apparent. In fact, the timing of the exposure may be more important than the amount. Exposure at a certain step of fetal development may have a dramatic effect, while the same exposure perhaps only a day or two later may have no effect or very little effect.

Lastly, hormone disrupters occur in complex mixtures in the human body. Each of us has several hundred synthetic chemicals in our blood. Every baby born throughout the world has been exposed in the womb to complex mixtures. Exactly how these chemicals will act together to interfere with normal biological functions over time is the question we have yet to answer.

UPDATE BY FRANCES CERRA WHITTELSEY
The importance of this story is that it shows the connection between the purity of the American food supply and conditions in poverty-stricken regions of the world. Even though DDT has been banned in America for nearly three decades, this persistent organic pollutant still contaminates our food supply through imports from countries still using the pesticide. It was particularly shocking for a breast cancer survivor to find DDT in the organic green tea she had been drinking to try to prevent the reoccurrence of her cancer. If Americans wish to have a food supply that its free of DDT, then we must give priority—for selfish reasons, if not humanitarian—to helping the impoverished people of Asia, Africa, and India fight malaria by means other than DDT.

Since publication of my article, diplomats from 122 countries finalized the text of a global treaty that will eliminate or minimize the use of persistent organic pollutants. Because of DDT's still-essential role in malaria prevention, the proposed treaty allows a health exemption for the chemical in malaria-prone countries. The treaty will be signed at a diplomatic conference in Stockholm on May 22 or 23, 2001, but it must then be ratified by 50 governments before it takes effect.

I am not aware of any mainstream press response to my story. There have been significant stories about the suffering and economic depression caused by malaria, and about the proposed global treaty, but none have connected the situation to the American food supply.

SOURCES OF INFORMATION:
On the global treaty: The United Nations Environment Program, www. chem.unep. ch/pops

On connection of DDT to cancer: Breast Cancer Fund (800) 487-0492, www.breastcancerfund.org

OTHER INFORMATION:
Physicians for Social Responsibility, Karen Perry: (202) 898-0150

World Wildlife Fund, Rich Liroff: (202) 778-9644

Frances Cerra Whittelsey: fwhittelsey @isa-ed.org

24 CENSORED

Pentagon Seeks Mega-Mergers Between International Arms Corporations

Source:
ARMS SALES MONITOR
January 2000
Title: "Arms Company of the Future: BoeingBAELockheedEADS, Inc?"
Authors: Anna Rich and Tamar Gabelnick
www.fas.org/asmp/library/asm/asm42.htm

Evaluator: Andrew Botterell, Ph.D.
Student Researchers:
Steve Quartz, Nathalie Manneville

A United States government task force has released its final report to the public recommending globalization of the U.S. defense industry, even if it results in the proliferation of conventional weapons.

The Defense Science Board's (DSB) Task Force on Globalization and Security is a 27-member appointed board, composed mostly of Department of Defense (DOD) and private industry representatives. The DSB encourages the Pentagon to facilitate transnational mergers of defense corporations in order to avoid eventual conflicts with European countries over global arms market shares. Overall, the DSB task force advocates reducing DOD's role in controlling arms exports, and holds little or no confidence in multilateral arms control agreements. The DSB recommends that the Pentagon automatically allow the export of military equipment, except when the United States is the sole possessor of the technology. However, since current U.S. practice allows arms exporters to out-source high-tech weaponry abroad before it enters the U.S. arsenal, such Pentagon exceptions would probably be rare. The task force recommends that the U.S. government stop worrying about protecting American military technologies since, in their judgment, most military technology will inevitably become available elsewhere in the future.

The DOD, State Department, and Congress lack consensus on these controversial issues. The Pentagon has conducted a variety of studies on globalization and related export control issues, and the State Department, anxious not to let its authority over arms export controls be usurped, has reportedly also done its own evaluations.

The DSB does acknowledge that its steps to maximize U.S. military capability may create tensions with other U.S. foreign policy objectives, particularly those achieved by limiting foreign access to U.S. defense technology, products, and services. Yet the DSB feels that "military dominance," rather than the promotion of U.S. foreign policy objectives and security, is the DOD's "core responsibility." The DSB considers U.S. State Department efforts to prevent or control conventional weapons proliferation naive at best. The DSB report describes international efforts to control conventional weapons proliferation, such as the Wassenaar Arrangement, as only "marginally successful."

A few large companies already dominate the American arms industry, and Europe's defense firms are rapidly consolidating as well. Germany's Daimler-Chrysler and France's Aerospatiale announced a planned merger to form the European Aeronautics, Defense and Space Co. (EADS), and BAE Systems now monopolizes the U.K. defense industry. Increased partnership between U.S. and EU defense corporations is needed, DSB warns, to avoid a protectionist "Fortress America" from going to war with a hostile "Fortress Europe" over market share.

The Federation of American Scientists is concerned that transnational arms mergers would create very powerful defense companies, further shifting control away from governments and toward private industry. Transnational companies will be eager to market their arms to many different countries, and will adapt the lowest common standards for exporting arms to other nations. With fewer controls and diffused production capabilities, conventional weapons will likely proliferate, posing long-term security risks around the world. Globalizing production of weapons is easy; globalizing responsibility for arms is a real challenge.

UPDATE BY TAMAR GABELNICK While embracing the idea of a globalized defense industry, the Pentagon and

U.S. arms makers have claimed that cumbersome U.S. export-licensing rules hinder exports to, and joint projects with, European and other allies. The Pentagon alleged that an overhaul of the U.S. arms export system was needed to avoid the creation of Fortress Europe, wherein consolidating European arms companies would shut American arms and technology out of the European market. With lightning speed and, according to the GAO, an inadequate analysis based on faulty anecdotal evidence, the Pentagon developed a set of 17 initiatives to expedite the arms export licensing process, especially to NATO members, Japan, and Australia. Despite protest by the State Department, which has the legal authority to decide arms export policy, the administration approved the Defense Trade Security Initiative (DTSI) in late May 2000.

The administration's initiatives will fundamentally alter the U.S. export licensing system, endangering a process that has helped control weapons diversion, unauthorized re-exports, and misguided sales. The most far reaching of the changes would grant to certain allies (beginning with the U.K. and Australia, with the possibility of including other countries) a license waiver for exports of unclassified weapons systems, effectively ending U.S. control over the transfer of arms to those countries. A similar arrangement with Canada had to be suspended in 1999 after Canadian firms transferred U.S. military technology to Iran and China. Other ill-advised reforms include loosening the rules on third-party transfers of U.S. weapons; creating broader export licenses to cover entire weapons systems (munitions, engines, and other sub-components were previously approved individually to allow for greater scrutiny); and speeding up the licensing process for NATO members (including making greater use of exemptions for transfers of technology and training). All will reduce the level of scrutiny of arms export decisions in the U.S. and oversight of U.S. weapons abroad.

The administration approved these major policy changes with little public debate or consultation of arms control experts. The mainstream media ignored the issue until the announcement of the completion of the reform package at the May 2000 NATO Defense Ministerial meeting. At that point, the coverage was minimal and presented the official view that the DTSI would promote bureaucratic efficiency and boost the defense industry's European business opportunities. Only the trade press covered the story throughout the spring, though again, the articles were geared toward their main audience, the arms industry. The arms control perspective was only provided in op-eds and newsletters written by the Federation of American Scientists and other arms control organizations.

For more information on the export reform process, visit the FAS website at: www.fas.org/asmp/campaigns/control.ht ml. Along with background information and articles on the subject, you will find official documents and government website links on DTSI. You can also contact Tamar Gabelnick at the Federation of American Scientists with any queries at (202) 675-1018.

25 CENSORED

Community Activists Outsit McDonald's

Source:
A-INFOS NEWS SERVICE
June 16, 2000
Title: "Residents Defeat McDonald's After Mammoth 552-Day Occupation"
Author: McLibel Support Campaign
www.mcspotlight.org

Faculty Evaluator:
Phil McGough, Ph.D.
Student Researchers: Stephen Hayth, Brian Baptista, Deanna Battaglia

On Sunday, December 13, 1998, local residents of Hinchley Wood, England, occupied the parking lot of their local pub to prevent McDonald's from building on the site. Their 24-hour-a-day sit-in campaign lasted 18 months, received national publicity, and galvanized community support against McDonald's. The community organized to become Residents Against McDonald's (RAM). RAM held numerous large public meetings in protest, set up marches, and delivered newsletters door to door throughout the community.

Their campaign forced McDonald's onto the defensive, stopping all work on the site.

RAM exposed how local planning laws allow companies to steamroll over the wishes of communities, ignoring expressed concerns over the quality of local lives and environment. Profiteering business chains have used planning law loopholes to continue to invade neighborhoods, often replacing green spaces and local facilities with their standardized, mediocre products.

Faced with widespread community-based opposition to the building of new restaurants throughout England, McDonald's tactics seem to favor the purchase of pubs precisely because of the national A-3 planning guidelines, which enable it to avoid the usual local planning applications and citizen objections. When McDonald's leases or purchases neighborhood pubs to avoid the usual local planning applications and guidelines, local residents become outraged and feel compelled to resist.

This time the residents were successful. After RAM's incredible 552-day continuous occupation, McDonald's threw in the towel and handed back the lease on the pub to the original owners. RAM celebrated a historic victory. Hinchley Wood residents can now join the growing list of places in which local communities have successfully defended themselves against huge controlling corporations.

RAM is now conducting a national survey of local planning departments throughout England about the issue of fast food units replacing local pubs. The United Kingdom Government Department of Transport and Regions has announced a review of the A-3 laws.

COMMENTS BY PROJECT CENSORED NATIONAL JUDGES

LENORA FOERSTEL: *Corporate Media in the Twenty-first Century and Project Censored:* The power now being exercised over our lives by corporations is unprecedented in U.S. history. This is particularly true with respect to the media, where massive mergers, shared board memberships, joint partnership ventures, and other forms of cooperation have allowed a handful of mega-corporations to create a new communications cartel.

The close working relationship between the U.S. government, the mega-corporations, and the media poses a chilling threat to U.S. democracy. This complicity can be seen in Project Censored's story of CNN's employment of U.S. army specialists in Psychological Operations (PSYOPS). Colonel Christopher St. John, commander of the Fourth Psychological Operations Group, states that "the cooperation with CNN was a textbook example of the kind of ties the American army wants to have with the media."

The government and corporate elite are not held accountable to the public. Their narrow focus on profits has led to the privatization of education and the rise of slave labor in the prison industry. The military-industrial complex blatantly weds corporate profits to expansionist foreign policy. Bruce L. Jackson, president of the U.S. Committee to Expand NATO, is also the director of strategic planning for Lockheed Martin Corporation, the world's largest weapons manufacturer. Like all defense contractors, Lockheed Martin encourages the expansion of NATO, which will create huge markets for the American weapons industry.

Pentagon spokesman Kenneth Bacon sees even the entertainment media as a propaganda arm of the military. He told reporters that "it only makes sense that we work with [the media] in any way we can to present the most positive portrayal of the military." Bacon announced that the Pentagon would ask motion picture and television stars as well as sports and broadcasting celebrities to promote the military in free advertisements.

Without the exposes published by alternative media and spotlighted by Project Censored, the public would have little or no knowledge of the links that exist between government and media that threaten the independent reporting required for a truly informed citizenry.

SHEILA RABB WEIDENFELD: This year's Project Censored stories cry out for public attention.

It's hard to believe that so many of these stories received minimal coverage. While the bombing of the Chinese Embassy in Belgrade by the United

States and NATO, for example, was widely reported in the context of a "tragic mistake," the real story was never told in the mainstream media. Equally alarming is the underreported story that the Environmental Protection Agency (EPA) plans to pump contaminated water into Denver's sewer system.

These are big stories—too big—to have gone relatively unnoticed by mainstream media. So are the stories on the damage genetically altered food does to the digestive system and the possible medical benefits of marijuana in treating certain types of cancer.

It's unbelievable. With all the resources at their command, one would think the *New York Times*, the *Washington Post*, Gannett, Knight, ABC Disney, GE/NBC or Viacom/CBS, and so on would be thrilled to pick up stories of this magnitude. But that is not how "pack" journalism works, where there is much reliance on spoon-fed news from press secretaries, corporate spokesmen, and outside PR companies. One of the problems may be the increasing concentration of media ownership.

Whatever the reason, the enterprising students and faculty of Project Censored should be congratulated. They found stories, often in obscure publications, that should shame the editors of our major newspapers and magazines.

JULIANNE MALVEAUX: Whatever happened to investigative reporting?

The real news during the 2000 election year was the stuff that didn't make the news. While I acknowledge my political bias, I am still puzzled that George W. Bush was given a pass on the facts of his life before age 40. He was a failed businessman who lost millions of dollars of other people's money. Sure, this was mentioned, but it was not examined in much detail. Life may begin at 40 for a privileged white man, but few people of color have the luxury of having all their prior mistakes wiped out when they seek employment.

Similarly, issues of the mechanics of democracy seemed highlighted in the 36 days after November 7, but there was so much that was neither investigated nor exposed. Why did the NAACP hearings get so little press attention? Had people simply decided that no matter what extraordinary steps had been taken to deny African Americans the vote in Florida, these steps did not bear full investigation and illumination? It has been frustrating to hear first-hand accounts, and then to be challenged to produce "proof" of voter fraud in Florida. The story will come out eventually, but too late to influence the selection of Mr. Bush as President.

If the press will cover up a candidate's record or the mechanics of an election, they'll also cover up the many ways that corporate power combines to disadvantage us as citizens and consumers. There are examples in some of the most censored stories that are examined this year, especially stories about the status of workplace safety and health, Monsanto's water monopoly, the corporate relationship with the United Nations, and immigrant servitude in Silicon Valley.

People sense that the media isn't telling the whole story about any number of things. This is why the drum of Internet rumors beats so loudly. The public will have more confidence in the press when the press uses its power to fully inform the public.

CARL JENSEN, founder and director emeritus of Project Censored: Twenty-five years of censored news! That amounts to 625 top censored stories selected from thousands of censored nominations over a quarter of a century. Stories that Project Censored has exposed to hundreds of thousands of people who would not have known about them otherwise. That is quite an accomplishment. But judging from the nominations for the new millennium year, it looks like we've still got a long way to go.

Some of the stories, such as pushing nuclear power plant construction in foreign countries, work-related injuries and illness on the job, and the hazards of low-level chemical exposure, reveal that there are serious issues that just won't go away. Others, such as recycled plutonium pancakes, genetic weapons for ethnic cleansing, and genetically engineered food, reveal there are always new issues deserving greater exposure.

Altogether I found the 25 nominations for 2000 to be an outstanding selection in terms of diversity, importance, and impact. Unfortunately, the post-election debacle was too late for the deadline set for the project. One must suspect there are some really important overlooked, undercovered, or censored issues that weren't part of the incomparable 24/7 media assault from November 7 to December 13.

While the public surely learned more than was necessary about hanging, swinging, dangling, and pregnant chads, they learned very little about the systematic nationwide election procedures that consistently disenfranchised minorities and the poor. If that isn't a page-one story in the major news media in 2001, I surely hope it will be exposed by Project Censored as a top censored story of the year.

In an earlier review of overlooked stories for my book *20 Years of Censored News*, I explored differences of censored subjects during political administrations. At the time, I found interesting differences between the censored stories exposed during the Reagan/Bush administrations and the Carter/Clinton administrations. Given the current change in administration from Democratic to Republican, I thought it might be interesting to revisit the differences.

There were significantly more political, international, and military stories exposed by the alternative media during the Reagan/Bush administrations than during the Carter/Clinton administrations. While there is no fully reliable way to explain these differences, one could speculate that there may have been more opportunities for the alternative media to expose political, international, and military chicanery during the Reagan/Bush era. And perhaps Carter and Clinton were more effective in monitoring these sectors during their administrations. It will be interesting to see if there is an observable variation in subject matter under the Bush Junior League administration.

Finally, as founder and director emeritus of Project Censored, I want to express my deep appreciation to Peter Phillips, the students and faculty at SSU, and our terrific panel of judges for their ongoing efforts to enhance Project Censored's reputation as an internationally respected champion of freedom of speech.

Censored 2001 Honorable Mentions

FOOD PYRAMID SCHEME
Source: IN THESE TIMES,
Aug 7, 2000
Author: Salim Muwakkil
www.inthesetimes.com

The United States Department of Agriculture practices racist food regulations.

Most minority Americans are lactose intolerant, unable to digest the milk sugar lactose. In these cases, the choice of cow's milk as food is a bad one. Yet the USDA continues to recommend that all Americans over the age of two acquire two to three servings of dairy products a day. Health officials estimated that 90 percent of Asian Americans, 70 percent of African Americans, 70 percent of Native Americans and 53 percent of Hispanics lack the lactase enzyme that enables them to digest milk sugar lactose correctly.

According to Dr. Milton Mills, a member of the Physicians Committee for Responsible Medicine (PCRM), the existing U.S. dietary guidelines are really a fundamental form of institutional racism. Mills feels that the indifference to lactose intolerance is another reflection of the federal government's lack of concern for minority Americans. In addition, the USDA refuses to encourage nondairy sources of calcium such as broccoli, kale, and beans. The USDA also fails to acknowledge the link between meat and dairy producers to many of the ailments that disproportionately affect many minority Americans.

The continuing influence of food producers in designing the USDA's dietary guidelines has prompted a lawsuit from the PCRM against the USDA and the Department of Health and Human Services (DHHS). The suit alleges racial bias and conflict of interest in the formulation of the food guideline pyramid. Chronic diseases affect American minorities, the law suit charges, and would be better served by dietary guidelines more inclusive of their needs.

THE THREAT TO THE NET

Source: THE PROGRESSIVE,
February 2000
Author: Pat Aufderheide
www.progressive.org

Broadband is not just the future of the Internet, it is the future of our communications system. Now, as cable companies are beginning to offer broadband, local governments are demanding open access: the ability to get on the broadband using any Internet Service Provider on the same terms as anyone else's. The cable companies are fighting for closed access, forcing everyone that uses their broadband service to go through their preferred Internet Service Providers.

Until the merger with Time Warner, AOL had been one of the leaders in the battle for open access. But that could now change. Time Warner, along with owning TV networks, movie studios, and more, is also the second largest cable operator in the country. With its merger to Time Warner, AOL will have to decide whether or not it is still for open access.

What AT&T does may be very important. AT&T, the country's largest cable company, is awaiting FCC approval for a merger with the country's third largest cable company, MediaOne. Once this happens, AT&T may be interested in joining forces with AOL/Time Warner down the line, placing a stranglehold on the Internet against any further competition.

Anyone running a small Internet business or a business that relies on Internet-related services (such as a content provider) would be forced to pay through the nose for broadband service or risk losing their business entirely. In addition, cable companies would be able to determine the speed at which any one of their users could operate depending on how much they are able to pay. Businesses and content providers that stand to lose the most are those without financial clout to begin with, widening the gap between the haves and the have-nots. It would also narrow the political and social information provided for free access.

PULP FACTS: PAPER, POLLUTION, AND THE PRESS

Source: EXTRA!, July/August 2000
Author: Miranda Spencer
Student Researcher: Molly Garrison

Millions of trees are sacrificed daily in order to publish our nation's newspapers and other print media. *USA Today* requires 11.8 million trees yearly, the *New York Times* requires 5.6 million, the *Los Angeles Times* requires 4.2 million, and finally, it takes 3.4 million trees a year to create the *Washington Post*.

Even more trees are sacrificed to produce the approximately 5.8 billion magazines and 24 billion newspapers that are published each year throughout the world.

While environmentalism continues as a hot topic with consumers, one of the most damaging environmental acts is the publication of your daily newspaper. Paper manufacturing uses more water per ton than any other product in the world and is one of the largest industrial consumers of energy. It's also highly polluting, creating air pollutants of sulfuric acid and carbon monoxide, effluents that are discharged into the waterways, and, the U.S. alone, some 12 million tons of solid processing waste each year, which usually gets land-filled or incinerated.

The printed media does a good job at hiding these facts because they often own the paper companies that provide their paper. For example, the Philadelphia Inquirer is part-owner of two paper companies, the Southwest Paper Mfg. Co. and the Ponderay Newsprint Co.

AOL'S LIBERAL BLACKLIST

Source: IN THESE TIMES,
May 29, 2000
Author: Kristin Kolb
www.inthesetimes.com
Student Researcher: Melanie Burton

America Online's (AOL) youth filters were screening out liberal sites with political content. AOL's youth filters are supposed to keep children away from pornography and violence on the internet, but they also seem to be designed to block out many liberal political organizations and allow conservative sites to fly through the filter with no problem. CNET News tested AOL's latest software, version 5.0, by pulling up more than 100 political sites in the "kids only" mode over a period of several days. AOL's filters for children consistently allowed the viewing of far more conservative sites such as that of the National Rifle Association, and not Democratic and liberal sites such as that of the Democratic National Committee.

CNET staff members were able to pull up conservative sites such as those of the Libertarian Party, the National Rifle Association, and a variety of gun manufacturers' sites. Sites such as those of Ralph Nader's Green Party, Ross Perot's Reform Party, the Coalition to Stop Gun Violence, and Safer Guns Now did not make it through the filter. These liberal sites produced the message "not appropriate for children" although none of the sites blocked contained depiction of nudity or even models in swimwear. Although much of this has now been corrected, it seems that AOL's intention was to keep more than just indecency away from children.

The filtering program was developed for AOL by The Learning Company, which is an educational software company owned by Mattel. The program was designed by reviewing submitted sites in order to develop a "whitelist" of sites approved for young children. AOL spokesman Rich D'Amato told CNET News that he was "unaware of any conservative bias" in the youth filters and explains that if some sites are included it is probably because someone submitted them.

Note: ProjectCensored.org used to be screened out by AOL for youth aged 15 years and under.

WAR GAMES

Source: YES! MAGAZINE, Fall 2000
Author: Carol Estes

More than 100 senior federal judges, the American Bar Association, several religious groups, most police chiefs, and the U.S. Sentencing Committee now oppose mandatory sentencing, yet Congress continues to ignore recommendations and impose more severe penalties.

More people are sent to prison in the U.S. for nonviolent drug offenses than for violent crimes, and penalties for drugs now sometimes exceed those for violent crimes. Blacks represent 11 percent of the drug users in the U.S., while 37 percent of people arrested on drug-related charges are black. Sixty percent of drug offenders in state prisons (42 percent in federal prisons) are black. These statistics show a racial inequality in the war on drugs. These inequalities arise from a battle about money and power, masked under the pretense of a strict drug policy. The war on drugs has turned the United States into the world's top jailer, a police state with a higher percentage of its population in jail than any other country.

Drugs are easier to get now than in the past. Drug-related deaths have dou-bled since 1979 (the year considered to be the height of the drug epidemic). Mandatory sentencing has been enforced in the legal system, leaving the court with no power to decide proper punishment. Federal District Judge Stanley Marshall points out the injustices in mandatory sentencing: "I've always been considered a fairly harsh sentencer, but it's killing me that I'm sending so many low-level offenders away for all this time." Mandatory sentencing fails to distinguish between major and minor players. A "kingpin" is in a better position to bargain down sentencing with information and power, while small time dealers and users have little options. Often, they go to jail for longer periods of time than the main supplier.

NEW CORPORATE WELFARE WAVE

Source: DOLLARS AND SENSE, November/December 1999
Author: Danielle Knight
Student Researcher: Andrew Cochrane

Forty nongovernment agencies (NGOs) have started a reform campaign to modify the public financing of private loans for environmentally destructive projects. Government-sponsored organizations known as export lending credit agencies and investment insurance agencies are using taxpayer dollars to insure risky overseas projects like China's Three Gorges Dam. The U.S. Bureau of Reclamation, probably the world's top dam-building agency, pulled out of the Three Gorges project in 1993, announcing it was "not environmentally or economically feasible."

Export credit agencies, of which the U.S.-based Export-Import Bank and Overseas Private Investment Corporation (OPIC) are examples, are bilateral finance agencies whose deals involve two nations or parties. They provide publicly backed loans, guarantees, and insurance to corporations from their countries that are seeking to do business in developing nations and emerging markets. The United States, Japan, and most Western European countries each sponsor at least one such agency.

Most export credit and public insurance agencies have minimal social and environmental restrictions, allowing them to back investments in potentially problematic projects like the Three Gorges Dam, which experts predict will displace as many as two million people living in the region. Pressure has been mounting for these agencies to consider human rights and environmental concerns when investing in an overseas project.

FRANCE'S 35-HOUR WORK WEEK
Source: CANADIAN DIMENSION,
February 2000
Author: Andres Hayden

A 35-hour workweek in France has shown positive economic results. As of January 1, 2000, a 35-hour workweek has been the legal standard in France. Since the 35-hour law was announced, unemployment has declined from 12.5 percent

to 11.1 percent due to renewed growth and the effect of shortened hours. This, combined with surging investor and consumer confidence, has disproved claims by employers and right-wing economists that the project would drive up labor costs, scare away investment, and destroy jobs.

A poll in September found that 84 percent of workers who have had their hours reduced said there were more advantages and 75 percent said their quality of life had improved. Spending more time with their family and children was the most commonly cited use of the additional free time. Other polls show high levels of satisfaction among 35-hour workers due to pride in their contribution to job creation. It can be expected to eventually create between 250,000 and 450,000 new jobs.

LET THE BIDDING BEGIN
Source: TEXAS OBSERVER,
May 12, 2000
Author: Gabriella Bocagrande
Student Researcher: Melanie Burton

Inter-American Development Bank is forcing Latin American privatization, to the detriment of public citizens.

The annual meeting of the Board of Governors of the Inter-American Development Bank in New Orleans concluded at the end of March. The Inter-American Development Bank is the Western hemisphere clone of the World Bank. In Spanish, the acronym for the Inter-American Development Bank is BID. Latin American countries are borrowing money to sell their public school, public health, and social security systems.

BID is pushing the countries to sell off other hunks of the hemisphere to private corporations by lending money to the governments of some of Latin America's poorest countries. With the money from these loans they are pushed to sell their social security and public health systems to private investors.

As a result, in Honduras, the cost of delivering a baby rose fifty-fold. In El Salvador social security and health workers went on strike to prevent the going-out-of-business sale of their public health services. Salvador's police force attacked striking doctors in a hospital, spraying the place with tear gas.

BID has also been bargain shopping for public schools. The International Youth Foundation (IYF), received a $1.1 million grant from BID to launch pilot projects for the young people in Ecuador, Guatemala, and Paraguay. Cisco Systems, a networking partner of the BID and IYF seems to have benefited the most with its Networking Academy Program in Mexico, Brazil, Uruguay, and Venezuela. Cisco Systems got privileged access to Latin American education budgets, just as educational systems were being privatized under pressure from BID. The budgets had just been increased with a BID loan, which the BID wouldn't make until the ministry privatized.

PEPPER SPRAY GETS IN YOUR EYES

Source: EXTRA!, April 2000
Author: Neil deMause
Student Researcher:
Katie June Anderson

Pepper spray, CS tear gas, and CN tear gas contain chemicals that can be deadly or carcinogenic. CN, or mace, is the most toxic of these agents. The CN formula used in Seattle at the peaceful protests against the World Trade Organization was 50 percent methylene chloride, a toxic solvent used in paint removers. Methylene chloride is reported to be a suspected carcinogen by Army research and OSHA (Occupational Safety and Health Administration). The Army and NATO no longer use CN because of its cancerous toxicity. The FBI proclaimed pepper spray its "official chemical agent" in 1987, and it was added to the arsenals of most police forces, replacing tear gas.

Chemical agents such as tear gas and pepper spray (also known as OC for oleoresin capsicum, its Latin name) are banned from warfare by international treaty, though domestic use is legal and widespread in the United States. These chemical weapons can cause a wide range of ongoing symptoms in healthy people. These include temporary blindness, respiratory problems, vomiting, diarrhea, fatigue, miscarriage, birth defects in future offspring, and disorientation. People with diabetes, asthma, and heart conditions are at an increased risk of illness or death when exposed to these agents.

In the streets of Seattle last fall,

chemical weaponry was used indiscriminately on a peaceful population, both demonstrators and bystanders. The media focused not on what the Southern California ACLU has called "a painful chemical 'street justice' without resort to criminal charges or the courts," but on the small amount of vandalism that occurred during the protests.

Many of the risks of these chemical agents are unknown. Despite widespread use, none of the agents sold for police purposes are monitored, tested, or regulated by any government agency for consistency, purity, toxicity, or even efficacy.

TO MANY ADJUNCT PROFESSORS, ACADEMIC FREEDOM IS A MYTH

Source: THE CHRONICLE
OF HIGHER EDUCATION,
December 10, 1999
Author: Alison Schneider
Student Researcher: Jennifer Swift

Parttime untenured faculty are increasingly subject to loss of their First Amendment rights to academic freedom. Adjuncts comprise nearly 50 percent of the professorate in the United States, yet many are being dumped for things tenure-track scholars do with impunity—teaching controversial material, fighting grade changes, organizing unions, and so on. Academic freedom has become more of a myth than reality to part-time professors. "I am so beaten down that I'm just hoping I keep the job I have," says one mathematics instructor who suspects she lost a post over union organizing. "If I'm in this article with my name, they won't rehire me. They'll come up with an excuse."

Jeffrey A. Schaler, a parttime psychology professor, was ditched by Chestnut Hill College for opining to tenured colleague Thomas Klee that addiction and mental illness are not diseases. Mr. Klee wrote an e-mail stating, "Mr. Schaler can think whatever he wants about mental illness, but Chestnut Hill's psychology department is on record with a specific theoretical orientation." So it seems clear that without the protection of tenure, a professor is vulnerable to dismissal for disagreeing with a particular theoretical perspective.

Randy Vanderhurst, a former instructor at Colorado Mountain College, was fired from the veterinary technician program for mentioning tampons and anal sex during a discussion of parasitic diseases in 1995. To illustrate the point that giardia survives sewage treatment he related how he had seen a tampon floating in water that had already gone through treatment. When the topic of cryptosporidium arose, he noted it was a particular problem for gay men because it can be transmitted through oral and anal sex.

In September, Ken Hardy sued Jefferson Community College in Kentucky for violating his free speech rights. In a 1998 lecture, Mr. Hardy asked students in his interpersonal communication course to deconstruct words used to oppress and offend. How did they evolve? How do they impede effective communication? The students bandied about examplesægirl, faggot, bitch, nigger—and Mr. Hardy repeated them during discussion. One student in a class of 22 took offense, saying that words like "nigger" had no place in a communications course. Five days later Hardy met with the academic dean, Mary Pam Besser. A month later, he was out of a job. Quint McTyeire, the college's lawyer, said, "What goes on in the classroom is not protected by the First Amendment. It's not a matter of public concern. It's a curricular issue."

CRYING AIDS

Source: TOWARD FREEDOM,
August 2000
Author: Tokunbo Ojo

The AIDS crisis in Africa may be a myth, because an AIDS diagnosis is seldom verified with actual tests. The conditions accepted as forming the problem of AIDS in the West bear little or no resemblance to that which is called AIDS in Africa. Recent findings say that approximately 99.2 percent of Africans don't have classic AIDS symptoms, including 97 percent of those presumed to be HIV-positive. Contrary to the Western practice of confirming an AIDS diagnosis with two or more laboratory tests, in Africa, AIDS is diagnosed, in most instances, without laboratory tests.

Based on the World Health Organization definition for African AIDS cases, many Africans are pronounced as AIDS victims if they show the following signs and symptoms: prolonged fever or a persistent cough for more than one month, 10 percent weight loss in two months, and chronic diarrhea. These problems are not necessarily rare in many African countries. Most African people die from symptoms that arise from known and treatable infectious diseases like malaria, pneumonia, or diarrhea as a result of poor hygiene and malnutrition. Societal illnesses are thus being listed as AIDS, a disease for which many people are more likely to blame the victim, instead of facing the socioeconomic realities of the region.

AIRPORTS' POISON CIRCLES

Source: EARTH ISLAND JOURNAL,
Winter 2000/2001
Author: Sharon Skolnick

U.S. airports are dangerous areas of pollution and increased cancer risk. A poison circle can extend for six miles around a single runway and is carried downwind 20 miles. Chemicals in the zone include nitrogen oxide, naphthalene, benzene, and formaldehyde, as well as others that harm human health and contribute to global warming.

Jet planes pollute much more on the ground than in the air. Additional dioxins from spilled jet fuel, diethelyne glycol from de-icing fluids, leaked engine oil, and jet exhaust particles seep into the ground, streams, and creeks boarding airports, endangering the health of downstream communities. Up to 90 percent of the aircraft hydrocarbon and carbon monoxide emissions occur as the planes idle and taxi.

Aviation is the only transport form not regulated in any significant way to reduce environmental impact. In 1998, the Environmental Organization of Copenhagen (EOC) published a report calling airports "environmental bombs" and noting that aviation "seems to be a 'sacred cow,' excluded from all legislation to minimize environmental impact and damage."

In 2000, President Clinton signed the $40 billion Airport Expansion Act (AIR-21). The act funds a 33 percent increase in airport construction and expansion. This will expand the already large circles of pollutants in the air around major airports, causing harm to the health of millions of people as well as the environment. The Federal Aviation Administration (FAA), which is supposed to regulate the airline industry, is also charged with promoting this act. Solutions do exist. Towing aircraft to and from terminals, using fuel vapor recovery procedures, and modifying jet fuel could reduce chemicals.

PLANNED DEPENDENCE

Source: TOWARD FREEDOM,
June/July 2000
Author: Barbara Aziz
Student Researcher: Erich Sommer

During the 1990s, the economy of Palestine has rapidly declined. New facts regarding the Palestinian economy have emerged since the creation of the Palestinian Authority (PA). As unproductive negotiations stretch out, the Palestinian economy is sliding back-

ward and is becoming weaker and more dependent on Israel than ever before.

Here are some of the facts:

➤Per capita GNP has fallen more than 21 percent since the signing of the Oslo accord, despite $3 billion in aid

➤Unemployment has increased 139 percent since 1993

➤Per capita consumption as declined 14 percent since 1992

The agricultural sector is the foundation of the economy. In 1970, during the early years of occupation, it provided 42 percent of the GNP of Palestine. By 1994 it had dropped to 24 percent. Israeli suppliers who can lower prices because of government farm subsidies undercut most fresh produce (once the pride of Palestinian farmers). As a result, the salaries of the Palestinians, especially the middle class, go back into Israel.

Some of the reasons Palestinians can't compete include bureaucratic and security obstacles. In addition, a maze of roadblocks and other communication problems are in part responsible for the general deterioration of the Palestinian industrial sector. Bypass roads, military areas, and Jewish settlements separate Arab towns and villages from one another.

ATROCITY AT MEDICINE LAKE

Source: EARTH FIRST!,
August/September 2000
Authors: Michelle Berditschevsky,
Peggy Risch

Geothermal mining threatens the sacred Native American Medicine Lake region in Northern California. In the 1980s, a large part of the Medicine Lake highland area was auctioned off to prospective energy companies by the Bureau of Land Management (BLM) and the Forest Service. The Medicine Lake Highlands encompass California's most diverse volcanic fields and are one of the major sources of water flowing into the Sacramento River. The highlands are also an ancient sacred prayer ground for many Native American tribes and a home to numerous plant and animal species.

By 1995, two multinational corporations had claimed ownership of the land with intent to develop two geothermal industrial "parks." Each of the complexes could cover up to eight square miles with power plants, well fields, toxic sump ponds, roads, above-ground steam pipes, and transmission lines, all within a half-mile southeast and two-and-a-half miles northwest of Medicine Lake. The beauty and serenity of Medicine Lake would be destroyed, not to mention the risk of chemical contamination into the ground, air, and water.

The Native Coalition along with other concerned groups have been trying to fight the corporations; the groups even sent delegates to Washington, D.C., to educate high-level decision makers on the sacred and environmental importance of the land. The damage done to the highlands would be irreversible and a major source of California's water could potentially be hazardous, but lawmakers have as of yet failed to see these issues as being more consequential than that of building another geothermal industrial "park."

BLOOD SHORTAGE REMEDY IS FOUND, BUT BANKS AND FEDS RESIST IT

Source: PROBE, February 1, 2000
Author: Jean E. Herskowitz
Student Researcher: Jeremiah Price

This year the United States will end up a quarter of a million pints of blood short of meeting the country's needs. This blood shortage could be curbed if the FDA and blood banks would allow the use of hemochromatosis-rich blood.

Twelve percent of all Americans have a condition called hemochromatosis, an iron overload in the blood. According to hematologist Victor Herbert, M.D., the iron-rich blood diluted 1:10 in adult recipients represents no risk at all. The U.S. Public Health Service's advisory committee meeting found that blood products obtained from persons with hemochromatosis do not carry any known increased risks to recipients attributable to hemochromatosis per se, and therefore may be a valuable resource to augment the diminishing blood supply. Despite the widespread approval among the medical community to use iron-rich blood, the FDA and the national blood organizations still have not lifted their ban on using it for transfusions.

One reason for the foot-dragging, Herbert asserts, is money. Blood banks charge hemochromatosis patients a fee to draw their blood. In addition recipients of the affected blood incur costs for the transfusions. The blood-letting fees paid by hemochromatosis patients typically range between $50 and $200. This is essentially pure profit since the blood is discarded, and doesn't need to be typed or tested.

"Blood banks currently gross $200 million a year charging hemochromatosis patients for phlebotomies," says Herbert. The reform proposal would redefine the hemochromatosis patients as blood donors. They would no longer have to pay to be bled and would contribute to the possible avoidance of future blood shortages.

VIEW FROM THE BOTTOM

Source: E MAGAZINE,
March/April 2000
Author: Jennifer Bogo
Student Researcher: Melanie Burton

Lead in baby powder can have serious health affects. The federal government has identified lead as the foremost environmental health threat to American children, yet infants are being exposed to lead in 10 brands of medicated baby powders on the market today.

Testing conducted by San Francisco's Center for Environmental Health (CEH) revealed that medicated powders under the brand names Ammens, Caldesene, Desitin, Dr. Scholl's, Gold Bond, Johnson & Johnson, Longs, Mexsana, and Walgreens contain trace amounts of lead (up to three parts per million).

The CEH has filed suit against the manufacturers of the powders and several retail distributors for silently exposing consumers, especially children, to lead. The CEH claims that the companies are in violation of California's Safe Drinking Water and Toxic Enforcement Act of 1986, which identifies chemicals known to the state to cause cancer or reproductive harm. Lead is listed for both.

The CEH found that all of the brands with detectable levels of lead contained the active ingredient zinc oxide, which is added to treat rashes and minor skin irritations. Dr. Janet Phoenix of the National Lead Information Center warns that "putting a product with lead on a child, even if it is not absorbed through the skin, may still result in ingestion or inhaling powder that's been dispersed through the air."

Phoenix says that although the levels of lead are low, all sources of lead exposure are cause for concern because the damage incurred is largely irreversible. When lead enters the body, it distributes to vital organs like the brain and kidney and settles in the bones. The effects range from reduced attentions and lowered intelligence to learning disabilities, impaired growth, and hearing loss.

Don Ryan, executive director of the Alliance to End Childhood Lead Poisoning, says that there is no excuse for the use of lead in consumer products.

THE BAN THAT WASN'T

Source: MOTHER JONES,
September/October 2000
Author: John R. Luoma & Vince Beiser

The Environmental Protection Agency (EPA) listed Dursban as a pesticide dangerous to children, but it went ahead and allowed continuation of sales for two more years.

Environmentalists, pediatricians, and consumer advocates called for a ban on Dursban, one of the most commonly used pesticides in the U.S. Instead, in June, a deal was made to phase out the over-the-counter sales of Dursban for household uses. Dursban, used in more than 800 products ranging from flea collars to bug sprays, will stay on the shelves until 2002.

The agreement with a subsidiary of Dow Chemical Co. was brought on by evidence that hundreds of children are poisoned by pesticides each year. Exposure to Dursban can cause headaches, numbness, vomiting, and diarrhea. In 1996 alone, 1,109 people reported being sickened by exposure to Dursban, and one person died. Some victims who are especially vulnerable to the pesticide suffer chronic problems ranging from learning and memory deficits to anxiety and fatigue.

The EPA is permitting the compound to continue to be used on golf courses and sprayed over communities for mosquito control. Although the deal limits the use of Dursban's active ingredient on tomatoes, apples, and grapes, it allows Dow to make and market millions of pounds for use on strawberries, broccoli, corn, and other crops. That means that farm workers and their children will continue to face exposure to the pesticide. Additionally, the deal does not protect consumers from nearly 40 other organophosphate pesticides that will remain in use. These compounds are similar to nerve gas and work in precisely the same way Dursban does. Dow and other pesticide manufacturers have claimed that doses sufficient to kill bugs present no risk to humans. Scientific findings show that children are especially sensitive to pesticide exposure. In 1996, Congress ordered the EPA to evaluate all pesticides by 1999. The agency has evaluated only two organophosphates in addition to Dursban and found enough risk to children to restrict all three.

URANIUM FALLS FROM THE SKY
Source: EARTH ISLAND JOURNAL, Summer 2000
Author: Gar Smith

After a Korean Airlines (KAL) Boeing 747 cargo plane crashed, hundreds of kilograms of depleted uranium (DU) debris were disbursed on the ground and a nearby freeway, exposing not only ground response units but thousands in local neighborhoods. DU is a known dangerous substance and requires full protective gear when workers are exposed.

Earth Island Journal revealed that many of the world's older jumbo jets carry large amounts of radioactive DU in the form of small, heavy counterweights hidden inside wingtips, tails, and elevators. Over the past 40 years, dozens of planes containing DU weights have crashed and burned in the U.S., Europe, and Asia. Thousands of people have been exposed to DU contamination from these crashes.

When contacted by the journal, U.S. Federal Aviation Administration spokesperson Mitch Barker stated that the FAA was aware of the problem but had not ordered the removal of DU components because the agency did not deem the situation "critical." Airline manufacturers have been quietly replacing DU counterweights with more expensive tungsten versions. In early 1998, the FAA conducted an "informal survey" of airlines in an attempt to determine how many planes were still flying DU components. "At that time," Baker reported, "most operators had not retrofitted their airplanes with tungsten weights. The owners were not required to report to us whether they had completed any changes on these counterweights."

CRIME SO IMMENSE

Source: TEXAS OBSERVER,
May 26, 2000
Author: James Galbraith

The Central Intelligence Agency (CIA) knew that the Bay of Pigs Invasion would fail but ordered it forward without passing this information on to President Kennedy, in hopes of promoting a full-scale invasion. When Kennedy refused to wage an air strike of Cuba, the CIA blamed him for the failure.

The CIA knew in advance that the date of the invasion had been leaked to the Russians, who had in turn relayed that information to Castro. In spite of this information, the head of the CIA, Allen Dulles, ordered the Bay of Pigs

Operation forward. The CIA's intention was for Kennedy to send in jets to bomb Cuba and for the Marines to join the brigade already on land. If this had happened the survivors would have been placed in a Cuban prison, which would have created an uproar by the American public and forced Kennedy to order a full-scale invasion. High-ranking officials within the CIA spread the myth that Kennedy was responsible for the failure of the invasion. Many Cubans continue to hold this belief when, in truth, the betrayal lies with Allen Dulles and the CIA.

MEDIA/PENTAGON BIGOTRY AGAINST GAYS

Source: NORTH COAST XPRESS,
Summer 2000
Author: Cliff Anchor

Since the enforcement of the noted "Don't Ask, Don't Tell" policy of the Clinton administration, incidences of anti-gay harassment have increased and even become commonplace in the United States military.

A Pentagon military survey under the climate of "Don't Ask, Don't Tell, Don't Pursue, Don't Harass" was implemented in March of this year in the wake of the murder of Private First Class Barry Winchell. The information for this survey was taken from the report *Conduct Unbecoming: Sixth Annual Report on "Don't Ask, Don't Tell, Don't Pursue, Don't Harass*," produced by the Service-Members Legal Defense Network (SLDN).

The survey found that of 71,500 service members surveyed, 80 percent said they heard derogatory anti-gay-bi-lesbian remarks this past year, 37 percent had witnessed or experienced targeted incidences of harassment, and 57 percent reported that they had not received training on "DA/DT/DP/DH." The policy, put into legislation in 1993, has, according to the SLDN, caused the surge of military hate crimes. The SLDN is an independent watchdog group and the sole legal aid assisting service members who are targeted under the military's anti-gay policy. According to the report by SLDN, the military's gay policy "reinforces the message that gays are second-class citizens who are not worthy of the rights and responsibilities of citizenship."

WATCHDOG SLAMS MONSANTO ADS

Source: THE OBSERVER (London),
February 28, 1999
Author: John Alridge

Monsanto, the United States giant of the genetically modified food industry, has been condemned for making "wrong, unproven, misleading and confusing" claims in an advertising campaign in England. The ruling, made by the Advertising Standards Authority (ASA), the industry's official watchdog, also included accusations that Monsanto expressed its own opinion "as accepted fact" and published "wrong" and "unproven" scientific claims in order to persuade the general public that foods from genetically modified crops are safe.

The series of commercials, by the London-based advertising agency Bartle Bogle Hegarty, began with a full-page ad that read: "Food biotechnology is a matter of opinions. Monsanto believes you should hear all of them." Over the next few weeks the company released further ads promoting the benefits of biotechnology, the safety of the genetically modified food crops, and its approval in twenty countries, including Britain. The ASA, in its report, uprooted the claims made by Monsanto and criticized the firm for wrongly giving the impression that genetically modified potatoes and tomatoes had been tested and approved for sale in Britain. The watchdogs also dismissed Monsanto's assertion that genetically modified crops were more environmentally friendly than ordinary crops.

RACISM AND CONSCRIPTION IN THE JROTC

Source: PEACE REVIEW,
Vol. 12:3 (2000)
Author: Marvin J, Berlowitz

The conscription of urban youths into the Junior Reserve Officer Training Corps (JROTC) is part of a movement for educational reform in the United States. Inner-city school districts, facing sharp declines in funding, are turning to the military for financial support in exchange for allowing the expansion of JROTC. Despite public objections, the number of JROTC programs has sharply increased from 1,464 to 2,267, and the latest defense authorization bill calls for an eventual 3,500 public schools to be militarized.

Structural changes because of globalization have led to increasing economic disparities between the wealthy and the poor. As a result the highest concentration of poverty is found among urban school children and racially oppressed groups. The advocates of JROTC use this unfortunate fact to make the privatization of public schools the central focus in educational reform. The Defense Department seeks "at risk" schools to transform into military academies for the purpose of future recruitment. The children enrolled in JROTC programs are trapped by economic conscription. They are pushed by poverty and the economics of racism, and pulled by the promise of military benefits. The strict and time-consuming requirements of the JROTC program deprive students of opportunities to enroll in college preparatory courses.

Critics of the program have identified numerous myths perpetuated by the Defense Department, such as claims that the program reduces violence among students, when in fact it contributes to violent acts such as hazing, crime sprees, "war games," and murders.

TAKING HEAD START TO A HIGHER LEVEL

Source: AFSCME PUBLIC EMPLOYEE, Spring 2000
Author: Jimmie Turner
Researcher: Brian Baptista

The American Federation of State, County, and Municipal Employees (AFSCME) is conducting a organizational effort aimed at Head Start employees nation-wide. Head Start employees prepare young children from low-income families to enter school. They are representative of the working class themselves, as most make less than $20,000 to $25,000 a year, without benefits. AFSCME believes that full-time workers should make adequate wages to support their families. Meanwhile, Head Start employees often fall below federal poverty guidelines.

Head Start employees are dedicated to helping low-income children while they struggle to maintain a healthy lifestyle for their own families. Following the successful examples of programs in Ohio and Pennsylvania, the AFSCME is attempting to help Head Start workers unionize.

Some Head Start administrators aren't supportive of the idea of unions. One employer "warned" his staff that a union has been requesting information about them, and that they should watch out for annoying calls. The plan backfired, as the employees started calling the union themselves.

BAY AREA REPORTER EJECTED FROM NAB

Source: SAN FRANCISCO BAY GUARDIAN, September 22, 2000
Student Researcher:
Christina Van Straalen

A *San Francisco Bay Guardian* reporter was forcibly ejected from the National Association of Broadcasters (NAB) convention in San Francisco two days after the paper published a front-page news package critical of the NAB.

The reporter, Steve Rhodes, was stripped of his press credentials and physically removed from the Moscone Center convention by two police officers summoned by NAB officials. Rhodes, who was covering the event, had not disrupted the convention, protested, nor done anything illegal. Several protest groups had been picketing outside the NAB meeting to protest the group's lobbying efforts against microradio stations in the U.S. NAB official Jack Knubel apparently made the decision to remove Rhodes, claiming that he "was part of the problem."

NAB is the national lobby group for the corporate media and has become an association of the media elite. At the Moscone Center convention, NAB officials also revoked the press credentials of Jenesse Miller and other credentialed reporters from the Independent Media Center.

APPROACHING $350 BILLION A YEAR, TRADE DEFICIT KEEPS GOING UP AND UP

Source: SOLIDARITY,
November 1999
Author: Steven Sack
Student Researcher:
Christina Van Straalen

The United States' growing trade deficit may have serious economic consequences in the near future. Now nearing $350 billion, the trade deficit is said to be unsustainable beyond two or three years, at which time it will cause inflation, an increase in the cost of imports, and possibly higher interest rates.

In the 1980s, when the trade deficit hit levels similar to its current level, the dollar fell by 50 percent. The current drop in the value of the U.S. dollar against the Japanese yen will make the price of Japanese imports more expensive. Imports from other countries may become more expensive as well. With higher interest rates, inflation, an increase in the price of imports, and the rate of unemployment also rising, the U.S. is looking at a wide range of future problems that stem from our current trade deficit trajectory.

The deficit issue is causing anger among the United Auto Workers and the United Steelworkers of America. If the U.S. reaches a $350 billion trade deficit, it could mean 4,900,000 lost jobs for the U.S. economy. However, many economists take a laissez-faire attitude toward trade deficits and seem prepared to let a huge chunk of the U.S. manufacturing base (especially the least technologically sophisticated end) slip away. They argue that we should concentrate on retraining workers and focus on opening up the world service market, where the U.S. appears to have a comparative advantage. But the union argues that even many service industries are vulnerable to foreign competition.

THE DECLINE OF THE SOCIAL SCIENCES IN PERU

Source: NACLA, Vol. 33, #4
January/February 2000
Authors: Carlos Ivan Degregori,
Javier Avila Molero

Under President Alberto Fujimori, the Peruvian government has withdrawn almost all state support for Peruvian universities and has abdicated the task of higher education to the private sector. Without state support of education, a dual system has emerged, with private universities that are well-funded and serve the wealthy, and public universities that are underfunded and serve the poor.

Influenced by private sector interests and Fujimori's neoliberal ideology, universities are almost universally focusing on highly technical business-oriented coursework. In public universities, already meager resources for investigative research in the social sciences have virtually disappeared.

SIGNAL DEGRADATION

Source: AMERICAN PROSPECT,
August 14, 2000
Author: Jerold Starr

Student Researchers:
Jaleah Winn, Eric Sommer

Proposed FCC rule changes, if put into place, will reduce educational programming requirements at conservative Christian radio stations. In June 2000 the House passed the National Broadcasting Freedom of Expression Act. The Act discontinues the educational requirement for noncommercial broadcasting licenses.

The new Act takes networks one step closer to being able to broadcast full-time sectarian religious programming on television and radio frequencies reserved for public educational broadcasting.

The assault on educational licenses by conservative religious broadcasters has its roots in the Reagan Revolution, when the FCC chairman Mark Fowler pledged "to take deregulation to the limits of existing law." Fowler's FCC abolished guidelines for local, news, public affairs, and nonentertainment programming and dropped almost all public interest standards in deference to "property rights" of broadcasters. Reagan's allies in Congress also rescinded appropriations for the Corporation for Public Broadcasting, while the FCC loosened PBS program underwriting guidelines to allow "trade names," "logos or slogans," and "product symbols" to appear before and after programs. Increasingly dependent on commercial sponsorship, public broadcasters drop experimental television and programs aimed at poor and minority viewers, while religious broadcasters get an unprecedented opportunity to proselytize.

In intervening years the religious right has utilized radio and television broadcasting as its most important tool. Since Reagan's deregulation, the number of Christian radio stations has doubled to 1,731 and the number of Christian television stations has tripled to almost 285, almost all of them conservative evangelical. Christian radio stations accounted for 8 percent of the total in 1981 and 10 percent in 1990. Today the proportion has risen to 14 percent. With an audience of 20 million, religious programming is now the third-largest radio format in the nation. And while most religious stations are on commercial frequencies, 23 television stations and well over 700 radio stations have been awarded noncommercial licenses.

THERE ISN'T ANY GOOD DAY: PORT TRUCKERS TAKE A BEATING

Source: DOLLARS AND SENSE,
May/June 2000
Author: Adria Scharf

The Federal Trade Commission enforces laws against small truckers but ignores mega-mergers involving industry giants.

The same week last fall that mega-corportions Exxon and Mobil announced their merger, the Federal Trade Commission (which oversees antitrust law) subpoenaed three low-paid truck drivers for "engaging in unfair methods of competitive pricing." Since the partial deregulation of the industry in 1980, working conditions and compensation for port truckers have badly deteriorated. The FTC suspected the three "owner operators" (truckers who own the rigs they drive) of breaching antitrust law. What was the drivers' offense? They planned to meet to talk about their shared problems and to discuss the possibility of affiliating with either the Teamsters or the Long-shoreman's union. The drivers targeted by the FTC haul containers out of ports in the United States. Today America's 40,000 port truckers net about $7 per hour after deducting expenses for repairs and fuel. They are not paid for the hours of mandatory time spent waiting to pick up their loads at the ports.

Theoretically, independent contractor status implies that the contractors are independent from the company with which they contract work. As self-employed entrepreneurs they are not subject to the control of that company. But a Savannah driver puts it another way. "The trucking companies treat drivers as employees, but don't want to accept the responsibility of being employers." Current data shows a drop in union trucking nationwide, from 57 percent in 1979 to 24 percent in 1990.

Today the shippers, deregulation's big winners, choose between dozens of trucking companies for each job. As large numbers of small firms undercut each other in the daily bid wars, the falling rates translate into ever-declining driver pay. In the absence of government regulation, there is no floor to the downward wage spiral.

CHAPTER 2

Director's Choice

Each year a number of important news stories appear in the alternative press after Project Censored's October 15th deadline. This year our staff made several recommendations for late stories to be included. The following was selected because of its importance and lack of attention in the post-election corporate media frenzy.

Democracy in Chains

BY LAURA CONAWAY
AND JAMES RIDGEWAY

Repinted with permission from the *Village Voice*, November 29, 2000

They meant to vote for Al Gore. Many came from the black, poor, education-deprived neighborhoods of Jacksonville, and had never cast a ballot before. But they got on the buses in Duval County, Florida, and they went to the polls. They did just what the Democratic organizers instructed: punch a hole in every page. And because the list of presidential contenders spilled over two pages,

thousands and thousands of them—an estimated one-third of the voters in some precincts—punched the hole for Gore, then invalidated their choice by stamping a minor-party candidate on the following leaf. In all, 27,000 Duval ballots had to be thrown out.

Black people had backed Gore by ratios as high as 10 to 1, but when they needed his help, he fled. If Al Gore winds up losing this election by the skin of few hundred votes, he can chalk up his defeat not to the avowed support of Floridians for George W. Bush, not to badly designed ballots, but to a centuries-old national system of labor, education, and politics designed to keep African Americans from rising above the legacy of chattel slavery. Gore and his lawyers can hunt until doomsday for enough votes to prove he won, but they'll never rescue the botched ballots of the barely literate nor a way to count the votes of minorities kept from the polls.

Duval County is only the starting point. Down to their foreshortened life expectancy, the black citizens there are the picture of a people held back. As recently as 1993, 47 percent of the county's residents were judged to be functionally illiterate, meaning they could read at a level no higher than ninth grade. Even well-educated citizens are often confused by the instructions in a voting booth, but those who can't make sense of an average newspaper have been disenfranchised long before Election Day. For this, some of Duval's black voters in particular were made to feel not merely unlearned, but dumb. "I kept looking around, pleading for help," a first-time voter told the *New York Times*. "But they just kept saying, 'Read it, read it.'"

Duval's African Americans were fortunate, in that at least they reached the polls. Hundreds of registered voters would tell the NAACP they were wrongly turned away from precincts across the state, because election clerks refused to accept their IDs, or polls in black districts closed early, or police set up roadblocks outside the halls. Despite their testimony, the U.S. Justice Department said no reason existed for the feds to intervene. After all, plenty of African Americans managed to vote, enough that they constituted 15 percent of Florida's turnout this year, up from 10 percent in 1996. With no help in sight, several black voters angrily filed suit. And where were the big white guys as this scene played out? Republican Bush retreated to his ranch in Texas, where he plotted to bar recounts and began shaping his cabinet. That self-proclaimed people's champion, Ralph Nader, pontificated about plans to run Greens for Congress, but said little about the problems of people in Florida. Gore scrambled for Washington, D.C., where he could keep his eye on the slave-built White House while turning a deaf ear to the pleas of African Americans for justice.

THIS MODERN WORLD
by TOM TOMORROW

WE'VE JUST RECEIVED WORD THAT 4,098 BALLOTS IN MISSISSIPPI MAY HAVE BEEN MISPUNCHED DUE TO THAT STATE'S COMPLICATED "ORIGAMI" BALLOT--WHICH REQUIRES VOTERS TO MAKE A *PAPER SWAN* OUT OF THEIR BALLOT BEFORE VOTING!

IN *WISCONSIN*, MEANWHILE, OFFICIALS BELIEVE 2,307 BALLOTS MAY HAVE BEEN AFFECTED BY LOCAL VOTING LAWS WHICH REQUIRE *REPUBLICAN* VOTERS TO SWALLOW A *LIVE HAMSTER* BEFORE THEY ARE ALLOWED INTO THE VOTING BOOTH!

WE'RE ALSO GETTING REPORTS OF TURMOIL IN *CALIFORNIA*, WHERE NOT ALL VOTERS WERE AWARE OF THAT STATE'S *"BACKWARDS DAY"* VOTING REGULATIONS--UNDER WHICH VOTERS ARE ACTUALLY SUPPOSED TO VOTE FOR THE CANDIDATE THEY WOULD MOST LIKE TO SEE *LOSE!*

After a year spent fulminating about education, Gore could have marched to Duval County and demanded to know why the schools there had failed so terribly that almost half the adults can't read a magazine. After building a campaign on pledges of better health care, he could have walked through the hospitals and cemeteries and asked why black babies die at a rate twice that of white ones. After riding the support of black citizens to a nationwide lead in the popular vote, he could have gone to the places where they lived, sat in their kitchens, and cried with them over the thousands of lost votes, the thousands of lost lives. Instead, Gore remained distant, aloof, mute, content to wave for the cameras as he passed out Thanksgiving meals—just like the other politicians. Behind the wall of white silence, you could almost hear the ghost of slavery, rattling its bones.

In the first hundred years after the Civil War, newly enfranchised African Americans had little real access to the polls. Finally, Congress took its most important step toward enfranchising black citizens since Reconstruction, by enacting the Voting Rights Act of 1965. The act banned any practice that denies or abridges the right to cast a ballot, including poll taxes, literacy tests, and the requirement that an applicant to vote get a character "voucher" from an already-registered voter. It also afforded protection to minorities who speak different languages, by ordering interpreters and translated ballots at the polls.

The effect of this act has been substantial. The statute has led to better registration rates for blacks, which are now comparable to those of whites, and to the election of black officials. Now, in each state of the old Confederacy, African Americans hold at least one congressional seat and a large number of state legislative seats. In fact, the Leadership Conference on Civil Rights notes, "the proportion of legislative seats held by blacks is approximately equal to their share of the population in several Southern states."

African American success at the ballot box has turned up the heat on the sim-

AND THIS JUST IN: MANY *DELA-WARE* VOTERS REPORTEDLY HAD DIFFICULTY WEAVING THE CLOTH TAPESTRY BALLOT MANDATED BY THEIR STATE'S ANTIQUATED *"JACQUARD LOOM"* BALLOTING PROCEDURE! CITIZENS' GROUPS CALL THE PROCESS UNFAIR AND ARE DEMANDING A *REWEAVING!*

Action McNews Network

IN FAIRNESS, WE SHOULD NOTE THAT THE NEWS NETWORKS *THEM-SELVES* ARE BEING CHASTISED FOR THEIR ELECTION NIGHT DECLARATION THAT *ALABAMA* VOTERS "MIGHT AS WELL JUST STAY HOME BECAUSE NO ONE CARES WHAT YOU THINK ANYWAY!"

Action McNews Network

COMING UP NEXT: OUR PANEL OF EXPERTS EXPLAIN WHY A *FEW MINOR MISTAKES* ARE *IN-EVITABLE* IN AN ADVANCED DEMOCRACY SUCH AS OURS.

FIRST, THESE MESSAGES.

Action McNews Network

mering resentment white conservatives carry toward minority voters, who often support candidates in a powerful bloc. That anger spills all across the country, but it is expressed most explicitly in the South. A day before the election, the *Economist* reported, the white Republican governor of Arkansas complained on national radio that Democrats were bringing in black voters on buses "as if they were cattle in a truck."

The will to discourage such heavy black turnout is great—which is why the Voting Rights Act exists. But the law depends on federal oversight, an element of enforcement that appears to have been dropped altogether in this election. Discrimination at the polls continues under one subterfuge or another, and in Florida has led to the filing of several suits in this election. Black voters in that state allege their votes weren't counted, and cite various gimmicks to keep people of color from voting, such as shunting them from one polling place to another until the polls closed.

Minority voters who were registered and had voted for years were told they didn't appear on voter lists; voters without Florida IDs were turned away, though the law says they can cast "affidavit ballots." In some counties, minority voters say they were asked for a photo ID while white voters were not, or turned away even when they showed up with a voter card and photo ID. People who lacked a photo ID or weren't on the voting list were put into a "problem line," where they were told voting officials were trying to call headquarters to find out what to do. But the lines were jammed and they just couldn't get through. Discouraged, voters gave up and went home. The Leadership Conference writes, "Poll workers reportedly were instructed by their supervisors to be particularly 'strict' in challenging voter qualifications because of aggressive voter registration and turnout efforts that had been made in their communities in connection with the November 7 election."

In a letter to Attorney General Janet Reno, Congresswoman Corrine Brown, who represents the Duval area, called for a federal investigation. "Clearly, we've got a major problem," wrote Brown, who said she has documented numerous cases of voters denied assistance. "Victims of and witnesses to Election Day irregularities and discriminatory practices at voting precincts have come forward in unprecedented numbers."

Even as Reno persisted in saying the federal government had little role in state elections—the same way presidents of old tiptoed around the issue of Southern segregation—civil rights leaders from reverends Al Sharpton and Jesse Jackson to Kweisi Mfume gathered testimony from black voters who'd been harassed. Even as liberal news outlets like Salon argued the allegations should be ignored in favor of a swift end to the election deadlock, African Americans prepared lawsuits for violations of the Voting Rights Act. Even as Gore and Bush wrangled over hanging chads, African Americans reckoned with a world in which they still don't count. "It is apparent to us that we, as Black people, do not matter in Florida," The *Ams-*

terdam News editorialized on November 22. "We all have been ignored by both the Democratic and Republican parties, for they simply saw no need to call upon us, except to mount a picket line or to go to jail, singing and acting ugly."

In part, the electoral disaster in Duval County can be seen as a simple snafu. Election officials there have said they won't list candidates over two pages again, a design that led to the disqualification of thousands of ballots. But the situation in Duval, where 27 percent of the residents are black, also stems from the lingering damages of slavery. Since the era when only the landed gentry were enfranchised, richer and better-educated people have been more likely to vote than the underprivileged. Today black kids across America funnel through underfunded schools, too often destined for curtailed job opportunities, dilapidated housing, and Third-World health care—hardly the kinds of conditions that augur a high turnout of informed voters.

Duval should be a center of affluence. It's home to Jacksonville (population 600,000), a naval air station, several large state offices, and an expanding financial hub. Scratch the surface, though, and you'll find nearly a quarter of the children living in poverty. Of Florida's 67 counties, Duval has the sixth-highest dropout rate. Statewide, Florida has not only an embarrassingly spiked rate of mortality among black babies, but its black adults have a much shorter life expectancy. Black women can expect to die about seven years younger than their white peers, as can black men, whose average age of death is 68.2 years. To find a similar average for white men, you'd have to look all the way back to 1959.

The creation of majority-black districts for local and state races has given African Americans a steady, if small, presence on town councils, in state assemblies, and on Capitol Hill. By gaining these measures of self-determination, African Americans have in part fulfilled the prediction of Marcus Garvey, who argued the only way for black people truly to be free was to found a nation-state of their own.

Though black people in the South were nearly unanimous in support for Gore, their votes were scattered across state lines and thus submerged through the electoral college as completely as if they'd never been cast.

Garvey's idea may sound revolutionary, but the courts have consistently ruled that without predominantly black districts, African Americans lack a fair chance at representation. When necessary, judges have redrawn electoral maps or scuttled at-large systems to ensure minorities have at least one seat.

Yet when it comes to electing a president, the Constitution mandates statewide contests and makes no provision for minority votes—whether from third-party backers or African Americans. As a result, white voters can easily overwhelm black ones, making places like Mississippi and Alabama near locks for Republican candidates, who then have little reason to consider minority concerns. Given the roots of the electoral college, this comes as no surprise. At the Constitutional Convention of 1787, none other than James Madison of Virginia objected to the direct election of presidents, on the grounds that it would put Southern states—with their large population of slaves—at an insurmountable disadvantage. Madison advocated a system in which states would receive a number of electors based on the size of the general population, franchised or not. That tilted the table in favor of white Southerners, whose votes carried more weight.

Today the electoral college, however inadvertently, continues to hold back African Americans, who even in relatively black states like Florida form only 15 percent of the population. Though black people in the South were nearly unanimous in support for Gore, their votes were scattered across state lines and thus submerged through the electoral college as completely as if they'd never been cast.

Plenty of African Americans get no protection from the Voting Rights Act at all. About 4 million U.S. citizens, most of them minorities, are denied the right to vote because their states disenfranchise convicted felons. A report by the Sentencing Project two years ago predicts that one quarter of all black men in seven states will soon be disenfranchised. In 13 states, this disenfranchisement is permanent, applying alike to those in jail, on parole, or free. According to the NYU School of Law's Brennan Center for Justice, which has

sued to overturn the felon statutes, such bans are a direct outgrowth of the antebellum South. "When Alabama adopted such a law in 1901," the Center said in a report, "John Knox, the politician presiding over the Constitutional Convention, stated that the aim of such provisions was to help preserve white supremacy without directly challenging the Constitution of the United States."

Today many prisoners of color are in jail because of the war on drugs, which has led to a quadrupling of the prison population since 1980, to nearly 2 million. Laws passed during this government assault have hammered away at black and Latino communities, calling for stiffer sentences for substances like crack cocaine, preferred by minorities, while remaining lenient on the powder preferred by whites. And though lots of these felons fit the demographics that vote Democratic, it was the Democratic Clinton administration that put its weight behind the effort to build more prisons to house more drug offenders.

In addition to routing former felons from the polling place, the laws can be used to intimidate and harass minority communities. A few months ago, nearly 12,000 Floridians were informed by the state Division of Elections that they had lost their voting rights because of felony convictions in other states, according to a report in Mother Jones. But the company hired by the state to compile that list of names made a massive mistake and misidentified thousands of people. When the error was fixed, 8,000 people were once again made eligible, but not before they'd been made to fear the loss of federally guaranteed voting rights.

About the time of the Civil War, the *New York Herald Tribune* referred to Florida as the "smallest tadpole in the dirty pool of secession." Which in no way made it any less a part of the Deep South. Like all the other Southern states, Florida killed itself after the war trying to substitute a somewhat more subtle form of slavery for the real thing. Black Codes, aimed at maintaining white supremacy through segregation, prevented whites and blacks from riding in the same railroad cars. Schools were segregated, with Florida outdoing all the other former members of the Confederacy by not only making sure white and black pupils used different sets of books, but ensuring that the books were stored separately. Poll taxes and the introduction of divisive primaries decimated the black vote.

With the toppling of segregation in the 1950s, white citizen councils sprang up to do openly what the robed Ku Klux Klan had done at night. The memory of the 1923 massacre at Rosewood was still fresh when Florida governor Leroy Collins in 1956 declared, "We are just as determined as any Southern state to maintain segregation."

Since World War II, "Florida's role as a shaper of what may or may not be the Deep South's last stand against creative federalism has been strangely underrated and usually ignored," Robert Sherrill writes in *Gothic Politics in the Deep South*. "One reason perhaps being that most of the country does not think of Florida as Deep South, forgetting that those Tallahassee legislators are operating about 20 miles from the Georgia border and about the same distance from Alabama. This is cracker country, moonshine country, stiff with the old social myths and political myopia."

Throughout the mid-1900s, Florida political deal makers viewed race as a legitimate topic. "The embers are always there," one mover and shaker told Sherrill. "You can fan it into flame or leave it smolder." When the Congress of Industrial Organizations tried to register black voters in Florida, George Smathers, the rising young political star who would become a senator, called the drive "the most dangerous invasion of carpetbaggers" since the Civil War. Today, the state is home to several of the most powerful white supremacists in the country, including Stormfront, an Internet-based hate group headquartered in West Palm Beach.

Though legally dead for more than a century, the chattel system re-emerged in Florida as late as 1991, when six sugar companies failed to pay migrant Caribbean workers promised wages, a practice labor groups likened to virtual slavery.

The aftereffects of slavery extend even to minorities newly arrived in this country. The large community of Haitian Americans centered around Miami is a case in point. As Papa Doc Duvalier instituted a reign of terror against his opponents in Haiti during the 1960s, Haitians fled their homeland in a steady stream. Working in the States, they sent much of their money home and waited patiently for things to improve, so they could return. They eagerly awaited the return to power of Jean-Bertrand Aristide, but after the American troops landed and Aristide came back, things only got worse.

In the last few years, Haitians here have abandoned their dream of going home and begun to seek U.S. citizenship. Across the Haitian communities, organizers patiently prepared people to become citizens, setting up community-based literacy programs and teaching people how to take the necessary tests and fill out government papers. These immigrants came from a nation with its own legacy of black slavery. Seventy years before Lincoln emancipated American slaves, the slaves of Haiti overthrew their white masters in a violent revolution, then created the first independent black state since Europeans colonized Africa. Wary of a similar uprising by freemen in this country, Thomas Jefferson recommended they be sent to live in Haiti. By the time Haitians began immigrating to the States in great numbers, they brought with them a rich tradition of self-determination, balanced by the fear of tyranny. It all came to a head with this election, when for the very first time, new Haitian American citizens, putting aside memories of election-day violence in their home countries, screwed up their nerve and went to the polls. What they encountered was a wall of resistance. "Several things happened," Marleine Bastien, a Haitian American organizer in Dade County, says. "They were told they couldn't vote because they didn't have a voter registration card. Some were threatened with deportation and intimidated in other ways. There were groups of people giving out information saying that voting Democratic is like voting for the devil and the Ku Klux Klan.

"Some ballots had Gore-Lieberman next to a punch line that really was for Bush-Cheney," Bastien continues. "People in line were prevented from voting because of polling deadlines, even if they were in line before 7 p.m., the cutoff time. Many of these people are in the service industry and use public transportation. Some precincts were closed as early as 4:30 in the afternoon. They were denied help even though there were Creole speakers available. Election officials ordered the Creole translators not to speak." One union observer working out of West Palm Beach says most votes of 2,000 Haitian union members were disallowed. "There was no Creole translation, but plenty of Spanish translators and a ridiculous ballot no one can understand," the observer says. "A lot of them just walked away. They didn't know what the fuck to do."

What happened to the Haitians is what has always happened to the Haitians: vicious intimidation and discrimination by public officials who consider them less than human. In this and countless other ways, they have become the new inheritors of slavery's legacy, adding another link in its chains.

CHAPTER 3

Censored Déjà Vu: What Happened to Last Year's Most Censored Stories

BY VICTORIA CALKINS, with assistance from Amy Bonczewski, Andrew Cochrane, Kathy McMills, and Karen Parlette

GUEST WRITER UPDATES: By Michel Chossudovsky, Samuel S. Epstein, Karl Grossman, Michael Parenti, Barbara Seaman, Larry Shaw

In medicine, we talk about Managed Care, in media, Managed News. Corporate media today is in the entertainment business. Market shares, advertising dollars, and political self interest drive the news. Stories about the decisions and manipulations of the powerful and news stories about challenges to power by the powerless are continually ignored or underreported in mainstream media. Only a strong alternative media system challenging mainstream media at every level will protect working people's interests and their rights to know. A strong alternative press, diversity of news sources (both foreign and domestic), ombudsmen, and reporters with tenure rights are needed to counterbalance the media elite's self interests. Anything less than this means a continued deterioration of informational freedom in the United States.

Here are in-depth updates on the top stories from *Censored 2000,* as well as stories from previous years that resurfaced in the news during the past year.

MULTINATIONAL CORPORATIONS PROFIT FROM INTERNATIONAL BRUTALITY

Multinational petroleum corporations have been collaborating with repressive governments who have histories of human rights violations. Although aware of the violations, the U.S. government continues to support and fund these countries and the corporations that operate there. The multinationals argue that through their presence and investment in a repressed country, human rights will improve, a posture they call "constructive engagement." In truth, a five-year look at corporations so engaged shows that any such improvement is a myth.

Any Export-Import Bank loan more than $10 million requires a State Department–conducted human rights assessment. March 1998, however, saw the U.S. State Department ignoring its own report of human rights abuses in Turkmenistan and paying out $96 million in Export-Import money to four U.S. natural gas companies located in that country. The White House announced that there had been improvement in Turkmenistan's human rights violations record but, on further investigation, this proved to include only a discussion with the Turkmenistan president and the

release of 10 political prisoners. Since Turkmenistan has some of the largest reserves of Asia's oil and gas, Mobil, Exxon, and Royal Dutch Shell, among others, still openly operate there.

Enron has called on the state of India to suppress and silence environmental opposition to their Dabhol power project, the largest power plant in the world. Enron paid local police to silence, imprison, and assault more than 3,000 protestors. Unocal similarly used Burma's military, who, through torture, murder, and rape, forced protesting villagers to work on Unocal's Yadana gas project.

Multinational corporations are against government-created sanctions to punish suppressive governments. Not only do they oppose the intrusion, but, as the American Petroleum Institute reported in a 1998 report entitled "Oil and Natural Gas Industry Promotes Human Rights Abroad," the use of "sanctions to punish regimes that abridge their people's human rights" denies local people the "rights enhancements" that oil companies confer. Human rights violations then become framed as a "necessary evil" to insure long-term improvement.

Although reportage of individual human rights issues has surfaced, the impact of energy companies globally on human rights has been ignored. Human

Rights Watch has seen slight improvement by some companies. BP Amico and Norway's Statoil have taken positive steps towards addressing human rights in Angola and Azerbaijan. However, most U.S. companies and their French counterparts (Exxon-Mobil or TOTAL) lag far behind in the human rights arena.

SOURCES: *Dollars and Sense,* May/June 1999, "Corporation Crackdowns: Business Backs Brutality," by Arvind Ganesan.

COVERAGE 2000: From looking at the mainstream media coverage this past year, it would seem as if the big-name oil companies had begun to take responsibility for their actions. But things are not always as they seem. Thanks to the Internet and its ability to publish information quickly and globally, environmental and human rights activists were able to make issues known faster than previously to a larger number of concerned people. In an Internet-enabled world, a big-name brand can be sullied almost overnight. This fact, combined with community demonstrations against corporations and media discussions of corporate actions, caused many multinationals to "spin" their companies and add environmental and community involvement agendas to their overseas policies.

Take Royal Dutch Shell, for example. In an article in the *Washington Post,* the corporation claimed that, because of their recent losses in court disputes and public knowledge of their human rights abuses overseas, they had adopted a new code of ethics for dealing with repressive governments. However, a senior Shell executive, who refused to be identified, said that Shell's policy is now withdrawal from communities where trouble follows their presence, not for any stated humanitarian reasons but because of their fear of repressive governments. In the spirit of "constructive engagement," Shell claims to also be fostering human relations with people in the communities where they are involved by sponsoring development projects, providing schools, and giving drugs to hospitals. They have also allowed activist groups to become involved in their planning process and now publish an environmental annex to their annual report.

In a July U.N. meeting, chief executives from 50 multinational corporations, including BPAmoco and Royal Dutch Shell, met with environmental organizations to pass the U.N. Global Compact. The compact lists universally recognized and specific labor, human rights, and environmental policies to which the corporations promised to adhere.

Yet it is doubted by some whether the Global Compact will realize any real changes. According to Phyllis Bennis, an analyst at the Institute of Policy Studies, the pact "...allows some of the world's biggest violators of core rights to use the U.N. logo to blue-wash their image.... There is no enforcement mechanism. The human rights and labor organizations that participate in the compact don't even play a monitoring role." Many key advocacy groups in the fight against corporations, including Greenpeace International, refused to participate in the process.

While the mainstream news sources focused on corporate attempts to "bluewash" their images, alternative, industry, and foreign news services continued to document human rights and environmental violations. *EarthFirst!* reported on almost daily widespread oil spills in Nigeria despite Shell's promise to correct environmental mistakes. Dispute continues over whether or not the problems are due to aging pipelines or sabotage from project protestors. And with a key court case against it dropped, Enron has moved forward with its controversial project in Turkmenistan.

The mainstream media, in fact, has well nigh ignored Enron's environmental and human rights activities, even domestically. In a flagrant disregard for environmental issues, the company is allowed to continue to operate a highly polluting Houston methanol plant because of a grandfather clause in the 1971 Texas Clean Air Act that former Texas governor and now-president George W. Bush extended in 1999. Enron was the biggest financial backer of the Bush campaign—which does not bode well for the future regulation of the petroleum industry abroad.

SOURCES: *Oil and Gas Journal,* November 1, 1999, "Petroleum and Human Rights: The New Frontiers of Debate," by John Bray; *The Progressive,* September 2000, "Meet Enron, Bush's Biggest Contributor," by Pratap Chatterjee;

EarthFirst!, September/October 2000, "Nigerian Military Opens Fire on Youths After Shell Oil Spill," by Felix Tuodolo; *Houston Chronicle,* January 28 & November 18, 2000; *Newsweek,* January 31, 2000, "Ubiquity and its Burdens," by Michael Hirsh and Kenneth Klee; *Washington Post,* July 27, 2000.

1999 #2 CENSORED STORY
PHARMACEUTICAL COMPANIES PUT PROFITS BEFORE NEED

Multinational pharmaceutical companies spend billions of dollars on research for highly profitable lifestyle drugs to treat such relatively benign non-life threatening conditions as impotence, baldness, canine Alzheimer's, and toenail fungus, while ignoring research for life-threatening diseases in Third World countries. Diseases such as malaria, tuberculosis, and acute lower respiratory infections killed 6.1 million people in 1998 alone. Only 1 percent of all new medicines brought to market by multinational pharmaceutical companies between 1975 and 1997 were designed specifically to treat the tropical diseases that plague poorer countries. Those that do (13 of every 1,223) were not specifically developed for this reason—most resulted from military research, variations of older drugs, or results of fluke veterinary accidents.

The pharmaceutical companies and their professional organization, Pharmaceutical Research and Manufacturers of America (PhRMA), claim that funds are being directed toward tropical disease research, but PhRMA refuses to release statistics. None of the 24 biggest drug companies has in-house research programs for tropical diseases unless they in some way affect the U.S. population.

It is known that the total amount of money spent worldwide on malaria research, including government programs, came to only $84 million in 1993; by contrast $1.5 *billion* is spent annually on the research and development of drugs for pets. Research for AIDS continues to be funded but only because it affects First as well as Third World countries. New drug breakthroughs for AIDS are typically too expensive for residents of poor countries. And although medicines for malaria and similar diseases are treatable, millions of infected people die each year who simply cannot afford those drugs that are available.

Corporate mergers have enhanced this inequity. Focus in the industry has shifted from healing to profits. In 1998, the pharmaceutical industry spent more than $10 billion on advertising, $74 million on lobbying, and another $12 million on campaign contributions. The U.S. government plays its role in this abuse by threatening countries that use less expensive and/or generic drugs with trade sanctions.

Doctors without Borders, winners of the 1999 Nobel Peace Prize, announced an international campaign to increase access to key drugs.

SOURCE: *The Nation,* "Millions for Viagra, Pennies for the Poor," July 19, 1999, by Ken Silverstein.

COVERAGE 2000: It took the combined efforts of Doctors Without Borders (DWB), Bill Gates, the World Trade Organization (WTO) protests, and President Clinton to bring media attention to the plight of the world's ailing millions. Slowly, hope is in the offing for these Third World sufferers, but not quickly enough; the global distribution of much-needed drugs continues to be blocked by the pharmaceutical industry's quest for profits.

DWB had already begun to campaign for international access to critical drugs in 1999. Shortly thereafter, the Bill and Melinda Gates Foundation donated $750 million to a global fund for children's vaccines, a fund estimated to eventually reach more than $4 billion. Not to be outdone, in his January budget proposal President Clinton outlined a $1 billion tax credit incentive for malaria, tuberculosis, and AIDS vaccine research aimed at relieving suffering in the global community. It was time for the drug companies, in Donald McNeil's words, "to turn their attention to diseases like sleeping sickness, malaria, tuberculosis, leishmaniasis and the various burrowing worms that kill or cripple millions each year in Africa, Asia, and South America."

It isn't always humanitarian motives that drive the research, however. As the drug supply for treating sleeping sickness, for instance, dwindled to near-zero, interest was revived when it was discovered that it might also prevent the growth of facial hair in women, promising soaring profits for pharmaceutical companies. This single example underscores the severity of the problem underdeveloped countries face: if there is no alternative profit promised from the development of a drug, then First World countries, world public health groups, or governments must underwrite the costs. The bottom line remains just that—no profit, no motive.

Pharmaceutical companies are beginning to respond to public pressure. Pfizer announced it would begin donating fluconazole, which cures AIDS-induced cryptococcal meningitis as well as yeast infections in women, to South Africans unable to afford it. But not all such gestures are without critique. One of the most abhorrent responses by the pharmaceutical industry to this international crisis is what DWB calls "drug dumping," donating expired or obsolete drugs in hopes of avoiding the costs of destroying or storing outdated inventory and coincidentally reaping substantial tax breaks.

Many Third World countries say they cannot wait for the charitable donations to begin. When the WTO spotlight shone on Ralph Nader's Consumer Project on Technology, attention was brought to the idea that poor countries could receive AIDS drugs by sidestepping expensive industry patents through two little-known WTO rules that permit the manufacture of generic drugs in the event of national health emergencies.

These exemptions provide a critical first-step for Third World countries. The pharmaceutical companies, however, call on the sovereignty of their drug patents to protect their profit margins, claiming that they are necessary to recoup high research costs. But some countries are contemplating declaring health emergencies in order to avoid U.S. patent restrictions and either import generic equivalents or bargain for lower prices. The cost of medicine varies widely, the same pill may cost dollars more in some countries than in others. Fluconazole, for instance, sells for between $3.60 per pill in Thailand to more than $27 each in Guatemala; the same pill by generic manufacturers sells from between 30 and 64 cents.

Recently, and not too surprisingly, more U.S. research firms are beginning to look at reinvesting in malaria research as the threat of global warming raises the possibility of mosquito-borne diseases invading the North American continent.

SOURCES: *San Francisco Chronicle,* November 24, 1999 & June 25, 2000; *salon.com,* December 15, 1999; *Pharmaceutical Technology,* March 2000, "AIDS and Drug access," by Jill Wechsler; *New York Times,* May 21, June 25, & July 9, 2000, "Medicine Merchants: A Special Report," by Donald McNeil, Jr., and September 21, 2000, "A Big Factor in Prescription Drug Pricing: Location, Location, Location," by Hal R. Varian; *Virginian Pilot,* May 25, 2000; *Baltimore Sun,* June 18, 2000; *salon.com,* December 15, 2000, "Warming to Malaria," by Arthur Allen.

FINANCIALLY BLOATED AMERICAN CANCER SOCIETY FAILS TO PREVENT CANCER

The American Cancer Society (ACS) has accumulated vast wealth, all the while maintaining its status as a charity institution. It is purported to be one of the largest nonprofit organizations in the world, and yet much of the ACS's donations have come from surgeons, drug companies, and corporations that profit from cancer cures and treatments.

The ACS Foundation Board of Trustees includes corporate executives David R. Bethune, president of Lederle Laboratories, a division of American Cyanamid, and Gordon Binder, CEO of Amgen, the world's foremost biotechnology company. Both companies produce cancer treatment drugs that have realized skyrocketing profits as the cancer epidemic grows.

More than half the funds raised by the ACS go toward overhead, executive salaries, and fringe benefits, while unpaid volunteers handle most direct services. Its 1998 cash reserves were reportedly in excess of $1 billion, including millions in real estate investments.

Nationally, only 16 percent of its funds go toward direct services to cancer victims, and conflicts of interest have affected approaches towards cancer prevention. The ACS has adopted a "blame the victim" attitude, which emphasizes faulty lifestyles rather than environmental influences as causes of cancer. The ACS has repeatedly refused to provide the scientific testimony congressional committees need to regulate occupational and environmental carcinogens.

The ACS's early detection stance towards breast cancer reflects the legacy of five radiologists serving as past foundation presidents along with the interests of large manufacturers of mammogram machines and film. The ACS recruited the help of AstraZeneca for its management of "Breast Cancer Awareness Month" in the United States. AstraZeneca Inc. manufactures the controversial cancer prevention drug, tamoxifen. In 1992 the ACS conducted a five-year trial of tamoxifen as a cancer prevention treatment on 16,000 healthy, yet "high risk" women in spite of evidence of numerous side affects, including increased risks of liver and uterine cancer as well as fatal embolisms.

Samuel Epstein charges the American Cancer Society with "losing the winnable war against cancer." The ACS fixates on damage control rather than cancer prevention, and has trivialized the escalating incidences of cancer, which have now reached epidemic proportions. Lifetime risks for the disease have reached one in two for men, and one in three for women. The American Cancer Society has misled the American public on its progress in the war against cancer while at the same time attacking alternative treatments and unorthodox therapy. Since this story first appeared in the *International Journal of Health Services*, more information on the ACS budget and its allocation of funds has become available. No information is yet available on salaries and benefits of national executives.

SOURCE: *International Journal of Health Services*, Vol. 29, No. 3, 1999, "American Cancer Society: The World's Wealthiest 'Non-Profit' Institution," by Samuel S. Epstein.

COVERAGE 2000: The American Cancer Society continues to conduct business as usual with little mainstream media coverage of its activities. There are a few notable exceptions.

The United Way of Los Angeles has changed its approach toward charitable donations, resulting in the ACS regional office standing to lose about $700,000 in United Way funding. Needless to say, it opposes the fundraiser's decision. Whether the United Way can adhere to its new policy or must capitulate to the demands of large national institutions like the ACS remains to be seen.

The Ohio Division of the ACS made local and regional news when its chief administrative officer was accused of embezzling nearly half the organization's $15 million annual budget. Daniel Stephen Wiant wired $6,936,250 from an ACS account to an investment banker in Kufstein, Austria, and then promptly left the country. The ACS Ohio Division was unaware the money was gone until six days later when notified by the FBI. The incident underscores the lax financial control within the organization. As the *Columbus Dispatch* commented, "[T]he claim by one society official that the organization has 'superlative' financial controls is simply unbelievable." Wiant had a recent criminal record spanning 10 years including convictions in Hawaii, California, and Ohio. The ACS started doing background checks on its employees since Wiant's hire, especially of those, like Wiant, who are put in charge of finances. Curiously, this incident followed an earlier embezzlement of $150,000 by another individual.

The *Dispatch* raised the issue of general ACS credibility, referring to a May 1998 survey that showed that while 96 percent of Americans recognize the organization by name, only 5 percent know what it does with its money. In his book, *Unhealthy Charities*, Thomas DiLorenzo points out that $140 million of the $556 million the ACS raised in 1998 went to administrative and advertising costs.

Information regarding ACS revenues and compensation for high level officials also found its way into print in 2000. A *National Journal* article listed the American Cancer Society's 1998 Internal Revenue filings. According to the IRS, the ACS had revenues totaling $241,577,836. The CEO at the time, John R. Seffrin, received a $325,000 salary along with $94,571 in benefits and allowances.

Incidentally, President Clinton's fiscal year 2001 budget is reported to include an unprecedented funding increase to explore the environmental causes of diseases like breast and prostate cancer. Undoubtedly, some of these funds will find their way to the American Cancer Society. Along the way, the investment practices of charitable foundations in general came under scrutiny. The Bill and Melinda Gates Foundation, the largest charitable foundation with a $22 billion endowment, spends much of its money on efforts to help "improve people's lives through health and learning." However, the *New York Times* discovered that while it supports charities like Cancer Lifeline and ACS, it also owns bonds in the Philip Morris tobacco company. Tamoxifen, championed by ACS, reappeared in the news. AstraZeneca's product remains controversial and has been challenged by reportedly more effective drugs, according to the San Antonio Breast Cancer Symposium. The symposium took place in late 1999, yet tamoxifen is still widely used. Despite new information, the Food and Drug Administration (FDA) is still conducting research on the drug.

The FDA has had its own problems with AstraZeneca this past year. In August, they had to caution the makers of tamoxifen against publishing misleading information in journal ads and promotional brochures, which suggesting that their drug was more effective than studies had actually demonstrated. They also understated its side effects. Such advertisements had appeared in journals targeting obstetricians, gynecologists, and other doctors who care for women.

SOURCES: *PR Newswire*, December 10, 1999, & March 14, 2000; *National Jour-*nal, Inc.*, January 15, 2000; *Los Angeles Times*, January 20, 2000; *International Journal of Health Service*, Volume 30, Number 2, 2000, "Legislative Proposals for Reversing the Cancer Epidemic and Controlling Run-Away Industrial Technologies," by Samuel S. Epstein; *Plain Dealer*, June 8, June 19, & August 24, 2000; *Columbus Dispatch*, June 11, & July 8, 2000; *New York Times*, June 11, 2000, "Charities' Investing: Left Hand, Meet Right," by Reed Abelson; *USA Today*, August 8, 2000.

2000 UPDATE BY AUTHOR SAMUEL S. EPSTEIN THE AMERICAN CANCER SOCIETY THREATENS THE NATIONAL CANCER PROGRAM

Operating behind closed doors and with powerful political connections, the American Cancer Society (ACS) is charged with forging a questionable and possibly illegal alliance with the federal Centers for Disease Control and Prevention (CDC) in attempts to hijack the National Cancer Program. The background to the ACS political agenda reveals a pattern of self-interest, conflicts of interest, lack of accountability, and nontransparency, to which the media have responded with deafening silence.

President Nixon's 1971 National Cancer Act, mandating the National Cancer Program directed by the National Cancer Institute (NCI), is under powerful attack by the ACS, the world's largest nonreligious charity. The ACS is lobbying to replace the 1971 Act by new legislation, assigning responsibility to and requiring coordination between the private sector, patient advocacy groups, and the public sector, the NCI, and CDC. Of major concern are the highly questionable close CDC–ACS relationship and efforts to divert emphasis and funds away from NCI's peer-reviewed scientific research to CDC's state and community public health programs primarily focused on screening and behavioral intervention.

The September 26, 1998, march, Coming Together to Conquer Cancer, brought several advocacy groups representing 125,000 survivors to Washington, D.C. However, it failed to create a community of scientists and patients unified by a common political agenda, and even strained their willingness to collaborate. The ACS was a minor and reluctant player in the march, recognizing that breast, prostate, and other advocacy groups posed a growing threat to its fundraising. However, the ACS deftly used the march to capture its PR fallout by creating the National Dialogue on Cancer (NDC), a purportedly independent forum co-chaired by former President George Bush and Barbara Bush, vice-chaired by Senator Dianne Feinstein (D-CA), and including Governors Tom Ridge of Pennsylvania and Tommy Thompson of Wisconsin. The NDC activities are managed by a 16-member steering committee, with representation from ACS, CDC, NCI, cancer survivors, the underserved, and the pharmaceutical industry, which meets behind closed doors; NCI's involvement has been nominal, at best.

In turn, the NDC leadership selected a group of more than 100 collaborating partners, including representatives of major advocacy groups, some of whom declined the invitation, while others failed to attend meetings or frankly suspected their agenda as a thinly disguised vehicle for furthering ACS special interests. On August 8, 1999, the NDC shocked its collaborating partners by suddenly announcing the formation of a National Cancer Legislation Advisory Committee to advise Senator Feinstein on rewriting the National Cancer Act. This 25-member committee was co-chaired by Dr. John Seffrin, CEO of the ACS, and Dr. Vincent DeVita, Director of the Yale Cancer Center and former NCI director, without any participation by the Steering Committee and NDC's collaborating partners. Apart from NDC's high-handed conduct and supposedly independent legislation committee spinoff, there are major concerns on interlocking ACS-CDC interests. CDC has improperly and possibly illegally funded ACS with close to $3 million for a sole source four-year cooperative agreement, and also the NDC with $100,000. In turn, ACS has made strong efforts to upgrade CDC's role in the National Cancer Program, and also to increase appropriations for its non-peer-reviewed cancer programs.

The relationship between the ACS, NDC, and the Legislation Committee raises fundamental questions on conflicts of interest. As reported in *The Cancer Letter*, a Washington, D.C., newsletter widely read within the cancer establishment, John Durant, former executive president of the American Society for Clinical Oncology, charged: "It has always seemed to me that this was an issue of control by the ACS over the cancer agenda…. They are protecting their own fundraising capacity… against competition by advocacy groups." More seriously, the leading U.S. charity watchdog, *The Chronicle of Philanthropy*, concluded: "The ACS is more interested in accumulating wealth than saving lives."

DeVita, the legislation committee co-chair, is also chairman of the Medical Advisory Board of CancerSource.com, a website launched by Jones & Bartlett (Sudbury, MA) that publishes the ACS "Consumers Guide to Cancer Drugs"; three members of the legislation committee also serve on the same board. Thus, DeVita appears to be developing his personal interests in a publicly funded forum. The ACS priority for tobacco cessation programs is inconsistent with its industry relationships. According to the *Cancer Letter*, Shandwick International, via its Division Management subsidary, which represents R.J. Reynolds, has been a major PR firm for the NDC and Legislation Committee. Also, Edelman PR, representing Brown & Williamson Tobacco Company, which handles publicity for Team KOOL Green championship auto racing, was hired by ACS to conduct voter education programs aimed at making cancer a major issue in the 2000 presidential campaign. Further improprieties relate to questionably legal ACS contributions to Democratic and Republican governors associations. "We wanted to look like players and be players," ACS explained.

More disturbing is ACS's three-decade track record of indifference and even hostility to cancer prevention. Examples include issuing a joint statement with the Chlorine Institute justifying the continued global use of persistent organochlorine pesticides, and also supporting the industry in trivializing dietary pesticide residues as avoidable risks of childhood cancer. ACS policies are further exemplified by its allocation of less than 0.1 percent of its $700 million annual budget to environmental and occupational causes of cancer.

In this connection, there are also growing and urgent concerns with regard to the NCI's imbalanced preoccupation with basic research, besides damage control—screening, diagnosis, and treatment—with minimal priorities and budgetary allocations for mission research on primary prevention and public outreach on avoidable causes of cancer. ACS, with its NDC and legislation spinoffs, has disqualified itself from any leadership role in the National Cancer Program. The public should be encouraged to redirect its funding away from the ACS to patient and prevention advocacy groups. The conduct of ACS, particularly its political lobbying and possibly illegal relationship to CDC, should be investigated by the House and Senate appropriations and oversight committees. Finally, Congress should ensure that the National Cancer Program directs the highest priority to cancer prevention.

2000 UPDATE BY BARBARA SEAMAN

Dr. Samuel Epstein's thoroughly documented exposé of pervasive conflicts of interest in the "cancer establishment," particularly the American Cancer Society (ACS), has already demonstrated a measurable impact. A major step toward full disclosure, which could lead to the reduction of female cancers, was taken on December 15, 2000, when a blue-ribbon government panel—the NIH's National Toxicology Advisory Committee—voted 8 to 1 to add prescription estrogens to the official list of "known carcinogens."

The ACS, along with much of the OB/Gyn establishment, has been so thoroughly influenced, lulled, perhaps even "brainwashed" by the prescription drug industry that 60 years—during which the frequency of hormone dependent female cancers has more than doubled in the United States—elapsed before the official labeling of steroid estrogens as carcinogens could be openly acknowledged. There was no suggestion that estrogen use be restricted or banned, but at meetings of the Toxicology Advisory Committee some scientists did express hope that prescribing physicians might become more cautionary. Toxicologist Michelle Medinsky stated, "They only discuss benefits. Listing might force it on the table.... Is knowledge power or is ignorance bliss? Everyone has to make their own decision."

My concerned colleagues and I have difficulty understanding why so many well-intentioned environmental cancer-prevention activists often fail to identify the estrogen products themselves in their research radar. Winning pieces on cancer factors in the environment that looked for estrogenic chemicals, phyto estrogens, xeno estrogens, and so on, seemed oblivious to the fact that prescription and veterinary estrogens should be placed in square one. It seems like a waste of research money to examine these other factors without looking simultaneously at exposure to prescription and (in so far as possible) veterinary estrogens in the same populations. To give one example, breast cancer activists on New York State's Long Island have investigated possible environmental causes of atypically high rates without also including questions on exposure to diethelstilbestrol (DES). In the post–World War II era, Long Island was one of the major "hotbeds" of routine DES-prescribing to pregnant women, based on the unjustified belief that it prevented miscarriages. This practice ended abruptly in 1971, when some of the daughters exposed in utero were diagnosed with reproductive tract abnormalities, particularly vaginal adenocarcinoma, which is often lethal. By 1978, when I served on the U.S. Surgeon General's task force on DES, an increased frequency of breast cancer in the DES-exposed mothers was also recognized. Twenty-three years later, in 2001, this finding was reconfirmed in the *British Medical Journal*, Volume 84, Number 1.

Estrogen Sea. "Veterinary" estrogens may be incurred through vocational exposure in laboratories and feedlots or through dangerously high dietary consumption of estrogen-fed meat and poultry. But further, most commercial estrogen products are not biodegradable by the stomach acids, and therefore residues are normally excreted in urine. Some eminent European scientists have posited in the *Lancet* that excreted estrogens in the food chain and water (supplied in the United States not only by women on prescription drugs, but by livestock as well) may have us "swimming in a sea of estrogens." This, the theory goes, would account for the lockstep rise in certain male cancers, and infertility in some aquatic creatures, along with the rise in female cancers.

In fact, the carcinogenicity of synthetic estrogens in laboratory animals that have similar patterns to humans was established in historic experiments performed by Michael B. Shimkin and Hugh C. Grady, and published in the *Journal of the National Cancer Institute* in 1940. In December 1947, less than a decade after estrogen products for treating menopause first came on the market, the *Journal Of Obstetrics and Gynecology* published Dr. Saul Gusberg's report on 29 cases of cancers and pre-cancers of the uterus associated with such therapy. By 1971, as mentioned, Dr. Arthur Herbst confirmed the tragic outcome of DES estrogens in pregnancy. In 1975 the FDA commissioner sent emergency notification to all U.S. physicians that four separate studies had confirmed a four- to eight-fold increase in uterine cancer in long-term users of estrogens for menopause.

By the 1990s it was demonstrated that adding progestin to the estrogen regimen gives considerable protection against uterine cancer, but, at the same time, raises the patient's risk of breast cancer to three times greater than taking estrogens alone. The longer a woman stays on hormones, the more her chances of uterine and breast cancer keep rising. If you have a uterus and take estrogens without progestins, you invite cancer of the uterine lining. If you add progestins to the estrogen you avoid the cancer "down there," but substantially increase your chances of getting it "up front" in your breast.

"Keep Her on Premarin." The major hormone-product manufacturers, including Ortho (Johnson and Johnson) and Wyeth Ayerst, are vigilant in censoring journalists and physicians who criticize or question their products. Hormone drugs are extraordinary sources of income simply because (unlike drugs for the sick) so many healthy women stay on them indefinitely. (For example, 12 million menopausal and postmenopausal U.S. women take estrogen alone, while 8.6 million take it in combination with progestin. Perhaps another 10 million to 14 million take birth-control pills.) Ortho is the world's largest manufacturer of oral contraceptives; while Wyeth Ayerst's Premarin (which stands for PREgnant MARes urINe) is the only prescription drug to remain in the top 50

bestsellers for more than half a century, and remained number one in 1999.

I am used to having Ortho and Wyeth Ayerst withdraw their ads from magazines to which I contribute, and their funds from medical conferences that include me on their programs. Indeed, when asked to speak at an event that may have industry sponsorship, I often warn the inviters that they may have to cancel me. Industry blacklists have become commonplace, extending to physicians and scientists, as well as journalists, who are deemed "unfriendly." But what I never expected was that Wyeth Ayerst would succeed in blackballing me at my own journalism school, Columbia University, where I was a Sloan Rockefeller Advanced Science Writing Fellow in 1967–68, the year that I began *The Doctors' Case Against the Pill*, the very book that first brought the hormone industry's wrath down upon me.

By the 1990s Kenneth Goldstein, then teaching the science writing courses, was accepting funds from Wyeth Ayerst for student junkets, sending them to cover pro-estrogen conferences, which they were expected to write up for a Wyeth Ayerst puff publication on menopause. One student became disturbed about the assignment and contacted me for advice. From the moment I confronted Goldstein, I was repeatedly excluded from speaking at any and all journalism school panels or forums on medical or population issues. Kenneth Goldstein retired recently, and I am waiting to see whether or not I am to be resuscitated.

A period of public comment follows additions to our federal lists of carcinogens. Manufacturers of hormone products, as well as some doctors who heavily prescribe them will, if true to form, object to this classification and try to have it modified. I hope that Project Censored readers who value full disclosure and informed consent will write to the NIH in support of the Toxicology Advisory Committee's long-overdue move. Comments (supporting or opposing) on estrogens can be sent to: National Institute of Environmental Health Sciences/National Toxicology Program (NIEHS/NTP), Dr. C. W. Jameson, EC-14, P.O. Box 12233, Research Triangle Park NC 27709. Copies may be sent to Barbara Seaman, c/o Project Censored, Seven Stories Press, 140 Watts Street, New York NY 10013. The exact language of the recommendation can be viewed in the *Federal Register*.

Barbara Seaman is a Project Censored National Judge.

1999 #4 CENSORED STORY

AMERICAN SWEATSHOPS SEW U.S. MILITARY UNIFORMS

Lion Apparel fits every criteria of a sweatshop and yet, in spite of laws prohibiting the use of public funds to purchase clothing from sweatshops, it is one of the top three suppliers of military uniforms to the U.S. Department of Defense (DOD).

The DOD has $1 billion invested in the garment industry and resells much of the military clothing it purchases at a markup, ranking it the fourteenth largest retail apparel outlet in the nation. Yet it has not joined private sector retailers in signing the Workplace Code of Conduct in response to the public outcry against sweatshop labor.

The Department of Labor, which can debar contractors who do not comply with wage or safety laws, never investigates compliance in spite of a 1996 General Accounting Office report which estimated that 22 percent of federal contractors have been cited by the Occupational Safety and Health Administration (OSHA) for violating safety standards.

Lion Apparel's manufacturing plants are in Appalachia, where there is little other choice for employment. Most of the factory's employees are women, supporting families on pay as low as $5.50 an hour. Workers must make do with antiquated equipment in a poorly heated building and are continually exposed to formaldehyde, a suspected carcinogen. Lion Apparel has been cited by OSHA 32 times in the last 12 years for workplace safety violations.

In 1997 Lion employees tried to unionize their shop. In response, management posted veiled threats that slyly evaded federal labor laws prohibiting union-busting plant closures. Eight employees fought back by sending a letter outlining Lion's threats to Vice President Gore, eight Kentucky congressmen, and the state's U.S. senators. The letter was mysteriously forwarded to Lion's management, abruptly ending all employee efforts toward unionization.

In spite of these charges, Lion Apparel has been praised by the Defense Logistics Agency (DLA), the procurement arm of the DOD, for its "finesse" in saving the government $4.5 million in military apparel costs. The DLA has in turn been awarded the Vice Presidential Hammer Award 51 times for its "efficiency."

Lion demanded a retraction of this article from *Mother Jones* but the magazine stood by its sources.

SOURCE: *Mother Jones,* May/June 1999, "An American Sweatshop," by Mark Boal.

COVERAGE 2000: There has been no direct news follow-up of this story aside from some brief local coverage when the city council of Bangor, Maine, deliberated on whether or not to purchase its fire department uniforms from Lion Apparel. Their decision, as it turned out, was directly influenced by information in Boal's *Mother Jones* article.

Otherwise it's been business-almost-as-usual at Lion Apparel. Three months after Boal's article appeared, Lion was awarded a DOD contract twice the size of its previous one. This new 10-year, $110 million contract is Lion's largest yet with the DOD. Lion, in conjunction with Vallen Corporation, will "manage procurement, inventory logistics, and distribution for military recruit clothing" for the military's entire Southeast region. A Lion VP made it clear that "the company will not manufacture the clothes, nor will it have control over who the DOD chooses as its supplier."

Instead, Lion/Vallen will perform supply chain management.

Mysteries remain over Lion's denial of the original *Mother Jones* allegations. Lion's Richard Lapedes claims that Lion Apparel is one of the most progressive companies in the country, and paints a workplace picture far different from the one described by the Lion employees Boal interviewed. But Boal documented Lion's 32 OSHA citations in 12 years, eight times as many as those received by other contractors during the same period. The Bangor City Council found Lion's average wage to be $8/hour compared to another company's $13/hour. Although Lion explicitly states that it is not a manufacturer in their newest DOD contract, they still have their old Air Force contract as well as a new USDA Forest Service uniform contract. Also, in refuting Boal's story, Lion had asserted that it now manufactures only fire protection clothing, and that they have not manufactured military uniforms in decades. Yet Lion continued to represent itself as a "manufacturer of government uniforms" as recently as early 1999.

The DOD's procurement practices are themselves questionable. For instance, Federal Prison Industries (FPI), the federally mandated supplier for government agencies, is taking a big bite of the market share of the apparel manufacturing industry, especially those companies that produce uniforms and personal issue items for the U.S. military. FPI is currently the largest supplier of textiles and apparel to the DOD. But the DOD's procurement practices have recently come under fire. A *New York Times* article reported on the Army and Air Force Exchange Service (AAFES) procurement of large quantities of apparel from Chentex, a suspected Nicaraguan sweatshop operation. Several members of Congress questioned such acquisitions, and U.S. labor-rights groups have mounted an intense campaign against further procurement. In light of such criticism, AAFES sent officials to Nicaragua to examine the Chentex operation. According to a spokesman, representatives found no problems.

News articles have appeared this year regarding the "frayed, patched, and

THIS MODERN WORLD
by TOM TOMORROW

obsolete gear" that servicemen are still being issued. Despite a $287.8 billion defense budget, soldiers are obliged to buy equipment themselves on an annual clothing allowance of only $255.60. This in turn forces them to purchase needed items from the Defense Logistics Agency (DLA).

SOURCES: *Small Business News,* January 1, 1999; *PR Newswire,* September 10, 1999; *Dayton Daily News,* October 9, 1999; *Bobbin,* January 1, 2000; *Bangor Daily News,* February 7 & July 4, 2000; *Commerce Business Daily,* June 27, 2000; *San Diego Union-Tribune,* August 30, 2000; *New York Times,* December 3, 2000.

1999 #5 CENSORED STORY

TURKEY DESTROYS KURDISH VILLAGES WITH U.S. WEAPONS

Turkey has been committing genocide against the Kurds that live within its borders using U.S.-made weapons. This fact alone should preclude the United States from selling Turkey anything, but it chooses to ignore the human rights abuses in order to maintain a military alliance with the strategically placed country.

The Kurds are the largest ethnic group in the world to have their own language, culture, and religion without their own state. They have lived for thousands of years in an area that now falls within the borders of Turkey, Iraq, Iran, Syria, and the Soviet Union. Of the 25 million Kurds spread throughout the Middle East, 15 million live in Turkey. In 1984 the Turkish Kurdistan Workers Party (PKK) started a separatist movement, which resulted in 40,000 Turkish Kurds dying since 1980, and 2 million being made homeless, exceeding the number of refugees in Kosovo where U.S. arms were not a factor.

The United States has sold or given Turkey weapons valued at more than $15 billion, mostly during President Clinton's first term. Turkey's war on the Kurds relies on weaponry from dozens of U.S. defense contractors. At the time of McKiernan's article, Turkey was waiting for a shipment of U.S.-made

armored personnel carriers (APCs). Amnesty International hoped to block the sale through its report on Turkish "anti-terrorist" activities, which documented the torture and sexual assaults of prisoners of all ages, including children. Nonetheless, the State Department allowed the sale to proceed.

Turkey's strategic Mideast location is well recognized. A 1980 agreement between the two countries allowed U.S. military bases into Turkey in exchange for U.S. help in modernizing the Turkish military. Several U.S. and NATO intelligence-gathering posts located in Turkey are critical to U.S. and NATO activities in Iraq. The United States also has an intense interest in the Caspian Sea oil reserves, and is lobbying to build a pipeline through Turkey to the Mediterranean Sea. The proposed pipeline would pass through the center of Kurdistan. Kurdish Guerrillas have vowed to block this project. They have already blown up sections of the Iraqi pipeline and Turkish oil fields in the southeast. Ironically, the United States supports the Kurds in Iraq since they oppose Saddam Hussein.

Turkey has been trying to get into the European Union (EU) for years, but the EU has rejected its petitions primarily because of its record of human rights violations. While the PKK has also been accused of perpetrating serious human rights abuses, the Turkish Army has been responsible for the majority of forced evacuation and destruction of Kurdish villages (more than 3,000), according to a human rights watchdog group in New York.

In an update to his original story, author Kevin McKiernan reports that he was asked by both CBS's *60 Minutes* and PBS's *NewsHour* to consult on Kurd-related stories. However, their interest was not on the plight of the Turkish Kurds and the U.S. involvement in their systematic annihilation, but on the sensationalism surrounding the arrest, trial, and sentencing (death by hanging) of PKK leader Abdullah Ocalan.

SOURCES: *The Bulletin of Atomic Scientists*, March/April 1999, "Turkey's War on the Kurds," by Kevin McKeirnan.

COVERAGE 2000: With little exception, the mainstream U.S. media has been "AWOL." in reporting on the role of U.S. arms in Turkey's war with the PKK. Media interest in the country's human rights abuses did surface, however, during three different circumstances: Turkey's petition to be included in the EU (mostly in the foreign press), the House resolution labeling Turkey's massacre and eviction of 1.5 million Armenians from 1915–1923 as genocide, and Ocalan's appeal to the European Convention on Human Rights. But few put all the issues together.

Author Kevin McKiernan reiterated his argument in several op-ed pieces around the country, this time focusing on a $4 billion contract for 145 attack helicopters. Although the U.S. government had earlier firmly stated that they would block the sale until Turkey changed its human rights policy, they sidestepped the issue completely by modifying their requirements, calling instead just for *improvement* in certain areas. Michelle Ciarrocca, a research associate at the World Policy Institute in New York City, joined McKiernan's fight, sending several pieces out to the wires documenting Turkey's record in the human rights arena. Ciarrocca states, "As U.S. weapons flows have increased, Turkey's human rights performance has worsened."

Time magazine's international edition reported on the heated competition for the $4 billion contract, with Bell Helicopter winning in the end, but only after pecuniary encouragement. Both Bell and Boeing contributed $650,000 to both Democratic and Republican presidential campaigns in 1996, and Bell another $102,000 in Election 2000. Additionally, Boeing contributed $100,000 to a Washington art opening of Ottoman Empire artifacts, and the Turkish Embassy in Washington signed a $1.8 million contract with former Congressman Bob Livingston, Gerald Solomon, and Stephen Solarz to lobby for the Turkish Government.

Foreign coverage picked up in May following the usual Turkish raids on Kurdish villages in Northern Iraq, even though Ocalan had called for a ceasefire from his prison cell the previous summer (obeyed by thousands of PKK fighters). *The Progressive's* Matthew Rothschild called U.S. readers' attention to the lack of coverage on the forays with U.S.-made weaponry and helicopters, and to a London article by Chris Morris. Morris notes, "Almost anywhere else in the world, thousands of heavily armed soldiers crossing an international border would be big news. But this latest Turkish incursion into Iraq will be greeted with barely a murmur in the west...." And he was right.

By year's end, Turkey got its helicopters and a $7.5 billion IMF loan, but its human rights record remained the worst in the world and it was still destroying Kurdish villages. Also, as Ciarrocca pointed out in the *Charleston Gazette,* the Clinton Administration remained the world's number one arms dealer no matter whose human rights were being violated (see *Censored 1998,* Censored #1, "Clinton Administration Aggressively Promotes U.S. Arms Sales Worldwide").

SOURCES: *Knight Ridder,* November 14, 1999; *Los Angeles Times,* March 3, 2000; *Knight Ridder,* March 21, 2000; *The Baltimore Sun,* April 28, 2000; *Guardian* (London), April 3, 2000, "Turks Pursue Kurds Inside Northern Iraq," by Chris Morris; *The Progressive,* May 2000, "Not All Invasions Are Equal," by Matthew Rothschild; *Charleston Gazette,* May 14, 2000; *Time* (international edition), May 22 & August 14, 2000; *Washington Post,* November 8, 2000.

1999 #6 CENSORED STORY

NATO DEFENDS PRIVATE ECONOMIC INTERESTS IN THE BALKANS

NATO and its member countries, fully aware of the numerous economic advantages to breaking up Yugoslavia, pursued a war over Kosovo in order to position the Western nations politically, economically, and militarily.

The media often depicts Kosovo as a poor, isolated region with little or no resources. Actually, it contains the most valuable resources in the Balkans—huge reserves of lead, zinc, cadmium, silver, gold, and coal estimated to be worth in excess of $5 billion. The Serbian state-owned Trepca mining complex holds the huge complex of mines, oil and gas refining prospects, and power and transportation futures. It is thought to be the largest piece of wealth not yet in the hands of U.S. and European capitalists.

Natural gas pipeline routes that carry Caspian oil to foreign markets may also have been a contributing factor in NATO's war against Serbia. On average, 1990 oil prices from the Caspian Sea amounted to approximately $5 trillion. But numerous problems exist with the various proposals for delivering Caspian oil to the West. Options for building pipelines through Iran and Russia are opposed by the United States for political reasons. The possibility of shipping the oil across the Black Sea from a pipeline at its eastern coast, the cheapest option, is environmentally unsound. The plan favored by the United States is to build the pipeline through the NATO-controlled Balkans.

The Caspian region has been touted as the successor to the Arabian Gulf as a source of world oil. But although the conflict there has been a major news story, few reports focused on the possible environmental consequences of the drilling, the lack of democracy in the region, and the unequal distribution of wealth. In November 1999, President Clinton took part in the formal signing of pipeline agreements with Turkey, Azerbaijan, Georgia, and Turkmenistan. Russia and Iran were not invited.

The role NATO plays in protecting the vital interests of multinational corporations is perhaps its principle justification for continuing existence after the end of the cold war. A leaked 1992 Pentagon planning document states, "It is of fundamental importance to preserve NATO as the primary instrument of Western defense and security, as well as the channel for U.S. influence and participation in European security affairs."

NATO has continually justified its intervention against the Yugoslavian military as an interdiction against genocide. However, subsequent investigations by forensic teams from 17 nations were unable to substantiate U.S. State Department claims of gross massacres and mass graves. The *New York Times* reported that after five months of investigation, they had not found even a fraction of the alleged hundreds of thousands massacred, nor any mass graves. (See also *Censored 2000*, Censored # 12, "Evidence Indicates No Pre-War Genocide in Kosovo and Possible U.S./KLA Plot to Create Disinformation.")

After the cease-fire, the U.S. military built the largest U.S. foreign base since Vietnam in Kosovo, the permanent, heavily fortified Camp Bondsteel. Additional U.S./NATO bases have been constructed throughout the Balkans.

Author Sara Flounders traveled in Yugoslavia during the 78-day NATO bombardment. "It was clear that NATO overwhelmingly targeted the civilian infrastructure," she wrote. Diverse investigations into war crimes by U.S./NATO forces against the Yugoslavian people are planned or ongoing, including the People's Tribunal in Athens, Greece, and an International Tribunal led by former Attorney General Ramsey Clark scheduled for June 2000 in New York City

SOURCES: *Women Against Military Madness*, November 1998, and *Sonoma County Peace Press*, April/May 1999, "The Role of Caspian Sea Oil in the Balkan Conflict," by Diana Johnstone; *Because People Matter*, May/June 1999 (Reprinted from *Workers World* July 30, 1998), "Kosovo: It's About the Mines," by Sara Flounders; *San Francisco Bay Guardian*, December 16, 1999, "Caspian Pipe Dreams," by Pratap Chatterjee.

COVERAGE 2000: U.S. and NATO interests continued to systematically exploit Balkan resources in 2000, a fact that went unnoticed by the U.S. mainstream media. For instance, although wire service stories pumped information back to the United States about the takeover of the Stari Trg mine, none spoke about NATO's role in privatizing the facility while placing the blame for its demise on former Serbian president Milosevic (see Flounders, below).

The Caspian Sea pipeline through Turkey, considered the environmentally safer alternative to shipping through the Bosporous straits (see Chatterjee, below), and newly discovered Caspian oil reserves captured the media spotlight. However, the trans-Balkan oil pipeline project by New York–based AMBO—the Albanian-Macedonian-Bulgarian Oil Company—a virtual fait accompli, remains completely unreported. Although widely circulated by the wire services, the consortium's activities were barely noted in business sections or on financial news shows.

The presidential campaign drew additional media attention to U.S. overseas oil interests. Marjorie Cohn notes that Dick Cheney has long lobbied to lift Iran sanctions in order to facilitate the movement of oil through the country. This is perhaps a harbinger of a shift in U.S. policy toward oil-delivering countries. Still, she notes, "Mr. Cheney's oily fingerprints are all over the Balkans as well."

And regarding Camp Bondsteel, Diana Johnstone, in a September 4, 2000, *In These Times* article quotes from the French *Figaro* magazine, June 9, 2000: "…Washington's European allies 'have the impression of having been taken for a ride: Anticipating tensions with a Europe on the way to unification and the loss of their bases in the EU, the United States may have decided to build itself a new bastion. A well chosen terrain: a Muslim region where European sentiments are inexistent, in the Balkans, near the Mediterranean, the

Near East, petroleum.'[meanwhile] …European allies, looking at this gigantic permanent military base on their doorstep, 'are beginning to wonder whether its implantation wasn't the real objective of the war.'"

The disinformation distributed by the U.S. mainstream press has produced skepticism about "NATOS's Balkan crusade" among apologetic humanitarian crusaders. Nonetheless, writes Paul Hockenos, "While the Western involvement in the Balkans isn't a grand imperialist plot, it is equally naïve to see it solely as an altruistic matter of human rights." Counters Johnstone, "…freedom and democracy must be developed by the people themselves, not by occupying armies and foreign administrators who know what is best, as dictated by IMF economists." (See *Censored 2000*, Censored # 20, "IMF and World Bank Contributed to Economic Tensions in the Balkans.")

SOURCES: *www.emperors-clothes.com*, February 28, 2000, "How it is Done: Taking over the Trepca Mines," by Diane Johnstone; *The Associated Press*, May 30, 2000; *The Baltimore Sun*, August 15, 2000, "Cheney Interests Can Affect Oil Policy," by Marjorie Cohn; *In These Times*, September 4, 2000, "A Humanitarian Crusade," by Diana Johnstone; *St. Petersburg Times*, September 26, 2000; *Agence France Press*, November 28, 2000.

2000 UPDATE BY AUTHOR PRATAP CHAT-TERJEE In June 2000 some 10,000 Caspian seals crawled ashore to die in the Kazakh port city of Aktau. Serikbek Daukeyev, Kazakhstan's environment minister, blamed multinational joint oil venture Tengizchevroil. "The effects of oil wastes and pesticides caused chronic toxic poisoning in the seals," he said. "Every year Tengizchevroil exceeds the set limit of waste emissions because of faulty equipment. Just this year the highest-permitted concentration has been exceeded by 200 percent." The news was completely ignored by U.S. media despite the fact that Tengizchevroil, which produces a third of Kazakhstan's crude output, is majority-controlled by two U.S. multinationals: 50 percent owned by Chevron and 25 percent by Exxon-Mobil. Similar cases of seal deaths have occurred in recent years along the Caspian. Last year 6,000 of the animals died in Azerbaijan while smaller numbers of deaths have been reported from the Turkmen and Russian sectors of the sea.

The media also ignored reports in December 1999 that Georgian scientists discovered several erosion sites along the western pipeline constructed by the Azerbaijan International Oil Consortium (17 percent owned by Amoco and British Petroleum each, 10 percent by Unocal and 8 percent by Exxon). Because of heavy rains the company was asked to stop oil transportation from Baku to Supsa.

Activists say that the environment is slowly facing catastrophe. "Environmental conditions of the Caspian Sea are degrading rapidly. The increased water level is damaging coastal areas, while increased oil concentration causes severe damage to the whole region," says Manana Kochladze of Friends of the Earth in Georgia. Despite these massive environmental impacts from oil drilling, the U.S. government is promoting multiple, major new oil pipelines to carry oil and natural gas across the Caspian Sea to western markets. For example, on September 22, 2000, U.S. Assistant Energy Secretary for International Affairs, David Goldwyn, told a seminar organized by the Middle East Policy Council: "Multiple east-west pipeline routes, we believe, are essential to the security of the region's infrastructure and development and thereby enhance U.S. energy security. Having a monopoly or even an oligopoly of transportation routes is not as good as having multiple routes in competition. Competition is going to give the countries the opportunity to make their own decisions on how to maximize their economic opportunities and also ought to drive down transportation costs."

Oil companies also strongly disagree with this policy. Julia Nanay, director of the Petroleum Finance Corporation, told the seminar that the government was choosing political interests over commercial interests in its pipeline strategy. "It has been the U.S. government's position to build these pipelines even at a time when it didn't know whether the energy resources would be there. So, in a sense, the U.S. government would be happy to see these pipelines built, drawing a line above Iran, even if they stood empty," he said.

Mr. Chatterjee welcomes comments and can be reached at Pratap Chatterjee, P.O. Box 14175, Berkeley, CA, 94712, USA; phone (510) 705-8970; fax (510) 705 8983; e-mail: pchatterjee@igc.org.

2000 UPDATE BY AUTHOR

SARA FLOUNDERS NATO TROOPS SEIZE MINING COMPLEX
Reprinted from the Aug. 24, 2000, issue of *Workers World*

Claiming they were concerned about controlling air pollution, some 3,000 NATO soldiers stormed a lead smelting plant in Zvecan at 4:30 in the morning of August 14. The plant was the only functioning industry in the vast Trepca mining complex in northern Kosovo, a few miles from the city of Mitrovica.

At 6:30 A.M., in a further attack that had nothing to do with air pollution, NATO soldiers closed down and confiscated the equipment of Zvecan's Radio S—the only station that dared to report information critical of NATO. The northern part of Mitrovica is the only remaining multiethnic part of Kosovo. Thousands of Serbs, Romani people, Slavic Muslims, other nationalities, and peoples of mixed backgrounds have been driven out of other areas by Kosovo Liberation Army thugs and vigilante groups. Many have fled to the north side of the Iber River. There, with the local Serbian population, they have resisted more than a year of KLA attacks in an economically devastated region.

The surprise attack by NATO shut down the only radio station and the main source of employment for the local population. The mines, with their smelting, refining and power centers, once constituted one of Yugoslavia's leading export industries and a main source of hard currency. It was the major source of jobs in the region.

Defending the predawn attack, Bernard Kouchner, the head of the United Nations Mission in Kosovo (UNMIK), said, "As a doctor and chief administrator of Kosovo I would be derelict if I allowed a threat to the health of children and pregnant women to continue for one more day." UNMIK is the police force set up by NATO to administer Kosovo. Kouchner has never had a word of criticism for the environmental havoc NATO created throughout the entire region with the use of depleted uranium weapons, the bombing of chemical plants, and the use of cluster bombs. If you find it hard to accept that NATO is suddenly concerned with pollution, it's worth looking for what is really at stake.

Most Valuable Piece of Real Estate. On July 8, 1998, *New York Times* reporter Christopher Hedges wrote, "The sprawling state-owned Trepca mining complex is the most valuable piece of real estate in the Balkans." Hedges described glittering veins of lead, cadmium, zinc, gold, and silver. The Stari Trg mine is ringed with smelting plants, 17 metal treatment sites, warehouses, freight yards, railroad lines, a power plant and the country's largest battery plant. It is the richest lead and zinc mine in Europe. There are also 17 billion tons of coal.

It was George Soros, the multibillionaire financier, who wrote Kouchner's script. Paris-based journalist Diana Johnstone, in a February 28 report, described a policy paper by the International Crisis Group (ICG). This is a think tank set up by Soros to provide guidance in the NATO-led reshaping of the Balkans. The think tank publicly called on Kouchner to take over the management of Trepca and to use the pretext of environmental hazards to shut the Zvecan smelter down.

The Soros group stressed that the takeover should happen before new elections in Yugoslavia so that the opposition could blame Yugoslav President Slobodan Milosevic for the loss of Trepca. The elections are now six weeks away. At the time this proposal was made there was no pollution—the lead smelter was not even in operation. It was closed for several months after the NATO bombing.

Production in this state-owned industry started again only two months ago, at great sacrifice and expense. The hard currency it could have earned was desperately needed to rebuild Yugoslavia's ravaged economy.

With the seizure of the smelting plant in Zvenca, NATO will control the entire Trepca complex. Proving once again that NATO is the military arm to insure primarily U.S. corporate control, the first move after seizing the complex was to turn it over to a consortium of private mining companies. This consortium—ITT Kosovo Ltd.—is a joint venture of U.S., French, and Swedish companies.

The most interesting partner in this deal to control Trepca is the U.S. company Morrison Knudsen International. On July 7 Morrison Knudsen merged with Raytheon Engineers and Constructors, a major military contractor that makes Patriot missiles and radar equipment for the Pentagon. This is an enormously lucrative deal. ITT Kosovo Ltd. will administer Trepca, appoint executives and a board of directors, develop the investment strategy, and skim the greatest profits from every possible deal. Those in the Albanian population who hold illusions that control by these corporations will mean the return of the thousands of well-paid, secure jobs with benefits that existed before the war should read the plans multibillionaire Soros has in store.

Once NATO has control of the whole industrial complex, according to the ICG, foreign investors will develop a very modern, highly profitable facility with a small workforce. In this outright theft of an industry that was built by the efforts of all the peoples of Yugoslavia, Soros's think tank recommends that the management and administration be made up of foreign executives "in order to prevent corruption"!

Copyleft Workers World Service: Everyone is permitted to copy and distribute verbatim copies of this document, but changing it is not allowed. For more information contact Workers World, 55 W. 17 St., NY, NY 10011; via e-mail: ww@workers.org. For subscription info send message to: info@workers.org. Web: www.workers.org)

1999 #7 CENSORED STORY
U.S. MEDIA REDUCES FOREIGN COVERAGE

Foreign news has been disappearing from American newspapers at an alarming rate. International news that does not involve violence, natural disaster, or financial calamity is not likely to receive coverage in the United States. The ethnic cleansing in Kosovo that led to a serious bombing campaign with risks to American lives, the nuclear confrontations between India and Pakistan, and other international crises of the past year or so came as total surprises to the U.S. public.

The *Indianapolis Star*, for example, has reduced foreign coverage by 23 percent over the last two decades. Beyond quantity, the trend involves an overall reduction in the prominence of international news. Even in metropolitan newspapers, readers can go for days without seeing a foreign news story crack the front pages. Television news programs, which once contained at least 40 percent foreign coverage, are now only 7 to 12 percent international.

International news began to fade in the 1970s with the end of the Vietnam War and the emergence of Watergate, the energy crisis, and other domestic concerns. American newspapers, magazines, and television stations have steered away from topics news managers fear will not stimulate public attention. Nationwide interviews suggest editors believe readers aren't interested in foreign news, but a survey of readers indicates quite the opposite is true.

Seeking greater profits through larger audiences, the media has been feeding the public a diet of crime news, celebrity gossip, and soft features. This comes at a time of increasing globalization and responsibility for the United States. America's mainstream media is failing in its obligation to inform the public about what's going on in the rest of the world.

SOURCE: *The American Journalism Review*, November 1998, "Goodbye-World," by Peter Arnett.

COVERAGE 2000: Although one wouldn't expect to see front-page, top-of-the-hour mainstream coverage on the media's own lack of foreign news reporting, the best response to Arnett's story (written especially as it was within the pages of an industry journal) would have been an increased presence of foreign news coverage in the U.S. media. Alas, there was not.

The Project on the State of the American Newspaper this past spring took a sampling of foreign coverage in 13 papers around the country and found only three or four international stories per paper appearing in any one day. Large metro dailies gave about 3 percent of their news hole to international news, and others devoted even less—as little as 2 percent. And in a follow-up to last year's story, the *American Journalism Review* surveyed foreign correspondents to see if more newspapers and newspaper chains had stationed reporters abroad. This, too, did not occur. The *Washington Post's* own ombudsman

took his paper to task for not offering "all the news—or even, with 25 correspondents, pretend to do so." (To its credit, however, the *Post* is noted as one of the best sources for foreign news.) One finds little improvement since Peter Arnett wrote that foreign news coverage had "almost reached a vanishing point" in many mainstream papers. Industry watchdogs are concerned.

Two years ago the American Society of Newspaper Editors and the Freedom Forum launched a campaign to boost foreign coverage. Last year the two groups took a series of workshops around the country and published a how-to booklet for editors (*Bringing the World Home: Showing Readers Their Global Connections*). Although newspapers are not providing more space for world news, some editors are finding work-arounds by giving international events a local spin. The *Spokesman-Review* in Spokane, Washington, for instance, recently ran a story discussing why nuclear tests in Pakistan were bad for wheat farmers in the Pacific Northwest. Before last year's WTO meeting in Seattle, the paper wrote an article about world trade.

In general, though, the media has not responded to the foreign press vacuum—mainstream media, that is. Peter Arnett, the author of our original story, is now a correspondent for ForeignTV.com, an Internet news site dedicated to the international news scene. Though hardly a threat to broadcast TV yet, its exposure has increased by links to notable Internet sites such as Microsoft's MSN.

An interesting editorial by Geneva Overholser examined the history of crime and crime coverage and in so doing made a noteworthy observation about international news coverage. Although the U.S. Justice Department has been announcing a significant decline in violent crime every fall since 1993, crime reporting has steadily increased in mainstream news sources, taking away valuable newsprint and space from other stories. Although Olserhaus also points to a slight reversal in this trend, news consumers in the meantime will continue to have to look to CNN and the Internet, alternative news sources, and the foreign press to find out what is happening in the world outside their borders.

SOURCES: *USA Today*, November 10, 1999; *Washington Post*, December 5, 1999 & December 24, 1999; *Milwaukee Journal Sentinel*, December 13, 1999; *American Journalism Review*, June 2000, "It's a Small World," by Charles Layton; *Gannett News Service*, October 23, 2000.

1999 #8 CENSORED STORY
PLANNED WEAPONS IN SPACE VIOLATE INTERNATIONAL TREATY

The 1967 international Outer Space Treaty prohibits nuclear-powered activities, deployment of weapons of mass destruction, or any endeavors in outer space that may cause "harmful contamination of space and celestial bodies [or] adverse changes in the environment of the Earth." Yet America's current military thrust, according to U.S. Space Command's *Vision for 2020*, is to militarize and control space through nuclear powered space-based weapons of devastating effectiveness.

A major stumbling block to space domination is obtaining the massive power needed to project space-based weapons into orbit. The U.S. military believes the answer is nuclear power. (The European Space Agency is pursuing solar-powered solutions.) The fact that our "fleets" in the ocean of space would have the power to destroy all of life is patently ignored. So is the 12 percent failure rate of our space missions. If anything had gone wrong during the 1999 "fly-by" of the Cassini space probe, the radiation of 72.3 pounds of plutonium fuel would have rained down on 75 percent of the world's population (see *Censored 1997*, Censored #1, "Risking the World: Nuclear Proliferation in Space"). NASA was willing to take that chance. Eight more plutonium-fueled space probe shots are planned, the first to be launched in 2003, the same year as the European Space Agency will be launching its solar-energized Rosetta space probe.

The military victories in Iraq and Kosovo credited to our satellite supremacy helped fuel these space control fantasies, but military might is not the only goal. As *Vision for 2020* states, "Due to the importance of commerce and its effects on national security, the U.S. may evolve into the guardian of space commerce...." This includes mining the moon, Mars, and other planetary bodies for minerals—and any other exploitation of space resources that might create corporate profits.

To further this futuristic vision, the Declaration of Space Leadership campaign, composed of corporations and their congressional allies, is making sure that NASA programs are funded at levels guaranteeing American leadership in space exploration. In addition, the children who will be taxpayers in 2020 are being brainwashed in our public schools into a knee jerk support of everything "space," including nuclear war for world dominance.

SOURCES: *Earth Island Journal*, Winter/Spring 1999, "U.S. Violates World Law to Militarize Space," by Karl Grossman; *Toward Freedom*, September/October, 1999, "Pyramids to the Heavens," by Bruce K. Gagnon.

COVERAGE 2000: Karl Grossman has continued to publish articles on this subject in numerous alternative news sources, and his Knight Ridder/Tribune News Service press wire, "We need to prevent an arms race in space," was followed by a lengthy, sympathetic cover story in *U.S. News & World Report* entitled, "The New Space Race." The June 2000 issue of *In These Times* included a piece by Jeffrey St. Clair whose facts and point of view reflected Grossman's and Gagnon's.

Elsewhere in the media, the *Denver Post* reported on a Cheyenne Mountain Operations Center missile defense technology test, citing critics' warnings against the expense and infeasibility of the technology and its power to ignite international conflict, as well as discussing the internal political forces affecting President Clinton's choice of whether to continue with the project. The *Minneapolis Star Tribune* pulled no punches in ridiculing the military's missile defense program, its fears of "rogue states" and "viciously anti-American" threats to U.S. security, and its use of scare tactics to coerce U.S. allies into supporting its race toward space domination. An editorial by Kitty Boniske, a member of the Women's International League for Peace and Freedom, referred specifically to the writings of Grossman and Gagnon. The Lancaster, PA, *Intelligencer Journal* covered a speech by Gagnon in which he stridently condemned the current government's culpability in plotting to "dominate space."

In September 2000, the *New York Times* ran a 1,400-word, front-section story on the American military's efforts to convert its air base in Thule, Greenland, to Ballistic Missile Defense use, quoting a Greenland government official as saying, "No one in Greenland wishes to take actions that would lead to recreating the atmosphere of the cold war era." Another official remarked, "The United States is very alone in the project." The article also addressed U.S. demands that Canada lend itself to America's space weapons agenda, quoting an editorial in Canada's *Globe and Mail* to the effect that "the national missile defense system is a dumb idea," and stating that Mr. Clinton should substitute "sense for macho posturing."

This article followed six months of outraged press in both England and Canada regarding U.S. machinations to make use of their countries to further its Space Command manifesto. The *Toronto Star* ran three stories between May and September, and the *Montreal Gazette* quoted Canadian Defense Minister Art Eggleton as angrily announcing, "We're not going to be blackmailed" when the Space Command threatened that they "would have absolutely no obligation to defend" Canada from attack if they did not put themselves at the disposal of the U.S. military space program. In England, stories ran strongly protesting the involvement of the Menwith Hill military base in a U.S. escalation of the nuclear arms race and calling Prime Minister Blair's willingness to participate in America's "Star Wars defence system" a "threat to Britain's security." References to Russia's possible retaliation to our disregard of the 1972 ABM Treaty were also made.

Interestingly, Karl Grossman's 1999 article figured in an Internet debate that raged for several months after *Censored 2000*'s publication. Don Hazen, former publisher of *Mother Jones*, started the debate in an editorial on his new Web-based alternative news service. Hazen disagreed about the value of the stories selected by the project. The Project Censored entries Hazen cited as "lame" included Grossman's "U.S. Violates World Law to Militarize Space." Grossman responded to Hazen's criticism by publishing a seven-page "Critique of the Critique" on the *San Francisco Bay Guardian* website (www.sfgb.com/censored-debate/), in which he substantiated the facts and sources for his story, its lack of mainstream coverage, the worsening of the situation since his 1999 article, the disastrous details of NASA's current experiments and future space weapons plans, and the many ramifications of the Army Space Command's philosophy and program. So far Grossman has had the last word, and the mainstream press coverage that has begun to leak out this year provides evidence of the reality and seriousness of his claims, especially in the face of the administration turnover. Whereas the Clinton Administration favored land-based missile defense, the Bush administration promises to pursue "a far more ambitious shield." Donald Rumsfeld, the new Secretary of Defense, is a leading proponent of Star Wars technology.

Unfortunately, sources have not picked up on the Cassini space probe, the Price-Anderson Act that limits U.S. liability in case of a nuclear accident, or the potential dangers of future nuclear-powered space shots.

Bruce Gagnon and the Global Network Against Weapons & Nuclear Power in Space have become increasingly active in the past year. The group can be contacted at www.globenet.free-online.co.uk.

SOURCES: *Knight Ridder/Tribune News Service*, November 6, 1999; *The Nation*, December 27, 1999, "Waging War in

Space," *The Progressive*, January 2000 and *Space News*, January 31, 2000, "Master of Space," *Earth Island Journal*, Spring 2000 & *Third World Resurgence* 116, "Astro Imperialism: War in Space," www.sfbg.com/censored-debate/, April 19, 2000, "A Critique of the Critique," and *NETWORK*, July/August 2000, "The Pentagon Prepares to 'Master Space,'" all by Karl Grossman; *U.S. News & World Report*, November 8, 1999; *Ashville Citizen-Times*, March 21, 2000; *Toronto Star*, May 3, May 7, and September 6, 2000; *Montreal Gazette*, May 3, 2000; *Minneapolis Star Tribune*, May 14, 2000; *In These Times*, June 12, 2000, "Star Wars: Episode Two. The Pentagon's Latest Missile Defense Fantasy," by Jeffrey St. Clair; *Independent (London)*, June 19, 2000; *Washington Post*, June 25 and December 30, 2000; *Denver Post*, July 7, 2000; *Observer*, August 6, 2000; *New York Times*, September 18, 2000; *Intelligencer Journal*, September 27, 2000

2000 UPDATE BY AUTHOR KARL GROSSMAN
The U.S. push to make space a new arena of war intensified since the 2000 Project Censored citation—and media underreporting on this drive continued.

For example, on November 20, 2000, because the U.S. plans contradict the intent of the basic international law on space—the Outer Space Treaty of 1967, which seeks to keep war out of space—there was a vote in the UN General Assembly to reaffirm the Outer Space Treaty and specifically its provision that space be set aside for "peace-ful purposes." Some 163 nations voted in favor. The United States abstained. Did you read about this anywhere? Did you hear it reported on the air?

Last year, too, the Department of Defense moved ahead with development of the Space-Based Laser. The "life-cycle budget" for the laser program "is estimated at $20–30 billion," said a statement from the Army's Redstone Arsenal. Where was this reported?

In 2000, too, Canada—and no one can say that Canada is a potential foe of the United States—continued its efforts to prevent the weaponization of space citing U.S. military space plans. In a speech October 19 at the UN, Marc Vidricaire, counselor of the Permanent Mission of Canada, said: "It has been suggested that our proposal is not relevant because the assessment on which it rests is either premature or alarmist. In our view, it is neither. One need only look at what is happening right now to realize that it is not premature." Where was this reported?

And it is easy for anybody—including journalists—to learn about what is happening. It's brazenly displayed on the website (www.spacecom.af.mil/usspace) of the U.S. Space Command. (The Space Command was set up by the Pentagon to "help institutionalize the use of space.") Among the plans displayed is *Vision for 2020*, its cover featuring a laser weapon in space zapping a target below, and opening with the declaration: "U.S. Space Command—dominating the space dimension of military operations to protect U.S. interests and investment. Integrating Space Forces into warfighting capabilities across the full spectrum of conflict." *Vision for 2020* then compares the U.S. effort to "control space" and from it the Earth below to how centuries ago "nations built navies to protect and enhance their commercial interests," how the great empires of Europe ruled the waves and thus the world. And *Vision for 2020* stresses the global economy. "The globalization of the world economy will also continue, with a widening between 'haves' and 'have-nots.'" The U.S. Space Command is prepared to help keep those "have-nots" in line.

The U.S. military documents make clear that missile defense, the extent of mainstream media reporting on U.S. plans for space warfare, is just one "layer" in a bigger program.

And, in 2000, with the Bush-Cheney takeover, the United States got an administration gung-ho for Star Wars, intimately linked to the right-wing organizations and aerospace corporations which with the U.S. military have been pushing it.

Exploring these links in December 2000, I called Bruce Jackson, vice president of corporate strategy and development for a major Star Wars contractor, Lockheed Martin. "I wrote the Republican Party's foreign policy platform," Jackson said in the interview. He was a delegate to the 2000 Republican National Convention, he noted, and "the overall chairman of the Foreign Policy Platform Committee." Amaz-

ing—a high official of the world's biggest weapons manufacturer having written the foreign policy platform of the new Bush administration.

Also amazing: a computer search on Jackson that came up with one article, in the *Washington Post*, about his chairing the foreign policy platform committee, which included comments from him. A little detail was not included: Jackson being Lockheed Martin's vice president of corporate strategy and development.

So it goes. Seven Stories Press will be publishing my *Weapons in Space* in 2001. A new video documentary I wrote and narrate, *Star Wars Returns* (available from the independent TV production company EnviroVideo at (800) ECO-TV46) will be out in 2001. But as a journalist all my working life, I so wish our media would do their job and provide people with information on a huge story of our time: the U.S. push to turn the heavens into a war zone.

2000 UPDATE BY AUTHOR BRUCE K. GAGNON What is our vision for the heavens? On a beautiful starry night do you look up to the moon and the stars and feel the connection to the ages? Can you imagine military bases on the moon and constellations of space-based lasers orbiting our planet? Can you envision the new military space plane, the successor to the shuttle, dropping off new space-based weapons systems and then returning to earth?

We are at a defining moment in history as the United States leads the rest of the world into this new space age that ripples with technological advances and challenges the peace and environmental movements to update our thinking and our organizing.

The ballistic missile defense system is sold to the American people as a way to protect us from attack by "rogue" states, or as they are now called, "states of concern." National missile defense is the $60 billion program to protect the continental United States from "attack." North Korea, one so-called possible enemy, has suspended its missile testing program and is now negotiating reunification with South Korea. China, another state of "concern," has only 20 nuclear missiles capable of hitting the United States, while we have 3,500 to "hit back." Chinese officials have been asking over and over again for the United States to join them in signing a global ban on weapons in space. The United States refuses to discuss such a ban, saying that there is "no problem."

Then there is the program called theatre missile defense (TMD) that aims to deploy these systems into the Middle East and Asia to "protect" U.S. interests and outposts. TMD will place weapons on ground launchers, ships, and airborne lasers so that the United States can hit "offending" ballistic missiles in their boost phase, right after launch.

The U.S. Space Command, with its logo "Master of Space," is also working hard to develop the space-based laser (SBL) program, the "follow-on" technology to missile defense. Its expressed intention is to use this program to protect corporate interests and investments around the globe as the gap widens between the "haves" and the "have-nots." The Space Command will become the military instrument by which corporations maintain their global control.

The $30 billion SBL program will soon begin construction of a test facility. The SBL, the real Reagan-era Star Wars program, will deploy a constellation of 20 to 30 lasers orbiting the earth with the job of knocking out competitors' satellites and hitting targets on earth. These lasers could very possibly be powered by nuclear reactors. Imagine what would happen if they tumbled back to earth....

We must call out to the public to help us keep space for peace. We must demand that the politicians rescind plans for "missile defense" and the space-based laser. We must say that space will be protected as a wilderness. The United Nations recognized this when they created the 1967 Outer Space Treaty that says no weapons of "mass destruction" can be put into the heavens. The treaty says that the heavenly bodies are the province of all human kind. We must call for the strengthening of this treaty, not its nullification.

Global Network Against Weapons & Nuclear Power in Space can be contacted at P.O. Box 90083, Gainesville, FL 32607; (352) 337-9274; www.space 4peace.org; globalnet@mindspring.com

LOUISIANA PROMOTES TOXIC RACISM

Southeast Louisiana, a region heavily populated with low-income and minority families, is one of the worst sites for toxic pollution in the country. The 175 industrial plants and seven oil refineries along this 100-mile stretch between Baton Rouge and New Orleans make it a veritable Who's Who of the petrochemical industry. More than 23 million pounds of toxins are released annually, compromising the health of the residents there so severely that the region is now called "Cancer Alley."

Substantial incentives offered by the Louisiana state government have attracted industry to the Cancer Alley area in one of the country's worse examples of environmental racism—the intentional location of undesirable industries in communities of color. According to an Environmental Protection Agency (EPA) report, the majority of toxins released into Louisiana's air are done so within the two zip code areas predominately inhabited by black residents. A 1987 study by the United Church of Christ's Commission on Racial Justice found that blacks were four times more likely to live in areas of high pollutants than were Caucasians. An investigation by the *National Law Journal* found government enforcement of environmental regulations ineffective and unjust; even when environmental regulations are enforced, fines are much lower in black communities than in white ones.

Although industry still has the support of Louisiana's state government, some local communities have begun to fight back. The town of Covenant waged a successful battle against the Japanese industrial giant Shintech, thwarting its plan to build a PVC (polyvinyl chloride) plant next door. Other communities were not so lucky. So heavily contaminated they had to be bought out by their polluters, they are now just toxic ghost towns.

SOURCES: *Southern Exposure*, Summer/Fall, 1998, "Toxic Gumbo," by Ron Nixon; *The Nation*, November 8, 1999, "Cancer Alley in Louisiana," by Barbara Koeppel. Mainstream (partial) coverage: CNN Cable, September 13, 1997; PBS News, September 27, 1998.

COVERAGE 2000: The story of Cancer Alley grabbed the attention of both the local and national media. The most extensive coverage was understandably on the local or regional level in Louisiana and the Southeastern United States. The New Orleans *Times-Picayune* ran a commendable series of articles on Cancer Alley and the underlying issue of environmental racism. They concluded that "economic and environmental decisions made over decades had exposed poor and minority communities around the country to more pollution and environmental hazards than the population as a whole." It also looked closely at the political fallout wrought by the Shintech controversy as well as medical studies, which focused on the health of the people living in the petrochemical corridor.

The Shintech controversy itself, on the other hand, has had national media attention. CBS's *60 Minutes II* focused on the plight of a Tulane law professor and his students who dared to oppose the building of the PVC processing plant. They talked about Cancer Alley, which provided the photographic backdrop for much of the piece. But it was NBC's *Nightly News* that brought the issue to the forefront of mainstream media. Reporters conducted interviews with local citizens, provided first-hand accounts of life in the shadow of industry, and explored the health problems the people of Cancer Alley faced on a daily basis.

There is conflicting medical research on Louisiana's petrochemical corridor. Industry leaders and state officials insist Cancer Alley is a myth. They point to statistics collected by the Louisiana Tumor Registry, part of the Louisiana State University Medical Center, which show no elevated cancer rates in the parishes of the region. The Registry's findings have been challenged, however, by the Louisiana Environmental Action Network (LEAN), an umbrella organization representing more than 70 environmental groups around the state, and by Attorney General Richard Ieyoub. LEAN has been critical of the Tumor Registry for years, charging that its studies are not aimed at answering key questions about the connection between cancer rates and the state's chemical industry. Attorney General Ieyoub expressed concern that the Louisiana Tumor Registry moves too slowly to pin down any cancer patterns that might affect children.

Environmental racism became an increasingly hot topic in the alternative media and minority newspapers. Larger, regional newspapers have also covered the issue when it relates to their own cities and towns. For instance, the *Atlanta Journal and Constitution* ran a story on a predominately black neighborhood in southeastern Atlanta, where citizens are exposed to more toxic emissions than any other Atlanta community.

However, examples of environmental racism aren't confined to the South. On the West Coast, the Navy let a fire at a toxic landfill located near the minority neighborhood of San Francisco's Hunter's Point smolder unchecked for almost three weeks before alerting the public. Across the bay, people in the predominately black community of Richmond have a disproportionately high ratio of cancers they blame on emissions from the nearby Chevron oil refinery. Residents and community activists there have been trying for years to solicit funds for necessary health and contaminate screening. And in Odessa, Texas, the mostly poor, minority residents live in an almost constant carcinogenic chemical soup emitted by Huntsman Polymers. A proposed $1 million settlement for Odessa's 6,000 residents seems a paltry compensation, and residents are determined to bring their plight to the attention of the Texas governor.

SOURCES: *New Orleans Magazine*, January 2000, "Cancer Tally," by Christine

L. Manalla; *The Times-Picayune*; March 18, May 22, May 24, & June 20, 2000; *60 Minutes II*, March 27, 2000, "Buying Judges?"; *NBC Nightly News*, May 26, 2000, "Health Problems in Mossville, Louisiana, Possibly Caused by Petrochemical Plants," by Fred Francis; *The Atlanta Journal and Constitution*, August 26, 2000; *The San Francisco Chronicle*, September 11–19, 2000; *Terrain*, Fall 2000, "Illnesses Raise Tempers Downwind of Chevron's Richmond Refinery"; *The Texas Observer*, September 22, 2000, "Hunstman's Odessa Syndrome," by Greg Harman.

1999 #10 CENSORED STORY

THE U.S. AND NATO DELIBERATELY STARTED THE WAR WITH YUGOSLAVIA

NATO and the United States forced the war with the Federal Republic of Yugoslavia (FRY). The U.S.-drafted Rambouillet ultimatum that preceded the bombing was not only a thinly veiled tactic to create an independent Kosovo state, but it also contained provisions no sovereign country in the world could possibly accept—the military occupation of all of Yugoslavia.

Clauses in Appendix B of the accords included the following conditions: NATO personnel could not be arrested, investigated, or detained for any reason; NATO was to receive an *unrestricted* right to travel through the Republic, which included the use of "airspace and territorial waters," the FRY transportation infrastructure, and "all of the electromagnetic spectrum"; and NATO personnel could arbitrarily arrest and detain Yugoslavian nationals. Fearing the loss of the FRY's sovereignty, President Milosevic refused to ratify the agreement and bombing started the next day. Curiously, NATO had carefully planned military operations several months in advance.

Analysts contend that Rambouillet was a trap for Milosevic, which gave NATO a pretext for bombing. As Ackerman notes in his update, "Henry Kissinger has said 'The Rambouillet text… was a provocation, an excuse to start bombing.'" Kosovar Albanians were forced into complicity with promises that NATO would bomb Serbia if they signed the agreement, and Milosevic didn't.

For months previously, the Serbian government had offered to negotiate. High-level government teams made many trips to Pristina to hold talks with nonviolent ethnic Albanians. The Albanians refused to negotiate, however, fearing opposition by the rising armed rebel movement, the hostile Kosovo Libertarian Army (KLA).

At Rambouillet, the older generation of nationalist leaders was precluded from entering negotiations with the multiethnic official Serbian delegation; they were overshadowed in the ethnic Albanian delegation by the KLA. By then the KLA was assured U.S. support. Genuine negotiations would have paid attention to the extensive ten-page proposal by the Serbian government, which included the following: equality of all citizens and guaranteed human rights; facilitated return of all citizens to their homes; safe unhindered access of the population to all international and national or nongovernmental humanitarian organizations for purposes of aid; and the widest possible media freedoms.

Although NATO's war against Yugoslavia was spun as a "humanitarian" war on behalf of the ethnic Albanians of Kosovo, it violated international law, killed thousands of people, destroyed the livelihood of millions, and left Kosovo province a shambles. Furthermore, NATO's air strikes triggered violent Serb retaliation against ethnic Albanians who were forced to flee to neighboring countries. They have since returned to a province under foreign military occupation, with no government administration or judicial system, at the mercy of a ruthless Albanian nationalist armed group, the Kosovo Liberation Army (UCK). From all appearances, this disastrous situation was driven by NATO's need to launch air strikes against Yugoslavia in time for its 50th anniversary celebration.

Meanwhile, the Clinton administration is encouraging further disintegration of Yugoslavia itself by inciting separatists in Montenegro, Voivodina, and the Sandjak region.

SOURCES: *Village Voice*, May 18, 1999, "The Real Rambouillet," by Jason Vest; *Extra*, July/August 1999, "Redefining Diplomacy," by Seth Ackerman; *In These Times*, August 8, 1999, "What Was the War For?" by Seth Ackerman;

CovertAction Quarterly, Spring/Summer 1999, "Hawks and Eagles: 'Greater NATO' flies to Aid of 'Greater Albania,'" by Diana Johnstone; Pacifica Radio Network, April 23, 1999, www.Pacifica.org, "Democracy Now," host, Amy Goodman. Mainstream Coverage: C-Span *Washington Journal*, April 22, 1999, San Husseini; *Washington Post*, "For the Record," April 28, 1999, p. A24; *Star-Tribune*, May 17, 1999, p. 6A; *Harper's Magazine*, July 1, 1999.

COVERAGE 2000: Most people are still unaware of Appendix B and the treacherous negotiations at Rambouillet. Those within the media who have tried to bring the information to the U.S. news public are primarily columnists or commentators. It wasn't until September 2000, after former State Department Spokesman James Rubin stepped down from the office, that he wrote in the London *Financial Times*, "The administration always understood that Rambouillet was a means to an end. Either a deal would be struck and NATO peacekeepers would be deployed to end the war, or, more likely the Serbs would reject any reasonable peace deal and that would convince the Europeans finally to support the Albanians through a NATO air campaign." Rubin had long been criticized for "stemming the flow of information" to journalists. Although journalists wonder whether or not his replacement will enjoy the same access to information Rubin had, questions exist as to whether the access was restricted by Rubin himself or at Albright's directive.

The war in Kosovo, cynically referred to as "Madeleine's War," remains painted as a NATO- and U.S.-backed humanitarian crusade to put down the "evil" Milosevic. Although it is unarguable that ethnic cleansing took place on both sides, until recently, media statistics reflected NATO-fed propaganda. Finally, "real" numbers began to appear in the U.S. press (long ago known throughout Europe). The massacres used as a springboard for NATO intervention in spring 2000 turned out to be grossly exaggerated, or even staged, as at Racak (see *Censored 2000*, Censored # 12, "Evidence Indicates No Pre-War Genocide in Kosovo and Possible U.S./KLA Plot to Create Disinformation"), and ethnic cleansing took on a whole new meaning as Albanians began to retaliate against the Serbs. As early as fall 2000, the media's honeymoon with NATO and Albright's cronies seemed over. Still, most of the U.S. media supported—and still supports—NATO's "humanitarian" efforts.

Disagreement even spilled over into the alternative press. *In These Times* ran a series of critical pieces exploring the "real" political motives behind the Kosovo war. According to Edward S. Herman, "The mainstream framing of the issues in the Balkans has had demonization at its core." He rejects the popular "liberal" viewpoint that outbursts against NATO equal "pro-Serb" sympathies. Instead, he says, "What is at stake is the real purposes and effects of NATO policy...." Herman advances the conclusions reached by David Chandler and Susan Woodward (author of *Masters of the Universe?*) that intervention by NATO-member countries since the early 1990s actually led to the ethnic cleansing the world eventually witnessed throughout the Balkans. He additionally supports the thesis that "humanitarian bombing created more pain and ethnic cleansing than existed prior to the supposedly humane action."

The U.S. manipulation of the forces that drove the tense situation in the region began to surface in foreign papers (and remains conspicuously absent in the U.S. media to this day). The CIA, it was divulged, had trained the KLA well before the NATO bombing began. KLA commander Shaban Shala admitted to having first met American, British, and Swiss intelligence agents as early as 1996. When the Organization for Security and Cooperation in Europe left Kosovo the week before the airstrikes began, they left their satellite telephones and global positioning systems in the hands of the opposition forces. "Several KLA leaders had the mobile phone number of General Wesley Clark, the NATO commander," the *Sunday Times* reported. (See *Censored 2000*, Censored #22, "U.S. and Germany Trained and Developed the KLA.")

To be commended is *Chattanooga Times*'s Reed Irvine's list of "Uncovered and Undercovered in 1999," which included "How Madeleine Albright started the war over Kosovo," and "Official lies about genocide in Kosovo."

SOURCES: *Boston Globe*, "A Question of Numbers," November 16, 1999, by James Carroll; *Chattanooga Times*, December 19, 1999, "Uncovered and Undercovered in 1999," by Reed Irvine; *Sunday Times*, March 12, 2000, "CIA aided Kosovo guerilla army," by Tom Walker and Aidan Laverty; *American Journalism Review*, April 2000, "State of Tension," by Dean Fischer; *Agence France Presse*, April 15, 2000; *In These Times*, September 4, 2000, "More Conspiracy Theories?" by Edward S. Herman; *Financial Times* (London), September 30, 2000, "A Very Personal War," by James Rubin.

1998 #1 CENSORED STORY

SECRET INTERNATIONAL TRADE AGREEMENT UNDERMINES THE SOVEREIGNTY OF NATIONS

The proffered intent of the Multilateral Agreement on Investment (MAI) was to safeguard the investments of multinational corporations. The corporate protections that the international trade treaty was meant to put into place, however, challenged the sovereignty of member nations by granting corporations rights that equaled or superseded the regulatory authority of nation-states and local governments. Additionally, MAI would have overreached the North American Free Trade Agreement (NAFTA) and the General Agreement on Tariffs and Trade (GATT) by allowing corporations to directly sue any level of government—state, municipal, or federal—for perceived financial losses (including future profits) due to legislative action, strikes, or boycotts. MAI would have thrust the world economy much closer to a transnational laissez-faire system where international corporate capital would hold free rein over the democratic wishes and socioeconomic needs of its people.

Update 1999: When the OECD decision to indefinitely suspend talks was announced, officials from the member countries agreed that it was imperative to continue discussing the need to protect overseas investment. France and Canada asserted that the World Trade Organization (WTO) not the OECD was the proper venue for such talks. The United States and OECD officials disagreed, pointing out that if a treaty agreement could not be reached with the 29-member OECD, it would not be reached with the 135-member WTO.

Anticipating the revival of MAI international trade rules within the framework of the WTO, critics and protestors from around the world converged on Seattle, Washington, from November 30–December 3, 1999, for the third ministerial WTO talks. What scanty press coverage the MAI received in the domestic press in 1999 came late in the year and in articles about the WTO ministerial meeting amidst critics' fears that MAI investment principles would be included in the negotiations.

SOURCES: *In These Times*, January 11, 1998, "Building the Global Economy," by Joel Bleifuss; *Democratic Left*,

Spring 1998, "MAI Ties," by Bill Dixon; *Tribune Des Droits Humains,* April 1998, "Human Rights or Corporate Rights?" by Miloon Kothari and Tara Krause; *The Washington Times,* December 5, 1998.

2000 UPDATE BY LARRY SHAW

THE DISAPPEARING WTO

Almost one year ago in late November 1999, 50,000 protesters converged on Seattle in an attempt to direct public attention to the World Trade Organization (WTO), and the process of global corporatization, which it promotes. Until that point, the WTO had received almost no U.S. media coverage, despite the fact that this extra-national organization had already forced the weakening of U.S. laws protecting clean air and endangered species. As a result of the protests, many people now know of the existence of the WTO and what the three letters stand for. However, most people still have almost no knowledge of its operations and effects. With the nation's interest piqued, it was hoped by the protesters that Seattle would be a starting point for the education of the public.

However, the WTO has disappeared from the media like the Cheshire cat, leaving only its smile. This writer conducted a study of newspaper coverage of the WTO to determine in what context the WTO has and has not been mentioned. The study was conducted for publications from January 1, 2000, to November 1, 2000, using a full-text search of the ProQuest database of 27 major U.S. daily newspapers, including the *Wall Street Journal, New York Times, Boston Globe, Chicago Tribune, USA Today, Christian Science Monitor, Los Angeles Times,* and *San Francisco Chronicle.* The study shows that mentions of the WTO were virtually nonexistent in articles covering issues related to attacks by the WTO on domestic environmental and human rights laws, that is, those issues most likely to turn public opinion against the WTO. In contrast, in articles covering other types of WTO news, the WTO was mentioned frequently and made headlines numerous times.

One of the major WTO-related stories of the year was an April 11 Federal Court ruling that thwarted the implementation of a weakened dolphin-safe labeling for tuna. The Federal Court ruled that the Commerce Department was attempting to prematurely implement the new labeling law without having even met the requirements of a weakened, 1997 version of the Marine Mammal Protection Act (MMPA). The dolphin protections in the initial, 1990 version of the MMPA were ruled trade-illegal twice under GATT, the parent treaty to the WTO. To avoid the embarrassment of having a foreign authority force the revision of a domestic environmental law, Congress weakened the dolphin protections and the tuna labeling requirements of the MMPA in 1997. In marked contrast with the fanfare that the MMPA received upon its inception, the delay of the implementation of the eviscerated dolphin-safe labeling was covered in only three of the major U.S.

dailies: *San Francisco Chronicle, Wall Street Journal* and *Los Angeles Times.* Even more striking was the fact that the five articles published in those papers did not contain a single mention of GATT or the WTO.

Portions of the U.S. Endangered Species Act (ESA) protecting endangered sea turtles have also been under attack by the WTO, as protesters dressed in sea turtle costumes tried to publicize in Seattle. On October 23, Malaysia continued the aggressions against the ESA by filing a complaint with the WTO charging that the United States had not yet lifted its ban on shrimp caught in a manner that kills sea turtles, as required by a previous WTO ruling. That news was covered in only a single article in one major U.S. daily, the *New York Times.* Furthermore, a June 1 study published in the scientific journal *Nature,* predicted that leatherback sea turtles will be extinct within 10 years unless fishing methods are substantially altered. Only four major U.S. dailies *(San Francisco Chronicle, New York Times, USA Today,* and *Christian Science Monitor)* covered the story, and none of the four articles mentioned the role the WTO has had in hampering the implementation of the Endangered Species Act.

Another dozen articles in the major dailies addressed issues relating to endangered sea turtles during the period of the study, and, again, none of the articles mentioned the WTO. Curiously, in a *San Francisco Chronicle* article about the *Nature* study, the headline

on the continuation page read "International Trade Agreements Slow Protection of Sea Turtles" even though there was no mention of international trade agreements anywhere in the article. When queried by this writer, the reporter said a discussion of the relationship to trade agreements had been in the story. An editor edited it out but the headline accidentally slipped through.

Another recent WTO-related development this year was the Supreme Court's consideration of Massachusetts's selective purchasing law, which prevented the state government from contracting with corporations doing business with the brutal totalitarian regime of Burma. Had the Supreme Court not decided against Massachusetts, the attack on the Massachusetts law would have escalated by resuming a pending WTO challenge mounted by Japan and the European Union. Of the 47 articles and commentaries that covered the story, 43 contained no mention of the role of the WTO. Coyly, nine of the 43 articles mentioned pressures from foreign countries without mention of the WTO. The *Los Angeles Times* went so far as to state cryptically that, in a sense, the Supreme Court case contains echoes of December's demonstrations against the World Trade Organization in Seattle. But the *New York Times* deserves the award for coyness when it reported that the European Community had lodged an official protest, and defenders of the Massachusetts law had tapped into some of the populist anger recently directed against the World Trade Organization, without actually mentioning that the official protest was a WTO challenge.

The WTO did, however, make numerous U.S. headlines this year for an export subsidies dispute between the United States and Europe, and for the grant of Permanent Normal Trade Relations (PNTR) status to China. Neither issue involved a direct attack by the WTO on domestic, environmental, or human rights laws. The export subsidies dispute with Europe was covered in nine articles in the major dailies, with mention of the WTO in all but one of the articles (a one-sentence squib in the *Wall Street Journal*) and the appearance of the WTO in three of the headlines. PNTR for China was covered in at least 1,063 articles and commentaries.

China's application for membership in the WTO was mentioned in 292 of the articles and commentaries, and referred to in 31 headlines. Although the articles often suggested a direct link between the grant of PNTR for China and China's admittance into the WTO, such was not the case. The relevance of the WTO is somewhat less direct and therefore less deserving of such frequent mention. Had the United States not granted PNTR to China, and if China does attain membership in the WTO, then, were the United States ever to apply trade sanctions against China, China could retaliate via the WTO.

In summary, of the articles covering developments in the Marine Mammal Protection Act, none of them mentioned the WTO; none of the articles covering news related to endangered sea turtles mentioned the WTO; only a single article nationwide mentioned Malaysia's resumption of aggressions against the Endangered Species Act via the WTO; and less than 10 percent of the articles about the Massachusetts-Burma law mentioned the WTO.

In contrast, with regards to the export subsidies dispute with Europe, the WTO was mentioned in nearly all of the articles, and appeared in one-third the headlines; and nearly 30 percent of the articles covering PNTR for China discussed the WTO. Furthermore, disregarding whether the WTO was mentioned or not, the 69 articles covering issues related to WTO attacks on U.S. environmental and human rights laws was substantially outnumbered by 1,080 articles covering other types of WTO-related news.

There has been a Cheshire cat–like disappearance of the WTO from the major U.S. daily newspapers. Only the smiling teeth of news, which do not involve WTO attacks on U.S. environmental and human rights laws, remain visible.

LARRY SHAW is a Seattle activist and the author and performer of "Sold Down the River," the anti-WTO song played from the Steelworkers' billboard truck during the protests in Seattle.

MONSANTO'S GENETICALLY MODIFIED SEEDS THREATEN WORLD PRODUCTION

Monsanto Corporation has been working to consolidate the world seed market and is now poised to introduce new genetically engineered seeds that will produce only infertile seeds at the end of the farming cycle. Farmers will no longer be able to save seeds from year to year and will be forced to purchase new seeds from Monsanto each year.

Monsanto has euphemistically called the process by which seeds are disabled the "technology protection system." A primary objective of Terminator Technology is to grant and protect corporate rights to charge fees for patents and products that are genetically modified. Terminator Technology offers no advantage by itself, but when coupled with the production of the strongest, highest yielding seeds, farmers may be compelled to buy single-season plants.

SOURCES: *Mojo Wire*, www.mother-jones.com/news_wire/broydo.html, and www.motherjones.com/news_wire/usda-inc.html, April 27, 1998, "A Seedy Business," by Leora Broydo; *Third World Resurgence #92*, "New Patent Aims to Prevent Farmers From Saving Seed," by Hope Shand and Pat Mooney; *Global Pesticide Campaigner & Earth Island Journal*," June 1998 & Fall 1998, "Terminator Seeds Threaten an End to Farming," by Chakravarthi Raghavan; *The Ecologist*, September/October 1998, Vol. 28, No. 5, "Monsanto: A Checkered History" and "Revolving Doors: Monsanto and the Regulators," by Brian Tokar.

2000 UPDATE BY MICHEL CHOSSUDOVSKY
SOWING THE SEEDS OF FAMINE IN ETHIOPIA

The "economic therapy" imposed under IMF–World Bank jurisdiction is in large part responsible for triggering famine and social devastation in Ethiopia and the rest of sub-Saharan Africa, wrecking the peasant economy and impoverishing millions of people.

With the complicity of branches of the U.S. government, it has also opened the door for the appropriation of traditional seeds and landraces by U.S. biotech corporations, which—behind the scenes—have been peddling the adoption of their own genetically modified seeds under the disguise of emergency aid and famine relief.

Moreover, under WTO rules, the agribiotech conglomerates can manipulate market forces to their advantage as well as exact royalties from farmers. The WTO provides legitimacy to the food giants to dismantle state programs (including emergency grain stocks, seed banks, extension services, and agricultural credit, and so on), plunder peasant economies and trigger the outbreak of periodic famines.

Crisis in the Horn. More than 8 million people in Ethiopia, representing 15 percent of the country's population, have been locked into "famine zones." Urban wages have collapsed and unemployed seasonal farm workers and landless peasants have been driven into abysmal poverty. The international relief agencies concur without further examination that climatic factors are the sole and inevitable cause of crop failure and the ensuing humanitarian disaster. What the media fail to disclose is that despite the drought and the border war with Eritrea, several million people in the most prosperous agricultural regions have also been driven into starvation. Their predicament is not the consequence of grain shortages but of "free markets" and "bitter economic medicine" imposed under the IMF–World Bank sponsored Structural Adjustment Program (SAP).

Ethiopia produces more than 90 percent of its consumption needs. Yet at the height of the crisis, the nationwide food deficit for 2000 was estimated by the Food and Agriculture Organization (FAO) at 764,000 metric tons of grain, representing a shortfall of 13 kilos per person per annum.[1] In Amhara, grain production (1999–2000) was 20 percent in excess of consumption needs. Yet 2.8 million people in Amhara (representing 17 percent of the region's population) became locked into famine zones and are "at risk," according to the FAO.[2] Whereas Amhara's grain surpluses were in excess of 500,000 tons (1999–2000), its "relief food needs" had been tagged by the international community at close to 300,000 tons.[3] A similar pattern prevailed in Oromiya, the country's most populated state, where 1.6 million people were classified "at risk" despite the availability of more than 600,000 met-

ric tons of surplus grain.[4] In both these regions, which include more than 25 percent of the country's population, scarcity of food was clearly not the cause of hunger, poverty, and social destitution. Yet no explanations are given by the panoply of international relief agencies and agricultural research institutes.

The Promise of the "Free Market" In Ethiopia, a transitional government came into power in 1991 in the wake of a protracted and destructive civil war. After the pro-Soviet Dergue regime of Colonel Mengistu Haile Mariam was unseated, a multi-donor financed Emergency Recovery and Reconstruction Project (ERRP) was hastily put in place to deal with an external debt of close to $9 billion that had accumulated during the Mengistu government. Ethiopia's outstanding debts with the Paris Club of official creditors were rescheduled in exchange for far-reaching macroeconomic reforms. Upheld by U.S. foreign policy, the usual doses of bitter IMF economic medicine were prescribed. Caught in the straightjacket of debt and structural adjustment, the new Transitional Government of Ethiopia (TGE), led by the Ethiopian People's Revolutionary Democratic Front (EPRDF), largely formed from the Tigrean People's Liberation Front (PLF), had committed itself to far-reaching "free market reforms," despite its leaders' Marxist leanings. Washington soon tagged Ethiopia alongside Uganda as Africa's post–Cold War free market showpiece.

While social budgets were slashed

under the SAP, military expenditure in part financed by the gush of fresh development loans quadrupled since 1989.[5] With Washington supporting both sides in the Eritrea-Ethiopia border war, U.S. arms sales spiraled. The bounty was being shared between the arms manufacturers and the agribusiness conglomerates. In the post–Cold War era, the latter positioned themselves in the lucrative procurement of emergency aid to war-torn countries. With mounting military spending financed on borrowed money, almost half of Ethiopia's export revenues was earmarked to meet debt-servicing obligations.

A Policy Framework Paper (PFP) stipulating the precise changes to be carried out in Ethiopia had been carefully drafted in Washington by IMF and World Bank officials on behalf of the transitional government, and was forwarded to Addis Ababa for the signature of the Minister of Finance. The enforcement of severe austerity measures virtually foreclosed the possibility of a meaningful post-war reconstruction and the rebuilding of the country's shattered infrastructure. The creditors demanded trade liberalization and the full-scale privatization of public utilities, financial institutions, state farms, and factories. Civil servants, including teachers and health workers, were fired, wages were frozen, and the labor laws were rescinded to enable state enterprises "to shed their surplus workers." Meanwhile, corruption became rampant. State assets were auctioned off to foreign capital at bargain prices and Price Waterhouse Cooper was entrusted with the task of coordinating the sale of state property.

In turn, the reforms had led to the fracture of the federal fiscal system. Budget transfers to the state governments were slashed, leaving the regions to their own devices. Supported by several donors, "regionalization" was heralded as a "devolution of powers from the federal to the regional governments." The Bretton Woods institutions knew exactly what they were doing. In the words of the IMF, "[the regions'] capacity to deliver

THIS MODERN WORLD

by TOM TOMORROW

RANDOM VIGNETTES FROM THE REPUBLICAN CONVENTION

1) LARRY KING SITS DOWN NEXT TO ME IN A STARBUCKS ONE MORNING. HE IS FRIENDLY, TALKATIVE--AND UTTERLY CAUSTIC ABOUT THE REPUBLICAN'S SHOW OF DIVERSITY.

WHITES IN THE AUDIENCE AND BLACKS ONSTAGE! ALL THE BLACKS ARE ONSTAGE!

IF THERE'S A BELLMAN AROUND, THEY INVITE HIM ON-STAGE!

2) ON A SHUTTLE BUS TO THE CONVENTION CENTER, A WHITE DELEGATE--WHOSE BOXES OF CAMPAIGN MATERIAL ARE BLOCKING THE AISLE--IS ASKED BY THE BLACK BUS DRIVER TO "MOVE TO THE BACK OF THE BUS."

YOU--WANT ME--TO MOVE TO THE BACK OF THE BUS?

I NEVER THOUGHT I'D HEAR THAT! HA, HA!

HA, HA.

effective and efficient development interventions varies widely, as does their capacity for revenue collection."[6]

Wrecking the Peasant Economy. Patterned on the reforms adopted in Kenya in 1991, agricultural markets were willfully manipulated on behalf of the agribusiness conglomerates. The World Bank demanded the rapid removal of price controls and all subsidies to farmers. Transportation and freight prices were deregulated serving to boost food prices in remote areas affected by drought. In turn, the markets for farm inputs, including fertilizer and seeds, were handed over to private traders including Pioneer Hi-Bred International, which entered into a lucrative partnership with Ethiopia Seed Enterprise (ESE), the government's seed monopoly.[7]

At the outset of the reforms in 1992, USAID under its Title III program "donated" large quantities of U.S. fertilizer "in exchange for free market reforms": "[V]arious agricultural commodities [will be provided] in exchange for reforms of grain marketing and [the] elimination of food subsidies. The reform agenda focuses on liberalization and privatization in the fertilizer and transport sectors in return for financing fertilizer and truck imports. These program initiatives have given us [an] 'entrée' in defining major [policy] issues."[8]

While the stocks of donated U.S. fertilizer were rapidly exhausted, the imported chemicals contributed to displacing local fertilizer producers. The same companies involved in the fertilizer import business were also in control of the domestic wholesale distribution of fertilizer using local level merchants as intermediaries.

Increased output was recorded in commercial farms and in irrigated areas (where fertilizer and high yielding seeds had been applied). The overall tendency, however, was toward greater economic and social polarization in the countryside, marked by significantly lower yields in less productive marginal lands occupied by the poor peasantry. Even in areas where output had increased, farmers were caught in the clutch of the seed and fertilizer merchants.

In 1997, the Atlanta-based Carter Center, which was actively promoting the use of biotechnology tools in maize breeding, proudly announced that "Ethiopia [had] become a food exporter for the first time."[9] Yet in a cruel irony, the donors ordered the dismantling of the emergency grain reserves (set up in the wake of the 1984–85 famine), and the authorities acquiesced.

Instead of replenishing the country's emergency food stocks, grain was exported to meet Ethiopia's debt servicing obligations. Nearly one million tons of the 1996 harvest were exported, an amount that would have been amply sufficient (according to FAO figures) to meet the 1999–2000 emergency. In fact the same food staple which had been exported (namely maize) was re-imported barely a few months later. The world market had confiscated Ethiopia's grain reserves.

In return, U.S. surpluses of genetically engineered maize (banned by the European Union) were being dumped on the horn of Africa in the form of emergency aid. The United States had found a convenient mechanism for "laundering its stocks of dirty grain." The agribusiness conglomerates not only cornered Ethiopia's commodity exports, they were also involved in the procurement of emergency shipments of grain back into Ethiopia. During the 1998–2000 famine, lucrative maize contracts were awarded to giant grain merchants such as Archer Daniels Midland (ADM) and Cargill Inc.[10]

Laundering America's GM Grain Surpluses. U.S. grain surpluses peddled in war-torn countries also served to weaken the agricultural system. Some 500,000 tons of maize and maize products were "donated" in 1999–2000 by USAID to relief agencies including the World Food Program (WFP), which in turn collaborates closely with the U.S. Department of Agriculture. At least 30 percent of these shipments (procured under contract with U.S. agribusiness firms) were surplus, genetically modified grain stocks.[11]

Boosted by the border war with Eritrea and the plight of thousands of refugees, the influx of contaminated food aid had contributed to the pollution of Ethiopia's genetic pool of indigenous seeds and landraces. In a cruel irony, the food giants were at the same time gaining control through the procurement of contaminated food aid over Ethiopia's seed banks. According to South Africa's Biowatch: "Africa is treated as the dustbin of the world. To donate untested food and seed to Africa is not an act of kindness but an attempt to lure Africa into further dependence on foreign aid."[12]

Moreover, part of the "food aid" had been channeled under the "food for work" program, which served to further discourage domestic production in favor of grain imports. Under this scheme, impoverished and landless farmers were contracted to work on rural infrastructural programs in exchange for "donated" U.S. corn.

Meanwhile, the cash earnings of coffee smallholders plummeted. Whereas Pioneer Hi-Bred positioned itself in seed distribution and marketing, Cargill

Inc. established itself in the markets for grain and coffee through its subsidiary Ethiopian Commodities.[12] For the more than 700,000 smallholders with less than two hectares that produce between 90 and 95 percent of the country's coffee output, the deregulation of agricultural credit combined with low farmgate prices of coffee had triggered increased indebtedness and landlessness, particularly in East Gojam (Ethiopia's breadbasket).

Biodiversity Up for Sale. The country's extensive reserves of traditional seed varieties (barley, teff, chick peas, sorghum, etc.) were being appropriated, genetically manipulated, and patented by the agribusiness conglomerates: "Instead of compensation and respect, Ethiopians today are getting bills from foreign companies that have 'patented' native species and now demand payment for their use."[13] The foundations of a "competitive seed industry" were laid under IMF and World Bank auspices.[14] The Ethiopian Seed Enterprise (ESE), the government's seed monopoly, joined hands with Pioneer Hi-Bred in the distribution of hi-bred and genetically modified (GM) seeds (together with hybrid resistant herbicide) to smallholders. In turn, the marketing of seeds had been transferred to a network of private contractors and "seed enterprises" with financial support and technical assistance from the World Bank. The "informal" farmer-to-farmer seed exchange was slated to be converted under the World Bank program into a "formal" market-oriented system of "private seed producer-sellers."[15]

In turn, the Ethiopian Agricultural Research Institute (EARI) was collaborating with the International Maize and Wheat Improvement Center (CIMMYT) in the development of new hybrids between Mexican and Ethiopian maize varieties.[16] Initially established in the 1940s by Pioneer Hi-Bred International with support from the Ford and Rockefeller foundations, CIMMYT developed a cozy relationship with U.S. agribusiness. Together with the U.K.-based Norman Borlaug Institute, CIMMYT constitutes a research arm as well as a mouthpiece of the seed conglomerates. According to the Rural Advancement Foundation (RAFI), "U.S. farmers already earn $150 million annually by growing varieties of barley developed from Ethiopian strains. Yet nobody in Ethiopia is sending them a bill."[17]

Impacts of Famine. The 1984–85 famine had seriously threatened Ethiopia's reserves of landraces of traditional seeds. In response to the famine, the Dergue government, through its Plant Genetic Resource Centre—in collaboration with Seeds of Survival (SOS)—had implemented a program to preserve Ethiopia's biodiversity.[18] This program, which was continued under the transitional government, skillfully "linked on-farm conservation and crop improvement by rural communities with government support services."[19] An extensive network of in-farm sites and conservation plots was established involving some

30,000 farmers. In 1998, coinciding chronologically with the onslaught of the 1998–2000 famine, the government clamped down on SOS and ordered the program to be closed down.[20]

The hidden agenda was to eventually displace the traditional varieties and landraces reproduced in village-level nurseries. The latter were supplying more than 90 percent of the peasantry through a system of farmer-to-farmer exchange. Without fail, the 1998–2000 famine led to a further depletion of local level seed banks: "The reserves of grains [the farmer] normally stores to see him through difficult times are empty. Like 30,000 other households in the [Galga] area, his family have also eaten their stocks of seeds for the next harvest."[21] And a similar process was unfolding in the production of coffee where the genetic base of the arabica beans was threatened as a result of the collapse of farmgate prices and the impoverishment of smallholders.

In other words, the famine itself, in large part a product of the economic reforms imposed to the advantage of large corporations by the IMF, World Bank, and the U.S. government, served to undermine Ethiopia's genetic diversity to the benefit of the biotech companies. With the weakening of the system of traditional exchange, village-level seed banks were being replenished with commercial hi-bred and genetically modified seeds. In turn, the distribution of seeds to impoverished farmers had been integrated with the "food aid" programs. WPF and USAID relief packages often include "donations" of seeds and fertilizer, thereby favoring the inroad of the agribusiness-biotech companies into Ethiopia's agricultural heartland. The emergency programs are not the "solution" but the "cause" of famine. By deliberately creating a dependency on GM seeds, they had set the stage for the outbreak of future famines.

This destructive pattern invariably resulting in famine is replicated throughout Sub-Saharan Africa. From the onslaught of the debt crisis of the early 1980s, the IMF–World Bank had set the stage for the demise of the peasant economy across the region with devastating results. Now, in Ethiopia, 15 years after the last famine left nearly 1 million dead, hunger is once again stalking the land. This time, as 8 million people face the risk of starvation, we know that it isn't just the weather that is to blame.

NOTES

[1] Food and Agriculture Organization (FAO), Special Report: FAO/WFP Crop Assessment Mission to Ethiopia, Rome, January 2000.
[2] Ibid.
[3] Ibid.
[4] Ibid.
[5] Philip Sherwell and Paul Harris, "Guns before Grain as Ethiopia Starves," *Sunday Telegraph*, London, April 16, 2000.
[6] IMF, Ethiopia, "Recent Economic Developments," Washington, D.C., 1999.
[7] Pioneer Hi-Bred International, General GMO Facts, www.pioneer.com/usa/biotech/value_of_products/product_value.htm#.
[8] United States agency for International Development (USAID), "Mission to Ethiopia, Concept Paper: Back to The Future," Washington, D.C., June 1993

[9]Carter Center, Press release, Atlanta, Georgia, January 31, 1997.

[10]Declan Walsh, "America Find Ready Market for GM Food," *The Independent*, London, March 30, 2000, p. 18.

[11]Ibid.

[12]Maja Wallegreen, "The World's Oldest Coffee Industry In Transition," *Tea & Coffee Trade Journal*, November 1, 1999.

[13]Laeke Mariam Demissie, "A vast historical contribution counts for little; West reaps Ethiopia's genetic harvest," *World Times*, October, 1998.

[14]World Bank, Ethiopia-Seed Systems Development Project, Project ID ETPA752, 6 June 1995.

[15]Ibid.

[16]See CIMMYT Research Plan and Budget 2000–2002, www.cimmyt.mx/about/People-mtp2002.htm#.

[17]Laeke Mariam Demissie, op. cit

[18]"When local farmers know best," *The Economist*, May 16, 1998.

[19]Ibid

[20]Laeke Mariam Demissie, op. cit.

[21]Rageh Omaar, "Hunger stalks Ethiopia's Dry Land," BBC, London, January 6, 2000.

MICHEL CHOSSUDOVSKY is Professor of Economics at the University of Ottowa, and the author of *The Globalization of Poverty*.

1998 #5 CENSORED STORY

U.S. WEAPONS OF MASS DESTRUCTION LINKED TO THE DEATHS OF HALF A MILLION CHILDREN

For the past seven years, the United States has supported sanctions against Iraq that have taken the lives of more Iraqi citizens than did the war itself. The Iraqi people are being punished for their leader's reticence to comply fully with U.S.-supported UN demands "to search every structure in Iraq for weapons of mass destruction." Ironically, 1994 U.S. Senate findings uncovered evidence that U.S. firms supplied at least some of the very biological material that the UN inspection teams are now seeking.

Although the United States defames the Iraqi government for damaging the environment and ignoring UN Security Council resolutions, it has itself engaged in covert wars in defiance of the World Court, and left behind a swath of ecological disasters in its continuing geopolitical crusade. Bill Blum considers the U.S. demands both excessive and hypocritical. A 1994 U.S. Senate panel report indicated that between 1985 and 1989, U.S. firms supplied microorganisms needed for the production of Iraq's chemical and biological warfare. The Senate panel wrote: "It was later learned that these microorganisms exported by the United States were identical to those the United Nations inspectors found and removed from the Iraqi biological warfare program." Blum writes that shipments included biological agents for anthrax, botulism, and E-coli. The shipments were cleared even though it was known at the time that Iraq had already been using chemical and possibly biological warfare since the early 1980s.

The real significance of "Made in America" is not only that the United States and its allies played a significant role in arming Iraq with weapons of mass destruction, but that those companies and politicians who were responsible for this lucrative but deadly policy were never held accountable.

SOURCES: *San Francisco Bay Guardian,* February 25, 1998, "Made in America," by Dennis Bernstein; *I.F. Magazine,* March/April 1998, "Punishing Saddam or the Iraqis," by Bill Blum; *Space and Security News,* May 1998, "Our Continuing War Against Iraq," by the Most Rev. Dr. Robert M. Bowman, Lt. Col., USAF (retired).

2000 UPDATE BY MICHAEL PARENTI
DEFYING THE SANCTIONS:
A FLIGHT TO IRAQ

Upon disembarking from the Olympic Airways plane that brings me to Iraq in November 2000, I can see some of the effects of the Western-imposed sanctions. What was once a busy international airport is now a desolate strip. Two lonely planes sit as if abandoned on the vast tarmac. There are no airport personnel to speak of, no baggage carts or utility vehicles, not even any visible security. On a wall inside the empty terminal is a handmade sign in Arabic and imperfect English; it reads: "Down USA." A large portrait of Saddam Hussein gazes down upon us. His image can be found along the road to the city, in the hotel, and on various public buildings.

I am part of an international delegation of Greeks, Britons, Canadians, and Americans. Included are journalists, peace advocates, and members of the Greek parliament. Margarita Papandreou, former first lady of Greece and devoted political activist, leads the group. It is an especially moving moment for her. It has been her dream for ten years to be able to fly directly to Baghdad. And ours is the first flight to Iraq by a state-owned commercial airline from the West in defiance of U.S./UN sanctions.

The Iraqi officials who greet us do not try to hide how pleased they are about our arrival. "Your presence is a statement against the inhuman means used against us. Iraq is a prosperous country capable of fulfilling the basic needs of the people but we are being prevented from doing so by the UN sanctions," one of them says. "Feel free to go anywhere and speak to anyone."

Killing Iraq. Most Americans do not know that Saddam Hussein was put into power by a CIA-engineered coup to stop the Iraqi revolution—which he did by massacring the communists and the left wing of his own Baath party. But in time Saddam proved to be a disappointment to his mentors in Washington. Instead of becoming the comprador ruler who opened his country to free-market capital penetration on terms that were thoroughly favorable to Western investors, he devoted a substantial portion of Iraq's export earnings to human services and economic development. In 1972, Iraq nationalized its oil industry, and was immediately denounced by U.S. leaders as a "terrorist" nation.

Before the six weeks of air attacks known as the Gulf War (which ended in February 1991), Iraq's standard of living was the highest in the Middle East. Iraqis enjoyed free medical care and free education. Literacy had reached about 80 percent. Most Iraqi youth were educated up through secondary school. University students of both genders received scholarships to study at home and abroad. In the eyes of Western leaders, Saddam was that penultimate evil, an economic nationalist, little better than a communist. He would have to be taught a lesson. His country needed to be bombed back into the Third World from which it was emerging.

The high explosive tonnage delivered upon Iraq during the Gulf War was more than twice the combined Allied air offensive of World War II. Within the first few days of bombing, there was no running water in the country. More than 90 percent of Iraq's electrical capacity was destroyed. Its telecommunication systems, including television and radio stations, were demolished, as were its flood control, irrigation, sewage treatment, water purification, and hydroelectric systems. Farm herds and poultry farms suffered heavy losses. U.S. planes burned wheat and grain fields with incendiary bombs and hit hundreds of schools, hospitals, rail stations, bus stations, air-raid shelters, mosques, and historic sites. Factories that produced textiles, cement, chlorine, petrochemicals, and phosphate were hit repeatedly. So were the refineries, pipelines, and storage tanks of Iraq's oil industry. Iraqi civilians and soldiers fleeing Kuwait were slaughtered by the thousands on what became known as the "Highway of Death." Also massacred were Iraqi soldiers who tried to surrender to U.S. forces on a number of occasions. In all, some 200,000 Iraqis were killed in those six weeks. Nearly all U.S. planes, Ramsey Clark notes, "employed laser-guided depleted-uranium missiles, leaving 900 tons of radioactive waste spread over much of Iraq with no concern for the consequences to future life."

Our delegation got a grim glimpse of the war's aftermath. We visited the Al-Amerya bomb shelter where more than 400 civilians, mostly women and children, had been incinerated by two US missiles. Blackened ossified body parts, including a child's hand, can still be seen melded into the ceiling. Along one wall is the irradiated shadow of a woman holding a baby in her arms, a ghoulish fresco created by the heat blast of the missiles. The shadow of another figure can be seen on the cement floor. The shelter has been made into a shrine, with candles, plastic flowers, and pictures of the victims. The guide notes that U.S. reconnaissance saw civilians using the shelter on a nightly basis during the early days of the bombing, yet it was still chosen as a target. In the ten years of "peace" since February 1991, an additional 400 tons of explosives have been dropped on Iraq, 300 people have been killed, and many hundreds wounded. The United States and United Kingdom, with the participation of France, imposed a no-fly zone over the northern region of the country, ostensibly to protect the Kurds. This newly found humanitarian concern did not extend to the Kurds residing on the Turkish side of the border. The next year, another no-fly zone was imposed in the south, reputedly to protect Shiite settlements, effectively dividing the country into three parts. By 1998, the French had withdrawn from both zones, but U.S. and British air attacks on military and civilian targets have continued almost on a daily basis, including strafing raids against Iraqi agricultural developments. Baghdad's repeated protests to the United Nations have gone unheeded. Since 1998, three members of the Security Council—Russia, China, and France—and various nonpermanent members have condemned the raids as illegal and unauthorized by the Security Council.

To drive the point home to us, on the second day of our visit, U.S. warplanes fired four missiles at the village of Hmaidi in the southern province of Basra, one of which struck the Ali Al-Hayaini school, wounding four children and three teachers. Several homes were also hit.

Picking Up the Pieces. Despite the years of bombings and the even greater toll on human life taken by the sanctions, visitors to Baghdad do not see a city in ruins. Much of the wreckage has been cleared away, much has been repaired. In our hotel there is running water throughout the day, hot water in the morning. Various streets in Baghdad are lined with little stores, surprisingly well-stocked with household appliances, hardware goods, furniture, and clothes (much of which has a second-hand look).

We see no derelicts or homeless people on the streets of Baghdad, no prostitutes or ragged bands of abandoned children, though there are occasional youngsters eager to shine shoes or solicit spare change. But even they seem to be wellfed and decently clothed. Obviously, despite all the destruction wrought by the sanctions, Iraq still has not undergone sufficient free-market "structural adjustment."

A British member of our delegation who has made more than a dozen trips to Iraq over the past decade sees some changes for the better. A few years ago, the cars all looked like "death traps"; tires were patched beyond recognition, windows were cracked, and doors were falling off the hinges, she tells me. Now the Iraqis seem to have procured vehicles that are in better repair. In addition, large swaths of the city used to be shrouded in complete darkness; now there are lights just about everywhere, though mostly on the dim side. There are more shops with more goods, "although 70 percent of the people can't buy anything." Still, "people used to feel hopelessly isolated and now there seems to be more hope and better morale," she concludes.

The Silent Cries of Children. Not everyone shows better morale. It is said that the most depressed officials in Iraq can be found in the Ministry of Health—not surprisingly, given the tragedies they confront. Aside from the 200,000 Iraqis slaughtered during the Gulf War, an additional 1.5 million civilians have died since 1991 as a result of the sanctions, according to UNICEF reports and the Red Cross, many from what normally would be treatable and curable illnesses. Of these victims, 600,000 are children under five years of age. Maternal mortality rates have more than doubled, and 70 percent of Iraqi women suffer from anemia. Given the tons of depleted uranium used during the Allied attacks, cancer rates have skyrocketed: the childhood leukemia rate is now the highest in the world. Most of the leukemia increase is in southern Iraq where the bombing was heaviest.

We visit a children's hospital in Baghdad. The familiar sight of skeletal-looking infants, racked with diseases that make it impossible for them to retain or digest nutrients, are no longer evident. Such dying children still can be found in parts of Iraq but not at this hospital. Instead we encounter something equally ominous: children suffering from acute forms of multiple malignancies. Shrouded mothers stand by the beds like mournful sentinels, their eyes filled with unspoken grief. The journalists, photographers, and TV crews in our delegation descend upon these sad people, clicking and flashing away with that intrusive irreverence that is the press's modus operandi. A mother weeps quietly against the wall. One of the doomed children smiles up at us, which almost causes me to start weeping.

Things are getting worse, a doctor tells us; more and more children are turning up with leukemia. The medical staff is overwhelmed. One doctor says he sees 300 patients in three hours: "We cannot treat them properly." Some of the hospital rooms are lined with incubators that contain what look like premature births. These turn out to be infants who are the products of depleted uranium, born with serious deformities and malfunctions, urgently in need of surgical intervention. The hospital lacks the special instruments needed to operate on infants, not to mention ordinary medications, anesthetics, antibiotics, bandages, intravenous sets, and diagnostic equipment. Iraq's excellent national health care system, with its universal coverage, is now in shambles because of the embargo.

Things were supposed to get better when the sanctions were eased in 1996, allowing Iraq to make "oil for food" sales. Since then, $32 billion in oil was sold abroad but only $8 billion worth of materials has reached Iraq, less than $5 or $6 a month per person. Another $10 billion has been allocated for "war compensation," in effect forcing the Iraqis to pay the costs incurred by the U.N. aggressors when destroying Iraq.

Another $11 billion in cash sits in Western banks. Worse still, many essential things needed to rebuild the infrastructure—including the technological, medical, educational, communicational, and industrial systems of the nation—are still not available. Under the deleterious "dual use" doctrine, many vital commodities and materials needed for humanitarian and civilian purposes are banned because they conceivably could also be used by the military: computers, components for electrical transmitters and water pumps, even glycerin tablets needed for heart ailments. (It would take millions of glycerin tablets mixed with nitrogen to make one small explosive.)

The Foreign Minister Speaks. Iraq's Minister of Foreign Affairs, Tariq Aziz, a calm congenial man, meets with our delegation. In clear and precise English, he makes the following points: Before 1990, the United Nations had placed sanctions upon only a few nations, such as Rhodesia and South Africa, on a voluntary basis. "It was left to the countries themselves and the world to implement those sanctions or not implement them." Hence the effects were mild. But since 1990, U.S. leaders with their so-called New World Order have imposed the severest embargo, "encircling Iraq with warships and airplanes that prevent even ordinary trips and ordinary cargoes." As with the sanctions against Yugoslavia, the minister notes, this policy has created a lot of suffering. "Therefore, when we say that this embargo is an international issue, it's not just anti-American propaganda. It's the truth. And it is quite horrid." The collapse of the Soviet Union has created a different international scene, he adds. With the end of the Cold War, "a new hot war and warm war" has been imposed on many nations, with Iraq as a prime target.

In spite of all the reports made by U.N. agencies themselves "informing the Security Council about the sufferings of the Iraqi people, and the deaths of so many children, and the deterioration of the Iraqi economy," Aziz reminds us, there is no likelihood of any change in U.N. policy on sanctions because of the Security Council veto wielded by the United States and Britain. Still the people of Iraq have not been merely passive victims. They have "refused to yield to American pressure and American blackmail." In addition, there is "the will of other peoples, the free women and men in this world" who refuse to support injustice and imperialism. After ten years, U.S. propaganda "is wearing thin," and "a lot of facts have become known to the peoples of the world" bringing a dramatic increase in support for Iraq—as measured by the growing number of air flights from various nations in defiance of the sanctions. Not only Iraq but its trading partners have sustained substantial commercial losses because of the ten-year embargo. In 2000, more than 1,500 international companies from 45 countries participated in the Iraqi trade fair. So, for both moral and legitimate commercial reasons, "the embargo is beginning to crack."

"Ten years ago," concludes Aziz, "we were told: history is over; from now on we will live according to the diktat of U.S. leaders in a Pax Americana. And those who do not accept this are 'rogue nations.'" But U.S. leaders are beginning to realize "that this new imperialism is not working.... Despite all its power, the United States is not God. It's not the Almighty. It's an imperialist force.... When a nation succeeds in refusing the dictate of imperialists," Aziz said, [and] succeeds in preserving its sovereignty, and its independence and dignity, that is an achievement." Aziz's closing plea was that we not rely on "the manipulated media" of the United States, Britain and Canada. "One of the basic human rights is that you have the right to make your own judgment, not to buy judgments made by others that might not be honest and true. So I hope that you will use this short visit to know what is going on in this country and what the realities are."

The "Realities." On the closing day of our trip, members of our delegation lay plans to carry on the battle against sanctions. These include: lobbying the U.N. Compensation Committee, which refuses to release the $11 billion in Iraqi "oil-for-food" earnings; joining with Women's International League for Peace and Freedom, and other NGOs to lobby the U.N. Security Council; lobbying the U.N. Human Rights Commission in Geneva and the parliament of the European Union; lobbying elected representatives and religious leaders in various countries; and sending messages through the Internet.

The sanctions wall is not about to crumble, but it is showing cracks. In 1998 Scott Ritter, chief U.N. weapons inspector in Iraq since 1991, resigned and accused the U.S. government of undercutting U.N. weapons inspectors. Meanwhile U.S. leaders and the press continued to portray Iraq as bent on nuclear aggression, despite the fact that Baghdad cooperated fully with U.N. inspectors who scoured the country in a vain search for weapons of mass destruction or the capacity to build them.

Also in 1998, Denis Halliday, U.N. Assistant Secretary General and Humanitarian Coordinator in Iraq, resigned in protest of what the sanctions were doing to that country. In early 2000, Hans von Sponeck, U.N. Humanitarian Coordinator in Iraq and Jutta Burghart, head of U.N. World Food Program in Baghdad, resigned in protest of the sanctions.

Still, the State Department and the U.S. media continue to blame Saddam, not the sanctions, for the misery endured by the Iraqi people. The claim that sanctions hurt ordinary Iraqis "is outweighed by the sad truth that Saddam Hussein is determined to keep portions of his population in poverty," intones a *Washington Post* editorial reprinted in the *International Herald Tribune* (November 14, 2000). The Iraqi leader, the *Post* assures us, is a "warmongering dictator" who needs to be contained by a still more severe application of sanctions. Upon being selected as the new U.S. Secretary of State in December 2000, General Colin Powell echoed this position, announcing that he would strive to "reenergize" the sanctions against Iraq. The Iraqi leadership could turn U.S. policy completely around by uttering just two magic words: "free market." All they would have to do is invite the IMF and World Bank into Iraq, eliminate free education and free medical care, abolish the minimal food ration that goes to every Iraqi, abolish the housing subsidies and transportation subsidies, and hand over the country's oil industry to the corporate cartels. To lift the sanctions, Iraq must surrender to the tender mercies of the free-market paradise as Yugoslavia has recently done under the newly minted, Western-sponsored president, Kostunica, and as so many other nations have done. Until then, Iraq will continue to be designated a "rogue nation" by those policymakers in Washington who themselves are the meanest profit-driven, power-mongering rogues on earth.

MICHAEL PARENTI's most recent books are *To Kill a Nation: The Attack on Yugoslavia* (Verso) and *History as Mystery* (City Lights).

1994 #9 CENSORED STORY

THE PENTAGON'S MYSTERIOUS HAARP PROJECT

The Pentagon's mysterious High-frequency Active Auroral Research Project (HAARP) at an isolated Air Force facility near Gakona, Alaska, marks the first step toward creating the world's most powerful "ionospheric heater." This joint effort of the Air Force and the Navy is the latest in a series of little-known Department of Defense (DOD) "active ionospheric experiments." Internal HAARP documents state, "From a DOD point of view, the most exciting and challenging" part of the experiment is "its potential to *control* ionospheric processes" for military objectives. Scientists envision using the system's powerful 2.8-10 megahertz (MHz) beam to burn "holes" in the ionosphere and "create an artificial lens" in the sky that could focus large bursts of electromagnetic energy "to higher altitudes... than is presently possible."

HAARP has remained extremely low-profile—almost unknown to most Alaskans and the rest of the country. HAARP surfaced publicly in Alaska in the spring of 1993 when the Federal Aviation Administration (FAA) began advising commercial pilots on how to avoid the large amount of intentional (and some unintentional) electromagnetic radiation that HAARP would generate. Despite protests of FAA engineers and Alaska bush pilots, the final Environmental Impact Statement gave HAARP the green light.

Scientists, environmentalists, and native people are concerned that HAARP's electronic transmitters could harm people, endanger wildlife, and trigger unforeseen environmental impacts. Despite critics and local public concern, testing of the HAARP prototype started in April 1995 (*Alaska*

Journal of Commerce, October 9, 1995). HAARP program director John Heckscher assures critics that "although HAARP is being managed by the Air Force and Navy, it is purely a scientific research facility that poses no threat to potential adversaries and has no value as a military target." Nonetheless, the authoritative *Jane's Defence Weekly* reported (April 1, 1995) potential military applications for HAARP.

SOURCE: *Earth Island Journal*, Fall 1994, "Project HAARP: The Military's Plan to Alter the Ionosphere," by Clare Zickuhr and Gar Smith.

2000 UPDATE BY MICHEL CHOSSUDOVSKY
IT'S NOT ONLY GREENHOUSE GAS EMISSIONS: WASHINGTON'S NEW WORLD ORDER WEAPONS HAVE THE ABILITY TO TRIGGER CLIMATE CHANGE

The important debate on global warming under UN auspices provides but a partial picture of climate change. In addition to the devastating impacts of greenhouse gas emissions on the ozone layer, the world's climate can now be modified as part of a new generation of sophisticated "nonlethal weapons." Both the Americans and the Russians have developed capabilities to manipulate the world's climate.

In the United States, the technology is being perfected under the High-frequency Active Aural Research Program (HAARP) as part of the ("Star Wars") Strategic Defense Initiative (SDI). Recent scientific evidence suggests that HAARP is fully operational and has the ability to potentially trigger floods, droughts, hurricanes, and earthquakes. From a military standpoint, HAARP is a weapon of mass destruction. Potentially, it constitutes an instrument of conquest capable of selectively destabilizing agricultural and ecological systems of entire regions.

While there is no evidence that this deadly technology has been used, surely the United Nations should be addressing the issue of "environmental warfare" alongside the debate on the climatic impacts of greenhouse gases.

Despite a vast body of scientific knowledge, the issue of deliberate climatic manipulations for military use has never been explicitly part of the UN agenda on climate change. Neither the official delegations nor the environmental action groups participating in the Hague Conference on Climate Change (CO6) (November 2000) have raised the broad issue of "weather warfare" or "environmental modification techniques (ENMOD)" as relevant to an understanding of climate change.

The clash between official negotiators, environmentalists, and American business lobbies has centered on Washington's outright refusal to abide by commitments on carbon dioxide reduction targets under the 1997 Kyoto protocol.[1] The impacts of military technologies on the world's climate are not an object of discussion or concern. Narrowly confined to greenhouse gases, the ongoing debate on climate change serves Washington's strategic and defense objectives.

Weather Warfare. World-renowned scientist Dr. Rosalie Bertell confirms "U.S. military scientists are working on weather systems as a potential weapon. The methods include the enhancing of storms and the diverting of vapor rivers in the Earth's atmosphere to produce targeted droughts or floods."[2] Already in the 1970s, former National Security advisor Zbigniew Brzezinski had foreseen in his book *Between Two Ages* that "technology will make available, to the leaders of major nations, techniques for conducting secret warfare, of which only a bare minimum of the security forces need be appraised…. [T]echniques of weather modification could be employed to produce prolonged periods of drought or storm."

Marc Filterman, a former French military officer, outlines several types of "unconventional weapons" using radio frequencies. He refers to "weather war," indicating that the United States and the Soviet Union had already "mastered the know-how needed to unleash sudden climate changes (hurricanes, drought) in the early 1980s."[3] These technologies make it "possible to trigger atmospheric disturbances by using Extremely Low Frequency (ELF) radar [waves]." [4]

A simulation study of future defense "scenarios" commissioned for the U.S. Air Force calls for "U.S. aerospace forces to 'own the weather' by capitalizing on emerging technologies and focusing development of those technologies to war-fighting applications. From enhancing friendly operations or disrupting those of the enemy via small-scale tailoring of natural weather patterns to complete dominance of global communications and counterspace control, weather modification offers the war fighter a wide range of possible options to defeat or coerce an adversary. In the United States, weather modification will likely become a part of national security policy with both domestic and international applications. Our government will pursue such a policy, depending on its interests, at various levels.[5]

The High-frequency Active Aural Research Program (HAARP). HAARP, based in Gokoma, Alaska, and jointly managed by the U.S. Air Force and the U.S. Navy, is part of a new generation of sophisticated weaponry under SDI. Operated by the Air Force Research Laboratory's Space Vehicles Directorate, HAARP constitutes a system of powerful antennas capable of creating "controlled local modifications of the ionosphere." Scientist Dr. Nicholas Begich—actively involved in the public campaign against HAARP—describes HAARP as "a super-powerful radiowave-beaming technology that lifts areas of the ionosphere [upper layer of the atmosphere] by focusing a beam and heating those areas. Electromagnetic waves then bounce back onto earth and penetrate everything—living and dead."[6]

Dr. Rosalie Bertell depicts HAARP as "a gigantic heater that can cause major disruption in the ionosphere, creating not just holes, but long incisions in the protective layer that keeps deadly radiation from bombarding the planet."[7]

Misleading Public Opinion. HAARP has been presented to public opinion as a program of scientific and academic research. U.S. military documents seem to suggest, however, that HAARP's main objective is to "exploit the ionosphere for Department of Defense purposes."[8] Without explicitly referring to the HAARP program, a U.S. Air Force study points to the use of "induced ionospheric modifications" as a means of altering weather patterns as well as disrupting enemy communications and radar.[9]

According to Dr. Rosalie Bertell, HAARP is part of an integrated weapons system, which has potentially devastating environmental consequences: "It is related to 50 years of intensive and increasingly destructive programs to understand and control the upper atmosphere. It would be rash not to associate HAARP with the space laboratory construction, which is separately being planned by the United States. HAARP is an integral part of a long history of space research and development of a deliberate military nature. The military implication of combining these projects is alarming. The ability of the HAARP/Spacelab/rocket combination to deliver very large amounts of energy, comparable to a nuclear bomb, anywhere on earth via laser and particle beams, is frightening. The project is likely to be "sold" to the public as a space shield against incoming weapons, or, for the more gullible, a device for repairing the ozone layer."[10]

In addition to weather manipulation, HAARP has a number of related uses:

"HAARP could contribute to climate change by intensively bombarding the atmosphere with high-frequency rays. Returning low-frequency waves at high intensity could also affect people's brains, and effects on tectonic movements cannot be ruled out."[11]

More generally, HAARP has the ability of modifying the world's electromagnetic field. It is part of an arsenal of "electronic weapons" that U.S. military researchers consider a "gentler and kinder warfare."[12]

Weapons of the New World Order. HAARP is part of the weapons arsenal of the New World Order under the Strategic Defense Initiative. From military command points in the United States, entire national economies could potentially be destabilized through climatic manipulations. More importantly, the latter can be implemented without the knowledge of the enemy, at minimal cost, and without engaging military personnel and equipment as in a conventional war.

The use of HAARP—if it were to be applied—could have potentially devastating impacts on the world's climate. Responding to U.S. economic and strategic interests, it could be used to selectively modify climate in different parts of the world resulting in the destabilization of agricultural and ecological systems.

It is also worth noting that the U.S. Department of Defense (DOD) has allocated substantial resources to the development of intelligence and monitoring systems on weather changes. NASA and the DOD's National Imagery and Mapping Agency (NIMA) are working on "imagery for studies of flooding, erosion, land-slide hazards, earthquakes, ecological zones, weather forecasts, and climate change" with data relayed from satellites.[13]

Policy Inertia of the United Nations. According to the Framework Convention on Climate Change (UNFCCC) signed at the 1992 Earth Summit in Rio de Janeiro: "States have in accordance with the Charter of the United Nations and the principles of international law, the… responsibility to ensure that activities within their jurisdiction or control do not cause damage to the environment of other states or of areas beyond the limits of national jurisdiction."[14]

It is also worth recalling that an international convention ratified by the U.N. General Assembly in 1997 bans "military or other hostile use of environmental modification techniques having widespread, long-lasting or severe effects."[15] Both the United States and the Soviet Union were signatories to the convention. The convention defines "environmental modification techniques" as "referring to any technique for changing—through the deliberate manipulation of natural processes—the dynamics, composition, or structure of the earth, including its biota, lithosphere, hydrosphere, and atmosphere or of outer space."[16]

Why then did the United Nations—disregarding the 1977 ENMOD Convention as well as its own charter —decide to exclude from its agenda climatic changes resulting from military programs?

European Parliament Acknowledges Impacts of HAARP. In February 1998, responding to a report of Dr.-Maj. Britt Theorin, Swedish Member of the European Paliament and longtime peace advocate, the European Parliament's Committee on Foreign Affairs, Security and Defense Policy held public hearings in Brussels on the HAARP program.[17] The Committee's "Motion for Resolution" submitted to the European Parliament "considers HAARP by virtue of its far-reaching impact on the environment to be a global concern and calls for its legal, ecological and ethical implications to be examined by an international independent body; [the Committee] regrets the repeated refusal of the United States Administration to give evidence to the public hearing into the environmental and public risks [of] the HAARP program."[18]

The Committee's request to draw up a "Green Paper" on "the environmental impacts of military activities," however, was casually dismissed on the grounds that the European Commission lacks the required jurisdiction to delve into "the links between environment and defense."19 Brussels was anxious to avoid a showdown with Washington.

Fully Operational. While there is no concrete evidence of HAARP having been used, scientific findings suggest that it is at present fully operational.

What this means is that HAARP could potentially be applied by the U.S. military to selectively modify the climate of an "unfriendly nation" or "rogue state" with a view to destabilizing its national economy.

Agricultural systems in both developed and developing countries are already in crisis as a result of New World Order policies including market deregulation, commodity dumping, and so on. Amply documented, IMF and World Bank "economic medicine" imposed on the Third World and the countries of the former Soviet block has largely contributed to the destabilization of domestic agriculture. In turn, the provisions of the WTO have supported the interests of a handful of Western agribiotech conglomerates in their quest to impose genetically modified seeds on farmers throughout the world.

It is important to understand the linkage between the economic, strategic, and military processes of the New World Order. In the above context, climatic manipulations under the HAARP program (whether accidental or deliberate) would inevitably exacerbate these changes by weakening national economies, destroying infrastructure, and potentially triggering the bankruptcy of farmers over vast areas. Surely national governments and the United Nations should address the possible consequences of HAARP and other "nonlethal weapons" on climate change.

MICHEL CHOSSUDOVSKY is Professor of Economics at the University of Ottowa, and author of *The Globalization of Poverty*.

NOTES

[1] The latter calls for nations to reduce greenhouse gas emissions by an average of 5.2 percent to become effective between 2008 and 2012. See Background of Kyoto Protocol at www.globalwarming.net/gw11.html.

[2] *The Times*, London, November 23, 2000.

[3] *Intelligence Newsletter*, December 16, 1999.

[4] Ibid.

[5] Air University of the U.S. Air Force, AF 2025 Final Report, www.au.af.mil/au/2025/ (emphasis added).

[6] Nicholas Begich and Jeane Manning, *The Military's Pandora's Box*, Earthpulse Press, www.xyz.net/~nohaarp/earthlight.html. See also the HAARP home page at www.haarp.alaska.edu/.

[7] See *Briarpatch*, January 2000 (emphasis added).

[8] Quoted in Begich and Manning, op cit.

[9] Air University, op cit.

[10] Rosalie Bertell, Background of the HAARP Program, November 5, 1996, www.globalpolicy.org/socecon/envronmt/weapons.htm.

[11] Begich and Manning, op cit.

[12] Don Herskovitz, "Killing Them Softly," *Journal of Electronic Defense*, August 1993 (emphasis added). According to Herskovitz, "electronic warfare" is defined by the U.S. Department of Defense as "military action involving the use of electromagnetic energy." *The Journal of Electronic Defense* at www.jedefense.com has published a range of articles on the application of electronic and electromagnetic military technologies.

[13] *Military Space*, December 6, 1999.

[14] U.N. Framework Convention on Climate Change, New York, 1992. See complete text at www.U.N.fccc.de/resource/conv/conv_002.html (emphasis added).

[15] See Associated Press, May 18, 1977.

[16]"Environmental Modification Ban Faithfully Observed, States Parties Declare," *UN Chronicle,* July 1984, Vol. 21, p. 27.

[17]*European Report,* February 7, 1998.

[18]European Parliament, Committee on Foreign Affairs, Security and Defense Policy, Brussels, doc. no. A4-0005/99, January 14, 1999.

[19]"EU Lacks Jurisdiction to Trace Links Between Environment and Defense," *European Report,* February 3, 1999.

CHAPTER 4

A Quarter Century of Censored News

BY PETER PHILLIPS AND PROJECT CENSORED

Censorship in the United States today is usually not deliberate, but rather comes under the heading of lost opportunities. Project Censored has been tracking these lost opportunities for the past 25 years. These stories are an archive of real news that has been ignored. Real news is media information that contributes to the lives and sociopolitical understandings of working people. Real news informs, balances, and awakens the less powerful in society. Real news speaks truth to power and challenges the hegemonic top-down corporate entertainment news systems.

The American people this past year experienced a national media event in the form of a Presidential election. We learned about voting machines, chads, dimples, and electoral inconsistencies. Pundits bemoaned the lack of a final decision and declared the impatience of the public for a quick finish. The media examined the Florida deadlock as if it were a street gang turf war with gang symbols, legalese weapons, and counter-punches that required a supreme police force to bring back law and order. The Florida news battle produced crisis viewing for millions and profitable easy coverage for the media.

Missing in the Presidential battles and the entire 2000 campaign were a number of essential issues that affect the American public in a real way, yet are ignored by the candidates and the corporate media.

GLOBALIZATION

Since the fall of 1999 there have been four major political demonstrations in the United States. The cities of Seattle, Washington D.C., Philadelphia, and Los Angeles each hosted either a major political party convention or global economic institution gathering or conference where thousands of activists protested and engaged in nonviolent civil disobedience.

Missing in Campaign 2000 was coverage of the core globalization issues these confrontations addressed. The World Trade Organization, World Bank, and International Monetary Fund are seen by many in the U.S. as top-down New World Order institutions that bypass the democratic process, and undermine working people in America and throughout the world. WTO business is conducted behind closed doors where committees and panels make decisions affecting the masses. The U.S. Clean Air Act, Marine Mammal Protection Act, and Endangered Species Act have all been undermined by WTO rulings. Deregulation of global logging, education, biotechnology, agriculture, health services are agenda topics slated for future WTO agreements. Furthermore, unions are concerned about the exportation of U.S jobs and the continuation of sweatshop exploitation abroad.

By their lack of discussion, it seems that both the Republicans and Democrats see continued globalization as desirable and inevitable. Media did not ask the hard questions about globalization's negative impacts and the issues remained unexamined in campaign 2000.

INTERNATIONAL ARMS SALES

In 1999, nation-states purchased over $30 billion worth of arms. These purchases represent huge expenditures for internal and external security at a

THIS MODERN WORLD   by TOM TOMORROW and RICHARD NIXON

THIS WEEK: MORE WISDOM FROM THE LATE, REVERED

RICHARD MILHOUS NIXON!

ACTUAL EXCERPTS FROM THE LATEST NIXON WHITE HOUSE TAPES RELEASED BY THE NATIONAL ARCHIVES!*

*TRANSCRIBED BY JAMES WARREN, CHICAGO TRIBUNE (AS REPRINTED IN HARPER'S)

WE'RE GOING TO (PUT) MORE OF THESE LITTLE NEGRO BASTARDS ON THE WELFARE ROLLS AT $2,400 A FAMILY...WORK, WORK. THROW 'EM OFF THE ROLLS. THAT'S THE KEY... I HAVE THE GREATEST AFFECTION FOR THEM. BUT I KNOW THEY'RE NOT GOING TO MAKE IT FOR 500 YEARS. THEY AREN'T. YOU KNOW IT, TOO.

THE MEXICANS ARE A DIFFERENT CUP OF TEA. THEY HAVE A HERITAGE. AT THE PRESENT TIME THEY STEAL, THEY'RE DISHONEST, BUT THEY DO HAVE SOME CONCEPT OF FAMILY LIFE. THEY DON'T LIVE LIKE A BUNCH OF DOGS, WHICH THE NEGROES DO LIVE LIKE.

direct cost to improvements in education, health care, human services, and economic development.

The United States is in the forefront of international arms sales, having promoted, sold, and delivered over $13 billion worth in 1999 alone. While candidate George W. Bush pledged increased support to the Pentagon, it has been the Clinton/Gore administration that actively supported global arms sales and worked towards the loosening up of licensing regulations. Neither presidential candidate, nor the media, were willing to address global arms proliferation and the consequent increase in tensions that are manifested as weapons are made more readily available. American solders face the continuing likelihood of being in armed conflicts with opponents using U.S.-made weapons.

With over 45 million people having died in regional wars since 1945, expanded weapons sales as a national policy is a huge humanitarian concern, and an issue worthy of presidential debate and media attention.

MEDIA MERGERS AND THE LOSS OF NEWS DIVERSITY

Since the passage of the Telecommunications Act of 1996, a gold rush of media mergers and takeovers has been occurring in the U.S. Over half of all radio stations have been sold in the past four years, and the merger upon merger of AOL–Time Warner–CNN has resulted in the largest media organization in the world. Less than ten major media corporations now dominate the U.S. news and information systems. Clear Channel alone owns over 800 radio stations. Ninety-eight percent of all cities have only one daily newspaper and these are increasingly owned by huge chains like Gannett and Knight Ridder. Lost to American voters is a diversity of political view-

YOU KNOW WHAT HAPPENED TO THE ROMANS? THE LAST SIX ROMAN EMPERORS WERE FAGS... YOU KNOW WHAT HAPPENED TO THE POPES? THEY WERE LAYIN' THE NUNS, THAT'S BEEN GOIN' ON FOR YEARS, CENTURIES. BUT THE CATHOLIC CHURCH WENT TO HELL THREE OR FOUR CENTURIES AGO. IT WAS HOMOSEXUAL AND IT HAD TO BE CLEANED OUT.

LOOK AT THE STRONG SOCIETIES. THE RUSSIANS. GODDAMN, THEY ROOT 'EM OUT. THEY DON'T LET 'EM AROUND AT ALL. I DON'T KNOW WHAT THEY DO WITH THEM. LOOK AT THIS COUNTRY. YOU THINK THE RUSSIANS ALLOW DOPE? HOMOSEXUALITY, DOPE, IMMORALITY ARE THE ENEMIES OF STRONG SOCIETIES.

THE UPPER CLASS OF SAN FRANCISCO IS THAT WAY. THE BOHEMIAN GROVE, WHICH I ATTEND FROM TIME TO TIME--IT IS THE MOST FAGGY GODDAMNED THING YOU COULD EVER IMAGINE, WITH THAT SAN FRANCISCO CROWD. I CAN'T SHAKE HANDS WITH ANYBODY FROM SAN FRANCISCO!

THIS MODERN WORLD--THE CARTOON THAT FEARLESSLY EXPOSES THE VENALITY OF DEAD EX-PRESIDENTS--CONSEQUENCES BE DAMNED!

points and news story sources that is vitally important for retaining an educated electorate in a democracy.

Efforts at rebuilding diversity in news sources through micro-power community radio and campaign finance reform, which would mandate access for all candidates on national media, have been strongly resisted by the National Association of Broadcasters (NAB). NAB, considered one of the most powerful lobby groups in Washington, works hard to protect the $200 billion of annual advertising and the $400 million candidates spend in each election cycle.

A recent Pew Research Center poll showed that over 77 percent of all journalists admitted that news stories that were perceived as important but dull are sometimes ignored, and more than a third stated that news stories that would hurt the financial interests of their news organization often or sometimes go unreported. How can we maintain a democracy with a news system that tends to choose stories for their entertainment value and profit potential over their importance?

MISSING NEWS

Missing news is censorship true and simple. Missing news in the presidential campaign for 2000 may well be a factor in why over 50 million eligible voters didn't bother to go to the polls. Without knowledge of these and other important political issues, voter apathy was rampant. The corporate media and its journalists have a First Amendment obligation to address all issues, ask broad inclusive questions, and demand articulation of future policies from the candidates. To do less is a rejection of the democratic process itself. Missing campaign stories in 2000 and this archive of censored news since 1976 is challenging indictment of corporate media's failure to support democracy in the United States. Freeing the media is a democratic challenge to the United States in the twenty-first century. I think we are up to the challenge and very capable of building a grassroots movement for real news in our society.

A special thanks to Dr. Carl Jensen for allowing us to use portions of his book, *20 Years of Censored News*, to compile these records. For more extensive follow-ups on these undercovered news stories, an excellent reference is *20 Years of Censored News* by Carl Jensen & Project Censored (Seven Stories Press, 1997). *20 Years* provides updates on the most censored stories for the years 1976 to 1995 and is available direct from the publisher (tel: (800) 596-7437), from the Quality Paperback Book Club, and in bookstores nationwide.

25 Years of Censored Stories

THE TOP TEN CENSORED STORIES OF 1976

1. JIMMY CARTER AND THE TRILATERAL COMMISSION (TLC).

Members of the TLC had agreed on Carter's potential as our next president as far back as 1970. Since the fall of 1973, Carter associated with the commission. Vice President Walter Mondale and many members of Carter's administration were also drawn from its membership rolls. **SOURCES:** "Report on the Governability of Democracies to the Trilateral Commission" in *The Crisis of Democracy* by Michael Crozier, Samuel P. Huntington, and Joji Watanuki (New York University Press, 1975); *Seven Days*, February 14, 1977, "From the Folks Who Brought Us Light at the End of the Tunnel," by William Minter, and "Trilateral RX for Crisis: Governability Yes, Democracy No," by Noam Chomsky; *The Review of the News*, August 18, 1976; *The Berkeley Barb*, July 30, 1976, by Gar Smith; *Jimmy Carter/Jimmy Carter*, by Gary Allen ('76 Press, Seal Beach, California, 1976); *American Opinion*, February 1976, "Carter Brings Forth a Cabinet," by Gary Allen; *New York*, December 13, 1976, "Carter's Little Kissingers," by Aaron Latham.

2. CORPORATE CONTROL OF DNA.

Since 1973, scientists have been creating new life forms from the DNA of other organisms, which could lead to the release of lethal new viruses. Federal guidelines are unenforceable and do not apply to private industry. **SOURCES:** *Mother Jones*, February/March 1977, "DNA: Have the Corporations Already Grabbed Control of New Life Forms?" by Jeremy Rifkin; *Science* magazine, October 15, 1976, "Recombinant DNA: A Critic Asks the Right to Free Inquiry;" *The Progressive*, March 1977, "Life from the Labs: Who Will Control the New Technology?"

3. SELLING BANNED PESTICIDES AND DRUGS TO THIRD WORLD COUNTRIES.

Drugs never approved by the FDA, and even some never tested, are marketed and sold in various Third World countries. According to a conservative estimate by the World Health Organization (WHO), approximately 500,000 people, the majority of them in Third World countries, are poisoned each year by banned pesticides and drugs. **SOURCE:** *Rolling Stone Magazine*, February 10, 1977, "Banned Chemicals Shipped Abroad," by David Weir.

4. WHY OIL PRICES GO UP.

While Americans fought one another in gasoline lines, elected U.S. representatives collaborated with the Organization of Petroleum Exporting Countries (OPEC) and Persian oil-producing nations to deliberately inflate the price of oil. The White House reported economic benefits from the increasing oil prices, and domestic oil producers realized increased profits. **SOURCE:** *Foreign Policy*, Winter Quarter, 1976, "Why Oil Prices Go Up—The Past: We Pushed Them," by Vivian H. Oppenheim.

5. THE MOBIL OIL/RHODESIA CONNECTION.
Mobil Oil kept alive a Rhodesian regime (known as Zimbabwe since 1980) that was "not only embargoed but condemned by virtually every nation on earth." By setting up a "paper chase," they disguised the fact that they were selling Rhodesia as much as $20 million a year in oil products. **SOURCE:** *Mother Jones*, September/October 1976, "Let's Make A Deal," by Richard Parker.

6. SOME OF OUR PLUTONIUM IS MISSING.
An unpublicized General Accounting Office (GAO) report revealed cases of inadequate security at nuclear plants, including using employee honor systems in lieu of posted guards, a lack of effective security screening for new employees, inadequate inventory methods, and the strategic "outmanning" of perimeter sentry guards. The government cannot account for 150,000 pounds of nuclear materials, 11,000 pounds of which is weapon-grade. **SOURCE:** *The Nation*, October 23, 1976, "Some of Our Plutonium is Missing," by Barbara P. Newman.

7. WORKERS DIE FOR CORPORATE PROFITS.
Untold numbers of injuries, illnesses, and deaths are caused by work hazards in America's industries. For example, in America's foundries, the Occupational Safety and Health Administration (OSHA) estimates that one out of every three foundry workers is injured annually, while the mortality rate among furnacemen is 76 percent greater than the rest of the working population in their age group. OSHA doesn't have the ability to investigate, let alone regulate and implement change in America's workplaces. **SOURCE:** *Seven Days*, February 28, 1977, "America's Foundries: Hell Aboveground," by Charles West.

8. KISSINGER USES THE CIA TO CHANGE INTELLIGENCE ESTIMATES.
While the conferences, accords, and summit meetings of the Strategic Arms Limitation Talks (SALT) were given substantial coverage in the media, the public was little aware of what really took place. For example, in 1976, then Secretary of State Henry Kissinger, with the collusion of the CIA, was accused of manipulating intelligence estimates for use in SALT talk negotiations. **SOURCE:** *Aviation Week and Space Technology*, September 13, 1976 and September 27, 1976.

9. WORTHLESS AND HAZARDOUS NON-PRESCRIPTION DRUGS.
Up to 500,000 different over-the-counter drugs generate at least $3.51 billion in sales every year. "[A]t least half… are worthless or of dubious value, and some may be harmful. Most of the products are labeled with misleading claims, and many are advertised with bold lies." While the industry invests in massive advertising campaigns, it spends comparatively little in developing and testing new drugs. **SOURCE:** *New Times*, September 17, 1976, "Non-Prescription Drugs—The Ultimate Confidence Game," by Daniel Zwerdling.

10. THE NATURAL GAS SWINDLE.
This investigative piece reports illegal and unethical activities of gas compa-

nies, company connections with government agencies, and motives for creating a natural gas shortage in the 1970s. Also noted is the Federal Power Commission's failure to issue injunctions against companies "sitting on" federal land leases, to report that gas companies greatly underestimated gas reserves, and to abide by its own mandate. **source:** *The Nation*, January 24, 1976, "The Natural Gas Swindle," by Robert Sherrill.

THE TOP TEN CENSORED STORIES OF 1977

1. THE MYTH OF BLACK PROGRESS.

Most of the indices of black poverty, illegitimacy, unemployment, and drug abuse have shown worsening conditions. Even those blacks who are considered successful are losing ground to their white counterparts. Black youth plays a major role in the crime problem. In New York City today, the number of black youths under 16 who have been arrested is almost ten times what it was in 1950. **source:** *The Progressive*, November 1977, "Black Progress Myth and Ghetto Reality," by Joel Dreyfuss.

2. THE WAR ON CANCER.

Forty percent of the National Cancer Institute (NCI) research funds go to contract research that is barely reviewed and invites abuse and poor quality work. Despite government estimates that 60–70 percent of cancer is caused by environmental factors, the American Cancer Society (the major political force behind the NCI) has refused to support such bills as the Toxic Substance Control Act and has never pushed a ban on any carcinogenic product. **sources:** *New Times*, November 25, 1977, "Cancer, Inc.," by Ruth Rosenbaum; *Politiks*, December 6, 1977, "Cancer Society Seeks Cure, Neglects Causes," by Jim Rosapepe.

3. JIMMY CARTER AND THE TRILATERAL COMMISSION: PART II.

Although the TLC was the top *Censored* story of 1976, it was renominated in 1977 since it continued to receive very limited press coverage. Jimmy Carter's major moves since taking over as president have been in accord with the TLC's recommendations. **sources:** *Penthouse*, November 1977, "Cartergate: The Death of Democracy," by Craig S. Karpel; *Esquire*, May 1977, "Where Jimmy Went Wrong," by Taylor Branch.

4. THE COST OF DECOMMISSIONING NUCLEAR POWER PLANTS.

The decommissioning of nuclear reactors is a problem that has not been resolved. The extremely high radioactivity that will surround shut-down plants—some of which may be hazardous for as long as 1.5 million years—will make it necessary for all reactors to eventually be completely decommissioned. **sources:** *The Progressive*, December 1977, "A Landscape of Nuclear Tombs," by Alexis Parks; *Environment*, December 1976, "The Cost of Turning It Off," by Steve Harwood, Kenneth May, Marvin Resnikaff, Barbara Schlenger, and Pam Tames.

5. THE BOTTLE-BABY SCANDAL IN THE THIRD WORLD.

Infant formula manufacturers began pushing their products on the Third World to ensure continued profits, relying on exploitative and deceptive tactics to sell them. Third World parents spend as much as 30-40 percent of their average daily wage for formula, while malnutrition and denial of natural immunities from formula feeding in Third World countries accounts for 35,000 deaths and untold instances of brain damage. Meanwhile, the profit margins on infant formulas have been documented at up to 72 percent.

SOURCES: *Mother Jones*, December 1977, "The Bottle Baby Scandal," by Barbara Garson; *Seven Days*, April 19, 1976, "Into the Mouths of Babes," by Leah Margulies.

6. THE MASS SLAUGHTER BY THE KHMER ROUGE.

The Khmer Rouge violated human rights in Cambodia and Vietnam through such abominable abuses as execution, starvation, cannibalism, torture, disease, and malnutrition. In January 1977, the American Security Council invited all three major networks to a conference on the subject; not one sent a correspondent.

SOURCES: *National Review*, September 2, 1977, "The Nation as a Concentration Camp," and April 29, 1977, "The New Vietnam"; *The Progressive*, September 1977, "Vietnam: A New Numbers Game," by Robert K. Musih; *TV Guide*, March 18, 1978, "Why Do Networks Play Down News From Cambodia?" by Patrick Buchanan; *Newsweek*, January 16, 1978, "A New Indochina War," by Kenneth Labich, with Holger Jansen and Lars-Erik Nelson.

7. THE COST BENEFITS OF ENVIRONMENTAL QUALITY.

American companies are fighting federal environmental and occupational health and safety regulations by warning that government controls would cause massive plant closings. In fact, according to the Environmental Protection Agency (EPA) and the Council on Environmental Quality, few would be shut down, many more jobs would be created than lost, and the price increases are balanced by the savings in pollution damage and health costs.

SOURCE: *The Nation*, October 29, 1977, "Environmental Balance Sheet: Cost Benefits of the Cleanup," by Stephen Solomon and Willard Randall.

8. ACID RAIN PORTENDS AN ECOLOGICAL DISASTER.

Acid rain, caused predominantly by oil and coal burning, smelting, and car exhaust, has been falling throughout most parts of the East coast of the United States. The pollution that causes the acidity (sulfuric and nitric acid) can originate thousands of miles from where the rain finally falls. Yet corporate opposition to air cleanup has been fierce.

SOURCE: *Mother Jones*, December 1977, "Look What They've Done to the Rain," by Alan MacRobert.

9. THE GLOBAL BATTLE FOR THE MINERAL WEALTH OF THE OCEANS.

In 1969, a United Nations (UN) resolution was passed saying that the ocean floor was a "common heritage of mankind." Third World nations interpret this to mean that all mining would be done under UN control. However, the American position would turn the mining control over to private corporations. **SOURCE:** *In These Times*, December 14, 1977, "Race to Control the Sea Floor," by David Helvarg.

10. THE UNTOLD SIDE OF THE ILLEGAL ALIENS STORY.

Most of the media coverage of illegal aliens has falsely concentrated on their role in draining welfare funds, creating unemployment, and not paying taxes into a system from which they benefit. Many employers benefit from illegal workers. The mainstream media tell only one side of the story of illegal aliens. **SOURCES:** *New West*, May 23, 1977, "California's Illegal Aliens, They Give More Than They Take," and "How Illegal Aliens Pay as They Go," by Jonathan Kirsch and Anthony Cook; *In These Times*, June 1, 1977, "Illegal Aliens: The New Scapegoat."

THE TOP TEN CENSORED STORIES OF 1978

1. THE DANGERS OF NUCLEAR POWER PLANTS.

In 1978, the Union of Concerned Scientists (UCS), a national public interest group, released a report which criticized the Nuclear Regulatory Commission's (NRC) failure to be a tough inspector of nuclear power plants. Contrary to the common perception that the nuclear industry is closely regulated, the UCS found that only 1 to 5 percent of safety-related nuclear power plant activities are inspected. NRC inspectors spend most of their time inspecting utility records, not the power plants themselves; most regulatory standards are drafted by the nuclear industry itself. **SOURCE:** *Union of Concerned Scientists*, November 26, 1978, "Scientists' Group Judges Federal Nuclear Safety Inspection Effort."

2. ORGANIC FARMING: THE SECRET IS IT WORKS!

Organic farmers, ignored by the press, may have the answer to some of the most critical health problems Americans face today. There is mounting evidence that the pesticides used in agriculture are responsible for cancer, mutations, birth defects, and many other health problems. **SOURCE:** *The Progressive*, December 1978, "Curbing the Chemical Fix: The Secret Is It Works," by Daniel Zwerdling.

3. THE GOVERNMENT'S WAR ON SCIENTISTS WHO KNOW TOO MUCH.

In 1964, Dr. Thomas Mancuso was commissioned by the Atomic Energy Commission (AEC) to measure how safe nuclear plants are for the people who work in them. He and two associates turned up alarming evidence that low levels of radiation, previously thought to be safe, can actually be quite deadly. Dr. Mancuso's contract with the government was promptly canceled and his research funds were cut off. He was forced into premature retirement and the government tried to take possession of his research findings. Mancuso was only one of several scientists the government sought to silence for challenging its view of nuclear safety. **SOURCE:** *Rolling Stone*, March 23, 1978, "The Government's Quiet War on Scientists Who Know Too Much."

4. U.S. EXPORTS DEATH: THE THIRD WORLD ASBESTOS INDUSTRY.

Research indicates that people who work in asbestos plants and inhale the asbestos fibers run a significantly higher risk of contracting lung cancer and other ailments. The asbestos industry has been aware of these health hazards since the 1930s and yet has done nothing about them. When the U.S. government began regulating the asbestos industry in the late 1960s, the asbestos manufacturers simply moved their factories to Third World nations where regulations were either minimal or nonexistent. **SOURCE:** *Guardian*, December 20, 1978, "Asbestos: U.S. Exports Death."

5. WINTER CHOICE: HEAT OR EAT.

More than 200 Americans died in the winters of 1975, 1976, and 1977, when utility companies shut off their gas and electricity service. At the same time, thousands of other Americans were forced to choose between heat, medication, food, or rent. Only Wisconsin, Maryland, and Rhode Island then had legislation to ban utility service shutoffs during winter. **SOURCE:** *Solidarity*, December 1, 1978.

6. AMERICA'S SECRET POLICE NETWORK.

The LEIU (Law Enforcement Intelligence Unit) is a virtually unknown organization linking the intelligence squads of almost every major police force in the United States and Canada. Although its members are sworn police officers who work for state and city governments, the LEIU is not answerable to voters, taxpayers, or elected officials. The organization not only withholds its files from the FBI and other federal authorities, but is also exempt from freedom of information laws, making its files more secret than even those of the CIA or FBI. **SOURCE:** *San Francisco Chronicle*, November 25, 1978, "Leaks to the Mob: U.S. Police Network's Big Problem"; *Penthouse*, 1976, "America's Secret Police Network," by George O'Toole.

7. THE SPECTER OF STERILITY.

Mounting evidence revealed that the average sperm count among American men dropped by frightening percentages since a landmark study done in 1951. The probable causes are those chemicals, such as herbicides and fungicides, with a composition similar to the pesticide DBCP, which are known to decompose very slowly and work their way up through the food chain. **SOURCE:** *Esquire*, April 11, 1978, "The Spectre of Sterility," by Raymond M. Layne.

8. THE SEARCH FOR DANGEROUS DAMS.

The need to identify America's dangerous dams is urgent. Of 49,422 large dams, about 39,000 have never been inspected by state or federal engineers. One scientific study concluded that, in any year, America's dams were 10,000 times more likely to cause a major disaster than were 100 nuclear power plants. **SOURCE:** *Smithsonian*, April 1978, "The Search for Dangerous

Dams—A Program to Head Off Disaster," by Gaylord Shaw.

9. IS YOUR DIET DRIVING YOU CRAZY?

There is mounting evidence that 6.4 million Americans now under mental health care, as well as 13.6 million in need of it, could be helped through proper nutrition. Yet the mental health aspect is the least funded in all nutrition research. **SOURCE:** *The Progressive*, May 1978, "Is Our Diet Driving Us Crazy?" by Jeanne Schinto.

10. WHO OWNS AMERICA? THE SAME OLD GANG.

The mass media have perpetuated the myth that class divisions in the United States are disappearing. Economic historians, however, tell us that the richest one percent owns a quarter of the population's net worth, and the top half of that one percent owns one-fifth of everything in America. **SOURCE:** *The Progressive*, June 1978, "Who Owns America? The Same Old Gang," by Maurice Zeitlin.

THE TOP TEN CENSORED STORIES OF 1979

1. THE CORPORATE CRIME OF THE CENTURY.

Corporate America "dumps" dangerous chemicals, toxic pesticides, and defective medical drugs and devices that have been restricted or banned in the United States on less wary Third World countries. *Every* pesticide that has been banned or restricted in this country has been exported elsewhere. When the U.S. nuclear industry encountered difficulties in selling reactors to American communities, it sold its power plants to less-developed countries. Most buyers were nations with strong regional rivalries. **SOURCE:** *Mother Jones*, November 1979, "The Corporate Crime of the Century," by Mark Dowie, Barbara Ehrenriech, Stephen Minken, Mark Shapiro, Terry Jacobs, and David Weir.

2. THE EMBASSY SEIZURE IN IRAN SHOULD NOT HAVE BEEN A SURPRISE.

If the mass media had accurately reported events in Iran in 1978 and 1979, the American people might not have been so shocked when militant Iranian students seized the American embassy and held more than 50 Americans hostage. The U.S. media were telling Americans that the Shah of Iran had a "broad base of popular support" while Amnesty International described Shah Pahlavi's regime as the "world's worst violator of human rights." The Shah's strong ties to the United States through Henry Kissinger and David Rockefeller served to inflame Iranian nationalists, climaxing with the seizure of the embassy. **SOURCE:** *Mother Jones*, April 1979, "The Iranian Hundred Years' War," by Eqbal Ahmad.

3. INTERNATIONAL PANEL FINDS U.S. GUILTY OF HUMAN RIGHTS VIOLATIONS.

A panel of U.N. jurists found the United States guilty of human rights violations against U.S. prisoners of certain races and socioeconomic classes, and against those holding unpopular political beliefs. This was never reported by the mass media. When queried for an explanation, media representatives explained that there is only room for one sizable "black story" at a time. **SOURCES:** *Village Voice*, September 10, 1979, "Seven International Jurists Journey to the Heart of Darkness," by Nat Hentoff; *New York Amsterdam News*, December 9, 1978, "Human Rights Violations Subject of U.N. Petition."

4. U.S. ELECTRONICS FIRMS OPERATE THIRD WORLD SWEATSHOPS.

Many American corporations looking for cheap labor and an escape from health and safety regulations and the unions, are setting up assembly branches in or contracting out jobs to Third World countries. The working conditions outside U.S. borders cut the average working life of workers to an estimated ten years. **SOURCE:** *The Nation*, August 25, 1979, "Asia's Silicon Valley," by Diana Roose.

5. OCCUPATIONAL DISEASE: IS YOUR JOB KILLING YOU?

OSHA reports that at least 100,000 workers die each year from illnesses attributable to the thousands of new and untested chemicals introduced into industrial products and processes. **SOURCE:** *The Progressive*, November 1979, "Dead on the Job," by Sidney Lens.

6. THE WORST NUCLEAR SPILL IN U.S. HISTORY GOES UNNOTICED.

The worst nuclear spill in U.S. history occurred when 100 million gallons of radioactive water containing uranium tailings breached from a tailing pond into the north fork of the Rio Puerco River in New Mexico. Samples of the river water indicated radioactivity 6,600 times the maximum standard for drinking water. The Rio Puerco flows into Lake Mead which supplies water for Southern California. Source: *Greenpeace Chronicles*, September 1979, "Worst Nuclear Disaster in U.S. History."

7. THE PRESS COVER-UP OF THE TRAGEDY IN EAST TIMOR.

Indonesian human rights violations rivaling those in Cambodia are occurring in East Timor with the support of the United States government but without the American public's knowledge. Neutral observers have estimated the number of people slaughtered at 50,000 to 100,000—almost ten percent of the population. The press, however, adheres to the Indonesian-U.S. State Department version of the situation that most of the lives were lost in the East Timorese civil war, which took place prior to the Indonesian intervention. **SOURCE:** *Inquiry*, February 19, 1979, "East Timor: The Press Cover-Up," by Noam Chomsky.

8. PBS, THE OIL NETWORK.

Oil companies are the primary underwriters of the Public Broadcasting System (PBS), making censorship a way of life. Examples given include controversial documentaries either dropped because they failed to conform to PBS's "journalistic standards," were termed "unsuitable for Americans," or reissued in a "reorganized or censored" form. **SOURCES:** *Washington Journalism Review*, April/May 1979, "The Horowitz Affair," by John Friedman; *Jump Cut*,

November 1979, "Racism in Public TV," by Joel Dreyfuss; *In These Times*, February 6, 1980 and March 5, 1980, "Public Television," by Pat Aufderheide; *San Francisco Chronicle*, June 12, 1978 and February 28, 1980, "The Oil Network," by Charles McCabe.

9. THE MOST POWERFUL SECRET LOBBY IN WASHINGTON.

The Business Roundtable, "the most powerful secret lobby in Washington," is known to include the chief executives of nearly 200 of the country's richest corporations. Assets of the member companies amount to $1.3 trillion, about half of the nation's total gross national product. In one way or another, the Business Roundtable has affected every American. **SOURCE:** *The New York Times Magazine*, December 9, 1979, "Big Business on the Offensive," by Philip Shabecoff.

10. THE 65 BILLION DOLLAR GHOST BANK IN WASHINGTON, D.C.

The Federal Financing Bank (FFB) is an obscure, off-budget government bank that works out of a small office in the Federal Treasury Building in Washington. It helps the government hide the true size of the national deficit and allows government agencies to pursue projects that Congress thought too costly or unnecessary. Sources: *Chicago Tribune Service*, December 16, 1979, "Buck Rogers' High Finance in Costly U.S. Space Venture," by James O'Shea; *Forbes*, March 15, 1976, "Ghost Bank."

THE TOP TEN CENSORED STORIES OF 1980

1. DISTORTED REPORTS OF THE EL SALVADOR CRISIS.

The U.S. media coverage of the outbreak of civil war in El Salvador was dangerously misleading. Either through willful misinformation or ignorance, the major U.S. media supported a misguided U.S. foreign policy by perpetrating a plethora of myths, including the popular position that the current government of the tiny Central American country is a "moderate" junta, struggling to maintain order in the face of left- and right-wing extremist minorities. **SOURCES:** *America*, April 26, 1980, "El Salvador's Agony and U.S. Policies," by James L. Connor; *Christianity and Crisis*, May 12, 1980, "El Salvador: Reform as Cover for Repression," by William L. Wipfler; *Inquiry*, May 5, 1980, "The Continuing Calamity of El Salvador," and November 10, 1980, "Central American Powder Keg," both by Anne Nelson; *The Nation*, December 13, 1980, "El Salvador's Christian Democrat Junta," by Penny Lernoux, and December 20, 1980, "The Junta's War Against the People," by James Petras.

2. NSA: BIG BROTHER IS LISTENING TO YOU.

The National Security Agency (NSA) has an annual appropriation of more than $2 billion and a staff of more than 22,000. Everything it does is classified. It monitors all electronic message traffic in the world. In 1973, the NSA reportedly retrieved more than 24 million individual communications including private, personal, and supposedly inviolable messages of ordinary Americans. **SOURCES:** *Penthouse*, November 1980, "Big Brother is Listening to You," by Harrison Salisbury; *The Progressive*, November 1980, "Somebody is Listening," by Loring Wirbell.

3. THE CONTINUING CENSORSHIP OF THE NUCLEAR ISSUE.

Three Mile Island (TMI), the worst accident in the history of the U.S. commercial nuclear energy program, proved to be a blessing for pro-nuclear propagandists. Using the catch phrase "no one died at TMI," they embarked on a slick nationwide campaign to resell nuclear power to the American public. Meanwhile, more than a half-dozen nuclear-oriented stories were nominated for "best censored" of 1980. **SOURCES:** *Harrowsmith*, June 1980, "The Silent Toll," by Thomas Pawlic; *In These Times*, November 19–25, 1980, "Uranium Rush Threatens New Jersey," by Ann Spanel; *Pacific News Service*, July 2, 1980, "Underground Tests Every Three Weeks," by Norman Solomon; *New York Times*, July 14, 1980, "2,300 Incidents Reported At Nuclear Plants in 1979," Associated Press.

4. THE BENDECTIN COVER-UP.

Richardson-Merrell Inc., the company that brought us thalidomide, has now produced another drug charged with causing birth defects: Bendectin. Numerous reports of birth defects suspected to be linked to Bendectin have been largely ignored and unreported. **SOURCES:** *Mother Jones*, November 1980, "The Bendectin Cover-Up," by Mark Dowie and Carolyn Marshall; *Science*, October 31, 1980, "How Safe is Bendectin?" by Gina Bari Kolata.

5. SOMETHING IS ROTTEN IN THE GLOBAL SUPERMARKET.

While modern technology has increased worldwide food production and raised per capita income, millions of landless peasants in Third World countries face starvation and malnutrition. Prime agricultural lands in Third World countries have increasingly been converted from subsistence crops to cash-generating export crops by vast transnational agribusiness firms. **SOURCE:** *The Nation*, February 9, 1980, "The Profits of Hunger," Richard J. Barnet.

6. THE CIRCLE OF POISON.

Banned pesticides are regularly exported from the industrial countries to the Third World. From 50 to 70 percent of the chemicals are used not to grow food for the hungry, but to grow luxury crops like coffee and bananas destined for the United States and Europe. **SOURCE:** *The Nation*, November 15, 1980, "The Circle of Poison," by David Weir and Mark Shapiro.

7. SPACE WARS.

Russia and the United States are locked into a race of time and technology to place super-sophisticated anti-satellite weapons in orbit above the earth. The technology would make a pre-emptive first strike feasible and make technological parity between the superpowers absolutely imperative. **SOURCES:** *New West*, April 21, 1980, "Space Wars," by

Jacques Gauchey; *Mother Jones*, August 1980, "No Need for Star Wars"; *Inquiry*, September 1, 1980, "Laser-Rattling in Outer Space," by David Ritchie; *Space For All People*, Newsletter for Citizens for Space Demilitarization, 1980 issues.

8. TOBACCO COMPANIES CENSOR THE TRUTH ABOUT CIGARETTES AND CANCER.

The American tobacco industry uses its substantial advertising revenue to discourage magazines from publishing stories on the health hazards of cigarette smoking. A *Columbia Journalism Review* survey over a seven-year period reported a "striking and disturbing" pattern that "advertising revenues can indeed silence the editors of American magazines." **SOURCES:** *ACSH News & Views*, February 1980, "Conspiracy of Silence?" by Beverly Mosher and Margaret J. Sheridan; ACSH press release, San Francisco, January 29, 1980, "New Report Says Tobacco Industry Uses Ad Revenue to Discourage Anti-smoking Magazine Stories."

9. THE OIL COMPANIES' MONOPOLY ON THE SUN.

Within the last five years, a powerful elite of multinational oil companies, aerospace firms, utilities, and other large corporations has been quietly buying into the solar industry. The group's aim appears to be to squeeze out smaller competitors and to control development so that alternative energy sources will never threaten its massive investments in fossil fuels and nuclear power. **SOURCES:** *New West*, August 11, 1980; *Mother Jones*, September/October 1980.

10. POISONED WATER, POISONED LAND.

Each year some 78 billion pounds of poisonous chemicals are dumped into 51,000 sites throughout the country where they can then enter the underground water supply. Many of these mixtures are lethal on contact, many are carcinogenic, and many can last in the environment for up to 100 years. Despite the enormity of this problem, the EPA has failed to monitor where the toxic wastes go. **SOURCES:** *Penthouse*, May 1980, "Poisoned Water," by Michael H. Browne; *The Progressive*, July 1980, "Poisoned Land," by Barry Jacobs.

THE TOP TEN CENSORED STORIES OF 1981

1. THE REAL STORY BEHIND OUR ECONOMIC CRISIS.

Testifying before the California Senate Committee on Industrial Relations, a UCLA professor, Maurice Zeitlin, stated that one basic cause of the worst economic crisis since the depression is that we no longer have a competitive economy, and that monopoly, militarism, and multinationalization are at the root of our economic crisis. **SOURCE:** *Voice*, January 1981, testimony by UCLA Professor Maurice Zeitlin, California Senate Committee on Industrial Relations, December 9, 1980.

2. INJUSTICE AT GREENSBORO AFTER KKK AND NAZI ATTACK.

One of the most flagrant miscarriages of justice in American civil rights history almost went unnoticed when, on November 3, 1979, members of the Ku

Klux Klan and the American Nazi Party murdered five Communist Workers Party demonstrators on the streets of Greensboro, North Carolina and the alleged murderers were acquitted. It was not until March 8, 1982, that the Justice Department impaneled a federal grand jury to hear evidence about the deaths of the five demonstrators. **SOURCES:** *The Institute for Southern Studies*, 1981, "The Third of November"; *Organizing Notes*, November/December 1981, "Greensboro, North Carolina: Two Years and No Closer to Justice."

3. BURYING AMERICA IN RADIOACTIVE WASTE.

Radioactive waste is accumulating daily throughout the United States and the government doesn't seem to know what to do with it. Radioactive trash is being dumped into our oceans—including prime fishing areas. Waste from atomic weapons production accounts for half the radioactivity as well as more than 90 percent of the volume of nuclear waste in the United States. **SOURCES:** *Mother Jones*, July 1981, "You Are What They Eat," by Douglas Foster; *Christian Science Monitor*, December 28, 1981, "Military's A-Waste—A Growing Problem," by Brad Knickerbocker: *This World, San Francisco Chronicle*, February 7, 1982, "Bury the Nuclear Dream," by Daniel Deudney; *Mother Jones*, January 1981, "Taking Apart Your Neighborhood Nuke," by John Ross.

4. A HUNGRY CHILD DIED EVERY TWO SECONDS IN 1981.

An estimated 50 million people quietly starve to death each year. In addition, according to a UN report released in 1980, more than one-half billion people —one out of every nine human beings —are severely malnourished. **SOURCE:** *Senior Scholastic*, October 16, 1981, "Earth's Hungry Millions," by Peter M. Jones.

5. OUR WATER IS RUNNING OUT AND WHAT'S LEFT IS BEING POISONED.

The country's water supply, once thought to be unlimited, is disappearing. Reservoirs across the United States are below capacity, and water levels are falling drastically in what is considered the world's largest freshwater underground reservoir, the Midwest's Ogalla aquifer. Meanwhile, the nation's remaining water is increasingly threatened by chemical contamination. The major villains are dangerous solvents and compounds released by industries. **SOURCES:** *The Progressive*, July 1981, "Wringing America Dry," by John Opie, and "Making Deserts Bloom," by Robert L. Reid; *National Wildlife Federation*, April 1981, "How Safe is the Water We Drink?" by Marvin A. Zeldin.

6. TRAINING TERRORISTS IN FLORIDA.

Guerrilla training camps are openly operating in Florida with the knowledge of the federal government. The activities appear to violate a number of federal laws that prohibit any organized attempt by private citizens to overthrow or undermine another government. **SOURCE:** *Pacifica National News Service*, Los Angeles, California, September 9, 1981, "The Miami Connection," by Ronnie Loveller.

7. THE INSANITY OF NUCLEAR WEAPONS.
Few Americans were informed about the true hazards of nuclear weapons. Several "censored" stories detail near-disastrous occurrences during 1981 including the accidental near-nuking of Scotland. **SOURCES:** *New Statesman*, November 27, 1981, "Accidents Will Happen," by Norman Solomon and Duncan Campbell; *Inquiry*, October 5, 1981, "Bombs Awry," by Fred Kaplan; *San Francisco Chronicle*, September 6, 1981, "How U.S. Spread Nuclear Power Around the World," by Howard Jaffe; *New West*, April 1981, "Where the Bombs Are," by David E. Kaplan; *Science*, May 22, 1981, "New A-bomb Studies Alter Radiation Estimates," by Eliot Marshal; *Washington Monthly*, January 1981, "Another A-bomb Cover-up," by Raymond E. Brim and Patricia Condon.

8. UNION BUSTING WITH BRIEFCASES NOT BLACKJACKS.
Companies are hiring a new breed of union busters known as labor relations consultants, most of them with advanced degrees in psychology, business, or industrial relations, whose sole intent is to prevent union organizing and to eliminate existing unions. **SOURCES:** *National Catholic Reporter*, April 17, 1981, "Congress, Labor Board Reports Blast 'Anti-Union' Consulting Firms"; *The Nation*, June 13, 1981, "Secrets of a Union Buster"; both by Kinsey Wilson and Steve Askin.

9. DEFENSE VULNERABILITY AND THE HIGH COST OF WHISTLE-BLOWING.
The central nervous system of America's military machine is a data processing network called Wimex. Unfortunately, this mighty communications system does not work. In 1973, John Bradley, an engineer originally charged with testing the Wimex prototype, discovered the problem. Since then he has been trying to convince people that the computers controlling the defense of the nation are dangerous, faulty, and may, in fact, trigger a holocaust. For his efforts, he was criticized, then transferred, and later fired. Then on March 8, 1982, the House Government Operations Committee substantiated his claims. **SOURCES:** *Inquiry*, September 1981, "The High Cost of Whistle-Blowing," by Rhonda Brown and Paul Matteucci; *San Francisco Examiner*, March 9, 1982, "Our Feeble Missile Attack Warning System."

10. CULTURED KILLERS—BIOLOGICAL WEAPONS AND THIRD WORLD TARGETS.
Biological warfare (BW) research was banned in 1969 due to public pressure. Existing BW stocks were to be destroyed and further research confined to "defensive purposes." Yet, in 1975, it was learned that a CIA project still maintained BW stocks at Fort Detrick, Maryland, with covert connections to "specific assassination plans." Source: *Science for the People*, July 1981, by A. Conadera.

THE TOP TEN CENSORED STORIES OF 1982

1. FRAUDULENT TESTING PROVIDES AN ILLUSION OF SAFETY.
Industrial Bio-Test (IBT), the largest testing lab in the country, conducted about one-third of the toxicity and cancer testing of chemicals in America. Its clients

included Proctor and Gamble, Armour, Upjohn, Dow, 3M, the Army, Department of Defense (DOD), the EPA, the FDA, and the WHO. In 1981, the former president of IBT and three ex-subordinates were indicted for allegedly fraudulent tests. Meanwhile, a major investigation by *Mother Jones* and the Center for Investigative Reporting into testing laboratories, standard-setting boards, and regulatory agencies that oversee the science of testing for safety, revealed that much of the research aimed at ensuring a safer world is either fraudulent or useless. **SOURCES:** *Focus/Midwest*, September 1982, "Testing Fraud," by Judith and Mark Miller; *Mother Jones* and the Center for Investigative Reporting, 1982, "The Illusion of Safety," by Mark Dowie, Douglas Foster, Carolyn Marshall, David Weir, and Jonathan King.

2. AMERICANS "BUGGED" BY SUPER-SECRET SPY COURT.

Unbeknownst to most Americans, there is a super-secret spy court in Washington, D.C.—the U.S. Foreign Intelligence Surveillance Court. It passes judgment on intelligence agency requests to spy on Americans in this country. The court's record is remarkable. Through 1981, it heard a total of 962 requests; it has issued 962 orders allowing electronic surveillance. **SOURCES:** *San Francisco Examiner*, October 24, 1982, "America's Super-Secret Spy Court," by Laurence McQuillan.

3. IS THIS THE END OF EQUAL OPPORTUNITY IN AMERICA?

The federal machinery for the protection of equal opportunity was almost totally destroyed. The Reagan administration has stripped away the traditional role of government in protecting the rights of disenfranchised citizens. **SOURCES:** *Equal Opportunity Forum*, January 1982, by Max Benavidez; *Labor Notes*, December 21, 1982, "Reagan Administration Dismantles Equal Opportunity Enforcement."

4. AGENT WHITE: THE SUPER AGENT ORANGE.

Residents of Cherokee County, North Carolina, believe that the herbicide picloram, known as "Agent White" in Viet Nam and stronger than Agent Orange, liberally applied to forest and farmland from one end of Cherokee to the other for as long as anyone can remember, is poisoning groundwater supplies. In 1976, less than one in seven people died in Cherokee from cancer, a figure below the national average. By 1979, nearly one in four died of cancer countywide—60 percent above the nation's average and nearly double the state average. **SOURCE:** *Inquiry*, March 15, 1982, "Agent White: It Kills Weeds, Bushes, Trees—and Maybe People," by Keith Schneider.

5. WHAT IS REALLY HAPPENING IN CENTRAL AMERICA?

The paradoxical media reports on El Salvador and the Nicaragua/Honduras situation have made it virtually impossible to ascertain what is really going on. But while the media reports from El Salvador, Nicaragua, and Honduras might be limited and often incomprehensible, we hear even less from Guatemala, where the situation may be even worse.

SOURCES: *Four Arrows: The Horror and the Hope* and various news sources.

6. RONALD REAGAN: AMERICA'S CHIEF CENSOR.

The Reagan administration has taken actions that increase the authority of government officials to classify data, cut back on the collection of statistics, eliminate hundreds of government publications, and reduce the staff of the National Archives. Furthermore, Reagan has tried to weaken the Freedom of Information Act although countless citizens regularly used the act to demand disclosures that benefit the lives of all Americans. SOURCES: *New York Times*, November 14, 1982, "Government Restricting Flow of Information to the Public," by David Burnham; *Columbia Journalism Review*, March/April 1983, "Keeping Government Honest"; *Organizing Notes*, May 1982, "Government Secrecy," by Maureen Weaver.

7. THE UNITED STATES AGAINST THE WORLD ON NUCLEAR ISSUES.

The United Nations General Assembly passed three resolutions concerning nuclear weapons and world peace. On all three, the United States was the lone dissenting vote. SOURCE: *New York Times*, December 10, 1982, "U.N., in 3 Votes, Asks Ban on Nuclear Arms Tests," by Eric Pace.

8. AMERICAN INDUSTRIALISTS TRADED WITH THE NAZIS.

Some of America's largest corporations collaborated with Nazi Germany during World War II. Such industrial and financial giants as DuPont, Rockefeller, Ford, Chase Manhattan Bank, ITT, General Motors, and Standard Oil collaborated with the Nazis either for monetary gain or because they were Nazi sympathizers hoping for a German victory. SOURCE: *Trading with the Enemy: An Exposé of the Nazi-Money 1933-1949*, by Charles Higham (New York: Delacorte Publishing, 1982); *San Francisco Chronicle*, February 9, 1983, review by Carl Vogel.

9. POLITICIANS AND FERTILIZERS THREATEN NATION'S FOOD SUPPLY.

The Congressional GAO predicted a food crisis that may dramatically overshadow the energy crisis over the next decade. President Reagan responded to this pessimistic forecast by encouraging America's farmers to take a record 82.3 million acres out of production. Meanwhile, 70 percent of the recommended fertilizers used by commercial farmers are useless. SOURCES: *The New Farm*, January-September 1982, "Testing... Testing" by George DeVault; *San Francisco Chronicle*, March 23, 1983, "One-Third of Farmland to Lie Idle."

10. TOXIC WASTE FIRMS TARGET INDIAN RESERVATIONS.

Corporate America wants Native American land for "chemical residual management facilities"—a trade term for toxic waste dumps. American Indian lands are attractive because they appear easily attainable to corporate boards as tribes begin suffering from recent cutbacks in federal funding. Also, the issue of tribal sovereignty can be used to corporate advantage. It is expected that monitoring and enforcing environmental laws would be much more difficult than on non-Indian land. **SOURCES:** *Native Self-Sufficiency*, May 1982, published by the Tribal Sovereignty Program, edited by Paula Hammett.

THE TOP TEN CENSORED STORIES OF 1983

1. ISRAEL: MERCHANT OF DEATH IN CENTRAL AMERICA.

President Reagan's policy objectives in Central America circumvent congressional objections with quiet help from Israel. Israel, now the fifth biggest exporter of arms in the world, is the largest supplier of weapons to Latin America. It is also a major source of training in intelligence and counter-insurgency techniques. **SOURCES:** *Covert Action Information Bulletin*, Winter 1984, "Israeli Arms in Central America," by Clarence Lusane; *New York Times*, December 17, 1982, "Israel Stepping Up Arms Sales to Central America," by Leslie H. Gelb.

2. THE U.S. NEVER DROPPED OUT OF THE ARMS RACE.

President Reagan contended that the United States needed to launch a massive military buildup to counter decades of stagnation and inactivity in the area of weapons development. Yet actions taken since the late 1960s make it clear that the United States has never fallen behind the Soviet Union in the arms race, and in fact led the race in most sectors. **SOURCE:** *Washington Post National Weekly Edition*, December 12, 1983, "We Never Dropped Out of the Arms Race," by Thomas J. Downey.

3. DETAILED SOVIET UNION NUCLEAR FREEZE PROPOSAL IGNORED BY THE UNITED STATES.

Following arms control talks, President Reagan consistently vilified Soviet Union representatives. The U.S. press provided front-page coverage of the Soviet military posture, yet a detailed proposal by the U.S.S.R. to remove the threat of nuclear war went virtually unreported. **SOURCE:** *Soviet Life Magazine*, December 1983.

4. AMERICA'S AGRICULTURAL DISASTER OF 1983—A PIK IN A POKE.

A new federal program called Payment In Kind, or PIK, was designed to reduce surpluses by giving farmers government-owned surplus crops which they can then sell in return for leaving their own croplands idle. The PIK program created a major national agricultural disaster, yet PIK is being touted as "one of the most successful farm programs in agriculture's history" and it appears it will be repeated in 1984. **SOURCES:** *The New Farm*, November 1983, "A PIK in a Poke," by Rodney Leonard; *Washington Post National Weekly Edition*, November 21, 1983, "Grain Trades and Conglomerates Benefit from PIK," by Ward Sinclair.

5. KAL 007 AND 269 INNOCENT PAWNS IN U.S.–U.S.S.R. SPY WAR.

On September 1, 1983, a Soviet jet shot down Korean Air Lines flight 007. It is now known that Korean Air Lines planes regularly fly over Soviet airspace to gather military intelligence. Some foreign government-owned airliners are regularly fitted in the United States with cameras and other devices for intelligence collection. **SOURCES:** *San Francisco Examiner*, September 4, 1983, "Aviation Experts Don't Rule Out Possibility KAL Jet Was Spying," by Knut Royce; *Denver Post*, September 13, 1983, "U.S. Spy Plane Capable of Interceding in Attack on Korean Jet," by Tom Bernard and T. Edward Eskelson; *The Progressive*, October 1983, "Collision Course"; *The Guardian* (London), December 17, 1983, "KAL 007: Unanswered Questions," by R.W. Johnson (reprinted in *World Press Review*, March 1984).

6. JOURNALIST CHALLENGES PRESS COVERAGE OF CENTRAL AMERICA.

We are still not getting the full story of what is happening in Central America. There are a variety of explanations for this, not the least of which is the intimidation and assassination of journalists. In addition, misinformation is regularly disseminated by our own State Department. **SOURCES:** *Billings Gazette*, August 31, September 4, 18, and 25, 1983, "Another Side of the Fight," by Peter D. Fox; *Columbia Journalism Review*, November 1983, "About-face on El Salvador," by Michael Massing; *Ithaca Times*, December 1, 1983, "A Conversion Story," by John E. Milich.

7. U.S. MEDIA NEGLECT SOUTH AFRICA POLITICS.

The U.S. media provided little coverage of Nelson Mandela's heroic fight against the apartheid regime in South Africa. Despite international condemnation of South Africa's racist policies, some 600 North American companies continued to do business with South Africa. U.S. investments there were estimated at $10 billion. **SOURCES:** *i.d.a.f. News Notes*, U.S. Committee of the International Defense and Aid Fund for South Africa, October 1983; *Daily World*, September 15, 1983, "South Africa, Poland, and the U.S. Press," by Tafataona P. Mahoso; *Washington Post National Weekly Edition*, March 26, 1984, "South Africa's Capital Connections," by Rick Atkinson.

8. THE CENSORED SAFETY RECORD OF THE U.S. NUCLEAR NAVY.

Since the 1950s, the U.S. Navy has testified annually before Congress that there has never been an accident involving a naval nuclear reactor, or any release of radioactivity that would significantly affect individuals or the environment. That statement stands in sharp contrast to a published list documenting 126 accidents involving nuclear-powered vessels. **SOURCE:** *Oceans Magazine*, July 1983, "When Incidents are Accidents: The Silent Saga of the Nuclear Navy," by David Kaplan.

9. DNA: U.S. KEY TO BIOLOGICAL WARFARE?

President Richard Nixon pledged we would never develop or use biological weapons and in 1972 signed the Convention on the Prohibition of the Development, Production, and Stockpiling of Bacteriological and Toxin Weapons. Yet over the years, under the guise of "defensive" research, the DOD has sponsored a broad program of studies involving the latest techniques of genetic engineering. **SOURCE:** *The Nation*, December 10, 1983,

"DNA—Key to Biological Warfare," by Charles Piller.

10. THE DEPARTMENT OF DEFENSE'S COST-PLUS CONTRACTING SYSTEM TAXPAYER SWINDLE.

The United States has a federal contracting system that encourages overruns, inefficiency, and fraud. Rockwell International, one of the nation's largest space and defense contractors, fired at least two employees for reporting contract fraud to NASA's Inspector General. **SOURCE:** *Common Cause*, March 1983, "Whistleblower!" by John Hanrahan.

THE TOP TEN CENSORED STORIES OF 1984

1. THE WELL-PUBLICIZED SOVIET MILITARY BUILD-UP SCARE WAS A LIE.

U.S. and military leaders lied about the Soviet arms build-up and falsified information in order to inflate Soviet military expenditures. By instilling fear in the American public, they hoped to realize higher military budgets. **SOURCES:** *Defense Monitor*, Vol. XII, #4, 1984, "Taking Stock: The U.S. Military Build-Up"; *Aviation Week & Space Technology*, February 13, 1984, "Soviet Defense Spending," by William H. Gregory.

2. REAGAN'S ATTACKS ON CIVIL LIBERTIES.

Four antiterrorist bills sponsored by President Reagan under the guise of fighting sabotage and assassination, criminalize domestic opposition to U.S. intervention in the Third World and authorize the FBI to investigate legal political activity. Two of the bills (HR5613 and S2626) make American citizens liable to criminal penalties for exercising their constitutional rights under the First Amendment. **SOURCES:** *Guardian*, July 25, 1984, "If These Laws Pass, Watch Out," and August 22, 1984, "FBI 'Terrorizes' the Solidarity Movement," by Eleanor Stein and Michael Ratner; *Wall Street Journal*, April 27, 1984, "White House Seeks to Broaden Authority to Thwart Growing Terrorism Threat."

3. NICARAGUA: FAIR ELECTIONS VERSUS AN UNFAIR PRESS.

Contrary to U.S. media predictions, the 1984 Nicaraguan national elections were not rigged by the ruling Sandinistas, nor were they the rubber-stamp of Soviet Communism. In fact, the elections were a model of fairness with the Nicaraguans choosing a "proportional representation" form of democracy based on Western European models. **SOURCE:** *Christianity and Crisis*, December 24, 1984, "What Really Happened on November 4?" by Andrew Reding.

4. CIA AND THE DEATH SQUADS— IMMORAL AND ILLEGAL.

A paramilitary apparatus was responsible for the deaths of thousands of Salvadoran leftists and peasants. The CIA continued to train, support, and provide intelligence to forces directly involved in Death Squad activities in violation of the Foreign Assistance Act of 1974. **SOURCE:** *The Progressive*, May 1984, "An Exclusive Report on the U.S. Role in El Salvador's Official Terror: Behind the Death Squads," by Allan Nairn.

5. WORST RADIATION SPILL IN NORTH AMERICA IS IGNORED.

A radioactive part from a discarded radiation therapy machine wreaked havoc throughout Mexico as it was sold and transported to various parties from Texas to Juarez. Sixty junkyard employees and an estimated 200 citizens of Juarez are expected to die or display symptoms of cancer or leukemia within the next few years. **SOURCES:** *Science*, March 16, 1984, "Juarez: An Unprecedented Radiation Accident," by Eliot Marshall; *Guardian*, June 20, 1984, "'Worst Radiation Spill in North America' Still Spreading," by Robby Newton and Ellen Kahaner.

6. THE RED-HERRING OF "LEFT-WING" TERRORISM.

The United States has attacked "left-wing" terrorism while supporting "right-wing" terrorism as a means of fighting communism. All terrorism should be a target of all nations concerned with democracy and human rights. Source: *Covert Action Information Bulletin*, Fall 1984, "The Fascist Network," by Edward S. Herman.

7. DEATH OF A NATION: THE TRAGEDY OF TRANSKEI.

The white minority government in Pretoria created the "independent" black state of Transkei as part of its apartheid policy. Transkei is a virtual wasteland, incapable of sustaining its burgeoning population. Blacks are being deported there by the tens of thousands yearly where they face a bleak future. **SOURCES:** *Christian Science Monitor*, April 3, 1984, "South African Blacks Struggle for Survival in Winter Recession," and April 30, 1984, "South African Relief Groups Find Better Ways to Combat Hunger," both by Paul Van Slambrouck; *New Statesman*, August 19, 1984, "South Africa: Drying Out," by Philip Willan; *U.S. News & World Report*, July 28, 1980, "Transkei: A Nation Only On the Map," August 22, 1983, "Another Deadly Famine Stalks Black Africa," both by Robin Knight.

8. ORWELL'S 1984 ARRIVED WHILE THE PRESS SLEPT.

The Reagan administration successfully implemented the largest censoring apparatus ever known in the United States, the National Security Directive-84. **SOURCES:** *Bill of Rights Journal*, December 1984, "They've Got a Secret," by Angus Mackenzie; *New York Times*, December 28, 1984, "Censorship of Its Employees Would Harm Government," by Thomas Ehrlich.

9. THREE STORIES THAT MIGHT HAVE CHANGED THE 1984 ELECTION.

Three potentially explosive political stories about Reagan cronies made available to America's press might have changed the results of the 1984 election if they had been published: the possible links to illegal activities and questionable practices of potential appointee, Paul Laxalt; the covert actions of Edwin Meese (later U.S. Attorney General) to undermine California's anti-war movement; and the suppression by the White House of a news story about the questionable business activities of Reagan's major political contributor, Charles Wick. **SOURCES:** *Mother Jones*, August

1984, "Senator Paul Laxalt, The Man Who Runs the Reagan Campaign," by Robert I. Friedman; *The Nation*, July 24, 1982, "The Senator and the Gamblers," by Bob Gottlieb and Peter Wiley; *Village Voice*, March 12, 1985, "Networks Knuckle Under to Laxalt: The Story That Never Was Aired," by Robert I. Friedman and Dan E. Moldea, *Village Voice*, February 26, 1985, "From the Man Who Brought You SWAT: Return of the Night of the Animals," by James Ridgeway; *San Francisco Bay Guardian*, February 20, 1985, "Meese Acknowledges Counter-Insurgency Role," by Paul Rauber, *Mother Jones*, November 1984, "What the Senate Didn't Know About Charles Z. Wick," by Seth Rosenfeld and Mark Shapiro.

10. MYTH OF THE PEACEFUL ATOM— UNITED STATES AND UNITED KINGDOM BREAK NUCLEAR TREATY.

The Nuclear Non-Proliferation Treaty calls for a clear distinction between civilian and military nuclear technologies. Still, nearly seven tons of plutonium from civilian reactors in Great Britain have been shipped to the United States for use in the manufacture of nuclear weapons. **SOURCES:** *Sanity*, November 1984, "Plutonium Lies"; and press releases, correspondence, and articles which appeared in British publications during 1984 (including *Daily Telegraph, New Scientist, The Guardian, Financial Times, New Statesman, New Society*, and *Nuclear Engineering International*) from Mr. David Lowry, Researcher, Energy Research Group, The Open University, Milton Keynes, England.

THE TOP TEN CENSORED STORIES OF 1985

1. FIERCEST AERIAL WAR IN AMERICA IS UNREPORTED IN U.S. PRESS.

While the President of El Salvador boasted about the decline in death squad killings, the people of El Salvador were victims of the most intense saturation bombing ever conducted in the Americas. U.S. military leaders often directed the missions and the bombs were supplied by the United States. More than one-fifth of the Salvadoran population of five million became refugees—a higher percentage than South Vietnam at the height of the Vietnam War. **SOURCES:** *The Nation*, June 1, 1985, "Remember El Salvador?", by Alexander Cockburn; *Refugee Legal Services*, Laredo, Texas, January 24, 1986, letter from Patrick M. Hughes, Director.

2. MILITARY TOXIC WASTE: MORE DANGEROUS AND NOT REGULATED.

While we are now becoming aware of the legacy of thousands of poisonous industrial waste sites, we haven't been told about the hundreds, perhaps thousands, of potentially more dangerous *military* toxic waste sites. There are two major differences between military and industrial waste. The military problem includes exposure to many different forms of radiation, weapon tests, and dangerous, obsolete weapons whose disposal poses a nearly insoluble problem, and they are not subject to the EPA regulations which govern industrial waste procedures. **SOURCE:** *Recon*, Winter 1986, "Pentagon Dumps Toxics On All of Us," by Will Collette.

3. STILL UNREPORTED: TEN YEARS OF GENOCIDE IN EAST TIMOR.

Amnesty International estimates that since 1975 up to 200,000 East Timorese, one-third of the population, have died as a result of Indonesian aggression. This tragedy still goes unreported by the American press. **SOURCE:** *Amnesty Action*, Summer 1985, "East Timor: A Decade of Killing, Torture, and Indonesian Claims of 'Normality.'"

4. THE REAGAN AUTOCRACY.

In 1982, President Reagan signed Executive Order 12291, setting up a framework for presidential management of the rule-making process. Under this order, the White House can nullify acts of Congress that the President considers too costly, in violation of the doctrine of separation of powers. Since then, the president has signed several executive orders that increase the power of the presidency and undermine the power of the law, the courts, Congress, and the people. **SOURCE:** *Harper's*, November 1985, "Liberty Under Siege," by Walter Karp.

5. MEDIA MERGER MANIA THREATENS FREE FLOW OF INFORMATION.

The drive for profits, coupled with the weakening of the Federal Communications Commission (FCC), paved the way for the specter of an international information cartel. As the FCC relaxed its rules on ownership and public service obligations, media firms bought and/or merged. **SOURCES:** *The Nation*, June 8, 1985, "Behind the Media Merger Movement," by Herbert Schiller; *San Francisco Chronicle*, December 23, 1985, "For Big Brother, It Was a Very Good Year," by Tom Shales, Washington Post Writers Group.

6. THE BIRTH DEFECT CRISIS AND THE ENVIRONMENT.

Conservative statistics reveal that 12 of every 100 babies born in the United States this year will have a serious, often incurable mental or physical health disorder. Recent studies have directly linked specific environmental and chemical agents to some of the defects that are increasing. **SOURCE:** *Mother Jones*, January 1985, "Terata," by Christopher Norwood, and "Manhattan Project for the Unborn," by Mark Dowie.

7. ADMINISTRATION RELEASES PHONY "STAR WARS" TEST RESULTS.

Officials of the Reagan administration reportedly covered up scientific failures with the "Star Wars" project in an effort to sell the program to a skeptical American public. While scientists working on the project were not allowed to talk to the press about test failures, administration officials did talk about successful test results. **SOURCES:** *New York Times*, December 4, 1985, "A 'Star Wars' Cover-Up?" by Flora Lewis; *In These Times*, November 6, 1985, "Scientists say no to Star Wars," by David Moberg.

8. THE DOOMSDAY COMMUNICATIONS SYSTEM.

The Ground Wave Emergency Network (GWEN) is a super-secret communications system designed to enable political and military leaders to establish and maintain communications during an extended nuclear war. **SOURCES:** *Recon*, Winter 1986, "National No-GWEN Alliance," by Lois Barber; *Physics and Society*, July 1985, "Estimating Vulnerability to Electromagnetic Pulse Effects," by John M. Richardson.

9. FEDERAL GOVERNMENT RIPS OFF THE HOMELESS.

The Homeless Task Force was to provide federal resources to the homeless by making "sharing agreements" with other federal agencies. A subcommittee of the House Committee on Government Operations released a 1985 study on homelessness. Few of the agreements actually provided relief to the homeless, and in some cases funds were misappropriated. Source: Pacific News Service, December 20, 1985, "Washington's Foot-Dragging Role in Dealing With the Homeless," by Polly Leider.

10. HIGH-TECH HEALTH HAZARDS: A NEW AMERICAN NIGHTMARE?

According to California labor statistics: "Poisonings are twice as common among semiconductor workers as they are among employees in other industries... and work-related illnesses occur three and one-half times more frequently in the semi-conductor industry than in manufacturing as a whole." Other high-tech health problems include respiratory disease, occupational asthma, chemical sensitization, hypertension, radiation hazards, reproductive problems, and cancer. Since 1980, cutbacks in OSHA funding and reductions in inspections have already worsened health matters in high-tech

fields. **SOURCES:** *The Progressive*, October 1985, "Dead End in Silicon Valley," by Diana Hembree; *Ms.* magazine, March 1986, "A New American Nightmare?" by Amanda Spake.

THE TOP TEN CENSORED STORIES OF 1986

1. CRITICIZING THE PRESIDENT'S POLICIES CAN BE DANGEROUS.

Political opponents of the Reagan administration's Central American policies became the targets of mysterious break-ins, IRS audits, FBI questioning, and physical surveillance. **SOURCES:** KRON-TV *"Target 4,"* February 18–20, 1987, "Heat on the Left" series, by anchor-reporter Sylvia Chase, producer Jonathan Dann, and Angus Mackenzie of the Center for Investigative Reporting; *San Francisco Examiner*, UPI, February 19, 1987, "Nicaragua Visitors: U.S. Harasses Us," by Neil Roland; *San Francisco Examiner*, March 13, 1987, "Info-Thieves Hit the Women's Building," by Warren Hinckle.

2. OFFICIAL U.S. CENSORSHIP: LESS ACCESS TO LESS INFORMATION.

Since 1980, the American Library Association has documented efforts by the Reagan administration to eliminate, restrict, and privatize government documents. The government also developed a new category of "sensitive information" to further restrict public access to a broad range of unclassified data. **SOURCE:** *American Library Association*, Washington Office, "Less Access to Less Information By and About the U.S. Government: II," December 1986.

3. PERSONAL PRIVACY ASSAULTED WITHOUT PUBLIC DEBATE.

In 1986, the Intelligence Authorization Bill for 1987, which was passed by Congress with little debate or press coverage, gave the FBI extraordinary powers to look into the most private files of Americans "suspected of being in the employ of a foreign power." Historically, this type of information was considered off-limits to government. **SOURCE:** *The National Reporter,* Fall/Winter 1986, "News Not In The News: Reach Out and Crush Someone," by Don Goldberg.

4. PRO CONTRA MEDIA COVERAGE— PAID FOR BY THE CIA.

Even though the CIA is prohibited from entering into "any paid or contractual relationship" with U.S. journalists, it has entered into such relationships with foreign journalists, even letting agency operatives pose as foreign reporters. Edgar Chamorro, former head of the Contra communications office, told the World Court that Honduran, Costa Rican, and Nicaraguan journalists were on the CIA payroll. **SOURCES:** *CovertAction Quarterly,* Summer 1986; *Columbia Journalism Review,* March/April 1987, "Contra Coverage—Paid For By The CIA," by Martha Honey.

5. PRESIDENT REAGAN AND THE FASCIST "WORLD ANTI-COMMUNIST LEAGUE."

President Ronald Reagan sent a congratulatory letter to The World Anti-Communist League (WACL)—described by one source as "largely a collection of Nazis, fascists, anti-Semites, sellers of forgeries, vicious racialists, and corrupt self-seekers." Members include Ferdinand Marcos, the Rev. Sun Myung Moon, and former OSS member U.S. Major General John Singlaub, retired. According to one exposé, the WACL is so extreme that the ultra-conservative John Birch Society shunned it and advised its members to do likewise. **SOURCES:** *UTNE Reader,* August/September 1986, "Moonies, Loonies, and Ronnie," by Eric Selbin; *Briarpatch,* November 1986, "In League with the Devil: The World Anti-Communist League," by George Martin Manz; *St. Louis Journalism Review,* March 1987, "Inside the League," by Scott and Jon Lee Anderson.

6. LETHAL NERVE GAS PRODUCTION IN RESIDENTIAL AREAS.

Although the military has been under orders from Congress since 1984 to dispose of nerve gases by 1994, the gases are currently being manufactured and tested in 46 U.S. communities in 26 states across the country—usually without the knowledge of residents. **SOURCES:** *Recon,* Winter 1987, "Nerve Gas in Residential Areas"; *New York Times,* February 28, 1985, "Research on Nerve Gas Suspended in Cambridge"; *USA Today,* March 11, 1987, "Risks Near Chemical Warfare Dumps Cited," by Wayne Beissert.

7. CONTRAGATE: THE COSTA RICA CONNECTION.

A $22 million lawsuit was brought against a group of U.S.-backed mercenaries operating in Miami and Central America with ties to Lt. Col. Oliver North and the Reagan administration. Alleged illegal activities included a conspiracy to murder contra leader Eden Pastora and the U.S. ambassador to Costa Rica, drug trafficking from Costa Rican contra air fields, a cover-up that included the torture and murder of a key journalistic source, and continued threats against the lives of the two veteran journalists who sought to expose the plot. **SOURCE:** *San Francisco Bay Guardian*, December 3, 1986, "Contragate: The Costa Rica Connection," and February 4, 1987, "Christic Institute Officials Detained in Costa Rica," both by Michael Emery.

8. U.S. AGENCIES CONDUCTED RADIATION TESTS ON HUMANS FOR 30 YEARS.

From the mid-1940s until the 1970s, federal agencies conducted heinous radiation exposure experiments on hundreds of people around the country. Some were reportedly volunteers, but for others there is no record of informed consent. A report on the testing was released by the House Energy and Commerce Subcommittee on October 24, 1986, but was not picked up by the media. **SOURCE:** *New York Times*, October 24, 1986, "Volunteers Around U.S. Submitted to Radiation."

9. IRRADIATED VETERANS: VA CAUGHT DESTROYING CLAIMS EVIDENCE.

In August 1986, the Veterans Administration (VA) was caught shredding thousands of case records of contested radiation injury claims. The shredding took place in spite of a federal court order placing all such records at the disposal of attorneys representing the injured veterans in a class-action suit.

SOURCE: *VVA Veteran*, November 1986, "Scandal Hints Plague VA"; January 1987, "The Scandal Deepens."

10. THE LETHAL PLUTONIUM SHUTTLE.

A space shuttle planned for launch in May 1986, was scheduled to carry an unmanned spacecraft fueled with 46.7 pounds of toxic plutonium-238. In case of an accident, the radiation that would be released "would be more than the combined plutonium radioactivity returned to earth in the fallout from all the nuclear weapons tests of the United States, the Soviet Union, and the United Kingdom." **SOURCE:** *The Nation*, February 22, 1986, "The Lethal Shuttle," and March 15, 1986, "Plutonium Cover-up?"; *Common Cause*, July/August 1986, "Red Tape and Radioactivity"; all by Karl Grossman.

THE TOP TEN CENSORED STORIES OF 1987

1. THE INFORMATION MONOPOLY.

The rapidly increasing centralization of media ownership raises critical questions about the public's access to a diversity of opinion. The prevailing corporate concern with the bottom line, coupled with traditional publishers' tendency to avoid controversy, fosters widespread self-censorship among writers, journalists, editors, and news directors. **SOURCES:** *EXTRA!*, June 1987, "The 26 Corporations That Own Our Media;" *Multinational Monitor*, September 1987, "The Media Brokers," both by Ben Bagdikian; *UTNE Reader*, January/February 1988, "Censorship in Publishing," by Lynette Lamb; *The Media Monopoly*, by Ben Bagdikian, Beacon Press, 1983.

2. THE UNITED STATES AND ITS CONTRA-DRUG CONNECTION.

Mounting evidence, with profound and alarming implications in terms of U.S. foreign policy and the Reagan administration's propriety, pointed to a large-scale Contra/CIA drug smuggling network. **SOURCES:** *The Christic Institute Special Report*, November 1987, "The Contra-Drug Connection," by The Christic Institute; *Newsday*, June 28, 1987, "Witness: Contras Got Drug Cash," by Knut Royce; *The Nation*, September 5, 1987, "How the Drug Czar Got Away," by Martin A. Lee; *In These Times*, April 15, 1987, "CIA, Contras Hooked on Drug Money," by Vince Bielski and Dennis Bernstein.

3. SECRET DOCUMENTS REVEAL DANGER OF WORLDWIDE NUCLEAR ACCIDENTS.

An NBC documentary on nuclear power failed to mention that NBC's owner, General Electric, is America's second largest nuclear power salesman and the third largest producer of nuclear weapons systems. Also unreported is the large number of nuclear accidents worldwide. This helps to explain the industry's undeserved reputation for safety. **SOURCES:** *Earth Island Journal*, Summer 1987, "Secret Documents Reveal Nuclear Accidents Worldwide," by Gar Smith with Hans Hollitscher; *EXTRA!*, June 1987, "Nuclear Broadcasting Company."

4. REAGAN'S MANIA FOR SECRECY: DECISIONS WITHOUT DEMOCRACY.

The Reagan administration is trying to control, interpret, manipulate, distort, and censor all forms of information the public might read about government decisions. Typical was the Department of Justice memorandum filed in a lawsuit that would have enabled Reagan to control the history of his involvement in the Iran/Contra scandal. **SOURCES:** *The Nation*, May 23, 1987, "History Deleted"; *Government Decisions Without Democracy*, December 1987, by People For the American Way; *FYI Media Alert 1987*, March 1987, "The Reagan administration & The News Media," by the Reporters' Committee for Freedom of the Press; *The American Library Association*, Washington Office, "Less Access to Less Information By and About the U.S. Government: IX," December 1987, by Anne A. Heanue.

5. BUSH'S PERSONAL AGENDA IN THE IRAN ARMS DEAL.

New evidence suggests that Vice President George Bush, far more than President Reagan, promoted the ill-fated secret arms shipments to Iran, took part in key negotiations, and conferred upon Oliver North the secret powers necessary to carry it out. It has also been charged that Bush actively promoted the Iran action for an economic motive—the desire to stabilize plunging oil prices. **SOURCES:** *Pacific News Service*, December 21, 1987, "Bush Had Oil Policy Interest in Promoting Iran Arms Deals," by Peter Dale Scott.

6. PENTAGON BIOWARFARE RESEARCH IN UNIVERSITY LABORATORIES.

The Reagan administration is pushing toward biowarfare. The research budget for infectious diseases and toxins increased tenfold since fiscal 1981. Most of the 1986 $42 million budget went to 24 U.S. university campuses where the world's most deadly organisms were being cultured in campus labs. When MIT's biology department voted to refuse Pentagon funds for biotech research, the Reagan administration forced it to reverse its decision. **SOURCES:** *Isthmus*, October 9, 1987, "Biowarfare and the UW," by Richard Jannaccio; *The Progressive*, November 16, 1987, "Poisons from the Pentagon," by Seth Shulman; *Wall Street Journal*, September 17, 1986, "Military Science," by Bill Richards and Tim Carrington.

7. BIASED COVERAGE OF THE ARIAS PEACE PLAN BY AMERICA'S PRESS.

Two separate studies monitoring U.S. press coverage of the five-country Arias Peace Plan revealed a startling bias in how America's leading newspapers covered the region following the historic pact. **SOURCES:** *San Francisco Bay Guardian*, January 6, 1988, "On Central America, U.S. Dailies Parrot Reagan Line," by Jeff Gillenkirk; *EXTRA!*, August/September 1987, "Media Put Reagan Spin on Arias Plan," by Jeff Cohen and Martin A. Lee.

8. DUMPING OUR TOXIC WASTES ON THE THIRD WORLD.

Traditionally, the majority of U.S. toxic waste exports have gone to Canada where regulations are less stringent than in the United States. However, there has been an abrupt increase in shipments to Third World countries where regulations are either nonexistent or loosely enforced. **SOURCES:** *The Nation*, October 3, 1987, "The Export of U.S. Toxic Wastes," by Andrew Porterfield and David Weir.

9. TORTURE IN EL SALVADOR: A CENSORED REPORT FROM MARIONA PRISON.

A report compiled by five imprisoned members of the Human Rights Commission of El Salvador was smuggled out of the Mariona men's prison. The report documented the routine use of torture on political prisoners in El Salvador. Three points were emphasized: the torture is systematic; the methods of torture are becoming more sophisticated; and torture is part of the U.S. counterinsurgency program there—with U.S. servicemen often acting as supervisors. **SOURCES:** *The Nation*, February 21, 1987, "After the Press Bus Left" and November 14, 1987, "The Press and the Plan," both by Alexander Cockburn; *San Francisco Examiner*, November 14, 1986, "In Prison, Salvador Rights Panel Works On," by Ron Ridenhour.

10. PROJECT GALILEO SHUTTLE TO CARRY LETHAL PLUTONIUM.

Despite scientific warnings of a possible disaster, NASA is pursuing plans to launch the Project Galileo shuttle space probe with enough plutonium on board to kill every person on earth. **SOURCE:** *The Nation*, January 23, 1988, "The Space Probe's Lethal Cargo," by Karl Grossman.

THE TOP TEN CENSORED STORIES OF 1988

1. GEORGE BUSH'S DIRTY BIG SECRETS.

Richard H. Meeker, president of the Association of Alternative Newsweeklies and publisher of *Willamette Week*, in Portland, Oregon, charges that if the average American voter had been reading the alternative press coverage of the 1988 election, George Bush would not have been elected president. Just 10 stories might have made a difference if the establishment press had bothered to investigate and report them with the same intensity as the alternative press. **SOURCES:** *San Francisco Bay Guardian*, November 2, 1988, "George Bush's Dirty Secrets," by Richard Meeker; *EXTRA!*, September/October 1988, "The GOP-Nazi Connection."

2. HOW THE EPA POLLUTES THE NEWS AND THE DIOXIN COVER-UP.

Reports of improvement in environmental pollution levels in 1988 were a deliberate attempt by the EPA to mislead and pacify the public. Equally disturbing, the news media has contributed to this disinformation campaign by treating EPA press releases as reliable news reports. **SOURCES:** *Columbia Journalism Review*, November/December 1988, "Dead Fish and Red Herrings: How the EPA Pollutes the News," by Jim Sibbison; *Greenpeace*, March/April 1989, "Whitewash: The Dioxin Cover-Up," by Peter Von Stackelberg.

3. PROJECT GALILEO: THE RISK OF A NUCLEAR DISASTER IN SPACE.

Despite the Challenger disaster, NASA plans to launch a shuttle on October 12, 1989, that will carry enough radioactive plutonium to kill every person on earth. NASA insists the risks of carrying the plutonium payload are minimal and that the possible scientific gains are substantial. But many scientists who are experts in the field of radioactivity are apprehensive. **SOURCES:** *The Long Island Monthly*, October 1988, "The Fire Next Time," by Karl Grossman; *EXTRA!*, September/October 1988, "Newsday Spikes Article on C*****ship," by Dennis Bernstein.

4. RADIOACTIVE WASTE AND THE DANGERS OF FOOD IRRADIATION.

Despite serious questions concerning effectiveness and consumer safety, the U.S. Department of Energy (DOE) plans to set up 1,000 food irradiation facilities around the country within the next 10 years. Research also indicates the evidence of somatic and genetic hazard from consuming irradiated foods is far greater than either the FDA or the proponents of irradiated foods are willing to admit. **SOURCES:** *The Workbook*, April/June 1988, "Food Irradiation: Its Environmental Threat, Its Toxic Connection," by Judith H. Johnsrud, Ph.D.; *Northern Sun News*, December 1988, "Update on Food Irradiation," by JoAnne Korkid.

5. ACID RAIN—ONE OF AMERICA'S BIGGEST KILLERS.

There is strong circumstantial evidence that acid rain is a significant threat to human health and lives. A study by Dr. Cedric Garland, Director of Cancer Epidemiology at the University of California at Berkeley, revealed a pattern of increased cancers occurring throughout the "acid rain belt" cutting across northeastern U.S. and eastern Canada. **SOURCE:** *Vanguard Press*, January 28, 1988, "Acid Rain Is Killing Five to 20 Times as Many Americans as AIDS," by Merritt Clifton.

6. AMERICA'S SECRET POLICE NETWORK—LEIU PART II.

The LEIU resurfaces 10 years later as we find that this secretive unofficial police intelligence organization is alive and well and more powerful than ever. It also is still virtually unknown. **SOURCES:** *Los Angeles Times*, June 24, 1988, "Intelligence Units Across U.S. Probe Alleged LAPD Leak," by William K. Knoedelseder, Jr., Kim Murphy, and Ronald L. Soble; *Penthouse*, December 1976, "America's Secret Police Network," by George O'Toole.

7. CHILDREN ARE PAYING THE THIRD WORLD DEBT WITH THEIR LIVES.

UNICEF Executive Director James Grant called for a world summit to save an estimated 3 million children who he said die each year from easily preventable diseases. More than 500,000 of those children died in 16 developing nations in 1987 because their debt-burdened governments had to cut back on social spending. **SOURCES:** *San Francisco Examiner*, December 21, 1988, "Children Hardest Hit By Resurgence of Global Poverty," by John Madeley, of the *London Observer*; *USA Today*, December 21, 1988, "World's Children Pay Debt With Their Lives," by Marilyn Greene.

8. A CONSTITUTIONAL CONVENTION IS JUST TWO VOTES AWAY.

There is a little-known, but potentially explosive and dedicated effort underway to call a constitutional convention to amend the U.S. Constitution. While some changes may be worthy, opponents worry that extreme changes could be made since there are no legal restrictions on what such a convention could do. **SOURCES:** *The Economist*, May 21, 1988, "The Constitution: Lid On to Keep the Worms Out"; *USA Today*, March 3, 1989, "Debate: We Shouldn't Tinker with Constitution."

9. UNITED STATES REFUSES TO ABIDE BY INTERNATIONAL COURT OF JUSTICE.

The World Court of the United Nations, also known as the International Court of Justice, passed down a ruling finding the United States in violation of international law as a result of the Reagan administration's support of the Contra war effort. **SOURCES:** *Los Angeles Times*, September 25, 1988, "U.S. Snub of World Court Won't Avert Day of Reckoning," op-ed article by Howard N. Meyer; *Congressional Record*, October 21, 1988, "The World Court," by Hon. Ted Weiss; *Our Right To Know*, Summer 1988, "The World Court and Nicaragua," by Howard N. Meyer.

10. THE ABUSE OF AMERICA'S INCARCERATED CHILDREN.

On any given day, there are an average of 2.5 million children of both sexes between the ages of five and nineteen years incarcerated in America's juvenile detention facilities. Of that number, more than 1.2 million are sexually abused by their peers. Nearly 150,000 more are being abused by their state-employed counselors and staff members. Sources: *Arete*, "I Cried, You Didn't Listen," by Dwight Boyd Roberts with Jack Carter; personal letter, February 21, 1989, from Jack Carter.

THE TOP TEN CENSORED STORIES OF 1989

1. GLOBAL MEDIA LORDS THREATEN OPEN MARKETPLACE OF IDEAS.

A handful of mammoth private organizations, driven by bottom line profit considerations, have begun to dominate the world's mass media. They confidently predict that by the 1990s, five to ten corporate giants will control most of the world's important newspapers, magazines, books, broadcast stations, movies, recordings, and video cassettes. **SOURCE:** *The Nation*, June 12, 1989, "Lords of the Global Village," by Ben Bagdikian.

2. TURNING AFRICA INTO THE WORLD'S GARBAGE CAN.

International sludge dealers have tried to dump U.S. and European waste onto at least 15 African countries, a trend exposed over the last couple of years by European environmentalists, but not widely covered by the U.S. press. **SOURCE:** *In These Times*, November 8, 1989, "Western Developmental Overdose Makes Africa Chemically Dependent," by Diana Johnston.

3. UNITED STATES SUPPORTS ONE OF THE MOST BRUTAL HOLOCAUSTS SINCE WORLD WAR II.

Mozambique's 14 million people are trying to resist brutal attack by the Mozam-bique National Resistance (RENAMO), a South African-armed and supported group. Funding for RENAMO is believed to come from South African sources as well as conservative, rightwing groups in the United States and Europe. **SOURCES:** *UTNE Reader*, November/December 1989, "The Hidden War in Mozambique," by Kalamu Ya Salaam; *20/20*, March 2, 1990, "Children of Terror," and "Against All Odds," by Janice Tomlin and Tom Jarriel; *RENAMO Watch*, February 1990, "RENAMO's U.S. Support."

4. DOES THE BUSH ADMINISTRATION REALLY WANT TO WIN THE WAR ON DRUGS?

Richard Gregorie, one of the nation's most successful Mafia prosecutors, was sent to Miami with orders to go after the top people in the cocaine business. When he began to target foreign officials from supposedly friendly nations, including General Manuel Noriega of Panama, intelligence and State Department officials told him to back off. Gregorie's charges were later validated by a Senate subcommittee, which concluded that foreign policy interests superseded the war on drugs. **SOURCES:** *NBC Nightly News*, February 22, 1989; *San Francisco Chronicle*, April 15, 1989, "Policy Reportedly Undercut Drug War," New York Times Service; Richard Gregorie, October 10, 1989, telephone interview.

5. GUATEMALAN BLOOD ON U.S. HANDS.

The Bush administration significantly strengthened ties with the Guatemalan military at the same time that human rights violations by the military rose sharply. **SOURCES:** *Guatemala Update,* February 1990, "U.S. Aid Said to Encourage Rights Violations," by Jana Schroeder; *Guatemala Human Rights Commission/USA,* January 24, 1990, "U.S. Citizen Kidnapped and Tortured in Guatemala," by Joanne Heisel.

6. RADIOACTIVE WASTE: AS CLOSE AS YOUR NEIGHBORHOOD LANDFILL.

If the NRC, the EPA, and the nuclear industry implement their latest plan— deregulating low level radioactive waste to "Below Regulatory Concern"— radioactive waste may be sent to both solid and hazardous waste incinerators, flushed down the drain to sewage treatment centers, and recycled into consumer products. **SOURCE:** *The Workbook,* April/June 1989, "NIMBY, Nukewaste In My Backyard?," by Diane D'Arrigo.

7. OLIVER NORTH & CO. BANNED FROM COSTA RICA.

In July 1989, Oliver North and other major "Contragate" figures were barred from Costa Rica. The order was issued by none other than Oscar Arias Sanchez, president of Costa Rica and winner of the 1987 Nobel Peace Prize, acting on recommendations from a Costa Rican congressional commission investigating drug trafficking. The commission concluded that the Contra resupply network in Costa Rica, which North coordinated from the White House, doubled as a drug smuggling operation. **SOURCE:** *EXTRA!,* October/November 1989, "Censored News: Oliver North & Co. Banned from Costa Rica."

8. BIASED AND CENSORED NEWS AT CBS AND THE WALL STREET JOURNAL.

The Wall Street Journal censored a top reporters for exposing how one of the nation's most respected television news departments, *CBS News,* broadcast biased news coverage of the Afghanistan war. The story, eventually published in the *Columbia Journalism Review,* charges that CBS's Kurt Lohbeck, a partisan of the mujahideen, favored one guerrilla commander and "served in effect as his publicist." Lohbeck is also charged with influencing other journalists' reporting of the war by feeding them disinformation, and with trying to set up an arms deal between Abdul Haq and a New Jersey arms manufacturer for 10,000 machine pistols. **SOURCES:** *Columbia Journalism Review,* January/February 1990, "Mission: Afghanistan," by Mary Williams Walsh; *Defense Media Review,* March 31, 1990, "*Wall Street Journal* and CBS: Case of Professional Courtesy?" by Sean Naylor; *The Progressive,* May 1990, "Afghanistan: Holes in the Coverage of a Holy War," by Erwin Knoll.

9. PCBS AND TOXIC WASTE IN YOUR GASOLINE.

The GAO, EPA, and the FBI are investigating sophisticated "waste laundering" schemes in which toxic wastes and solvents are mixed with gasoline, diesel, and industrial fuel. At least one of the plans revealed connections to organized crime. The GAO told Congress that although the EPA had received information on a waste firm's suspected organized crime connections, it would not share the information with GAO officials. **SOURCE:** *Common Cause Magazine*, July/August 1989, "Toxic Fuel," by Andrew Porterfield.

10. SOMETHING FOUL IN THE CHICKEN INDUSTRY AND THE USDA.

The number of cases of salmonella rose to 2.5 million per year, leading to an estimated 500,000 hospitalizations and 9,000 deaths. This national epidemic was caused by a massive leap in consumer demand for chicken as a "healthier food" and by the failure of the U.S. Department of Agriculture to adequately inspect processing plants. **SOURCE:** *Southern Exposure*, Summer 1989, "Chicken Empires," by Bob Hall and "The Fox Guarding the Hen House," by Tom Devine.

THE TOP TEN CENSORED STORIES OF 1990

1. THE GULF WAR: TRUTH WAS THE FIRST CASUALTY.

Many journalists were slow in uncovering the fact that just days before the invasion of Kuwait, the White House was lobbying Congress not to apply sanctions against Iraq. Further, the U.S. ambassador to Iraq was telling Saddam Hussein that the United States had "no position" concerning Iraq's border dispute with Kuwait. Nor was there any coverage of the secret August 23 offer by Iraq to pull out of Kuwait and release all hostages (which President Bush rejected). **SOURCES:** *Image Magazine*, October 14, 1990, "The First Casualty," by Mark Hertsgaard; *Editor & Publisher*, October 20, 1990, "Storytelling from the Persian Gulf," by Debra Gersh; *The Quill*, October 1990, "Imperial Thoughts," by Mike Moore; *The Spotlight*, October 8, 1990, "Saddam Was Bush-Whacked On Invasion," by John McBrien.

2. THE S&L CRISIS: THE SOLUTION IS WORSE THAN THE CRIME.

The Resolution Trust Corporation (RTC) —the government's S&L caretaker—is now the nation's largest operator of financial institutions, yet it was established with neither any meaningful public debate nor with any serious consideration of alternatives. No war, no defense program, no social program, no other scandal has ever cost what the S&L bailout will cost. **SOURCES:** *Progressive Review*, August 1990, "No-Fault Capitalism Meets Lemon Socialism," by Sam Smith; *Wall Street Journal*, August 9, 1990, "Viewpoint: Biggest Robbery in History—You're the Victim," by Michael Gartner.

3. THE CIA ROLE IN THE SAVINGS AND LOAN CRISIS.

Links have been found between S&Ls, organized crime figures, and CIA operatives. If S&L funds went to the Contras or other covert operations, it would help explain where at least some of the money went. **SOURCES:** *Houston Post*, "Savings and Loan" series starting February 4, 1990, by Pete Brewton; *The Nation*, November 19, 1990, "The Looting Decade," by Robert Sherrill"; *Columbia Journalism Review*, November/December 1990, "The Mob, The CIA, and the S&L Scandal," by Steve Weinberg.

4. NASA SPACE SHUTTLES DESTROY THE OZONE SHIELD.

"Every time the space shuttle is launched... 25 percent of the ozone is destroyed," says physician Dr. Helen Caldicott. Valery Burdakov, co-designer of the Russian "Energiya" rocket engine, said the history of ozone depletion correlates closely with the increase of chlorine discharged by solid fuel rockets. **SOURCES:** *Sonoma State University Star*, May 8, 1990, "Doc Caldicott Prescribes Medicine," by Mindi Levine; *Earth Island Journal*, Fall 1990, "Soviets Say Shuttles Rip Ozone Layer," by Gar Smith; *San Francisco Chronicle*, August 21, 1990, "Group Says Space Shuttle Damages Earth's Ozone," by David Sylvester.

5. CONTINUED MEDIA BLACKOUT OF DRUG WAR FRAUD.

Michael Levine, the latest "drug war" insider to "go public," retired from the U.S. Drug Enforcement Agency (DEA) after 25 years as a leading undercover agent. In his exposé of the DEA he says, "The only thing we know with certainty is that the drug war is not for real." **SOURCES:** *EXTRA!*, July/August 1990, "Ex-DEA Agent Calls Drug War a Fraud," by Martin A. Lee; *The Humanist*, September/October 1990, "A Funny, Dirty Little Drug War," by Rick Szykowny.

6. WHAT REALLY HAPPENED IN PANAMA IS A DIFFERENT STORY.

It now appears that the legal implications of the invasion of Panama, the Bush–Noriega relationship, and the actual post-invasion conditions in Panama were all misrepresented to the American people. Perhaps the most fraudulent news coverage dealt with the true numbers of civilian and combat fatalities. **SOURCES:** *Panama Delegation Report*, March 1, 1990, by the Central American Human Rights Commission; *San Francisco Bay Guardian*, September 26, 1990, "The Hidden Body Count," by Jonathan Franklin; *CBS News, 60 Minutes*, September 30, 1990, "Victims of Just Cause," by Mike Wallace; *Washington Post*, June 30, 1990, "How Many Died in Panama?" letter from the Guatemalan Human Rights Commission, by Joanne Heisel; *The Nation*, June 18, 1990, "The Press and the Panama Invasion," by Marc Cooper.

7. THE PENTAGON'S SECRET BILLION DOLLAR BLACK BUDGET.

The Pentagon has a secret stash called the "Black Budget" that costs taxpayers $100 million a day. The "Black Budget" funds every program the President of the United States, the Secretary of Defense, and the Director of the CIA want to keep hidden. Source: *Rolling Stone*, 9/6/90, "How the Pentagon Hides Its Secret Spending," by Tim Weiner.

8. THE BILL OF RIGHTS HAD A CLOSE CALL IN 1990.

An anti-crime bill was introduced in Congress which, had it been enacted and signed into law, would have essentially nullified the Bill of Rights. Fortunately, neither the Senate version, introduced by Senator Phil Gramm (R-Texas), nor the House version, introduced by Representative Newt Gingrich, (R-Georgia), passed either chamber. **SOURCE:** *The*

Spotlight, August 6, 1990, "Repressive Gingrich Bill: Dangerous Attack on Rights" and 10/15/90, "Danger to Bill of Rights," by Mike Blair.

9. WHERE WAS GEORGE DURING THE IRAN-CONTRA AFFAIR?

New material from Oliver North's diaries provides additional evidence that George Bush played a major role in Iran-Contra from the beginning, passing up repeated opportunities to cut the transactions short. **SOURCE:** *Washington Post*, July 10, 1990, "Outlook: Where George Was," by Tom Blanton, National Security Archive.

10. AMERICA'S BANKING CRISIS: COMING TO A BANK NEAR YOU.

The same economic conditions that led to the demise of the S&L industry have been eating away at commercial banks, and the same kinds of accounting gimmicks that hid the S&L crisis are now being used to cover up the commercial banking crisis. **SOURCE:** *Dollars & Sense*, October 1990, "If You Liked the S&L Crisis… You'll Love the Banking Crisis," by John Miller.

THE TOP TEN CENSORED STORIES OF 1991

1. CBS AND NBC SPIKED FOOTAGE OF IRAQ BOMBING CARNAGE.

CBS and NBC refused to broadcast uncensored footage taken deep inside Iraq at the height of the air war. The footage, initially commissioned by NBC from two producers whose earlier work had earned the network seven Emmy awards, substantially contradicted U.S.

administration claims that civilian damage from the American-led bombing campaign was light. **SOURCE:** *San Francisco Bay Guardian*, March 20, 1991, "Sights Unseen," by Dennis Bernstein and Sasha Futran.

2. OPERATION CENSORED WAR.

A secretive Bush administration, aided and abetted by a press more interested in cheerleading than in journalism, persuaded the American people to support the Gulf War by media manipulation, censorship, and intimidation. In addition, reporters in the Gulf were routinely and openly censored and harassed by military public-affairs officers. **SOURCES:** *Editor & Publisher*, July 13, 1991, "Military Obstacles Detailed"; *San Francisco Bay Guardian*, March 6, 1991, "Inside the Desert Storm Mortuary," by Jonathan Franklin; *Progressive Review*, March 1991, "Collateral Damage, What We've Lost Already," by Sam Smith.

3. VOODOO ECONOMICS: THE UNTOLD STORY.

By September 30, 1992, when the fiscal year ends, the federal government's outstanding debt—which took some 200 years to reach $1 trillion in 1981—will total $4 trillion. Incredibly, as of October 1991, the interest alone on the federal debt will be the nation's single largest expenditure this year, exceeding even the military budget. A two-year investigative research effort by *Philadelphia Inquirer* reporters Donald L. Barlett and James B. Steele reveals that the rules by which the economy operates have been rigged, by design and default, to favor the privileged, the powerful, and the influential. **SOURCES:** Knight-Ridder Newspapers, November 2–8, 1991, "Caught in the Middle," by Donald L. Barlett and James B. Steele, of the *Philadelphia Inquirer*; *USA Today*, October 1, 1991, "Interest to Take Largest Slice of Budget Pie," by Mark Memmott.

4. THE 250 BILLION DOLLAR S&L POLITICAL COVER-UP.

An investigative television documentary revealed that high administration officials had lied to prevent the public from knowing the full scope of the S&L crisis before the 1988 election. **SOURCES:** Center for Investigative Reporting and PBS-TV *Frontline*, October 22, 1991, "The Great American Bailout."

5. OPERATION ILL WIND— DOD'S UNTOLD SCANDAL.

Northrop Corporation's former CEO, Thomas V. Jones, kept the company thriving despite scandals involving overseas payoffs, illegal Watergate contributions, and falsified tests on U.S. jet parts used in the Persian Gulf War. Northrop was just another culprit unearthed by a massive investigation into possible fraud and bribery in securing defense contracts. **SOURCES:** *Common Cause Magazine*, November/December 1990, "The Devil and Mr. Jones," by John Hanrahan; *St. Louis Journalism Review*, March 1991, "The Documents Were Sealed and the Public Shut Out," by Philip Dunn.

6. NO EVIDENCE OF IRAQI THREAT TO SAUDI ARABIA.

Satellite photos of Kuwait that President George Bush used to rally a surprised nation to support a war in the Persian Gulf did not prove Bush's claim of an imminent Iraqi invasion of Saudi Arabia. In fact, the photos showed no sign of a massive Iraqi troop buildup in Kuwait. **SOURCES:** *St. Petersburg Times*, January 6, 1991, reprinted in *In These Times*, February 27, 1991, "Public Doesn't Get Picture with Gulf Satellite Photos," by Jean Heller.

7. FREEDOM OF INFORMATION ACT IS AN OXYMORON.

The erosion over the past 10 years of the 25-year-old Freedom of Information Act (FOIA) coincides with a new and particularly hostile attitude towards the public's right to know that came in with the Reagan and Bush administrations. The executive branch and federal courts are exploiting the law's exemptions to circumvent the FOIA. **SOURCE:** *Common Cause*, July/August 1991, "The Fight To Know," by Peter Montgomery and Peter Overby.

8. CORPORATE AMERICA'S ANTI-ENVIRONMENTAL CAMPAIGN.

Companies with questionable environmental records are adopting an array of tactics and attack strategies aimed at disrupting environmental and citizen groups. Some of the more recent anti-environmental innovations include multimillion dollar SLAPP suits, the harassment and surveillance (including electronic) of activists, the infiltration of environmental groups by "agent provocateurs," and the creation of dummy ecology groups to ferret out whistleblowers. Another disturbing trend is the proliferation of groups such as "The

Oregon Committee for Recycling," an industry front group whose real purpose was to lobby *against* a recycling initiative on the state ballot. **SOURCES:** *E Magazine*, November/December 1991, "Stop the Greens," by Eve Pell; *Greenpeace News*, May 10, 1991, "Clorox Company's Public Relations 'Crisis Management Plan.'"

9. INSLAW SOFTWARE THEFT: CONSPIRACY AT THE JUSTICE DEPARTMENT?

In a little publicized legal battle, the Inslaw Corp. charged that the U.S. Department of Justice robbed it of its computer software program, conspired to send the company into bankruptcy, and then initiated a cover-up. **SOURCES:** *In These Times*, May 29, 1991, "Software Pirates," by Joel Bleifuss; *Random Lengths*, 10/3/91, "Software To Die For," by James Ridgeway.

10. THE BUSH FAMILY AND ITS CON-FLICTS OF INTEREST.

No president in recent history has had the blatant familial conflicts of interest that George Bush has. Examples include links to crime families, vested interests in the petroleum industry, and direct involvement in the poster child of the S&L fiasco, Silverado Savings & Loan. **SOURCES:** *San Francisco Examiner*, July 28, 1991, "Crime-Linked Firms Hired Prescott Bush"; *Santa Rosa Press Democrat*, July 19, 1991 and August 6, 1991, "Neil Bush's New Boss" and "Son's S&L Not Closed"; *SPIN*, December 3, 1991, "See No Evil," by Jefferson Morley; *The Texas Observer*, July 12, 1991 and August 6,

1991, "Oil in the Family" and "Global Entanglements," by David Armstrong.

THE TOP TEN CENSORED STORIES OF 1992

1. THE GREAT MEDIA SELL-OUT TO REAGANISM.

Reaganism ushered in the era of giant, monopolistic media empires. Take, for example, the three big networks—ABC, CBS, and NBC. Each was acquired by corporations that might have been deemed unqualified under earlier FCC standards. In return, big media dispensed relentlessly positive news about Reaganism and the great trickle-down dream. **SOURCE:** *Mother Jones*, May/June 1992, "Journalism of Joy," by Ben H. Bagdikian.

2. CORPORATE CRIME DWARFS STREET CRIME AND VIOLENCE.

While the press continues to frighten the public with stories of street crime and violence, corporate violators run rampant and unwatched by the major media. Public corruption, environmental degradation, financial fraud, procurement fraud, and occupational homicide are on the rise. **SOURCE:** *Multinational Monitor*, December 1991, "Corporate Crime & Violence in Review," by Russell Mokhiber.

3. CENSORED ELECTION YEAR ISSUES.

While the presidential candidates and the media were focusing on alleged infidelities, family values, and rap music lyrics, other far more important issues were ignored or underreported during the 1992 election. These include George

Bush and Iran-Contra, the awarding of ambassadorships and federal advisory committee appointments to major Bush campaign contributors, homelessness, Dan Quayle's "Council on Competitiveness," the rising death rate of Iraqi children in the months after the Gulf War, and covert operations run from a clandestine airfield at Mena, Arkansas, while Bill Clinton was governor. **SOURCES:** *Common Cause Magazine*, April/May/June 1992, "George Bush's Ruling Class," by Jeffrey Denny, Vicki Kemper, Viveca Novak, Peter Overby, and Amy Young; *Washington Post*, January 9, 1992, "A Profound Silence on Homelessness," by Mary McGrory; *The Progressive*, May 1992, "Deregulatory Creep: Dan Quayle Clears the Way for Industry," by Arthur E. Rowse; *San Francisco Examiner*, "This World," October 11, 1992, "46,900 Unspectacular Deaths," by Mike Royko; *Unclassified*, February/March 1992, "The Mena, Arkansas, Story," by David MacMichael.

4. UNITED STATES: THE WORLD'S LEADING MERCHANT OF DEATH.

The leading arms merchant in the world is the United States, which has provided over $128 billion in weaponry and military assistance to more than 125 of the world's 169 countries since 1982. **SOURCES:** *World Press Review*, September 1992, "The World's Top Arms Merchant," by Frederick Clairmonte; *The Human Quest*, July/August 1992, "War 'Dividends'—Military Spending Out of Balance with Needy," by Tristram Coffin.

5. IRAQGATE AND THE QUIET DEATH OF THE WATERGATE LAW.

Representative Henry B. Gonzales (D-TX), chair of the House Banking Committee, launched an intensive investigation into the Iraqgate scandal. Gonzalez charged that the Bush administration was instrumental in building up Iraq militarily, including supplying nuclear, chemical, and biological weaponry, and that it was blocking investigations into these actions. In September 1992, the Senate quietly killed legislation that was necessary to renew the Watergate Law, which had previously assured independent investigations of criminal acts by top officials. **SOURCES:** *CovertAction Information Bulletin*, Fall 1992, "Bush Administration Uses CIA to Stonewall Iraqgate Investigation," by Jack Colhoun; *War & Peace Digest*, August 1992, "BNL-Iraqgate Scandal," by Kevin Sanders; *The Paper* of Sonoma County (CA), October 22, 1992, "Is Bush a Felon?" by Stephen P. Pizzo; *New York Times*, October 20, 1992, "The Patsy Prosecutor," by William Safire.

6. "WE ARE WINNING THE WAR ON DRUGS" WAS A LIE.

President Bush's claim that "we are winning the war on drugs" was false. In fact, despite glowingly positive rhetoric, drug deaths in the United States are rising at a much higher rate than drug arrests. **SOURCES:** *In These Times*, May 20, 1992, "Drug Deaths Rise as the War Continues," by Mike Males; *EXTRA!*, September 1992, "Don't Forget the Hype: Media, Drugs and Public Opinion," by Micah Fink.

7. TRASHING FEDERAL REGULATIONS FOR CORPORATE CONTRIBUTIONS.

In his State of the Union address on January 28, 1992, President George Bush declared a 90-day "moratorium" on new federal regulations. There was a direct correlation between the regulations that were halted and the industries that contributed most heavily to the Bush/Quayle campaign and/or the Republican National Committee. **SOURCES:** *The Nation*, March 23, 1992, "Bush's Regulatory Chill: Immoral, Illegal, and Deadly"; *The Progressive*, May 1992, "Deregulatory Creep: Dan Quayle Clears the Way for Industry," by Arthur E. Rowse.

8. GOVERNMENT SECRECY MAKES A MOCKERY OF DEMOCRACY.

In 1991, some 6,500 U.S. government employees classified 7,107,017 documents, over 19,000 documents per day. Our information policy is in disarray, with widespread over-classification and an inefficient and costly information system. **SOURCE:** *Issues in Science and Technology*, Summer 1992, "The Perils of Government Secrecy," by Steven Aftergood.

9. HOW ADVERTISING PRESSURE CAN CORRUPT A FREE PRESS.

The Center for the Study of Commercialism invited 200 media outlets to a press conference in Washington, D.C. to announce the results of its study documenting dozens of instances of advertiser censorship in the media. Not a single radio or television station or network sent a reporter. Only two newspapers, the *Washington Post* and the *Washington Times*, bothered to attend. **SOURCE:** Center for the Study of Commercialism, March 1992, "Dictating Content: How Advertising Pressure Can Corrupt a Free Press," by Ronald K.L. Collins.

10. PENTAGON'S POST-COLD WAR BLACK BUDGET IS ALIVE AND PROSPERING.

Every day, close to $100 million flows through underground pipelines from the U.S. Treasury to the Pentagon to fuel the national security machinery of the United States. The "Black Budget" is the secret treasury of the nation's military and intelligence agencies. The secrecy of the system defies the Constitution, which requires the government to publish a complete and accurate account of all federal spending. **SOURCE:** *Mother Jones*, March/April 1992, "The Pentagon's Secret Stash," by Tim Weiner.

THE TOP TEN CENSORED STORIES OF 1993

1. THE UNITED STATES IS KILLING ITS YOUNG.

According to the UN Children's Fund: nine out of ten young people murdered in industrialized countries are slain in the United States; the U.S. homicide rate for young people ages 15 to 24 is five times greater than that of Canada, its nearest competitor; the U.S. poverty rate for children is more than double that of any other major industrialized nation; since the 1970s, while other industrialized nations were bringing children out of poverty, only the United States and Britain slipped backward. **SOURCES:** *Dallas Morning News*, September 25, 1993, "UN Says U.S. Dangerous for

Children," by Gayle Reaves; *USA Today*, June 16, 1993, "Report: 12 Million Kids Go Hungry in USA."

2. WHY ARE WE REALLY IN SOMALIA?

The decision to send U.S. troops to Somalia was based more on potential oil reserves found there than on the tragic images of starving Somalis, which dominated the major media in late 1992 and 1993. **SOURCES:** *Los Angeles Times*, January 18, 1993, "The Oil Factor In Somalia," by Mark Fineman; *Propaganda Review*, No. 10, 1993, "Somoilia?" by Rory Cox; *EXTRA!*, March 1993, "The Somalia Intervention: Tragedy Made Simple," by Jim Naureckas.

3. THE SANDIA REPORT ON EDUCATION: A LESSON IN CENSORSHIP.

The results of an investigation of states' public education by Sandia National Laboratories, a scientific research organization, did not reveal a seriously deficient educational system in dire need of profound changes such as a nationwide voucher program. Instead, the report revealed a steady or slightly improving trend in public education on nearly every measure employed in the survey. Nonetheless, the report was suppressed. **SOURCES:** *Phi Delta Kappan*, May 1993, "Perspective on Education In America," by Robert M. Huelskamp; *The Education Digest*, September 1993, "The Second Coming of the Sandia Report," reprinted from *Phi Delta Kappan*.

4. THE REAL WELFARE CHEATS: AMERICA'S CORPORATIONS.

There are five major areas of government giveaways to corporations: the retention of patents and profits by universities and private firms on products developed with public funds; the jettison of questionable debt by corporations under Chapter 11 of a new bankruptcy code; the mining of valuable minerals and metals from federal lands without paying royalties; taxpayer subsidies of the nuclear power industry; and undervalued timber sales to the logging industry. **SOURCE:** *Multinational Monitor*, January/February 1993, "Public Assets, Private Profits: The U.S. Corporate Welfare Rolls," by Chris Lewis, Laurence H. Kallen, Jonathan Dushoff, David Lapp, and Randal O'Toole.

5. THE HIDDEN TRAGEDY OF CHERNOBYL HAS WORLDWIDE IMPLICATIONS.

A devastating book on the far-reaching dimensions of the 1986 Chernobyl disaster explodes many of the Chernobyl myths propagated by Soviet authorities and eagerly accepted by the international nuclear establishment. **SOURCE:** *The Nation*, March 15, 1993, "Chernobyl—The Hidden Tragedy," by Jay M. Gould.

6. U.S. ARMY QUIETLY RESUMES BIOWARFARE TESTING AFTER TEN-YEAR HIATUS.

Although few people outside of Dugway, Utah, are aware of it, the U.S. Army has brought biological warfare testing back to a site it had declared unsafe a decade earlier. **SOURCES:** *Salt Lake Tribune*, January 27, 1993, "Army Resumes Biological-Agent Tests at Dugway After 10-Year Cessation," July 28, 1993, "Dugway to Test Disease-Causing Agents at Remote Lab," both by Jim Woolf; September 21, 1993, and "Dugway Base Cited for 22 Waste Violations," by Laurie Sullivan; *High Country News*, August 9, 1993, "Biowarfare is Back," by Jon Christensen; *High Desert Advocate*, September 15, 1993, "Utah Biowarfare Oversight Group Wants to Do Its Work Behind Closed Doors."

7. THE ECOLOGICAL DISASTER THAT CHALLENGES THE EXXON VALDEZ.

Man-made "lakes" and ponds saturated with selenium from agricultural run-off are threatening our drinking water and wildlife. Hardest hit is the Kesterson National Wildlife Refuge in California's San Joaquin Valley. The selenium crisis has grown to extraordinary proportions in California, with selenium runoff now threatening the entire 500-mile-long Central Valley as well as the water supply for Los Angeles. SOURCES: *Sports Illustrated*, March 22, 1993, "The Killing Fields," by Robert H. Boyle.

8. AMERICA'S DEADLY DOCTORS.

According to estimates, 5 to 10 percent of doctors—some 30,000 to 60,000—could be hazardous to your health. A study by the Public Citizen's Health Research Group concluded that medical negligence in hospitals alone injures or kills 150,000 to 300,000 Americans each year. SOURCE: *Woman's Day*, October 12, 1993, "Deadly Doctors," by Sue Browder.

9. THERE'S A LOT OF MONEY TO BE MADE IN POVERTY.

Huge national and international corporations, such as ITT, General Motors, and American Express, own and finance a growing "poverty industry" that targets low-income, blue-collar, and minority consumers for fraud, exploitation, and price gouging. SOURCE: *Southern Exposure*, Fall 1993, "Poverty, Inc. Why the Poor Pay More—And Who Really Profits," by Mike Hudson, Eric Bates, Barry Yeoman, and Adam Feuerstein.

10. HAITI: DRUGS, THUGS, AND THE CIA.

Few Americans are aware of our secret involvement in Haitian politics, including the CIA's attempted intervention in Haiti's election and the agency's role in trafficking drugs from Colombia and the Dominican Republic into the United States. SOURCES: *New York Times*, November 1, 1993, "Key Haiti Leaders Said To Have Been In The CIA's Pay," by Tim Weiner; *Pacific News Service*, October 20, 1993, "What's Behind Washington's Silence on Haiti Drug Connection?" and November 2, 1993, "A Haitian Call to Arms," both by Dennis Bernstein; *San Francisco Bay Guardian*, November 3, 1993, "The CIA's Haitian Connection," by Dennis Bernstein and Howard Levine; *Los Angeles Times*, October 31, 1993, "CIA's Aid Plan Would Have Undercut Aristide in '87–'88," by Jim Mann.

THE TOP TEN CENSORED STORIES OF 1994

1. THE DEADLY SECRETS OF THE OCCUPATIONAL SAFETY AGENCY.

In the early 1980s, a study by the National Institute for Occupational Safety and Health (NIOSH) revealed that 240,450 American workers had been exposed to hazardous materials.

NIOSH was instructed to inform affected workers so they could arrange for cancer screening. However, the Reagan Administration refused to fund a $4 million pilot notification program and opposed legislation that would have required it. Fewer than 30 percent of the workers covered by the studies have been notified. **SOURCES:** *Health Letter*, March 1994, "Unfinished Business: Occupational Safety Agency Keeps 170,000 Exposed Workers in the Dark About Risks Incurred on Job," by Peter Lurie, Sidney Wolfe, and Susan Goodwin.

2. POWERFUL GROUP OF ULTRA-CONSERVATIVES HAS SECRET PLANS FOR YOUR FUTURE.

In 1981, 160 new-right political leaders calling themselves the Council for National Policy (CNP) launched a political federation to coordinate their own political agenda. One of their members, R.J. Rushdoony, a leader of the Christian Reconstruction movement, argues that right-thinking Christians should take "dominion" over the United States and do away with the "heresy" that is democracy. After the public inauguration of the group the CNP went underground, meeting quarterly behind closed doors. **SOURCE:** *In These Times*, August 8, 1994, "Right-Wing Confidential," by Joel Bleifuss.

3. THE SECRET PENTAGON PLAN TO SUBSIDIZE DEFENSE CONTRACTOR MERGERS.

The Pentagon is secretly funneling taxpayer dollars to giant military contractors in order to underwrite expenses connected with acquisitions and merg-

ers. Norman Augustine, chairman of Martin Marietta, a billion-dollar defense contractor, argued that the federal government would over the long term reap lower costs from these defense mergers. Under the plan, Augustine's company would get $270 million from the Pentagon to cover expenses related to the purchase of a subsidiary from General Electric. **SOURCE:** *Newsday*, July 28, 1994, "Flak for Defense Merger," by Patrick J. Sloyan.

4. POISONING THE PUBLIC WITH TOXIC INCINERATORS.

Government officials knew dioxin was a byproduct of incineration, and EPA scientists knew dioxin accumulates through the food chain. Despite this knowledge, incineration has rapidly gained approval throughout the country as the "profitable answer" for disposal of the nation's stockpile of toxic waste and garbage. **SOURCE:** *Government Accountability Project*, September 1994, "Poisoning Ourselves: The Impact of Incineration on Food and Human Health, An Executive Summary," by Mick G. Harrison, Esq.

5. EPA RETREATS ON OZONE CRISIS.

The United States first banned chlorofluorocarbon aerosols (CFC), a prime suspect in ozone depletion, in the 1970s. DuPont planned to stop CFC production in 1994, but the EPA asked the company to continue production until 1996, putting the United States in a bad position to argue for the phase-out of CFCs by developing countries. **SOURCES:** *In These Times*, January 24, 1994, "Full of Holes: Clinton's Retreat on the Ozone Crisis," by David Moberg.

6. 1947 AEC MEMO REVEALS WHY HUMAN RADIATION EXPERIMENTS WERE CENSORED.

An Atomic Energy Commission memorandum issued in 1947 ordered all documents suppressed and marked "Secret" that referred to the illegal Cold War radiation experiments by the Department of Defense on unsuspecting humans which "might have adverse effect on public opinion or result in legal suits." Although documentation of the inhumane program was publicly available as early as 1986, it was only after the 1993 disclosures by a small daily newspaper and by Secretary of Energy Hazel O'Leary—with all the victims dead and most of the perpetrators retired—that the news media put it on the national agenda. **SOURCES:** *Secrecy & Government Bulletin*, March 1994, "Protecting Government Against the Public," by Steven Aftergood; *Columbia Journalism Review*, March/April 1994, "The Radiation Story No One Would Touch," by Geoffrey Sea.

7. 60 BILLION POUNDS OF FISH WASTED ANNUALLY.

The UN Food and Agriculture Organization reported in April 1994 that roughly 60 percent of the fish populations they monitor are fully exploited or depleted. As large-scale fishing technologies have taken over the world's oceans, they have become less and less selective in their catch, often throwing overboard fish that were too small, or too large, to be processed by factory trawlers. **SOURCE:** *Mother Jones*, July/ August 1994, "Special Report: A Farewell To Fish?" by Peter Steinhart, Hal Bernton, Brad Matsen, Ray Troll, and Deborah Cramer.

8. THE RETURN OF TUBERCULOSIS.

Tuberculosis, thought to be a disease of the past, has surged back with a vengeance and now kills more people than any other infectious or communicable disease in the world—despite the fact it is curable and treatment costs are not prohibitive. **SOURCE:** *World Watch*, July/August 1994, "Why Don't We Stop Tuberculosis?" by Anne E. Platt.

9. THE PENTAGON'S MYSTERIOUS HAARP PROJECT.

The High Frequency Active Auroral Research Project (HAARP) is the latest in a series of little-known DOD experiments for the military which burns "holes" in the ionosphere. HAARP surfaced publicly in Alaska only when the FAA began advising commercial pilots on how to avoid the large amount of electromagnetic radiation that HAARP would generate. Scientists, environmentalists, and native people are concerned that HAARP's electronic transmitters could harm people, endanger wildlife, and trigger unforeseen environmental consequences. **SOURCE:** *Earth Island Journal*, Fall 1994, "Project HAARP: The Military's Plan to Alter the Ionosphere," by Clare Zickuhr and Gar Smith.

10. NEWS MEDIA MASK SPOUSAL VIOLENCE IN THE "LANGUAGE OF LOVE."

The media is inaccurately characterizing spousal violence. The murder of an ex-wife and boyfriend becomes a "love triangle" and the mass killing of a woman and her coworkers becomes a "tragedy of spurned love." This kind of reporting has real consequences because it affirms a batterer's most common excuse for assault, "I did it because I love you so much." **SOURCE:** *USA Today*, March 10, 1994, "Crimes Against Women: Media Part of Problem for Masking Violence in the Language of Love," by Ann Jones.

THE TOP TEN CENSORED STORIES OF 1995

1. TELECOMMUNICATIONS DEREGULATION: CLOSING UP AMERICA'S "MARKETPLACE OF IDEAS."

The Telecommunications Deregulation Act stealthily moved through Congress under the guise of "encouraging competition," though in reality, it will have the opposite effect—creating huge new concentrations of media power. It eliminates current antitrust regulations, dismantles limitations on the number of radio stations that can be owned by a single company, and lifts the current FCC ban on joint ownership of a broadcast radio or TV license in the same market—allowing a single company to have 100 percent control over the three primary sources of news in a community. **SOURCE:** Consumer Project on Technology, 7/14/95, "Federal Telecommunications Legislation: Impact on Media Concentration," *TAP-INFO*, an Internet Newsletter, by Ralph Nader, James Love, and Andrew Saindon.

2. THE BUDGET DOES NOT HAVE TO BE BALANCED ON THE BACKS OF THE POOR.

The Washington-based Center for Study of Responsive Law identified 153 federal programs that benefit wealthy corporations and cost taxpayers $167.2 billion annually. In comparison, federal support for food stamps, housing aid, and child nutrition costs $50 billion a year. Congress could balance the budget by cutting "aid to dependent corporations." **SOURCE:** *Public Citizen*, July/August 1995, "Cut Corporate Welfare Not Medicare," by John Canham-Clyne.

3. CHILD LABOR IN THE U.S. IS WORSE TODAY THAN DURING THE 1930S.

Every day, children across America are working in environments detrimental to their social and educational development, their health, and even their lives. As yet, there is no comprehensive national data collection system that accurately tracks the numbers or conditions of working youths. Cultural beliefs about the benefits of work for children are strong, and various PACs lobby successfully to keep child labor laws from being strengthened. **SOURCE:** *Southern Exposure*, Fall/Winter 1995, "Working in Harm's Way," by Ron Nixon.

4. THE PRIVATIZATION OF THE INTERNET.

The federal government has been gradually transferring the backbone of the U.S. portion of the global computer network to companies such as IBM and MCI as part of a larger plan to privatize cyberspace. The crucial step was taken on April 30, 1994, when the National Science Foundation shut down its part of the Internet, leaving the corporate giants in charge. Cyberspace speech is already less free than speech in traditional public forums since it is more expensive and subject to the whims of private censors who are not accountable to the First Amendment. **SOURCE:** *The Nation*, July 3, 1995, "Keeping On-line Speech Free: Street Corners in Cyberspace," by Andrew L. Shapiro.

5. U.S. PUSHES NUCLEAR PACT BUT SPENDS BILLIONS TO ADD BANG TO NUKES.

Even as the United States urged the rest of the world to indefinitely extend a treaty requiring signatories to work toward elimination of nuclear weapons, the U.S. Department of Energy planned a multibillion dollar project to resume production of tritium—a radioactive gas used to enhance the explosive power of nuclear warheads. **SOURCE:** *Washington Post*, May 1, 1995, "U.S. Seeks Arms Ingredient As It Pushes Nuclear Pact," and 5/28/95, "House Bill Would Order Nuclear Reactor As New Source of Tritium," both by Thomas W. Lippman.

6. RADICAL PLAN FROM NEWT GINGRICH'S THINK TANK TO GUT THE FOOD AND DRUG ADMINISTRATION.

A powerful bloc of critics in the drug industry has joined hands with some members of Congress in pushing to overhaul the FDA. These critics claim the FDA is too tough on drug companies, unnecessarily inhibits innovation, and delays approval of new drugs and medical devices. **SOURCE:** *Mother Jones*, September/October 1995, "Agency Under Attack," by Leslie Weiss.

7. RUSSIA INJECTS EARTH WITH NUKE WASTE.

For more than three decades, the Soviet Union secretly pumped billions of gallons of atomic waste directly into the Earth and, according to Russian scientists, the practice continues today. **SOURCE:** *The New York Times*, November 21, 1994, "Poison in the Earth: A Special Report; Nuclear Roulette for Russia: Burying Uncontained Waste," by William J. Broad.

8. MEDICAL FRAUD COSTS THE NATION $100 BILLION ANNUALLY—OR MORE.

No one really knows how much money is stolen from the medical system every year. Although Medicare and Medicaid were created in 1965, no monitoring measures were established until 1978. Unfortunately, it did not take health care providers long before they developed a series of "medscam" techniques. **SOURCE:** *Mother Jones*, March/April 1995, "Medscam," by L.J. Davis.

9. U.S. CHEMICAL INDUSTRY FIGHTS FOR TOXIC OZONE-KILLING PESTICIDE.

Methyl bromide (MB) is a pesticide that is at least 50 times more destructive to the ozone layer, atom for atom, than chlorofluorocarbons. For 60 years, MB has been used to kill pests in soil and buildings and on agricultural products. Under the Clean Air Act, the EPA has mandated a halt to MB production in, and imports to, the United States in 2001—but manufacturers and agricultural users have mounted a formidable campaign to delay the ban. **SOURCE:** *Earth Island Journal*, Summer 1995, "Campaign Against Methyl Bromide: Ozone-Killing Pesticide Opposed," by Anne Schonfield.

10. THE BROKEN PROMISES OF NAFTA.
The promises of prosperity that the North American Free Trade Agreement (NAFTA) would bring the United States and Mexico were most loudly proclaimed by USA*NAFTA, a pro-NAFTA business coalition. Now, some two years after the agreement became law, USA*NAFTA's own members are blatantly breaking the coalition's grand promises with resulting economic and environmental repercussions in both the United States and Mexico. **SOURCES:** *CovertAction Quarterly*, Fall 1995, "NAFTA's Corporate Con Artists," by Sarah Anderson and Kristyne Peter; *Mother Jones*, January/February 1995, "A Giant Spraying Sound," by Esther Schrader.

THE TOP TEN CENSORED STORIES OF 1996

1. RISKING THE WORLD: NUCLEAR PROLIFERATION IN SPACE.
While much press coverage was devoted to the failed Russian space probe that crashed into the South Pacific along with its payload of 200 grams of plutonium-238, virtually no attention was paid to the launch of NASA's Cassini probe which carried 72 *pounds* of the same substance. **SOURCES:** *CovertAction Quarterly*, Summer 1996, "Risking the World: Nuclear Proliferation in Space"; *Progressive Media Project*, May 1996, "Don't send plutonium into space," both by Karl Grossman

2. SHELL'S OIL, AFRICA'S BLOOD.
In the wake of Nigeria's execution of nine environmental activists, evidence has indicated that Shell had fomented civil unrest in Nigeria, contributed to unfair trials, bankrolled Nigerian military action against protesters, and failed to use its leverage to prevent the unjustified executions. **SOURCES:** *San Francisco Bay Guardian*, February 7, 1996, "Shell Game" by Vince Bielski; *Texas Observer*, January 12, 1996, "Shell's Oil, Africa's Blood," by Ron Nixon and Michael King; *Editor & Publisher*, March 23, 1996, "Rejected Ad Flap," by M.L. Stein; *World Watch*, May/June 1996, "Dying for Oil," by Aaron Sachs, July/August 1996, "Eco-Justice in Nigeria," by Chris Bright; *Bank Check*, February 1996, "IFC Pulls Out of Shell Deal," by Andrea Durbin.

3. BIG PERKS FOR THE WEALTHY HIDDEN IN MINIMUM WAGE BILL.
The publicized intent of the Small Business Job Protection Act of 1996 was to raise the minimum wage from $4.25 to $5.15 an hour. However, the bill included at least 10 other significant provisions that may negate its positive aspects. **SOURCE:** *The New Republic*, 10/28/96, "Bare minimum: Goodies for the rich hidden in wage bill" by John Judis (reprinted in Santa Rosa Press Democrat, October 13, 1996).

4. DEFORMING CONSENT: THE PR INDUSTRY'S SECRET WAR ON ACTIVISTS.
Multimillion dollar clients of major public relations firms are creating false nonprofit organizations that target activists and proposed legislation that threaten big business. **SOURCES:** *CovertAction Quarterly*, Winter 1995/1996, "The Public Relations Industry's Secret War on Activists," by John Stauber and

Sheldon Rampton; *Earth Island Journal,* Winter 1995/1996, "Public Relations, Private Interests," by John Stauber and Sheldon Rampton.

5. WHITE-COLLAR CRIME: WHITEWASH AT THE JUSTICE DEPARTMENT.

While white-collar crime costs America 10 to 50 times more money than street crime, the DOJ shows little interest in prosecuting white-collar criminals. Business organizations claim the federal government restricts business with unnecessary and heavy-handed regulations. **SOURCE:** *CovertAction Quarterly,* Summer 1996, "White-Collar Crime: Whitewash at the Justice Department," by David Burnham.

6. NEW MEGA-MERGED BANKING BEHEMOTHS = BIG RISK.

The massive consolidation of the nation's banking resources has resulted in 71.5 percent of U.S. banking assets being controlled by the 100 largest banking organizations. Since the Federal Reserve has capped the amount that financial institutions have to pay into the government's bank insurance fund, a bailout would come directly from U.S. taxpayers should any new megabank fail. **SOURCE:** *Multinational Monitor,* June 1996, "The Making of the Banking Behemoths," by Jake Lewis.

7. CASHING IN ON POVERTY.

Corporate America is making huge profits off the 60 million poor people who must pay from 240–2,000 percent interest to pawn shops, check-cashing outlets, rent-to-own stores, finance companies, and high-interest mortgage lenders. These highly profitable businesses are increasingly owned or subsidized by Wall Street giants. Sources: *The Nation**, May 20, 1996, "Cashing in on Poverty," by Michael Hudson; *The Houston Chronicle**, July 15, 1996, "Bordering on Scandal: What Some Pay for Credit," by Michael Hudson (*excerpted from the book, *Merchants of Misery: How Corporate America Profits From Poverty*, edited by Michael Hudson, Common Courage Press, 1996).

8. BIG BROTHER GOES HIGH-TECH.

Information on individuals can now be obtained by governments and corporations using new surveillance, identification, and networking technologies without the need for warrants and formal investigations, threatening privacy rights. **SOURCES:** *CovertAction Quarterly,* Spring 1996, "Big Brother Goes High-Tech," by David Banisar; INSIGHT, August 19, 1996, "Access, Privacy and Power," by Michael Rust and Susan Crabtree, September 9, 1996, "New Surveillance Camera Cheers Police, Worries ACLU"*, by Joyce Price (*reprinted from the *Washington Times*).

9. U.S. TROOPS EXPOSED TO DEPLETED URANIUM DURING GULF WAR.

The Pentagon failed to warn Gulf War troops of the dangers of depleted uranium (DU) weapons and let them perform DU battlefield cleanup without the necessary protective clothing. Exposure is linked to many illnesses, including "Gulf War Syndrome." **SOURCES:** *Military Toxics Project's Depleted Uranium Citizens' Network,* January 16, 1996 (release of report), "Radioactive Battlefields of the 1990s: A Response to the Army's Unreleased Report on Depleted Uranium Weaponry," by Pat Broudy, Grace Bukowski, Leonard Dietz, Dan Fahey, John Paul Hasko, Cathy Hinds, Damaica Lopez, Dolly Lymburner, Arjun Makhijani, Richard Ochs, Laura Olah, Coy Overstreet, Charles Sheehan Miles, Judy Scotnicki, and Nikki F. Bas, edited by Rebecca Solnit; *Multinational Monitor*, January/February 1996, "Radioactive Ammo Lays Them to Waste," by Gary Cohen; Swords to Plowshares, November 7, 1995 (presentation), "Depleted Uranium: Objective Research and Analysis Required," by Dan Fahey; *The Vva Veteran*, March 1996, "Depleted Uranium: One Man's Weapon, Another Man's Poison," by Bill Triplett; *National Catholic Reporter*, January 19, 1996, Depleted Uranium, First Used In Iraq, Deployed in Bosnia," by Kathryn Casa.

10. FACING FOOD SCARCITY.

The world's stock of grains has fallen to its lowest level in two decades, and world grain prices will double by 2010, a sharp departure from World Bank projections. **SOURCES:** *World Watch*, May/June 1996, "Facing Food Scarcity" and "Japanese Government Breaks With World Bank Food Forecast," both by Lester R. Brown

THE TOP TEN CENSORED STORIES OF 1997

1. CLINTON ADMINISTRATION AGGRESSIVELY PROMOTES U.S. ARMS SALES WORLDWIDE.

Over the course of the Clinton administration, the United States has become the world's leading arms merchant. U.S. weapons are used in almost every global conflict, taking a devastating toll on civilians, U.S. military personnel, and the economies of many developing nations. **SOURCES:** *The Bulletin of Atomic Scientists*, October 1996, "Costly Giveaways," by Lumpe, Lora; *In These Times*, August 1, 1997, "Guns 'R' US," by Martha Honey.

2. PERSONAL CARE AND COSMETIC PRODUCTS MAY BE CARCINOGENIC.

Unbeknownst to many consumers, presumably safe personal care and cosmetics products such as Crest toothpaste and Cover Girl makeup contain potential carcinogens. Many Americans mistakenly believe that the FDA regulates and monitors the cosmetic industry. Although the FDA has the power to pull products it considers unsafe from store shelves, it rarely does. **SOURCES:** *In These Times*, February 17, 1997, "To Die For," and March. 3, 1997, "Take a Powder," both by Joel Bleifuss; *Chicago Tribune*, July 29, 1997, p. 3, zone C.

3. BIG BUSINESS SEEKS TO CONTROL AND INFLUENCE U.S. UNIVERSITIES.

Corporations avoid incurring research costs by endowing professorships, funding think tanks and research centers, sponsoring grants, and contracting for university services. Federal tax dollars fund about $7 billion worth of research to which corporations can now buy access for a fraction of the actual cost. University presidents often sit on the boards of directors of major corporations, and captains of industry dominate university boards of trustees, hiring chancellors and presidents with pro-industry biases. **SOURCES:** *CovertAction Quarterly*, Spring 1997, "Phi Beta Capitalism"; *Dollars and Sense*, March/April 1997, "Big Money on Campus," both by Lawrence Soley.

4. EXPOSING THE GLOBAL SURVEILLANCE SYSTEM.

Unknown to its citizens and most government officials, New Zealand's largest intelligence agency has been helping its Western allies spy on countries throughout the Pacific region for the last 40 years. In the late 1980s, the United States convinced New Zealand to join a highly secret global intelligence system, ECHELON, which allows spy agencies to monitor most of the telephone, e-mail, and telex communications carried over the world's telecommunication networks. **SOURCE:** *CovertAction Quarterly*, Winter 1996/1997, "Secret Power: Exposing the Global Surveillance System," by Nicky Hager.

5. UNITED STATES COMPANIES ARE WORLD LEADERS IN THE MANUFACTURE OF TORTURE DEVICES FOR INTERNAL USE AND EXPORT.

An Amnesty International report listed 100 companies that produced and sold instruments of torture; 42 were U.S. firms, giving the country the dubious distinction of leading the world in the manufacture of equipment designed to cause devastating pain. **SOURCES:** *The Progressive*, September 1997, "Shock Value: U.S. Stun Devices Pose Human Rights Risk," by Anne-Marie Cusac; *Chicago Tribune*, March 4, 1997; *Washington Times*, March 4,

6. RUSSIAN PLUTONIUM LOST OVER CHILE AND BOLIVIA.

On November 16, 1996, Russia's Mars 96 space probe broke up and burned while descending over Chile and Bolivia, scattering its remains across a 10,000-square-mile area. The probe carried about one-half pound of plutonium, and no one seems to know where the canisters went. The amount of plutonium that was "lost" is a potentially devastating health hazard. **SOURCE:** *CovertAction Quarterly*, Spring 1997, "Space Probe Explodes, Plutonium Missing," by Karl Grossman.

7. NORPLANT AND HUMAN LAB EXPERIMENTS IN THIRD WORLD LEAD TO FORCED USE IN THE UNITED STATES.

Low-income women in the United States and the Third World have been the unwitting targets of a U.S. policy to control birth rates. **SOURCES:** *Ms.*, November/December 1996, "The Misuses of Norplant: Who Gets Stuck?" by Jennifer Washburn; *Washington Free Press*, March/April 1997, "Norplant and the Dark Side of the Law," by Rebecca Kavoussi; *Human Events*, May 16, 1997, "BBC Documentary Claims That U.S. Foreign Aid Funded Norplant Testing On Uninformed Third World Women," by Joseph D'Agostino.

8. LITTLE-KNOWN FEDERAL LAW PAVES THE WAY FOR NATIONAL IDENTIFICATION CARD.

Buried in the Illegal Immigration Reform and Responsibility Act of 1996 is the framework for establishing a national ID card for the American public. This piece of legislation was slipped through without fanfare or publicity.

SOURCES: *WITWIGO*, May/June 1997, "National ID Card is Now Federal Law and Georgia Wants to Help Lead the Way," by Cyndee Parker; *New York Times*, September 8, 1996, Section 6; p. 58, column 1; related article in the *San Francisco Chronicle*, September 19, 1996, p. A1.

9. MATTEL CUTS U.S. JOBS TO OPEN SWEATSHOPS IN OTHER COUNTRIES.

Since the inauguration of the North American Free Trade Agreement (NAFTA) and the General Agreement on Tariffs and Trade (GATT), the toy industry's American labor force has been reduced by over half; many of those lost jobs have reappeared in other countries notorious for their sweatshop practices. SOURCES: *The Nation*, December 30, 1996, "Barbie's Betrayal: The Toy Industry's Broken Workers," by Eyal Press; *The Humanist*, January/February 1997, "Sweatshop Barbie: Exploitation of Third World Labor," by Anton Foek.

10. ARMY'S PLAN TO BURN NERVE GAS AND TOXINS IN OREGON THREATENS COLUMBIA RIVER BASIN.

The Oregon Environmental Quality Commission has approved the building of six new toxic waste incinerators. A partial list of the chemicals to be incinerated includes nerve gas, mustard agents, bioaccumulative organochlines such as those found in dioxin, furans, chloromethane, vinyl chloride, PCBs, and arsenic, as well as metals like lead, mercury, copper, and nickel. SOURCE: *Earth First!*, March 1997, "Army Plans to Burn Surplus Nerve Gas Stockpile," by Mark Brown and Kayrn Jones

THE TOP TEN CENSORED STORIES OF 1998

1. SECRET INTERNATIONAL TRADE AGREEMENT UNDERMINES THE SOVEREIGNTY OF NATIONS.

The Multilateral Agreement on Investment (MAI) is supposed to protect the foreign interests of multinational companies. However, the agreement threatens to undermine the sovereignty of nations by assigning power to corporations that is almost equal to those of the occupied countries. Countries who do not relax their environmental, land-use, and health and labor standards to meet the demands of foreign firms may be accused of acting illegally. SOURCES: *In These Times*, January 11, 1998, "Building the Global Economy" by Joel Bleifuss; *Democratic Left*, Spring 1998, "MAI Ties" by Bill Dixon; *Tribune Des Driots Humains*, April 1998, "Human Rights or Corporate Rights?" by Miloon Kothari and Tara Krause, *Denver Post*, August 2, 1998; *Charleston Gazette*, September 7, 1998; *San Francisco Chronicle*, April 10, 1998; *Washington Times*, March 21, 1998.

2. CHEMICAL CORPORATIONS PROFIT OFF BREAST CANCER.

Pharmaceutical companies are profiting from breast cancer by selling known carcinogens on the one hand, and then the "cures" for the resulting cancers on the other. SOURCES: *Rachel's Environment and Health Weekly*, December 4, 1997, "The Truth About Breast Cancer," by Peter Montague; *Green Guide*, October 1998, "Profiting Off Breast Cancer," by Allison Sloan and Tracy Baxter.

3. MONSANTO'S GENETICALLY MODIFIED SEEDS THREATEN WORLD PRODUCTION.

Monsanto Corporation is poised to sell genetically engineered "terminator seeds" which will produce only infertile plants, preventing farmers from saving seed and forcing them to purchase subsequent crop seed directly from Monsanto. Genetic engineering is still a new science, and no one can reliably predict the results from introducing genetically altered plants into the environment. **SOURCES:** *MoJo Wire* (www.motherjones.com/news_wire/broydo.html), April 27, 1998, "A Seedy Business," by Leora Broydo; *Third World Resurgence,* #92, "New Patent Aims to Prevent Farmers from Saving Seed," by Chakravarthi Raghavan; *Earth Island Journal,* Fall 1998, "Terminator Seeds Threaten an End to Farming," by Hope Shand and Pat Mooney; *The Ecologist,* September/October 1998, "Monsanto: A Checkered History" and "Revolving Doors: Monsanto and the Regulators," both by Brian Tokar.

4. RECYCLED RADIOACTIVE METALS MAY BE IN YOUR HOME.

The DOE, NRC, and the radioactive scrap metal industry are calling for a relaxation in standards for "decontaminated" radioactive metal. The current standards are already lax enough to allow low levels of radioactivity in items as intimate as spoons, dental fillings, and IUDs. **SOURCE:** *The Progressive,* October 1998,"Nuclear Spoons," by Anne-Marie Cusac.

5. U. S. WEAPONS OF MASS DESTRUCTION LINKED TO THE DEATHS OF A HALF-MILLION CHILDREN.

U.S. supported sanctions over the last seven years have claimed more Iraqi civilian lives than did the war itself. DU weapons abandoned during the Gulf War and more recently Operation Desert Fox are causing sharp rises in birth defects and childhood cancer. **SOURCES:** *San Francisco Bay Guardian,* February 25, 1998, "Made in America," by Dennis Bernstein; *I.F. Magazine,* March/April 1998, "Punishing Saddam or the Iraqis," by Bill Blum; *Space and Security News,* May 1998, "Our Continuing War Against Iraq," by the Most Rev. Dr. Robert M. Bowman, Lt. Col., USAF (retired).

6. UNITED STATES NUCLEAR PROGRAM SUBVERTS U.N.'S COMPREHENSIVE TEST BAN TREATY.

The United States used a "virtual" nuclear weapons testing program in March, 1998, to circumnavigate the U.N. Comprehensive Test Ban Treaty (CTBT) and to justify propping up its aging nuclear arsenal with new, more powerful weapons. Many nations claimed the test was a "hostile act," but the United States, itself critical of India's underground testing only two months later, claimed it was "fully consistent with the spirit and letter of the CTBT." **SOURCE:** *The Nation,* June 15, 1998, "Virtual Nukes—When is a Test Not a Test?" by Bill Mesler.

7. GENE TRANSFERS LINKED TO DANGEROUS NEW DISEASES.

Genetic engineering is becoming increasingly suspect in the resurgence and emergence of life threatening diseases.

At least 30 new diseases have emerged in the past 20 years, and older infectious ailments like malaria and tuberculosis are returning with renewed vigor. SOURCES: *Third World Resurgence*, #92, "Sowing Diseases, New and Old," by Mae-Wan Ho and Terje Traavik; *The Ecologist*, May/June 1998, "The Biotechnology Bubble," by Mae-Wan Ho, Hartmut Meyer, and Joe Cummins.

8. CATHOLIC HOSPITAL MERGERS THREATEN REPRODUCTIVE RIGHTS FOR WOMEN.

Catholic hospitals are merging with secular hospitals at an alarming rate across the country, threatening access to women's reproductive health care, in vitro fertilization, fetal tissue experiments, and assisted suicide. The Roman Catholic Church is now the largest private health-care provider in the country. SOURCE: *Ms.*, July/August 1998, "Women's Health: A Casualty of Hospital Merger Mania," by Christine Dinsmore.

9. U. S. TAX DOLLARS SUPPORT DEATH SQUADS IN CHIAPAS.

Members of special Mexican military units trained by U.S. Army Special Forces with U.S. drug-war money are perpetuating atrocities against indigenous peoples. SOURCES: *Slingshot*, Summer 1998,"Mexico's Military: Made in the USA," by the Slingshot collective; *Dark Night Field Notes/Zapatismo*, "Bury My Heart At Acteal," by Darrin Wood.

10. ENVIRONMENTAL STUDENT ACTIVISTS GUNNED DOWN ON CHEVRON OIL FACILITY IN NIGERIA.

Chevron corporation used Nigerian armed forces to police its facility off the coast of Nigeria and gun down several of the 121 student demonstrators peaceably gathered to protest the destruction of the Niger Delta wetlands by the oil-producing facility. SOURCES: *Era Environmental Testimonies*, July 10, 1998, "Chevron in Nigeria," by Environmental Rights Action/Friends of the Earth Nigeria; Pacifica Radio (www.pacifica.org), September 1998, "Drilling and Killing: Chevron and Nigeria's Oil Dictatorship," by Amy Goodman and Jeremy Scahill.

CHAPTER 5

Junk Food News 1877–2000

BY CARL JENSEN, Founder and Director Emeritus, Project Censored,
with Victoria Calkins, and research assistance by Amy Bonczewski

In 1877, John B. Bogart, an editor with the *New York Sun*, offered a definition of news that has not only endured but, indeed, seems to have become
even more widely adhered to in recent years. Bogart wrote, "When a dog
bites a man, that is not news, because it happens so often. But if a man
bites a dog it's news." His definition implies that there is a need for a sen-
sationalistic aspect for an event to become news. It's an ingredient that now
appears to be endemic in the press. "Man bites dog" is the classic example
of Junk Food News.

Our annual Junk Food News (JFN) effort evolved from criticism of Project
Censored by news editors and directors who argued that the real issue isn't
censorship—but rather a difference of opinion as to what information is
important to publish or broadcast. Editors often point out there is a finite
amount of time and space for news delivery—about 23 minutes for a half-
hour network television evening news program—and that it's their responsibility to determine which stories are most critical for the public to know.
The critics said I wasn't exploring media censorship, but rather I was just
another frustrated academic criticizing editorial news judgment.

This *appeared* to be a legitimate criticism, so I decided to review the stories that editors and news directors consider to be most the important and
worthy enough to fill their valuable news time and space. In the course of
this research, I didn't find an abundance of hard-hitting investigative journalism—quite the contrary. Indeed, what I did find is the journalistic phenomenon I call Junk Food News, which, in essence, represents the flip side

of the Top 25 Censored Stories announced annually by Project Censored. The typical Junk Food News diet consists of sensationalized, personalized, and homogenized inconsequential trivia that is served up to the public on a daily basis. While it may not be very nourishing for the public, it's cheap to produce and profitable for media proprietors.

Junk Food News is served up to the public in a number of predictable varieties:

BRAND NAME NEWS: Britney Spears, Brad Pitt, Madonna, Robert Downey Jr., John F. Kennedy Jr.

SEX NEWS: Ricky Martin's sexuality, Ellen Degeneres and Anne Heche, Pamela Anderson's breasts.

YO-YO NEWS: The stock market is up or down, the crime rate is up or down, unemployment is up or down, inflation is up or down, the interest rate is up or down.

SHOWBIZ NEWS: "Survivor," "Big Brother," "Who Wants To Marry a Multimillionaire?" and "Who Wants To Be a Millionaire?"

CRAZED NEWS: The latest Internet craze, dot-com craze, diet craze, fashion craze, drug craze, video game craze, and, of course, the always newsworthy latest crazed killer.

ANNIVERSARY NEWS: Commemorating the Columbine shooting, Oklahoma bombing, JonBenet Ramsey murder, Princess Diana accident, and, the ultimate anniversary, the Millennium.

SPORTS NEWS: Super Bowl, Super Salaries, Super Injuries, and Super Drug Problems

POLITICAL NEWS: The biannual political news season, when congressional candidates promise you anything to be elected, and the 2000 election that added "pregnant chads" to the political lexicon.

Given the diversity, *enormity*, and *propensity* of the media for Junk Food News, it is readily apparent the problem is not a lack of time and space for news. The problem is the quality of the news selected to fill that limited time and space. Today we're suffering from news inflation—there seems to be more of it than ever before—but it isn't worth as much as it used to be.

News should be nutritious for society. We need more steak and less sizzle from the press. The news should warn us about those things that make our society ill, whether economically, politically, or physically. And there is a significant amount of such news out there, as Project Censored has revealed each year since 1976.

Ever since 1984, when Clara Peller's "Where's the beef?" commercial became a national slogan, Project Censored has identified and announced the top Junk Food News stories of the year. Members of the national Organization of News Ombudsmen have participated as judges in the effort since 1988 and we appreciate their input and first-hand knowledge.

Ombudsmen, an invaluable yet rare presence on daily newspapers, generally defend the quality of news published but also acknowledge the problem of sensationalism. One ombudsman said, "Media types are gossips at heart who love scandal, controversy, and bad news (all prime ingredients of news). Newspaper folk are driven to get it first—the scoop—generating the feeding frenzy."

Another ombudsman suggested the public had some responsibility, saying, "I'm not bothered by a little JFN, just as I can tolerate some of the junk food it's named for. As long as there is showbiz there's going to be showbiz reporting, and there's nothing wrong with that. What's wrong is a way of eating that relies too heavily on empty calories and fat—and a diet of 'news' that consists mostly of trivia, gossip, and mockery."

One ombudsman, less charitable about the journalist's role, said "We're getting too damned lazy and… we underestimate the intelligence of our readers and listeners." Another suggested the solution for the press is to "satisfy the appetites of all of its readers without stuffing them too full of 'junk.'"

There has been little change in the make-up of the top junk food news stories in the past 16 years. The leading category of JFN is show business news, with about 30 percent of the stories. It's followed by brand name news, sex news, and political news. This year's JFN stories, selected before the 2000 election debacle, follow the pattern set since 1985.

In last year's *Censored* yearbook, I predicted: "The news media in 2000 will be dominated by the quadrennial explosion of political junk food news. The media will loudly decry the trivialization of the presidential election and the influence of money but then go on to portray it as an expensive horse race, characterized by endless polls, political scandals, and unending 20-second television sound bites." About the only thing I missed was the intrusion of the Supreme Court and those pesky chads.

While we, as a nation, have been conditioned to Junk Food News, it's still not too late to get off the JFN diet before we become fatally addicted to it. To do this, we all have to participate. Corporate-level media heads should start to earn their unique First Amendment privileges. Editors should rethink their news judgment. Journalists should persevere in going after the hard stories. Professors of journalism should emphasize ethics and critical analysis and educate more muckrakers and fewer buckrakers. The judicial system should defend the freedom of the press provision of the First Amendment with more vigor. And the public should show the media that it's more concerned with the high crimes and misdemeanors of its political and corporate leaders than with television fantasies and Britney Spears's belly button.

The effort will be worth it. America today is a pale imitation of what it should or could be. More than ever, we need a free, impartial, and aggressive press to expose the conditions that tear our nation apart.

My first published use of the term Junk Food News was in an article I wrote for *Penthouse* magazine in March 1983. The article focused on a comparison of the *New York Times* coverage of two news events that occurred in 1981. In one case, the New York State Worker's Compensation Board ruled that a telephone company supervisor had been killed by prolonged exposure to microwave radiation. It was the first official finding in the United States that long-term exposure to microwaves could cause death.

That information appeared to provide the basis for a significant news story. Experts at the time, and even to this day, suggest that our nation is engulfed daily by microwave pollution that might endanger our health and lives. Studies have linked sustained microwave exposure to headaches, dizziness, fatigue, irritability, loss of judgment, leukemia, cataracts, heart trouble, cancer, central nervous system disorders, and genetic damage. *The New York Times*, America's "newspaper of record," devoted just three column inches to the death of the telephone company supervisor.

For comparative purposes, later that year, *The New York Times* devoted five column inches to a story headlined "London Zoo Says Panda is Pregnant." Throughout 1981, the *Times* ran 20 separate stories about pandas, which took up more than 100 column inches, while it referred back to the microwave death just once. Some of the newsworthy headlines in the *Times* devoted to pandas included: "London's Giant Panda to Get U.S. Valentine," "Panda Mating," "British Panda on Way to the U.S.," "London Zoo Says Panda is Pregnant," and, subsequently, "Panda's Birth is No Surprise."

Personally, I have nothing against pandas. With the possible exception of Great Dane puppies, they may indeed qualify as the cutest animals on the planet. I am, however, intrigued by their awesome ability to attract the attention of our leading news media.

I have often wondered if this might have been one of Richard Nixon's final jokes on the press. Pandas first burst onto our news scene in a major way when then-President Nixon gave two musk oxen to China. In response Chou En-lai gave the United States two giant pandas—Hsing-Hsing and

Ling-Ling. I've often wondered how much coverage our two musk oxen received in the Chinese media.

It may seem that I have been carried away by the pandas myself. Nonetheless, when the nation's most prestigious newspaper devotes twice as much space to the pregnancy of a panda in a London zoo as it does to the death of an American citizen from microwave radiation in New York City, it's time to question the judgment of our news media managers.

The bottom line is that while the nation's most prestigious newspaper essentially ignored a story about death from microwave radiation that potentially affects millions of people, it found the space to report the intimate details of a panda couple—a classic Junk Food News story that, without media coverage, would affect few of us.

Joseph Pulitzer, the renowned American journalist and publisher, once said, "We are a democracy, and there is only one way to get a democracy on its feet in the matter of its individual, its social, its municipal, its state, its national conduct, and that is by keeping the public informed about what is going on." Joseph Pulitzer, whose will provided for the establishment of the Pulitzer Prizes, did not have Britney Spears or pandas or the following JFN stories of 2000 in mind when he said that.

(A John Bogart update for the record: On September 9, 2000, Stephen Maul, 24, a San Francisco furniture mover, was arrested for biting his dog, an 80-pound Labrador puppy named Boo. He also made national news. And, to complete the panda saga, we must note that two new Chinese pandas, Mei Xiang and Tian Tian, made national news when they arrived at the National Zoological Park in Washington, D.C., on December 6, 2000.)

2000 TOP 10 JUNK FOOD NEWS STORIES

1. *Survivor*
2. Elian Gonzalez
3. The millionaire bride ("Who Wants to Marry a Multi-Millionaire?")
4. Britney Spears
5. *Who Wants to Be a Millionaire?*
6. Whitewater and the private lives of the Clintons
7. Napster
8. Tie: The Ellen Degeneres and Anne Heche break-up/ JonBenet Ramsey
9. Ricky Martin's sexuality
10. Tie: Brad Pitt's wedding/Dot-coms and IPOs

The year 2000, opening to the fizzle of the Y2K panic and turning at its close on the counting of pregnant chads, seemed to befuddle both the media and news consumers. In the interim, reporters shrank from dicey news and converged on the simple, easily assimilated entertainment that now all too often masquerades as journalism. Dan Hortsch, public editor for *The Oregonian*, contends that stories like Whitewater and Elian Gonzalez are legitimate stories, but that they are "overreported or are just not covered thoughtfully, or consistently." Dot-coms and IPOs may be legitimate business stories, for instance, but overreporting is what pushed them onto our Top 10 list. Likewise, as Elian shouted, "Leave me alone!" to scores of waiting photographers, few reporters were looking into more telling aspects of the drama such as the conservative Cuban-American hold on Miami's political structure and the more reasonable posture of moderate Cuban Americans across the country. The Elian Gonzalez tug-of-war finally ended with infamous front-page photo spreads of the SWAT team seizure of a frightened boy, later seen smiling in his father's arms on inside pages.

The Top 10 JFN for 2000 succeeded in edging out other equally dubious headline stories by small margins. Runners-up were Harry Potter, the breakup of Microsoft, gas prices at the pumps, Madonna's baby (see also 1996 JFN, #1), Olympic human interest stories, and the ongoing print and air wave saturation by Britain's royal family, in this case Prince William's eighteenth birthday, and an ongoing fascination with the gone-but-not-forgotten Princess Di.

Other stories our judges wished would fade from American consciousness were the anniversaries of the Columbine shootings and the JFK Jr. plane crash. In a few instances ombudsmen nominated their own Junk Food News

THIS MODERN WORLD   by TOM TOMORROW

favorites: the 2000 elections (just wait until next year), the Super Bowl, and newly minted dot-com billionaires.

In fact, stories of instant wealth and sexual exposés (sometimes ludicrously intertwined) dominated our Top 10. Our Junk Food News "winner," the mid-summer reality TV/game show *Survivor,* pitted 16 strangers against an isolated South Sea island—and each other—for $1 million and fame. Who would have thought that the ultimate winner would have been the smug corporate trainer/motivational speaker, Richard "Machiabelly" Hatch, the naked fat guy? The CBS summer ratings' success spawned an entire new subculture which included "Survivor" parties, office pools, and additions to the American lexicon of vacuous phrases such as "the tribe has spoken" (accompanying Regis Philbin's "Is that your final answer?").

Overnight millionaires became the paradigm for the Great American Hero. Two popular paths to riches (less risky than dot-comming or IPO-ing, as winter 2000–2001 demonstrated) were to either get money (and lots of it) by answering inane questions on a TV game show (*Who Wants to Be a Millionaire?* was the highest rated TV show ever) or, in the case of Darva Conger, by marrying a complete stranger—stand-up comic and real estate developer Rick Rockwell. Although the "millionaire bride" chose instant annulment when unappealing stories about the groom's real life began to surface, lucrative offers poured in including the chance to be Regis's co-host and to do a nude *Penthouse* spread.

Not to be outdone, belly-button baring Britney Spears, teenybopper role model and most searched-for subject on Lycos, kept the media hopping as she bounced between classy and trashy. Celibate?—yes according to Ms. Spears; a Lolita?—yes, too, by the looks of a *Rolling Stones* magazine cover. Vacillating between porn queen and prom queen suits her bankroll well;

Ms. Spears, at 19, has sold more than 20 million albums. A fuzzy sexual image also seems to serve Latin heartthrob Ricky Martin well; he continues to refuse to say if he is gay—or not. Who wants to know? Everyone, it seems, including entertainment interrogator Barbara Walters. The breakup of Ellen and Anne (see also 1996 JFN, # 8), however, was the gay event of the year, culminating with the tragic news of "poor" Anne wandering deliriously in a rural California town after the public announcement of the breakup. While breaking up is hard to do, Brad Pitt finally succumbed to Eros and tied the knot. And so it goes in Tinseltown, on and on like the Energizer bunny, providing fodder for so much of what we call "the news."

On the more prosaic side, Napster put the question of intellectual property rights into the pop culture limelight and turned the music industry forever on its head. In the White House, the Clintons were vindicated in the Whitewater case (bad news for "Hillary haters"). "Whitewater [was] a force of its own and hard to ignore, but the special prosecutor drove much of the coverage, and to what end?" wonders ombudsman Hortsch.

Kenneth Starck, ombudsman at the *Cedar Rapids Gazette*, notes, "Like a one-eyed Odysseus, the news media these days scan the environment for that single story that will captivate an audience. Television is particularly prone to obsessing over what attracts viewers. There's little effort, if any, to examine the news for its social relevance. Maybe news execs think the audience is so dumb it can't pay attention to more than one news story at a time. Another problem is the intermingling of talk shows posing as journalism. Real journalists should distance themselves from the blabbermouths."

Once again Project Censored would like to thank the members of the Organization of News Ombudsmen who helped select this year's junk food news. The job of news ombudsmen—to keep the news media on the high road of journalism—often goes unnoticed. Empowered by their editors or publishers to critique published articles and take in and investigate claims from readers and viewers of inaccurate, unfair, unbalanced, or tasteless news reporting, they then make appropriate recommendations for clarification or correction. All too many newspapers do not employ ombudsmen (also known as readers' representatives, readers' advocates, or public editors). Those who don't, might, if the reading and listening public were to expect and demand it.

JUNK FOOD NEWS, 1984–1999

Unfortunately, gathering together the JFN stories of the past 16 years made two things abundantly clear: news reporting has *not* gotten better, and some stories just won't go away. News ombudsmen Emerson Law Stone finds the 25-year trend in junk news reporting troubling. "The grievous part is not just that Junk News has increased markedly, not just that it has infected the traditional news sources, but that those traditionalists continue to deny that it is so, that they do 'hard news.'... Junk eye-candy and ear-candy now often dictate news selection, broadcast length, and placement in the newscast in such once-solid outlets as network evening news. Even the august *New York Times* succumbs now and then. Weekly newsmagazines? Routinely...."

And now, here are Project Censored's winners for the "junk eye- and ear-candy" that dominated the news each of the last 16 years.

1984

1. Octogenarian Clara Peller's "Where's the beef?!" commercial for Wendy's

1985

1. Coca Cola's formula change—new-old-classic-Cherry-Coke
2. Guru Baghwan Shree Rajneesh's lavish lifestyle, Oregon commune, and 85 Rolls Royces
3. *Rambo*: the movie, the doll, the craze
4. The Wall Street merger craze
5. The stock market yo-yo
6. Lee Iacocca saves Chrysler and writes a book
7. Chicago Bears' William "The Refrigerator" Perry
8. *Fatal Vision*: real-life murders become bestselling book, miniseries
9. Halley's Comet
10. Prince Charles and Princess Di (continued from 1984)

1986

1. Clint Eastwood's campaign for mayor of Carmel
2. The 15th anniversary of Disney World (and an all-expenses paid junket to Orlando for 10,000 lucky journalists)
3. The 75th anniversary of the Oreo cookie
4. The Vermont romance of Jessica, the cow, and Bullwinkle, a 700-pound moose
5. The wedding of Prince Andrew and Sarah Ferguson
6. Herb the Nerd, Burger King's answer to Clara Peller
7. The Super Cockroach contest
8. Philippine First Lady Imelda Marcos's shoe collection
9. The weekly media ritual of the White House lawn arrivals and departures of Ronald and Nancy Reagan and their dog

1987

1. The trials and tribulations of TV evangelist Jimmy Bakker and his wet-eyed wife, Tammy Faye
2. Junk Food tarts Jessica Hahn (Jim Bakker), Donna Rice (presidential candidate Gary Hart), and Fawn Hall (Ollie North's secretary) hustle to turn sins into profits
3. Princess Di sets an all-time record in America's Index of Leading Magazine Cover Stories (along with the Stock Market Crash of 1987, for those of you who want to know)
4. Celebrity heartbreaks—Madonna and Sean Penn, Di and Charles, Brigitte Nielsen and Sly Stallone, Bess Meyerson and Andy Capasso, and Liz Taylor and Malcolm Forbes
5. Long Island garbage barge makes a 62-day, 6,000-mile odyssey to six states and several foreign countries before being sent home
6. Olliemania: Col. Oliver North T-shirts, posters, yo-yos, and buttons
7. "Weird" Michael Jackson
8. The Loch Ness Monster revisited; alas, the $1.64 million "scientific" search produced no monster, but plenty of headlines
9. The California Raisins: TV cartoon raisins dancing to Marvin Gaye's "Heard It on the Grapevine" promote the California raisin industry, make a TV special, and record a hit single
10. *Vanna Speaks*, autobiography of *Wheel of Fortune* spinner Vanna White

1988

1. Political trash and trivia of the 1988 election: the endless polls, Dan Quayle's malapropisms, and the media's fascination with itself
2. Trapped whales
3. The Mike Tyson/Robin Givens marital bout
4. Television talk shows
5. The Age of Aquarius and the White House—Nancy Reagan consults the stars
6. 25th JFK assassination anniversary
7. Mickey Mouse's 60th birthday
8. *The Last Temptation of Christ*: fundamentalists protest at movie theaters across the country
9. The last temptation of Jimmy Swaggart: fundamentalist evangelist publicly confesses to "being entertained" by prostitutes
10. The Emperor's death watch: the nation's media rushes to Tokyo to record the final breath of Emperor Hirihito

1989

1. Zsa Zsa Gabor stands trial for slapping a cop
2. Roseanne Barr's off-tube antics
3. Jim and Tammy Faye Bakker: Jimmy gets 45-year prison term
4. The feuding Bryant Gumbel, Willard Scott, Jane Pauley, and Deborah Norville; The *Today Show* goes from news show to early morning soap
5. *Batman*
6. Billionaire real estate heiress Leona Helmsley, "The Queen of Mean," goes to jail for tax evasion
7. Pres. George Bush, Sr. trivia, from fishing fiascoes to Millie, the First Dog
8. VP Dan Quayle
9. Malcolm Forbes' $2 million birthday bash in Morocco
10. The 20th anniversary of Woodstock

1990

1. Donald Trump's marital problems
2. Roseanne Barr's crotch-grabbing rendition of the national anthem
3. The New Madrid (Missouri) Earthquake prediction
4. Milli Vanilli surrenders its Grammy when caught lip-synching their hit album
5. Women sportswriters in male locker rooms
6. Madonna's wardrobe (or lack of it)
7. *The Simpsons*
8. Teenage Mutant Ninja Turtles
9. The president, George Bush, Sr,. hates broccoli
10. The quirky nighttime soap, *Twin Peaks*

1991

1. The William Kennedy Smith rape trial
2. Elizabeth Taylor's wedding—again
3. *Lady and the Tramp*
4. The Gulf War
5. Pee Wee Herman's misadventures at the movies
6. Magic Johnson, the media's first AIDS victim
7. Nancy Reagan's biography
8. The Annette Bening/Warren Beatty Baby Boom
9. The Julia Roberts/Keifer Sutherland almost-wedding
10. Almost Presidential candidate Mario Cuomo's definite indecision

1992

1. Dan Quayle misspells "potato"
2. Madonna's best-selling bare-all, *Sex*
3. TV character Murphy Brown and Vice President Dan Quayle on "family values"
4. The final days of Johnny Carson
5. Royal scandal: Fergie and Di, the naughty royal wives
6. Woody Allen vs. Mia Farrow
7. Clinton paramour Geniffer Flowers
8. The Barbara Bush/Hillary Clinton cookie bake-off
9. The Elvis stamp election
10. The U.S. Olympic "Dream Team"

1993

1. Wife-shooter Amy Fisher (17) and her 39-year-old lover, the husband Joey Buttafuoco (later convicted for statutory rape)
2. Woody Allen and Mia Farrow, again
3. Bill Clinton's $200 haircut
4. Madonna, still
5. John Wayne Bobbitt's severed penis
6. The Michael Jackson allegations
7. Burt and Loni Reynolds' divorce
8. Late night talk show Armageddon: Letterman vs. Arsenio Hall vs. Leno vs. Chevy Chase
9. Heidi Fleiss, the Hollywood Madam
10. *Jurassic Park* "dinosauritis"

1994

1. The O.J. Simpson case
2. Ice-skating hussy Tonya Harding
3. More Roseanne Barr
4. Michael Jackson and Lisa Marie Presley
5. The British Royals
6. John Wayne and Lorena Bobbitt (the movie, the pity)
7. Singapore caning of American teenager, Michael Fay, for malicious mischief
8. The Information Super Highway
9. Whitewater-gate
10. Woodstock II

1995

1. More O.J. Simpson
2. The compromising position of Hugh Grant
3. Kato Kaelin (see Story #1): aspiring bad actor gives testimony
4. Mike Tyson returns from prison
5. Windows 95, the media-hype circus
6. Michael Jackson: near-death collapse, Sony deal
7. Jerry Garcia's demise
8. Colin Powell: "no" to presidency, all-around "Mr. Nice Guy"
9. Mickey Mantle and his liver
10. Shannon Faulkner storms the bastion of the all-male Citadel

1996

1. Celebrity pregnancies: Madonna, Melanie Griffith, Christie Brinkley, Rosie O'Donnell, and Jane Seymour
2. The British Royals
3. The Macarena
4. The Kennedy's auction and JFK Jr.'s wedding
5. Dennis Rodman, from NBA to Hollywood
6. Lisa Marie Presley dumps Michael Jackson
7. O.J. Simpson, part III: the wrongful death suit
8. Ellen DeGeneres comes out
9. The "anonymous" Clinton satire, *Primary Colors*
10. Sex scandal of Clinton advisor, Dick Morris

1997

1. Sports announcer Marv Albert's hairpiece, indictment for sexual assault (bites a woman)
2. Princess Di and the British Royals
3. Frank and Kathie Lee Gifford
4. Michael Jackson's baby, Prince Michael
5. JonBenet Ramsey
6. The Tyson/Holyfield match
7. O.J. Simpson, part IV: the Goldman civil case
8. Tie: Andrew Cunanan's killing spree/ the anniversary of Elvis's death
9. Howard Stern
10. The Paula Jones sexual harassment suit

1998

1. President Clinton's sex life and "Zipper-gate" including Monica Lewinsky, Linda Tripp, Kathleen Willey, Vernon Jordan, the cigar, and "the dress"
2. The Spice Girls
3. *Titanic*
4. Paula Jones
5. The British Royal Family
6. JonBenet Ramsey
7. John Glenn, the geriatric astronaut
8. Jerry Springer
9. Viagra
10. Jerry Seinfield

1999

1. The purple Teletubby, Tinky Winky, is menace to society, says Jerry Falwell
2. Pokémon
3. Y2K
4. Millennium
5. Pamela Anderson Lee's breasts
6. *Star Wars*
7. Clinton: the Clintons search for a house, Monica searches for an apartment, the release of Monica's book, and the Hillary's-side-of-the-story interview
8. The Columbine shootings, teen shootings in general, killer class-mates, and Marilyn Manson delays video release
9. The John F. Kennedy Jr. plane crash
10. George W. Bush and cocaine

CHAPTER 6

Manifestations of Media Bias: The Case of the New York Times Reporting on Indonesia and East Timor

BY EDWARD S. HERMAN

Media bias takes many forms, some not easy to recognize without close examination and comparing how the media treat similar matters with different political implications. The study of bias is complicated by the fact that no media institution or system suppresses everything inconvenient to its agenda, and even the Soviet press elicited denunciations from the Minister of Defense that they were playing into the hands of the enemy by featuring information on drug use and the demoralization of Soviet forces in Afghanistan.[1] The periodic surfacing of similar "negative" information in the U.S. mass media confuses some people, grateful for the morsels and unable or unwilling to see that they are only morsels.

This contrarian information is also the basis for the occasional rhetorical suggestion that as media critics derive much of their information from the mainstream media, their claim of serious bias is self-refuting. This is a fallacy: some, and sometimes a great deal, of the critic's information is obtained outside the mainstream media, and the media's critical facts are

---

[1] Bill Keller, "Soviet Official Says Press Harms Army," *New York Times*, January 21, 1988.

usually easily absorbed without effect, overwhelmed by the biased language, frames, placement, and flood of acceptable information and disinformation that supports the favored line. Obviously we are speaking only of particular topics on which the media have policies and agendas that make truthfulness inconvenient. A media institution may be seriously biased in dealing with labor disputes or policy toward Saddam Hussein and Iraq, but very objectively report news on the conflict between Coca Cola and Pepsi and many other topics.

Censorship and bias are intimately connected, and government agendas and censorship are frequently transmuted into media censorship through common biases and media dependence on official sources. For example, when Indonesia, after having invaded East Timor in 1975, was intensifying its killing there in 1977 and 1978, the Carter administration collaborated with Indonesia both by supplying more arms and by issuing no public protests or reports on the ongoing mass killing. The *New York Times's* news coverage of East Timor fell to zero in those two years, perfectly adapting to official policy, but also reflecting the paper's (and mainstream media's) heavy news dependence on official sources. This was de facto news censorship by the *Times* (et al.), because there were many nonofficial sources that could have been tapped but weren't.[1] In notable acts of hypocrisy, in later years the paper several times editorialized on how unfortunate it was that "most of the world wasn't looking" when Indonesia invaded East Timor (July 25, 1980) and how regrettable it was that East Timor "was largely ignored until last November 12 [1991], when Indonesian troops killed 50 East Timorese" (ed., January 21, 1992)—as if its own news and editorial policies had not contributed to these results.

As noted, the comparative method is helpful in demonstrating bias, and it can yield dramatic results. In what follows I will examine how The *New York Times*, the distinguished "paper of record," has used words, framed issues, treated information sources, and made—as well as institutionalized—errors in dealing with Suharto, East Timor, and Indonesia, in comparison with its treatment of official enemies like Pol Pot and Slobodan Milosevic.[2]

---

[1]For a full account of this history, and the neglect of optional sources, see Noam Chomsky and Edward Herman, *The Washington Connection and Third World Fascism* (Boston: South End Press, 1979), pp. 129–217.

[2]Citations below not otherwise attributed are from articles in *The New York Times*. For more illustrations and a discussion of other forms of bias, see Edward Herman, *The Myth of the Liberal Media: An Edward Herman Reader* (New York: Peter Lang, 1999), especially chapter 5.

LANGUAGE AND TONE

Although General Suharto's takeover of Indonesia in 1965–1966 was accompanied by the killing of 700,000 or more civilians, and despite the fact that his invasion and occupation of East Timor, which led to the death of some 200,000 in a population of only 700,000, has never been recognized by the United Nations, his rule was consistently supported by the U.S. government and its allies. The language and tone of the news reports in the *New York Times* have paralleled this government support, treating the Indonesian dictator gently. Thus, while Pol Pot was referred to as a "despised killer" and "mass murderer" who committed "genocide," and Milosevic was carrying out a "genocidal campaign" in Kosovo and "ravaged" Kosovo with "horrors," the words "despised killer" or "mass murderer" have never been applied to Suharto by *Times* reporters or editorial writers, nor have the words "genocide," "ravaged," or "horrors" been applied by them to Indonesian operations in East Timor, with the single exception of Anthony Lewis's use of the word "horror" (August 12, 1994). In Barbara Crossette's words, Indonesia and Suharto have merely had "a troublesome reputation in human rights" (June 23, 1996).

Times reporters—and other mainstream reporters as well—have regularly found that Pol Pot and Milosevic were personally responsible for the deaths associated with their rule and policies. Thus, Philip Shenon refers to Pol Pot "the man responsible for the deaths of more than a million Cambodians" (April 11, 1998), and the editors call him the person "who ordered more than a million people killed" (June 24, 1997). But in describing Suharto's deadly takeover of Indonesia, *Times* reporters have long resorted to the passive voice and have found it difficult to identify an agent who did the killing. There was "a wave of violence that took up to 500,000 lives," or "more than 500,000 Indonesians are estimated to have died in a purge of leftists in 1965" (Seth Mydans, August 7, 1996 and April 8, 1997), or "650,000 people are believed to have died" (Colin Campbell, November 28, 1982). The victims in Indonesia just "died," whereas Cambodians and Kosovo Albanians were killed and massacred, with particular individuals the responsible agents. Note also the use of the word "purge" instead of slaughter or murder, and the making of the victims into "leftists" although many thousands were merely peasant farmers.

Reporter Steve Erlanger wrote about East Timor that "This is one of the world's sadder places, where 100,000 to 200,000 people died from 1974 in a brutal civil war and the consequent invasion through combat, execution, disease and starvation" (October 21, 1990). Here also we see the use of the passive voice and absence of a clear agent; but in addition, there is serious misrepresentation of the facts—the civil war was short and left small numbers dead; and the invasion was not "consequent" to a brutal civil war, except in Indonesian propaganda. Furthermore, the listing of the sources of deaths, with "combat" placed first, prior to "executions," and adding in disease and starvation, lessens Indonesian responsibility for the deaths of a larger fraction of the population than died in Cambodia under Pol Pot. Making Indonesia's invasion a response to a "brutal civil war," and identifying the sources of deaths as combat first, then a mixed bag, constitutes a complete apologetic package.

Times reporters have even had numerous explicitly positive statements about the approved dictator and genocidist. Suharto is a "profoundly spiritual man" according to Nicholas Kristof, a "reforming autocrat" for Steven Erlanger, and a man with benevolent motives, who simply "failed to comprehend the intensity of people's discontents" according to Seth Mydans.[1]

FRAMING

Another language abuse observable in *Times* reporting is the repeated reference to the East Timorese resisters to the Indonesian occupation as "separatists." The UN never recognized the Indonesian invasion-occupation, but the U.S. government did, and *Times* reporting practice followed. Beyond

---

[1]Kristof, "Suharto: A King of Java Past, Confronts Indonesia's Future," June 2, 1998; Erlanger, "Suharto Fostered Rapid Economic Growth, and Staggering Graft," May 22, 1998; Mydans, "Suharto Besieged, Steps Down After 32-Year Rule in Indonesia," May 21, 1998.

THIS MODERN WORLD   by TOM TOMORROW

making the resistance forces "separatists," during the period from July 19, 1985, through September 22, 1999, *Times* reporters regularly datelined their articles from East Timor "Dili, Indonesia," just as apologists for the Iraq invasion-occupation of Kuwait in 1990 might have regarded the exiled government of Kuwait as "separatist" and datelined any reports from that country "Kuwait City, Iraq." This normalization of Indonesia's aggression-occupation has allowed *Times* reporters to frame the ongoing struggle there as between an implicitly legitimate occupation and "separatists" who refuse to recognize reality, rather than a liberation movement fighting for self-determination and independence.

Times reporter Seth Mydans refers to the "long separatist war" and a "generation of insurgent warfare" in East Timor, thereby subtly making the killing there a result of the stubborn behavior of separatists, not the Indonesian invader (April 26, 1999). He never mentions an Indonesian "invasion," only that Indonesia was "annexed… after its colonial ruler, Portugal, withdrew." Nor does he mention any "long and brutal war of pacification" carried out by the Indonesian army, only that East Timor has become a "tropical island with little joy," rife with "violence and terror," the only named source of the violence being "insurgent warfare." This is straightforward apologetics for Indonesian terror.

Over the years *Times* reporters have used three other frames of apologetics for Suharto's dictatorship and mass killings. One is that Suharto's takeover and slaughters of 1965–1966 were induced by an attempted Communist coup. They were "a result of a failed coup" (Shenon, August 27, 1993), which "touched off a wave of violence" (Mydans, August 7, 1996), or "followed an onslaught from the left" (Henry Kamm, June 17, 1979). These formulas, invoked repeatedly, suggest that the holocaust was provoked

and thus may be justified by the prior "onslaught." In the case of Pol Pot, by contrast, although his forces suffered terrible damage from U.S. bombing and state violence, and starvation and disease were already rampant when his forces took over in April 1975, *Times* reporters have never mentioned these as background facts relevant to a discussion of Pol Pot's subsequent actions.

Another major apologetic frame is that Suharto brought "stability" to Indonesia and the area. "Throughout Mr. Suharto's rule, Indonesia has been a bulwark of stability in Southeast Asia" (Seth Mydans, January 10, 1998). "Stability and a constitutional succession are desired even by Mr. Suharto's harshest critics [the reporter remains to go unnamed]" (Steven Erlanger, November 11, 1990). Things may look undemocratic, but "Ms. Megawati's outspokenness breaks the rules of Indonesian-style consensus politics" (Mydans, July 29, 1996). Whereas the Sukarno government was "a military threat to its neighbors and an international bully," under Suharto "Indonesia has become a stabilizing influence" (Barbara Crossette, April 20, 1986). In contrast with Saddam Hussein, "Mr. Suharto isn't hoarding anthrax or threatening to invade Australia" (David Sanger, March 8, 1998). Note that neither Crossette nor Sanger regard Suharto's invasion and murderous occupation of East Timor as international bullying or equivalent to a "threat" to invade another country. Joseph Stalin brought a kind of stability to the Soviet Union, just as Suharto did to Indonesia, but he was never a "bulwark of stability" in the pages of the *Times*.

In addition to stability, Suharto brought "growth," which in the *Times* has regularly been introduced to counterbalance repression and terror. (Stalin also brought growth, but the *Times* has never allowed this as an offset to his terror.) "It has been Indonesia's remarkable prosperity that has cemented [Suharto's] control" (David Sanger and Seth Mydans, January 18, 1998). This insight on *cemented control* preceded Suharto's downfall by four months. "The signs of success are everywhere in this increasingly prosperous nation of 190 million people" (Mydans, June 21, 1996). This third apologetic frame—of terror counterbalanced by growth—was encapsulated in the title to Philip Shenon's "As Indonesia Crushes Its Critics, It Helps Millions Escape Poverty" (August 27, 1993).

SOURCING

A *Wall Street Journal* article of July 14, 1998 showed that in reality the "trickle-down" of Indonesian growth to the millions never took place, and that the government and World Bank claim of a large-scale reduction in poverty was a big lie.[1] In reaching this conclusion the *Journal* article authors spoke with a variety of retired Indonesian officials and former U.S. officials and consultants. The *Times* and other mainstream media, however, had always been content to pass along the claims of Indonesian and World Bank officials, as Shenon did in his article on "Millions Escape Poverty." Interestingly, the *Wall Street Journal* bombshell was never cited in the *New York Times* or *Washington Post*, nor did it lead them to do any further investigative work on the subject. They were satisfied to leave intact the propaganda claim and misinformation protecting our ally in Indonesia, much favored by the large oil companies and with Suharto himself, referred to by a Clinton administration official as "our kind of guy."[2]

Even in dealing with Indonesian terror, the *Times* has relied heavily on the terrorists and shown minimal investigative zeal in checking out or following up their claims. Indonesia refused to let reporters visit East Timor "because of the government's belief that they will not be objective." (Barbara Crossette, March 20, 1988). Crossette suggested no other possible reason for Indonesian official reticence. Similarly, citing an Indonesian official, Henry Kamm reported that "because of continuing insecurity, the former colony remains a restricted area" (April 19, 1978). It is noteworthy that Kamm interprets the Indonesian occupation as noncolonial. And for this reporter, claims of terrible things going on in East Timor are qualified by the fact that "the bulk of the testimony has come from highly partisan members or supporters of Fretilin" (Kamm, February 15, 1981). In reporting the reason for restrictions on entry given him by Indonesian officials in 1978 Kamm never suggested that this was from a "highly partisan" source. This makes explicit Kamm's and the *Times's* own partisan identification with the Suharto dictatorship.

INSTITUTIONALIZED LIES

Bias is also frequently evidenced by the institutionalization of lies. Thus, from the moment of the Indonesian invasion of East Timor on December 7, 1975, *Times* news reports and editorials reported that Indonesia's "incursion" took place in the midst of a civil war, that Indonesia was "providing support for the anti-Fretilin forces,... which had seemed to be winning the

---

[1]Marcus Brauchli, "Speak No Evil: Why the World Bank Failed to Anticipate Indonesia's Crisis, " *Wall Street Journal*, July 14, 1998.
[2]Quoted in David Sanger, "Real Politics: Why Suharto Is In and Castro Is Out," *New York Times*, October 31, 1995.

civil war handily against pro-Indonesian forces until Jakarta began to intervene."[1] In fact, the civil war had ended in September, but Indonesian propaganda maintained that it was only helping "pro-Indonesian forces" in its December invasion, and the *Times* passed along this disinformation in both news articles and editorials. It also repeated the Indonesian claim of a "lightning takeover" of East Timor, when in fact Indonesian forces had only occupied Dili. The former claim—that Indonesia had only intervened in a civil war—made the invasion more palatable than if it had been to reverse a victory and end East Timor's new found independence; and accepting the lie of a lightning takeover made it easier to accept the aggression as a settled matter. The U.S. State Department repeated these propaganda claims from the day of the invasion onward, and the *New York Times* followed in its wake.

And the initial lies have been repeated many times since. East Timor "was taken by force by Indonesia in 1975 as separatists were trying to proclaim independence," stated Philip Shenon in a September 17, 1992, news article. Shenon makes the East Timorese "separatists" even before the Indonesian aggressors had occupied the area. In a more fuzzy version of this apology, Clyde Haberman said that Indonesia annexed East Timor "in the confusion that followed the withdrawal of Portugal in 1974" (October 13, 1989).

And what was the U.S. role in the Indonesian invasion and occupation? The U.S. "furnished most of the weapons that Indonesia used for its invasion—although the United States intended that these weapons be used only for Indonesia's self-defense" (Henry Kamm, February 15, 1981). In the same article Kamm says that although President Ford and Secretary Kissinger visited Suharto on the eve of the invasion, "there is no evidence that they discussed the invasion with him." But given the importance of the invasion, the timing of the visit, the subsequent U.S. behavior supporting the invasion, and the improbability that U.S. collusion would be acknowledged, Kamm's citing only a lack of evidence is atrocious reporting and de facto apologetics. He never indicates how he knows U.S. weapons-use intentions, and he fails to mention the contradictory fact of a quadrupling of the U.S. flow of weapons after the invasion and during the savage pacification that ensued, along with the failure of the U.S. government to protest the aggression and killing (and, in fact, protection of Indonesia against any effective international action).[2]

---

[1] For these and other quotes from *Times* news articles and editorials, see Chomsky and Herman, *Washington Connection*, pp. 129-172.

[2] Then-U.S. Ambassador to the UN, Daniel Patrick Moynihan, brags in his autobiography about his success in blocking any effective international action against Indonesia in 1975. See *A Dangerous Place* (Boston: Little Brown, 1978), p. 247.

THE MORE THINGS CHANGE,
THE MORE THEY STAY THE SAME

In the light of the U.S. intervention allegedly on behalf of human rights in Kosovo, and Richard Holbrooke's role there, it is interesting to note that back in 1977, when Holbrooke was Assistant Secretary for East Asian and Pacific Affairs, he stated that "I want to stress I am not remotely interested in getting involved in an argument over the actual number of people killed [in East Timor]. People were killed, and that is always a tragedy but what is at issue is the actual situation in Timor today…"[1] The "actual situation" for Holbrooke was that Indonesia had firm control (which was a lie even then), so that any ongoing killing is an internal Indonesian problem. As for the numbers killed in the past, "we are never going to know anyway." So let us move on to issues, like perhaps the number Pol Pot was killing!

Things haven't changed one iota. Pol Pot's victims in Cambodia aroused a frenzy here in the mid to late 1970s, whereas the unworthy victims of our friend Suharto were treated in very muted fashion in light of "the actual situation"—that our friend had allegedly established control by aggression. A little more than two decades later, the worthy victims in Kosovo moved Holbrooke and his fellow officials to anguish over the "genocide." The numbers killed in Kosovo were urgently important; the search for mass graves was intense. On the other hand, when our Indonesian ally interfered with the August 30, 1999 UN-sponsored referendum in East Timor, killing thousands and creating hundreds of thousands of refugees, the Clinton administration was "regretful" but suffered no anguish, was not interested in numbers and mass graves, and claimed that this was an internal Indonesian business. It never threatened Indonesia with sanctions let alone the Kosovo solution, and when the administration very belatedly intervened to call off its friend, that sufficed. There was no demand that graves be located and victims identified, nor any call for reparations or the establishment of an international tribunal to try criminals.

And once again the *Times* followed the same pattern. It provided extensive and indignant coverage of the Serb treatment of Kosovo Albanians, using the word "genocide" in 52 news articles and 16 editorials and opinion columns on the conflict in 1999. There were numerous front page articles and pictures, and generous and uncritical attention was given to the work of the War Crimes Tribunal. The paper maintained a steady focus on Serb president Slobodan Milosevic, his trials and tribulations, his misdeeds,

---

[1]Quoted in Chomsky and Herman, *Washington Connection*, p. 148.

his status as an "indicted war criminal," and the evidence of war crimes committed and mass graves found in Kosovo.[1]

But the paper's treatment of Indonesia's assault on East Timor from 1998 through 2000 was of a different order. Although highly credible sources estimated that the Indonesian army and army-sponsored militias killed between 3,000 and 6,000 civilians even before the referendum was held—twice or more than the number of deaths in Kosovo in the year before the NATO bombing—the *Times* failed to report those estimates, and its reporters and editors never once used the word genocide to describe the ongoing terror in 1999. In the months before the referendum, the frame used by reporter Seth Mydans was not one of an aggressor and massive human rights violator being opposed by an oppressed people seeking freedom, or a terror state trying to prevent a UN-organized free election. Instead, in a rerun of the old *Times* apologia in which Indonesia intervened in a war between "separatists" and "pro-Indonesia forces," Mydans posed the struggle as one of "integrationists" fighting "separatists," with an uncertain outcome.[2]

Following the withdrawal of Indonesia from East Timor in November 1999, the paper's modest interest in the area flagged. In contrast with its continuing attention to Kosovo, there was no interest in numbers killed or mass graves and minimal reporting on or concern over the condition of the survivors in East Timor. In a rare article by Seth Mydans on the problem of bringing justice for the atrocities in East Timor, he writes that the referendum was followed "by a campaign of revenge, in which most of the territory's buildings were ruined, perhaps 1,000 people killed, scores of women raped and more than a quarter of the population of 800,000 forcibly transported across the border into Indonesian West Timor."[3] Mydans does not mention the 3,000–6,000 killed before the referendum, and he fails to discuss why the United States and its allies did not intervene to prevent this catastrophe, which was underway many months before August 30, 1999, and known by Western authorities to pose a still greater post-referendum threat. He also fails to explain why the Great Powers didn't immediately insist on the repatriation of the several hundred thousand East Timorese driven into West Timor and left to be abused by the Indonesian army and militias. He discusses the stymied process of bringing the criminals to jus-

---

[1] For a fuller account, see Edward Herman and David Peterson, "The NATO–Media Lie Machine," *Z Magazine*, May 2000.

[2] Seth Mydans, "With Peace Accord at Hand, East Timor's War Deepens," *New York Times*, April 26, 1999.

[3] Seth Mydans, "And Justice For All?," *New York Times*, October 22, 2000.

tice, left to a powerless UN and Indonesia itself. But he doesn't explain why the Great Powers haven't insisted on reparations from Indonesia, and why they don't seem interested in finding mass graves and organizing a War Crimes Tribunal in this case, in contrast with their great energy in pursuing Yugoslav war criminals.

I can envision some years hence the *Times* editorializing on how regrettable it was that "the world wasn't looking" when thousands of East Timorese died in West Timor long after Indonesia withdrew from East Timor, and how unfortunate that justice was "largely ignored" as Indonesia's war criminals escaped scot free. The Times and its media confreres have averted their eyes here as in the past in accord with State Department priorities; news policy once again follows the official agenda and reinforces state policy, and the unworthy victims suffer accordingly while their tormenters remain unpunished.

CONCLUDING NOTE

In sum, we are dealing with a durable relationship between official and media policy, with the media (in this case, the *New York Times*) functioning here as a virtual propaganda arm of the state. But this propaganda service is hard to see, as the mainstream media all perform this service, have furious debates among themselves and criticize the government—within narrow bounds—and speak with great confidence and indignation on the crimes of enemy states while evading, obfuscating, and suppressing information in dealing with the crimes of "our kinds of guy." As shown here, with regrettable brevity, comparing their treatment of friends and enemies, worthy and unworthy victims, throws considerable light on their structured and systematic bias.

THIS MODERN WORLD

by TOM TOMORROW

CHAPTER 7

The Media Oligarchy: Undermining Journalism, Obstructing Democracy

BY NORMAN SOLOMON

In December 2000, nearly a full year after the announcement of plans for America Online to purchase Time Warner, the Federal Trade Commission approved the deal. Despite much-ballyhooed "concessions" by the two merging conglomerates, AOL Time Warner signifies more extreme concentration of media power. The benefits for investors are evident, but merger-mania continues to undermine journalism.

"Freedom of the press is guaranteed only to those who own one," A.J. Liebling remarked several decades ago. Today, as Ben Bagdikian has documented, half a dozen corporations own media outlets that control most of the news and information flow in the United States. The current situation is terrific for the profits of those with the deepest pockets, but bad for democratic possibilities.

The latest huge wave of media consolidation can be traced to the day in September 1999 when the Viacom–CBS story broke. News coverage depicted a $37 billion match made in corporate heaven. It was (at that point) the largest media merger in history. With potential effects on the broader public kept outside the story's frame, what emerged was a rosy picture. "Analysts hailed the deal as a good fit between two complementary companies," the Associated Press reported flatly. The news service went on to quote a media analyst who proclaimed: "It's a good deal for everybody."

"Everybody"? Well, everybody who counts in the mass media calculus. For instance, the media analyst quoted by AP was from the PaineWebber investment firm. "You need to be big," Christopher Dixon explained. "You need to have a global presence." Dixon showed up again the next morning (September 8) in the lead article of the *New York Times,* along with other high-finance strategists. An analyst at Merrill Lynch agreed with his upbeat view of the Viacom–CBS combination. So did an expert from ING Barings: "You can literally pick an advertiser's needs and market that advertiser across all the demographic profiles, from Nickelodeon with the youngest consumers to CBS with some of the oldest consumers."

In sync with the prevalent media spin, the *New York Times* devoted plenty of ink to assessing advertiser needs and demographic profiles. But during the crucial first day of the *Times* coverage, foes of the Viacom–CBS consolidation did not get a word in edgewise. There was, however, an unintended satire of corporate journalism when a writer referred to the bygone era of the 1970s: "In those quaint days, it bothered people when companies owned too many media properties."

The *Washington Post,* meanwhile, ran a front-page story that provided similar treatment of the latest and greatest media merger, pausing just long enough for a short dissonant note from media critic Mark Crispin Miller: "The implications of these mergers for journalism and the arts are enormous. It seems to me that this is, by any definition, an undemocratic development. The media system in a democracy should not be inordinately dominated by a few very powerful interests." It wasn't an idea that the *Post's* journalists pursued.

Overall, the big media outlets offer narrow and cheery perspectives on the significance of merger mania. News accounts keep the focus on market share preoccupations of investors and top managers. Numerous stories explore the widening vistas of cross-promotional synergy for the shrewdest media titans. While countless reporters are determined to probe how each company stands to gain from the latest deal, few of them demonstrate much enthusiasm for exploring what's at stake for the public.

With rare exceptions, news outlets covered the Viacom–CBS merger as a business story. But more than anything else, it should have been covered, at least in part, as a story with dire implications for democratic discourse. And the same was true for the announcement that came a few months later, on January 10, 2000, when a hush seemed to fall over the profession of journalism.

A grand new structure, AOL Time Warner, was unveiled in the midst of much talk about a wondrous New Media world to come, with cornucopias of bandwidth and market share. On January 2, just one week before the portentous announcement, the head of Time Warner had alluded to the transcendent horizons. Global media "will be and is fast becoming the predominant business of the twenty-first century," Gerald Levin said on CNN, "and we're in a new economic age, and what may happen, assuming that's true, is it's more important than government. It's more important than educational institutions and non-profits."

Levin went on: "So what's going to be necessary is that we're going to need to have these corporations redefined as instruments of public service because they have the resources, they have the reach, they have the skill base. And maybe there's a new generation coming up that wants to achieve meaning in that context and have an impact, and that may be a more efficient way to deal with society's problems than bureaucratic governments." Levin's next sentence underscored the sovereign right of capital in dictating the new direction. "It's going to be forced anyhow because when you have a system that is instantly available everywhere in the world immediately, then the old-fashioned regulatory system has to give way," he said.

To discuss an imposed progression of events as some kind of natural occurrence is a convenient form of mysticism, long popular among the corporately pious, who are often eager to wear mantles of royalty and divinity. Tacit beliefs deem the accumulation of wealth to be redemptive. Inside corporate temples, monetary standards gauge worth. Powerful executives now herald joy to the world via a seamless web of media. Along the way, the rest of us are not supposed to worry much about democracy. On January 12, 2000, AOL chief Steve Case assured *NewsHour with Jim Lehrer* viewers that "nobody's going to control anything." Seated next to him, Levin declared: "This company is going to operate in the public interest."

Such pledges, invariably uttered in benevolent tones, were bursts of fog while Case and Levin moved ahead to gain more billions for themselves and maximum profits for some other incredibly wealthy people. By happy coincidence, they insisted, the media course that would make them richest was the same one that held the most fulfilling promise for everyone on the planet.

Journalists accustomed to scrutinizing the public statements of powerful officials seem quite willing to hang back from challenging the claims of media magnates. Even when reporting on a rival media firm, journalists who work in glass offices hesitate to throw weighty stones; a substantive critique of corporate media priorities could easily boomerang. And when a media merger suddenly occurs, news coverage can turn deferential overnight.

On March 14, 2000—the day after the Tribune Co. announced its purchase of the *Los Angeles Times* and the rest of the Times Mirror empire—the acquired newspaper reported on the fine attributes of its owner-to-be. In a news article that read much like a corporate press release, the *Times* hailed the Tribune Co. as "a diversified media concern with a reputation for strong management" and touted its efficient benevolence. Tribune top managers, in the same article, "get good marks for using cost-cutting and technology improvements throughout the corporation to generate a profit margin that's among the industry's highest." The story went on to say that "Tribune is known for not using massive job cuts to generate quick profits from media properties it has bought."

Compare that rosy narrative to another news article published the same day by the *New York Times.* Its story asserted, as a matter of fact, that "the Tribune Co. has a reputation not only for being a fierce cost-cutter and union buster but for putting greater and greater emphasis on entertainment and business."

The corporate priorities of mass media are hardly mysterious or clandestine. "It is not necessary to construct a theory of intentional cultural control," media critic Herbert Schiller commented in 1989. "In truth, the strength of the control process rests in its apparent absence. The desired systemic result is achieved ordinarily by a loose though effective institutional process." In his book *Culture, Inc.: The Corporate Takeover of Public Expression,* Schiller went on to cite "the education of journalists and other media professionals, built-in penalties and rewards for doing what is expected, norms presented as objective rules, and the occasional but telling direct intrusion from above. The main lever is the internalization of values."

Self-censorship has long been one of journalism's most ineffable hazards. The mergers rocking the media industry are heightening the dangers. To an unprecedented extent, large numbers of American reporters and editors now work for just a few huge companies, a situation that hardly encourages unconstrained scrutiny of media conglomerates as they assume unparalleled importance in public life.

The mergers also put a lot more journalists on the payrolls of mega-media institutions that are very newsworthy as major economic and social forces. But if those institutions are paying the professionals who provide the bulk of the country's news coverage, how much will the public learn about the internal dynamics and societal effects of these global entities?

Many of us grew up with tales of journalistic courage dating back to colonial days. John Peter Zenger's ability to challenge the British Crown with unyielding articles drew strength from the fact that he was a printer and publisher. Writing in the *New York Weekly*, a periodical burned several times by the public hangman, Zenger asserted in November 1733: "The loss of liberty in general would soon follow the suppression of the liberty of the press; for it is an essential branch of liberty, so perhaps it is the best preservative of the whole."

In contrast to state censorship, which is usually easy to recognize, self-censorship by journalists tends to be obscured. It is particularly murky and insidious in the emerging media environment, with routine pressures to defer to employers that have massive industry clout. We might wonder how Zenger would fare in most of today's media workplaces, especially if he chose to denounce as excessive the power of the conglomerate providing his paycheck.

Americans are inclined to quickly spot and automatically distrust government efforts to impose prior restraint. But what about the implicit constraints imposed by the hierarchies of enormous media corporations and internalized by employees before overt conflicts develop?

"If liberty means anything at all," George Orwell wrote, "it means the right to tell people what they do not want to hear." As immense communications firms increasingly dominate our society, how practical will it be for journalists to tell their bosses—and the public—what media tycoons do not want to hear about the concentration of power in few corporate hands? Orwell's novel *1984* describes the conditioned reflex of "stopping short, as though by instinct, at the threshold of any dangerous thought... and of being bored or repelled by any train of thought which is capable of leading in a heretical direction."

In the real world of the early twenty-first century, bypassing key issues of corporate dominance is apt to be a form of obedience: in effect, self-censorship. "Circus dogs jump when the trainer cracks his whip," Orwell observed, "but the really well-trained dog is the one that turns his somersault when there is no whip." Of course, no whips are visible in America's modern newsrooms and studios. But if Orwell were alive today, he would surely urge us to be skeptical about all the somersaults.

Does America have a military-industrial-media complex? Whether you consider the question in terms of psychology or economics, some grim answers are available.

Forty years ago, a farewell speech by President Dwight Eisenhower warned about the "conjunction of an immense military establishment and a large arms industry." He said: "In the councils of government, we must guard against the acquisition of unwarranted influence, whether sought or unsought, by the military-industrial complex. The potential for the disastrous rise of misplaced power exists and will persist." That potential has been realized, with major help from media.

Rather than scrutinize the merchants of militarism, large news organizations have been inclined to embrace them. (In some cases, as with NBC and General Electric, network owner and arms contractor are one and the same.) The Pentagon's key vendors can rest assured that big TV and radio outlets will function much more as allies than adversaries.

On television, the recruitment ads for the armed forces symbolize the cozy—and lucrative—ties between the producers of fantasy violence and the planners of vast carnage. Military leaders have good reasons to appreciate the nation's entertainment media for encouraging public acceptance of extreme violence.

In the late summer of 2000, when the Federal Trade Commission issued a report that faulted media companies for marketing violence to children, various politicians expressed outrage. But few of them came close to taking on the National Association of Broadcasters, a trade association with a fitting acronym. The NAB has a notable record of nabbing the public airwaves for private gain.

In practice, big money rules the airwaves, and that's the way the NAB likes it. The industry swung its mighty lobbying arm to knock down a proposal—approved by the Federal Communications Commission —to license low-power radio stations. (During 2000, National Public Radio helped by participating in the successful effort to persuade Congress to block low-power stations.) The specter of community-based "microbroadcasting" has worried the NAB, which sees wealth as a vital precondition for control of broadcast frequencies.

The NAB has championed some new laws, like the landmark Telecommunications Act of 1996 that made it possible for a single corporation to own several radio stations in the same city—and hundreds of stations across the country. Now, more than ever, cookie-cutter stations from coast to coast are beaming identical syndicated garbage to millions of listeners.

As autumn 2000 got underway, the NAB held its annual radio convention in San Francisco. The keynote speaker was a former chairman of the Joint Chiefs of Staff. "Colin Powell is a true national hero," said NAB's president. A decade earlier, Powell had won great media acclaim for overseeing the Gulf

War slaughter of Iraqi people—200,000 of them in a six-week period, according to a Pentagon estimate. At the time, America's broadcasters and their cable television colleagues presented the bloodshed as a glorious exercise of military prowess, rendered on TV screens as dramatic video games.

Political bluster tells us that children should not be overly exposed to media images of simulated violence—but it's A-O.K. to depict the real thing as a big feather in the nation's patriotic cap. The military-industrial-media complex takes its toll with deeply ingrained patterns of newspeak and doublethink. Orwell recognized such patterns long ago.

American media's high comfort level with sanctioned violence—imaginary or real—has a numbing effect on people of all ages. Meanwhile, the dominant weave of propaganda and militarism is, for some, a brocade embossed with gold.

In September 1998, Colin Powell joined the management board of America Online. In January 2000, the retired general voted with other members of the board to approve AOL's purchase of Time Warner. (Powell's stake in the deal was appreciable, as he held AOL stock options worth $13.3 million.) His son Michael Powell was one of the five FCC commissioners voting on whether to approve the merger of AOL and Time Warner.

One of the most insidious prerogatives of media giants is that they largely filter out news about challenges to their own power. Dissent was not on the agenda inside the NAB convention. But I was glad to be among the more than one thousand people who marched nearby, in the streets of San Francisco, to confront the dire centralization of media ownership. "Perhaps unsurprisingly, the corporate media responded to protests against their own power with a news blackout," reported Rachel Coen of the media watch group FAIR (where I'm an associate). "The NAB protests received no mainstream press or broadcast coverage outside the Bay Area, and precious little press attention even locally."

In late 2000, after a decade filled with round-the-clock media sensations, the United States ended up with one that was truly portentous. The post-election battle for the White House stood in sharp contrast to countless ersatz stories that gained enormous coverage during the 1990s. The overtime fight between Al Gore and George W. Bush was certainly historic—but their partisan version of a demolition derby may not have been as profound as we thought.

While Americans finished Thanksgiving turkey leftovers with no president-elect in sight, the sizzling media fixations of previous years seemed notably trivial. In retrospect, how would one rank the uproar about Tonya Harding and Nancy Kerrigan? All the obsessive and protracted O.J. mania? The cable TV–driven frenzy over little Elian?

After such breathless stories, the network anchors were proud to be reporting on truly weighty events as Gore and Bush operatives went all-out. But ironically, the "better" the story got—the more that Democrats and Republicans clashed, litigated, and spun at a frenetic pace—the farther it moved from the essence of political leverage in America.

Nearly 3,000 years ago, the Greek poet Homer was serving as a darn good media critic when he lamented, "We mortals hear only the news, and know nothing at all."

A few centuries after Homer, another poet, Francis Quarles, offered some advice that still resonates with wisdom. "Let the greatest part of the news thou hearest be the least part of what thou believest, lest the greater part of what thou believest be the least part of what is true."

Fast forward to 1920, when the great writer and hell-raiser Upton Sinclair observed that "journalism in America is the business and practice of presenting the news of the day in the interest of economic privilege."

In the waning weeks of 2000, with journalists and many of the rest of us transfixed with the slugfest in Florida, each twist and turn of the story took us further away from the strongest muscle behind American politics—big money.

If we're attentive to the breaking news of the day, we're apt to know a lot of isolated facts. But truth is another matter.

On the surface, in news coverage of historic events, what we see is what we get. But what about what we don't see?

"In the American republic," journalist Walter Karp wrote in 1989, "the fact of oligarchy is the most dreaded knowledge of all, and our news keeps that knowledge from us." His words, first appearing in *Harper's* magazine, are even more acutely relevant today. "By their subjugation of the press, the political powers in America have conferred on themselves the greatest of political blessings—Gyges's ring of invisibility."

If a wealthy few have inordinate power to dominate government decision-making, and most of their manipulations occur behind Oz-like curtains, then what are we to make of the feverish media spectacle that unfolded in Florida?

A convincing case could be made—but you didn't hear it on network television—that the 2000 presidential election was stolen by both of the two major parties as they ran campaigns fueled with hundreds of millions of dollars from wealthy individuals and large corporations. No matter who the next president turned out to be, those benefiting from the fact of oligarchy had already won. Most Americans had good reasons to count themselves among the losers.

One of the great paradoxes of modern journalism is that unusual and extraordinary events seem to be the most newsworthy—but in the long run, key realities of our lives are shaped by what's usual and ordinary.

The news coverage filling our screens is routinely the product of haste, with little exploration beyond the surface. Generally, the sizzle of the moment prevails—which is understandable, since novelties tend to be more captivating than chronic situations. But over time, barraged with accounts of the atypical, our society can easily lose sight of what matters most.

"When a dog bites a man, that's not news, because it happens so often," journalist John Bogart commented many decades ago. "But if a man bites a dog, that is news." This assumption is apt to sound like common sense. It's certainly common, but is it really sensible? After all, we have much more reason to be concerned about dogs biting people than the other way around.

If something happens all the time, it's unlikely to be "news"—but it ultimately may be far more significant than the latest sensation.

In late 2000, American television showed what it could do when the stakes were obviously high and the story was complex. For more than a month, the intensity of post-election coverage was remarkable—especially on the nation's cable news channels. From West Palm Beach, Miami, and Tallahassee to Austin and Washington, the biggest TV outlets used state-of-the-art technologies to bring us vivid accounts of dramatic history in the making.

Now, let's imagine what could happen if the great powers of the networks concentrated on cumulatively momentous day-to-day events that usually get scant media attention. The reportage might sound something like this:

➤"Welcome to our continuing coverage of 'Malnutrition 2001.' As widespread hunger in America wears on, news analysts wonder if the country is beginning to run out of patience. How long can the public accept delays in resolving this crisis while millions of children keep going to bed hungry? With the latest developments…"

➤"Joining us now on another special broadcast of 'National Health Crisis' are investigators who've been examining why upwards of 42 million Americans—15 percent of the population—still don't have health insurance. We'll also hear some harrowing examples of what this has meant during the last few hours, in human terms, at clinics and hospitals across the country…"

➤"Welcome to 'Poverty 2001: America's Children Held Hostage.' Tonight, a series of reports from the frontlines where kids are the first casualties. Among those most affected by grievous inequities are black youngsters. Nearly 50 percent of them are living below the official poverty line..."

▶"Cruel and usual punishment continued today in the nation's jails and prisons, where some 2 million people remain behind bars. Meanwhile, experts say the evidence of institutionalized racism is clear. As one defense attorney put it, 'African Americans constitute 14 percent of drug users nationally but represent 35 percent of drug arrests, 55 percent of drug convictions and 75 percent of prison admissions.' One out of every 35 black people in the United States is now incarcerated. For the latest on this phenomenal story, we go to our team of correspondents, starting with..."

▶"Clinics and emergency rooms are filled again tonight as a perennial epidemic of domestic violence continues to afflict American households. All kinds of people are suffering as a result, but the overwhelming preponderance of the victims are women and children. Stay tuned for this special report, 'The War At Home: Counting the Casualties'..."

▶"Thousands of Americans were injured on the job again today, and some of the mishaps turned out to be deadly. We have on-the-spot reports from correspondents at hospitals across the nation..."

And so it could go, with networks defining big news to include what affects large numbers of people on a daily basis. But we're accustomed to a very different approach: Stories about singular events keep preoccupying media outlets and commanding our attention.

Meanwhile, on a daily basis, media outlets encourage us to accept as normal the privatization of public space. One manifestation of that trend has been

THIS MODERN WORLD   by TOM TOMORROW

the renaming of sports edifices. "Corporations are seizing the names of our beloved parks and stadiums, and replacing these with their own," the Commercial Alert organization complained in a June 2000 letter to newspapers across North America. The letter added: "There is no law that says that you have to call a sports venue what a big corporation wants you to call it."

In recent years, several dozen companies have bought major-league naming rights. Baseball teams now play in Tropicana Field (Tampa Bay), Bank One Ballpark (Phoenix), Coors Field (Denver), Network Associates Coliseum (Oakland), Pacific Bell Park (San Francisco), and Safeco Field (Seattle). Pro basketball games are happening at branded sites from Continental Airlines Arena in northern New Jersey to American Airlines Arena in Miami to Arco Arena in Sacramento. Football and hockey are in the same groove.

A decade ago, we might have been very surprised to see the Washington Redskins playing host to gridiron foes at a place called FedEx Field. Now, "to help us stop the commercial degradation of sports," Commercial Alert wants sportswriters and fans to call stadiums "by their nicknames, not corporate names." But such advice runs counter to the current momentum.

The logic of auctioning off the rights to name public places is often remarkable. For instance, your local library system might be called the Starbucks Public Library or the Random House of Books. This would guard against tax levies and prevent the need to increase library fines or charge admission.

Likewise, museums that drain the U.S. Treasury could pay their own way. One day, we might matter-of-factly refer to the Smithsonian Burger King Museum. And private cultural institutions could also balance their books while participating in the entrepreneurial renaissance. New York's famed Guggenheim Museum and the Metropolitan Museum of Art could become Nike Museum and the Exxon Mobil Museum of Art.

Children who go to public school now routinely wear shirts without paying attention to the values of the dollar. Instead of freeloading their way through childhood with some kind of anachronistic nod to a welfare state, students could meet taxpayers partway by submitting to the discipline of wearing T-shirts with specified commercial logos, as per contracts negotiated between school districts and corporations.

Given the importance of wiping out vestiges of New Deal sentimentalism, Social Security could be named something like the Citibank of America System. Other public-sector naming rights could be opened to competitive bids. And because the goal of reducing taxes runs parallel to a multitude of privatization options, it would be shortsighted to bypass a potentially great source of federal revenues—the renaming of monuments.

The magnificent marble shrines dedicated to our third and sixteenth presidents could draw capitalization from aesthetically minded firms that wish to combine reverence for heritage with promotion of their cutting-edge technologies. How about the Jefferson/Cisco Memorial and the Lincoln/Microsoft Memorial?

The Pfizer drug conglomerate would pay a pretty penny for a multiyear lease on the Washington Monument's naming rights. "The Viagra Monument" might sound strange at first but soon could roll off millions of tongues as easily as "FedEx Field."

Then there's the Capitol Building. A tasteful sign across the front facade might identify the national legislature as the U.S./AOL Time Warner Congress. To defray some of the governmental operating costs that burden every working American, both chambers could bear additional names such as the Disney Senate and the Viacom House of Representatives. Nearby, the General Electric Supreme Court might serve us well.

Meanwhile, rather than allowing the mansion at 1600 Pennsylvania Ave. to continually deplete the public coffers, any president with a bipartisan spirit would be pleased to live in the AT&T White House, honoring a firm that has given millions to both the Democratic and Republican parties. And there are plenty of other opportunities to gain top dollar from the corporate community.

So, let's start getting used to the kind of news broadcasts that we can learn to accept as perfectly normal: "Speaking in the Dow Chemical Rose Garden today, the president called on the AOL Time Warner Congress to boost appropriations for the Merrill Lynch Kodak Defense Department. The Secretary of McDonald's State urged full appropriations for the Fox Dreamworks Space Weapons Station and added that further deployment of Philip Morris nuclear missiles will be necessary in order to safeguard the security of the United States of Archer Daniels Midland America..."

Inside the temples of true believers, ardent faith has a way of prevailing. And so, in the dot-com era, vast numbers of followers seem eager to fulfill a sacred digital future.

Implicit and largely unspoken, the virtual Ten Commandments of dot-comity are now widespread:

I. You shall have no other gods before media synergy.

II. You shall not bow to any image above those of the profits. Technology and venture capital are marvels that turn the Internet into a cosmic pathway for the commerce of life.

III. You shall not take the name of the Lord your Market in vain. It has little use for those who squander opportunity. It will not hold guiltless those who fail to appreciate Its transformative powers.

IV. Remember the stock exchange and keep it holy. You may pause and reflect on the meaning of your labor, but for the long days and during after-hours trading—with the help of cable TV networks and online brokerage firms as well as some of the hottest investment websites around—the Lord your Market blesses every breath you take and hallows it, especially when earnings soar.

V. Honor your father and mother, for they made possible a balanced portfolio, taking into account the strengths of blue chips and Nasdaq, with careful attention to the most auspicious high-tech initial public offerings.

VI. You shall not fail to make a killing, within the constraints of mortal fallibility, which must be reduced to aggregate the momentum of digital technologies and the markets. In the Canaan of the Web, you shall revere those who develop software to let there be cyberlight, making new fiduciary horizons dawn and rendering mere human form secondary.

VII. You shall not adulterate the potential of dot-comity to raise our eyes to the heavens of capital formation, IPOs, and long-term advancement of New Media.

VIII. You shall not steal. Above all, entrepreneurial fortunes depend on respect for intellectual property rights.

IX. You shall not undermine the dot-com faith that rockets the blessed of us to seven figures and beyond. You should participate in all manner of fascination with interfaces between the technical and the financial, subjecting them to interminable media discourse, while bypassing qualitative evaluation of "content" and thus minimizing public debate about the cultural and political messages most widely promoted by centralized New Media power.

X. You shall not covet the trademarked, copyrighted, patented, or encrypted products of competitors, but you shall be free to attempt capture of fabulous wealth available to a small percentage of adherents. Take full advantage of the Internet and satellite technology that was massively subsidized by the federal government decades ago, but do not hesitate to claim that the Lord your Market has made it all possible and therefore the private sector deserves all its divine profits, and more, if only government would get out of the way.

The virtual commandments need not be belabored or even mentioned; they are mainly internalized by the faithful. Every month, hundreds of hours on national television and many large vats of ink go to prayerful meditations on how to better understand and analyze the Lord our Market, seeking to assess Its will to be done. Sanctified by an inexhaustible fountain of media reports and discussions, the Lord our Market reaches new and transcendent levels, nearing the iridescent light to shine on the human condition.

Some fundamentalist believers in dot-comity insist that the literal words of the Lord their Market include this admonition: "As for others who fail utterly in the glorious quest for rich holiness of the techno-age, you shall not be distracted by their misfortune nor attempt significant aid. For I, the Lord your Market, am a zealous god, smiting each generation with inequities that favor the best and lay low those who cannot glorify the Lord their Market. This need not bother the followers who embrace me and with steadfast devotion keep my commandments."

NORMAN SOLOMON writes a syndicated column on media and politics. His latest book is *The Habits of Highly Deceptive Media: Decoding Spin and Lies in Mainstream News.*

CHAPTER 8

Missing the Movements

BY MARRIANNE MANILOV

Corporate media coverage of the emerging antiglobalization movement missed the story. Media covered protestors instead of issues. Coverage showed images of anarchists breaking windows instead of providing the history, context, strategy, and leadership behind the antiglobalization movement. Focus on conflict over substance also meant that other interconnected movements, including the Prison Industrial Complex and the Independent Media Center movements, were missed by the corporate media entirely.

SEATTLE: CREATING A MEDIA IMAGE

"Two teenagers with Leonard Nimoy haircuts and real Star Trek uniforms had come, they said, 'to Vulcanize the revolution.' The black-clad anarchists seemed happiest burning American flags, though—let's be clear—they, too had issues with the fascist state police. A half-dozen publicity gofers were trying to drum up enthusiasm for a screening of *Steal This Movie*, the upcoming Abbie Hoffman biopic. And then there were the clowns. 'We're here for a picnic,' one of them solemnly informed me. 'And it has been a very poor picnic. No pies. No cake.'" (*The American Prospect*, September 11, 2000)

The media coverage of the antiglobalization movement in 2000 used the street demonstrations against the WTO in Seattle—a tactic—to define the movement. The image carried on television the most, the black-masked anarchist breaking a window, led much of the coverage throughout the year while the issues around the demonstrations were lost. "Teamsters and turtles," a phrase coined from a media photo in a Seattle street, originally referred to the alliance between labor and environmentalists. But over the year, "teamsters and turtles," like the black-masked anarchists, became just an image the mainstream media used to describe the antiglobalization movement.

The reality of the marches in Seattle, however, was that they were vast and diverse. Many people came to represent their various constituencies. Religious groups from around the world were there, as were intellectuals and authors. International solidarity movements like Free Burma and Free Tibet marched alongside people from South Africa and South America. Young people from the campus sweatshop movements, youth of color from the emerging Prison Industrial Complex movement, and a large contingent of Seattle high school students participated, as did many others. Yet media put them all into the frame of "protestor" and the breadth of the movement was lost in the coverage. Intense intellectual debate occurred in Seattle. Many articles, opinion pieces, and position papers were written and presented. Strategy sessions were held. But most of the efforts that didn't include street theater were not covered by the mainstream media.

The majority of those who attended Seattle to demonstrate in the street were committed to and used the tactics of nonviolence. But the demonstrators were shrunk to a soundbite and an image. The focus on the picture of the anarchists and the words "teamsters and turtles" are easily decoded: Anarchists=fringe, white, youth, violent. Teamsters=old, "tough" labor. Turtles=wacky, protectionist environmentalists whose focus is on animals over jobs.

This representation grew stronger in the coverage throughout the year 2000. Over the year, the image and soundbites hurt the movement as public opinion grew to believe the media mythology. By the end of 2000, at the year anniversary of Seattle, the media said the globalization movement was dying out. The meal the mainstream media had cooked and served the American public of Seattle was a young, wacky, radical, and violent group lacking vision and direction was done, and they were clearing the plates. By the end of 2000, this image of the "Seattle protestor" had become a media stereotype similar to the "welfare queen." The myth of the "Seattle protestor" had become so strong that it no longer mattered what the truth was about the movement or the people who came to Seattle and changed history.

THE PROTESTOR MYTH

The tactics used in Seattle—colorful demonstrations, large puppets, non-violent blockades—became larger than life in the media. Despite the fact that Seattle involved close to two weeks of debates, town hall meetings, small group meetings, policy discussions, and position papers, the media coverage in 2000 of Seattle only focused on a few hours. Those few hours were when anarchists broke the windows of downtown Seattle businesses, often in full view of the police. Some journalists accurately reported that property damage was done by a small contingent of people who were often stopped by other demonstrators, who called out "No violence" or "Shame." The images that many newspapers photographed, journalists led with, and TV carried, however, were of the property destruction. After Seattle, the media stayed stuck in Seattle, in the few hours of the events that occurred there, and used this image to frame all activities in the antiglobalization movement. In other post-Seattle demonstrations it simply no longer mattered who you were, because now you were labeled "a protestor" or "a person who was in Seattle." After Seattle, the image that sold papers—property damage and black-clad youth—overwhelmed the issue coverage.

One of the worst examples of this was Edward Wong reporting for the *New York Times*. Close to the year anniversary of Seattle, Wong was covering a serious academic conference hosted by the International Forum on Globalization (IFG). The IFG, a think tank of writers, intellectuals, and organizers from around the world, had held policy meetings for five years prior to Seattle and had published a book of writings against globalization. The conference included renowned authors, Harvard-trained academics, and national leaders from many countries including India, Malaysia, and Canada. In an article headlined "Summit in New York," Wong reframed them in one sentence: "But there were no black masks or tear gas in evidence yesterday, and the attendees appeared as well-mannered as their counterparts in the United Nations complex overlooking the East River." (Edward Wong, *New York Times*, September 6, 2000, "Summit in New York: The Protestors: A Quiet Forum at Tome Hall Opposed the East River Forum.")

"For two weeks prior to Seattle, the media began to do substantive stories on the issues around globalization," IFG Director Jerry Mander said. "After that the media coverage changed. The media missed the connections between globalization and environmental damage, poverty, human rights abuses, and financial breakdown. We all became protestors, anarchists. Here we were in New York, some of the top thinkers and policy makers internationally against globalization and the *New York Times* actually acted as if we were anarchists who had put on suits."

Jerry Mander also noted that the media had swallowed the idea put out by Clinton, the WTO, and the IMF that the protesters were hurting the poor. "The reality was that the G-77, a group of the world's poorest countries, met in Havana and issued an unanimous statement of support for the protesters," Mander said. None of the corporate media in the U.S. covered the G-77 statement. The protestor myth was carried throughout the news coverage in the year 2000. Even in U.S. stories that included some sense of what was happening in the movement or had analysis on an issue, the lead called out the images of Seattle and reinforced the myth.

THE VIOLENCE MYTH

"Waging their war on economic globalization with firebombs and rocks, some 5,000 protestors marched Tuesday on the IMF and World Bank Summit, turning Prague into a smoky battle zone." (AP Worldstream, September 26, 2000)

One of the main media myths that was created in Seattle and carried on through the year 2000 was that violence and property destruction were an integral part of the movement. During Seattle, the media often danced around the issue, using images in the first three paragraphs of an article that talked about property destruction but then side-stepping the issue with a disclaimer such as "of course, the majority of those in Seattle were nonviolent."

This kind of coverage is similar to crime coverage where journalists describe the crime in lurid detail and call the person an "accused gang mem-

ber." Coverage that leads with violence and images encourages the reader to form an opinion early on about who is right and who is wrong. Guilt or innocence, whether a source is valid or not, is established by the media in the first couple of paragraphs. If the beginning of an article carries a picture or a story about a protestor in graphic description, the rest of the article carries that image or story. The use of these images over and over, out of context, creates a myth that often takes on a life of its own.

For the antiglobalization movement in the year 2000, the media frame of "violent protestors" became more direct as the year went on.

One of the low points in media coverage was a *New York Times* article in June. Talking about Seattle it reframed even its own coverage from 1999: "In the protests, demonstrators, some wearing gas masks, hurled Molotov cocktails, rocks, and excrement at delegates and police officers," read the article. Although the *Times* ran a correction, it was indicative of the kind of rewriting that was being carried out in the media. Shannon Hall, assistant editor for TomPaine.com, and David Corn of *The Nation* both wrote about the mistake.

At the same time, nonviolence as a tactic was given excellent coverage in the *New York Times Magazine* in the year 2000. In the cover article "The Hidden Revolution" in November, young people involved in bringing down Milosevic were given the kind of intellectual and strategic coverage denied the antiglobalization demonstrators. Although similar in tactics—both movements use nonviolence and culture to undermine authority—the Otpor movement was covered in a manner that said it was legitimate and important.

The antiglobalization movement, on the other hand, using the same tactics to talk about a lack of democracy in the U.S., was made to seem radical and irrelevant. The article quotes one Otpor leader about his tactics:

"Activists were trained in how to play hide-and-seek with the police, how to respond to interrogation, how to develop a message in posters and pamphlets and how to transfer fear from the population onto the regime itself..."

The *Times* calls these young people "revolutionaries" in a serious tone and gives background on the intellectuals, books and strategy behind the Otpor movement—including training by the U.S. government and funding by U.S. donors. The coverage of the antiglobalization movement, in contrast, was very different. According to *Los Angeles Times Magazine* on August 13, 2000: "Breakfast is over and it's time to get back to the Revolution. The vegan bread, snatched from a bakery's discard pile, sits on the table, next to the tubs of organic yogurt and cups of certified Fair Trade coffee. Two dozen members of the Student Alliance to Reform Corporations (STARC) hold hands in a ring around the center of a room in Eugene, Oregon."

The antiglobalization movement is looked down on for using the same tactics of nonviolence and creating a culture of resistance—albeit against a democratically elected government, rather than a dictatorship. Still, nonviolent protest to overthrow a dictatorship is clearly legitimate in the media's eyes while nonviolent protest to change corporate control of institutions that control public life, without accountability or oversight, is not.

Many people who were demonstrating approached journalists and tried to talk about the coverage frame while the media was still covering the demonstrations. Van Jones, executive director of the Ella Baker Center for Human Rights, is one of the leaders of the emerging Prison Industrial Complex movement. He traveled to Seattle and Los Angeles with contingents of youth of color who were protesting the fact that "young people are losing their summer opportunities and scholarships." Jones sees that young people of color are interested in making the links in the global prison boom. "There is an increase of security forces and police weapons worldwide. That's a part of globalization, controlling the people," he said.

Jones was part of the effort to hold media on the ground accountable for their coverage of the demonstrations. In one instance, Jones saw a photographer taking pictures of kids smashing windows and approached him. "I asked why not take pictures of those who were admonishing them, why ignore all the people who were nonviolent," Jones said. "The photographer told me he'd take care of it. He said 'I'll write it in the cut line below the photo.' I said: 'That won't matter.' There was real struggle on the ground to hold journalists accountable but to no avail."

The *L.A. Times* piece that appeared in June was part of the coverage looking at the kind of people coming to demonstrations at the Republican and

Democratic conventions. By the time of the conventions, protestors were being thoroughly framed as lacking credibility, strategy, and sanity. The media, rather than covering the issues that were central to each of the demonstrations, or even the civil liberty violations taking place, covered all the events as the police versus the crazy "Seattle protestors."

An exception to this in the mainstream media was the coverage in salon.com. Jesse Walker, writing for salon.com in August, wrote directly about the repression of the demonstrators and put it in a political context: "Many U.S. cities have been militarizing their police forces recently, with the fed's enthusiastic support. The number of paramilitary police units has taken off in the last 10 years, as has, naturally, the number of times they've been deployed. This has brought about an insidious change in police thinking, outside of the special units as well as within them. When you see yourself as part of a military force, you stop thinking of individual crimes and start thinking in terms of containment."

Walker goes on to report that this strategy in Seattle meant that officers didn't arrest those who were, in their view, destroying property but stayed in their police lines because "stopping them would have meant breaking with the day's containment strategy."

This kind of analysis of why so many police could not stop a handful of people from destroying property was an important part of the Seattle story. It also created a context for what happened in the streets of Philadelphia and Los Angeles. The demonstration in Philadelphia at the Republican convention was a broad base of people focused on the Prison Industrial Complex, yet the coverage focused on the conflict between police and demonstrators and the arrests. "The media missed the issue. Here we had a large number of people who were protesting prisons sent to prison," Van Jones said.

MISSING THE MOVEMENT: MISSING THE HISTORY, MISSING THE ORGANIZING EFFORTS LOCALLY AND NATIONALLY

Media Coverage framed the entire globalization movement as people who showed up to protest in Seattle. "The media did what they always do badly, they covered it as an event and not a movement," said John Anner, Executive Director of the Independent Press Association. "They acted like Seattle just happened out of thin air when of course if you were reading the alternative press, you knew about these struggles for a long time and Seattle was no surprise."

The lack of historical context through interviews with movement leaders was astounding. Even those journalists who didn't know about Seattle before it happened chose not to investigate the roots of the issues. The campus sweatshop movement, for example, has organizing roots that are important. Efforts like the one led by Charles Kernaghan and the National Labor Committee in New York against Kathie Lee Gifford and those led by Young Shin and the Asian Women Immigrants Association (AIWA) in San Francisco against dressmaker Jessica McClintock changed the public perception of sweatshops as a distant issue.

"Before this group of predominantly women of color stood in front of Jessica McClintock stores and told the dressmaker that even if she subcontracted far away, it was still her responsibility if those dresses were made by children and in sweatshops. The 'we subcontracted' excuse seemed to fly," Anner said. AIWA's campaign simply changed the whole debate. It focused the debate on the fact that sweatshops were no just overseas, but right here."

The Nike Campaign, led by Global Exchange, who worked with the AIWA campaign and the campus sweatshop movement, followed these leads. But like so much of the history of the antiglobalization movement, these simple connections were never made.

Other connections were missed in the coverage during the year 2000. While the media made a point of covering white protestors who were told to leave by black residents in D.C., they missed covering demonstrations that went against the "protestor myth" they had created.

After the D.C. demonstrations around the World Bank, the mainstream U.S. media failed to cover similar demonstrations in the streets of Chiang Mai in northern Thailand in May of 2000. The Thailand demonstrations against the Asian Development Bank (ADB) were important because they flew in the face of the portrayal of the movement by the U.S. media. As International Forum on Globalization fellow Walden Bello wrote in January 2001 for the Independent Media Center: "With the majority of protestors being poor Thai farmers, the Chiang Mai demonstrations showed that the anti-globalization base went beyond middle class youth and organized labor in advanced countries. Equally important, key organizers of the Chiang Mai actions, like Bamrung Kayotha, one of the leaders of the Forum of the Poor, had participated in the Seattle protest, and saw Chiang Mai not as a discrete event but as a link in the chain." (Independent Media Center, January 1, 2001)

The reality was that the globalization movement was made up of a broad group of people working towards and achieving a number of goals. Yet corporate media coverage at the year anniversary of Seattle said the movement was pretty much over, that labor and environmentalists had split, and that street demonstrators were wearing thin.

Mainstream media covering the antiglobalization movement missed local organizing efforts in cities like Portland and elsewhere but they also missed major national victories. Environmental groups led by Friends of the Earth, for example, researched and found genetically modified corn and traced it to tacos in Taco Bell. The effort was so successful it forced a recall of many brands of tacos found at Safeway and other major stores. A coalition of environmental groups also brought lawsuits against Aventis S.A., the producers of the genetically modified corn, StarLink. Most importantly, they brought the problems in the food source to the attention of everyday consumers. Yet this victory and many others were not framed as part of the antiglobalization movement.

The movement of people to control their food was worldwide. The mainstream media didn't understand the adage "think globally, organize locally" and were not able to put together different organizing efforts that had connections into in-depth coverage. The planting of hemp by U.S. farmers, cheese that was illegal to eat in France, and seed farmers in India needed to be connected for the U.S. public and covered as part of the antiglobalization movement.

Of course, if international street protests were not media-worthy to the U.S. press, organizing efforts weren't either. The protestor myth meant that farmers in India who started the genetically modified food movement and who maintained ongoing organizing efforts in 2000 were not covered. "I think the entire planet owes the Indian farmers who have turned back genetic engineering a big debt right now," Ruckus Society Director John Sellers said in an interview. "I think they catalyzed the movement."

The Zapatistas in Mexico, and the solidarity movements around South Africa and Central America, all have bridges to the antiglobalization movement. Instead, the leaders were defined as young people roving to three or four international protests. The issue campaigns and ongoing organizing efforts led by experienced people who often had deep connections across the U.S. and abroad were missed.

"Just think about South Africa," the Independent Press Association's Anner said. "International solidarity is one of the founding principles of the antiglobalization movement. I've been active in that work since '78 or '79. This has been covered in the alternative media for so long now. We were all reading the *National Guardian* at that time and they were talking about globalization then."

Independent media and the Internet were the ways that many of those working on the issue of globalization came to find out about Seattle. Magazines like *In These Times*, *Z*, and a host of others covered the issues and the movement long before Seattle became a household word.

THE PRISON INDUSTRIAL COMPLEX
AND INDEPENDENT MEDIA CENTER MOVEMENTS

While media spent its time covering select demonstrations, it missed emerging movements in the U.S. entirely. Whether formal parts of the globalization movement or just participants in demonstrations, the Prison Industrial Complex and Independent Media Center movements promise to stand up and take on major issues in the next five years.

One of the new emerging movements where youth of color are involved in the Prison Industrial Complex movement started in California. The PIC movement cut its teeth on Proposition 21 in California and continued to organize. Many of the leaders and young people went to the globalization demonstrations, learned nonviolent direct action tactics and took them back to their local efforts. More importantly, there were intellectual and strategic bridges forged against some of the corporations responsible for helping the U.S. put two million people behind bars.

"Young people in the Bay Area went to Seattle and learned about nonviolent protest," Ella Baker Center Executive Director Van Jones said. "In February of 2000, these same youth held an overnight protest in a public school to bring to light the amount of money being taken away from education and spent on prisons. No one in the media asked 'How did these young

THIS MODERN WORLD   by TOM TOMORROW

NOTE: The satirical commentary which follows will undoubtedly provide most readers with more cartoon satisfaction than they ever dreamed possible. However, a recalcitrant minority may find this week's offering predictable, heavy-handed, or otherwise disagreeable. Fortunately, there's something for them as well:

A RAINY DAY FUN GAME!

That's right! You see, we've *deliberately inserted* numerous mistakes throughout the following four panels. Can you spot them all? We believe the attempt to do so will provide untold hours of non-partisan entertainment!

people get involved? How do they see themselves?' I think people would be surprised to see how much cross fertilization there is between movements."

This cross-fertilization is partly thanks to the emerging globalization movement's own media movement, the Independent Media Center movement. Spawned in Seattle, the Independent Media Center movement or "IMC" first started reporting in Seattle, on the WTO and the protests. The IMCs are local collectives that cover issues around social and economic justice. To tell their own story, they set up shop in Seattle and began reporting with an open door policy. Anyone could report. Anyone could upload. People roamed the streets of Seattle with reporter notebooks, IMC reporter tags, cell phones and video cameras. They told the story of the movement from diverse perspectives, unedited.

"There were a large number of people who watched Seattle on the web," Jones said. "The people who did this had a different understanding of what happened, and not just what happened but the pace. Some of it was exciting; some of it was boring. Some of it was drums; some of it was sitting. But this is what it is like to be in a day-long or week-long effort or to be involved in organizing. The mainstream media was all chaos all the time, cut and paste for their 15 seconds."

Andrea Buffa, executive director of Media Alliance, has watched and participated in the IMC movement. According to Buffa, the IMC Seattle website during the week of demonstrations in Seattle in November 1999 got 1.5 million hits, more than CNN. They continue to this day to get large numbers, especially during the national elections and when demonstrations or issues around the world in the antiglobalization movement are moving.

"Most progressives agree that IMCs are the most exciting development in alternative media in the last five years," Buffa said. "This is the solution.

DID YOU *SPOT THE MISTAKES?*

1. When Sparky says "we," he is clearly referring to government officials and their apologists, of which he is neither. Whoops!

2. Amtrak doesn't really operate a "clue train."

3. An actual defender of the I.M.F. would be unlikely to phrase his arguments in quite this manner.

4. Sparky is talking about the protesters-- but Biff's rejoinder seems to refer to the third world nations affected by I.M.F. structural adjustment policies. Whoops again!

SPECIAL NOTE TO READERS PLANNING TO LET US KNOW THAT OUR ENTIRE POINT OF VIEW IS A MISTAKE: Ha, ha! Good one! We sure didn't see that coming!

We know that the ownership of papers effects coverage. It isn't about the owners stepping into the newsroom and saying 'don't cover this.' It can be the trickle-down effect where the journalist knows which stories the editors like and which ones are going to help them move up in the ranks." According to the Seattle IMC collective, they seek to "generate alternatives to the biases inherent in the corporate media controlled by profit, and to identify and create positive models for a sustainable and equitable society."

The Independent Media Center movement, which had just a few articles written about it (most notably in the *Boston Globe*), remained below the radar screen despite its growth to many U.S. cities and a number of countries. According to Buffa, 450 people showed up in Seattle to be journalists for the movement, 800 in D.C., and 1,400 in Los Angeles. During the presidential elections, the IMC Seattle site got 100,000 hits a day.

But the fact that the media missed the movements doesn't surprise Buffa. "Reporters don't have good community contacts anymore, they don't have good sources, they don't follow trends," Buffa said. "Partly reporters might also believe their own reporting. They are reporting that there are no social justice movements and the ones that exist are ineffective and full of rag tag losers who have nothing better to do with their time."

MARRIANNE MANILOV is a writer and organizer in San Francisco and the recipient of a fellowship from the Prentice Foundation. She is currently at work on her first book about Ka Hsaw Wa, a human rights leader from Burma, and his work on a landmark U.S. court case that holds a corporation accountable for forced labor and torture abroad for the first time. She is a Senior Consultant with the media group We Interrupt This Message.

CHAPTER 9

Building a Movement for Media Democratization

BY ROBERT A. HACKETT

Project Censored has identified critical flaws in America's corporate media system. Through its strong domestic market and the export of not just particular media products but its entire model of organizing the media, that system influences the flow of news, ideas, and entertainment around the world. Any citizen, any social movement, concerned with promoting social equality, justice, and democracy within and between nations will sooner or later have to confront and challenge an increasingly globalized corporate media system. Why is that the case?

Essentially, transnational corporations in the communication and information industries have become key bulwarks of global capitalism both ideologically and economically.[1] Since the 1980s, the emerging global media system has vastly enhanced the communication infrastructure of international commerce, constituted a crucial site of investment (think of Nasdaq), and through its news, movies, television programs, and other media formats

An earlier version of this chapter was published in *Studies in Political Economy* 63 (Autumn 2000), where the dozens of media activists interviewed are identified by name. The journal's web site is www.carleton.ca/spe. The research has been supported by the Social Sciences & Humanities Research Council of Canada.

[1] Robert W. McChesney, *Rich Media, Poor Democracy: Communication Politics in Dubious Times* (Urbana and Chicago: University of Illinois Press, 1999), chap. 2.

created a cultural environment which promotes the politics and values of consumerism and free market fundamentalism.

Undoubtedly, the global communication system has enhanced (unevenly) the affluence of a minority of the world's countries and people. It has also sometimes contributed to the political liberalization of old-style authoritarian regimes like those of Eastern Europe. On the other hand, the journalism offered in such a hyper-commercialized, corporate-dominated system in many ways contradicts fundamental democratic values and ideals, such as equal opportunity for informed participation by all citizens in discussing and deciding matters of public concern. In journalism, as Project Censored's work highlights, marketing imperatives are overriding the ethos of public service. Affluent consumers and business are relatively well-served with a press that reflects their generally conservative political dispositions. The rest of us are offered a steady diet of trivia and scandal—"junk food news." Unprecedented transnational media concentration creates potentially centralized power over the public agenda. Increasingly, newsrooms promote or censor stories based not on their relevance to the public, but rather their ability to help or hurt the commercial and political interests of the media empires.

Some people argue that new media technology, particularly the Internet, is the solution to the "democratic deficit" of the corporate media system. But the Internet, while an extremely valuable organizing tool for grassroots activists, is not likely to fundamentally shift the balance of political power. Quite apart from the inequalities in access to computers and telecommunication networks, the Net itself is becoming commercialized and colonized by many of the same corporations which dominate the conventional media.[1]

While they offer some openings for alternative and progressive views on particular issues, the dominant transnational media on the whole are significant obstacles to movements promoting progressive social change. Any fundamental challenge to the current distribution of wealth and power within global capitalism is also a challenge to the dominant media. How can ecologically sustainable economies be achieved without addressing a media/advertising complex that cultivates the desire for limitless consumption? Can a level playing field for diverse political parties be achieved in the U.S. without bitter opposition from the television networks, who have a vested interest in hyper-expensive political advertising? Can ethnic and gender equality be achieved while media representations and employment practices

---

[1]McChesney, *Rich Media*, chap. 3; Donald Gutstein, e.con: *How the Internet Undermines Democracy* (Toronto: Stoddart, 1999).

continue (despite some progress) to stereotype, marginalize, or underrepresent women and minorities? Can social programs and workers' rights be sustained in the long run when the agenda-setting media are closely tied to the corporate elite and its interests? Can progressive social movements succeed when they are demonized, trivialized, or ignored by the media on which they generally depend to reach broader publics?[1] And most crucially, can democracy itself flourish without a political communication system which nurtures equality, community, and informed engagement with public issues?[2]

The pivotal role of the media leads Robert McChesney to observe, "Regardless of what a progressive group's first issue of importance is, its second issue should be media and communication, because so long as the media are in corporate hands, the task of social change will be vastly more difficult, if not impossible, across the board."[3]

Encouragingly, there are growing signs of organized grassroots activity within many countries to challenge the "corporatization" of public communication. Such activism for media democratization takes different forms in different national contexts, and I do not attempt a global overview here.[4]

In the U.S. and Canada alone, there are hundreds of local and national projects and groups engaged in one or more of the following dimensions of media activism, each of which is typically associated with specific kinds of actors.[5] These forms include building autonomous or "alternative" media

---

[1] Todd Gitlin, *The Whole World is Watching: Mass Media in the Making & Unmaking of the New Left* (Berkeley: University of California Press, 1980), pp. 258, 271. For a useful overview of influences on the media, see Pamela J. Shoemaker and Stephen D. Reese, *Mediating the Message: Theories of Influences on Mass Media Content*, 2nd edition (White Plains, NY: Longman, 1996).

[2] McChesney, *Corporate Media*, p. 5.

[3] McChesney, *Corporate Media*, p. 71.

[4] For a short overview of media reform activism, see John Nichols and Robert W. McChesney, *It's the Media, Stupid* (New York: Seven Stories Press, 2000).

[5] For an overview of many media democratization groups and projects, and a guide to activist resources, see Don Hazen and Julie Winokur (eds.), *We the Media: A Citizens' Guide to Fighting for Media Democracy* (New York: The New Press,1997), and Peter Phillips and Project Censored, *Censored 1999: The News that Didn't Make the News* (New York: Seven Stories, 1999), esp. Appendix D. The categorization below draws from Marc Raboy, "Communication, Politics, and Society: The Case of Popular Media in Quebec," in Janet Wasko and Vincent Mosco (eds.), *Democratic Communications in the Information Age* (Toronto: Garamond, 1992; New Jersey: Ablex, 1992), pp. 175-76; Robert A. Hackett and Yuezhi Zhao, *Sustaining Democracy? Journalism and the Politics of Objectivity* (Toronto: Garamond, 1998), pp. 206–213; and Laura Stein, "Media and Democratic Action: Introduction," Peace Review 11/1 (March 1999), pp. 5-8.

independent of state and corporate control, which add diversity to the media system insofar as they give voice to the marginalized, convey counter-hegemonic information, and/or offer models of organization and communication more democratic than the dominant commercial media.[1]

Other major avenues of activism include the media education movement, which is especially advanced in Europe, and media analysis and monitoring projects such as Fairness and Accuracy in Reporting (FAIR) and Project Censored in the U.S., and NewsWatch in Canada. Also present are campaigns and publicity strategies to use and enhance openings for progressive voices within the existing media (media skills training, media relation strategies to gain access by achieving newsworthiness, etc.). We see also satirical "culture jamming," which aims to subvert the intended meanings of commercial and corporate media, and challenges to ideological hegemony and the logic of the marketplace from within mainstream media. Culture jamming is represented by the struggles of journalists and other media workers and public interest interventions in legal, regulatory, and political arenas to challenge the processes and substance of state policy towards media. Efforts to build national and international coalitions around "the cultural environment," "media and democracy," "press and broadcasting freedom," or "the right to communicate" are ongoing as well. In some countries—as diverse as New Zealand, India, Brazil, Sweden and Finland—such commitments are also represented directly in elected legislatures from emerging progressive political parties.[2]

Behind their diversity, democratic media activism displays a fairly consistent and enduring commitment to change media messages, practices, institutions, and contexts (including state communication policies), in a direction which enhances democratic values and subjectivity, as well as equal participation in societal decision-making. A Polish public broadcasting planner suggests that a key principle of democratic public communication is the ability of each segment of society "to introduce ideas, symbols, information, and elements of culture into social circulation" so as to reach all other segments of society.[3] This is at the heart of the progressive project of a more equitable distribution of economic, social, cultural, symbolic, and informational resources.

[1]Hackett and Zhao, *Sustaining Democracy?*, pp. 206–213; Greg Ruggiero, *Microradio & Democracy: (Low) Power to the People* (New York: Seven Stories Press, 1999).
[2]Nichols and McChesney.
[3]Karol Jakubowicz, "Stuck in a Groove: Why the 1960s Approach to Communication Democratization Will No Longer Do," in Slavko Splichal and Janet Wasko (eds.), *Communication and Democracy* (Norwood, NJ: Ablex, 1993), p. 41.

To be sure, there are important ambiguities within the concept of media democratization. Debates over censorship, pornography, and hate speech suggest the sometimes uneasy combination of commitments to social solidarity, egalitarian social transformation, and individual freedom from state or corporate power.

Nevertheless, media democracy manifestos exhibit an impressive degree of convergence around the goals of expanding the range of voices accessed through the media, building an egalitarian public sphere, promoting the values and practices of sustainable democracy, and offsetting or counteracting political and economic inequalities found elsewhere in the social system.[1]

Indeed, Jakubowicz suggests adopting the term "communicative democracy" rather than "democratic communication," in order to underscore that the idea of democracy itself is premised upon communication between equals.[2]

It is probably premature to describe these various forms of media activism as a coherent social movement, but they are laying the groundwork for one. In the rest of this chapter, I reflect on both the obstacles that such a movement would face, and the social resources it could draw upon. The chapter concludes with some suggestions for strategic priorities.

OBSTACLES TO A MEDIA DEMOCRATIZATION MOVEMENT

Without doubt, a media democracy movement will face formidable obstacles. Of the relatively few published case studies from which to draw historical lessons, one of the best is McChesney's analysis of an early U.S. media reform movement: the coalition to support public broadcasting and oppose the commercialization of radio as it emerged as a mass medium in the 1930s.[3] Within a few years, that coalition's goal of reserving significant spectrum space for public interest, noncommercial broadcasters had been decisively defeated; conversely, the dominance of the corporate networks was entrenched through legislation and regulatory practice. The reformers failed partly due to their own avoidable shortcomings—their political incom-

---

[1]Programmatic statements reviewed include the "People's Communication Charter" and "Viewer's Declaration of Independence," in Kate Duncan (ed.), *Liberating Alternatives: The Founding Convention of the Cultural Environment Movement* (Cresskill, NJ: Hampton Press, 1999), pp. 175–183, and Campaign for Press & Broadcasting Freedom, *21st Century Media: Shaping the Democratic Vision* (London: CPBF, 1996).

[2]Jakubowicz, "Stuck in a Groove," pp. 49–50.

[3]Robert W. McChesney, *Telecommunications, Mass Media & Democracy* (New York: Oxford University Press, 1993), esp. pp. 252–270.

petence, their lack of coordination, and in some cases, their elitist sympathies which militated against organizing a popular base. Moreover, the onset of the Depression drastically shifted national priorities towards more obviously bread-and-butter issues.

Other obstacles confronting the reformers, however, were more fundamental and long-term—primarily, the ideological, political, and structural power of their main opponents, the broadcasting corporations. The American corporate media, McChesney argues, "have actively and successfully cultivated the ideology that the status quo is the only rational media structure for a democratic and freedom-loving society." More broadly, American political culture since the early twentieth century has virtually precluded public discussion of the fundamental weaknesses of capitalism, forcing media reformers to argue defensively that commercial broadcasting is a special case of market failure.[1] This constraint has been reinforced by the near-absence of a viable Left, and by the dominant culture's sanitized images of capitalism.

In the 1930s the structural power of corporate media was already evident in their dominance over politicians' access to voters and over the terms of public debate, including debate about media issues themselves. Today, the weapons of globalized media conglomerates include their sheer financial resources and their ability to use cross-promotional synergy, brand-name recognition, distribution muscle, high entry costs, and economies of scale. Oligopolistic markets give them the power to marginalize or take over smaller players. They also have the ability to pre-empt or co-opt politically troublesome opposition through token concessions.

Canada, Britain, and many other Western countries succeeded, where the U.S. failed, in establishing a viable, mass-audience public broadcasting service, one which could to some extent counterbalance the democratic shortcomings of a purely corporate, commercial system. Today public broadcasting around the world faces severe challenges. These include declining audiences related to channel multiplication, the decline of social democratic governments in western Europe, governmental pressure to become more commercial, the resulting identity crisis and dislocation, right-wing attacks on its perceived left-liberal bias, and broader critiques that see it as obsolete or irrelevant.[2]

---

[1] McChesney, *Telecommunications*, p. 264.
[2] Karol Jakubowitz, "Public Service Broadcasting in the Information Society," *Media Development* 46/2 (1999): pp. 45–49; William Hoynes, "Democracy, Privatization and Public Television," Peace Review 11/1 (1999), pp. 33–39.

The broader context for public broadcasting's crisis is the worldwide hegemony of market liberalism, and the process of media globalization. The flipside of the concentrated power of global media capital is the social and political indeterminacy of the groups that would potentially benefit from media democratization. For the most part, they are diffused, marginalized, and/or difficult to mobilize. The apathy of media audiences is not surprising during "normal" times of social and economic stability in the advanced capitalist societies. There is no widespread popular clamor for participation in mass communication (on the production side), nor for more access to a greater range of views (on the consumption side). If anything, given marketing and cultural pressures towards social fragmentation, many consumers want fewer voices and less complexity in their daily media fare, not more. Many consumers also identify with the branded images, products, programs, and celebrities that constitute the corporate mediascape.

The culture of consumerism and the sheer burdens of daily life militate against all movements for social change, but especially one with goals as seemingly remote from daily concerns or immediate successes as media democracy. According to some theorists, accessible and diverse media programming may be a "merit good" like education, training, or health; left to themselves, consumers "tend to take less care to obtain it than is in their own long-term interests."[1]

The current absence of mass involvement in media democratization, however, should not be taken as unduly discouraging. Demands for participatory communication are historically more frequent in times of revolutionary upheaval when people's stories, actions, and protests are prominent in public communication. Michael Traber identifies three such waves of change. The eighteenth-century middle-class revolutions in France and America established the democratic rights of the individual vis-a-vis despotic government. The early "utopian" years of twentieth-century socialist revolts in Mexico and Russia posited a second generation of human rights in which the state has, in principle if not practice, a positive role in promoting citizens' well-being, including their access to the means of communication. The third wave of communication rights derives from the postwar Third World anticolonial struggles; these "solidarity" rights emphasize the duty of states and social organizations to place common human interests before national and individual interest.[2]

---

[1]Jakubowicz, "Public Service Broadcasting," p. 47.
[2]Michael Traber, "Changes of Communication Needs and Rights in Social Revolutions," in Splichal and Wasko (eds.), *Communication and Democracy*, pp. 19–31.

During more stable periods, however, demands for expanded public communication rights are typically confined to advocacy groups, creative cultural producers, alternative journalists, mainstream media workers, scholars, and others with occupational or political incentives to seek media access.[1] Indeed, some of the most articulate and energetic spokespeople for media democracy, at least in the U.S., have come from their ranks. But the interests of these groups are not identical, and in many cases they are marginalized, lacking the power resources strategically to intervene in a media system dominated by huge companies which integrate production and distribution.

Moreover, without brand-name products to sell, media democracy groups in a market economy are perpetually short of money. Typically, they depend on supporters' donations, short-term contracts, memberships, government or foundation grants, or sponsorship by institutions, such as the several trade unions which help underwrite the British Campaign for Press and Broadcasting Freedom (CPBF). While the CPBF itself has largely maintained its democratic autonomy, such funding is elsewhere often tied to specific projects or institutional agendas. Even foundation grants, a major funding source for progressive groups in the U.S., have important limitations. They increase the sense of rivalry between groups pursuing the same funders, and they are often time-consuming to pursue: unlike their right-wing counterparts, "liberal" foundations still tend to fund specific projects rather than long-term institution-building.

---

[1]Jakubowicz, "Stuck in a Groove," pp. 38, 42.

THIS MODERN WORLD

by TOM TOMORROW

SOCIAL BASES FOR A MOVEMENT

While the obstacles are formidable, there are also deep and persistent social bases for media democratization. I do not want to suggest that social movements simply reflect existing tensions and interests; they have a creative role in raising new issues and forging new identities. But, extrapolating from the political economy approach to communications analysis, it is possible to suggest some of the structural conditions and social dynamics most favorable to media democracy activism.[1]

The conflicting interests and inequalities generated within a capitalist social structure have spurred various forms of social, cultural, and political resistance, most classically the organized workers' movement and socialist parties. Communicative democracy can be seen as a product of the ways that subordinate social classes constitute themselves through their own media and culture.[2] The struggles of workers and social democratic parties have been a major backbone in western Europe of both the Left press, and advocacy for reformist state media policies. The CPBF in Britain is an exemplar. It was founded in 1979 as an alliance between journalists, academics, and public sector workers facing hostile press coverage, and print media unions facing technological annihilation. CPBF attempted to increase workers' influence over media employment and coverage, and to influence, with some success, the communications policy stance of the Trade Union

---

[1] Vincent Mosco, *The Political Economy of Communication* (Newbury Park: Sage, 1996).
[2] Armand Mattelart, "Introduction: For a Class and Group Analysis of Popular Communication Practices," in A. Mattelart and S. Siegelaub (eds.), *Communication and Class Struggle Vol. 2: Liberation, Socialism* (New York: International General, 1983); cited in Mosco, *Political Economy*, p. 230.

Congress and the Labour Party during its long stay in opposition. While Britain's current "New Labour" government clearly has no interest in challenging the media conglomerates, CPBF continues to be probably the most impressive progressive advocate of media reform in western Europe.[1] It also inspired the formation, in 1996, of a fledgling Canadian counterpart to oppose growing press concentration. It was spearheaded by several media unions and the country's largest progressive advocacy coalition, the Council of Canadians. In the U.S., unions have to date shown little interest in coalitions for media reform, preferring to put most of their eggs in the basket of conventional public relations strategies. There are signs, however, that under pressure from media mega-mergers, layoffs, and management assaults on editorial integrity, once reticent American media workers are becoming less reluctant to join unions and form alliances.[2]

Indeed, while the point has been contested, some political economists regard the cultural industries as more fertile sites for worker resistance, compared to other industrial sectors. Bernard Miege points to the tendency to define divisions, the inherent "creativity crisis," and the tension between different technical and social "logics" at work in cultural industries.[3] One challenge and opportunity for a media democratization movement is to find the common ground between worker resistance from within, and the demands for media access and diversity from without.

Some forms of nationalism generate localized resistance to the logic of globalized capitalism. The centrality of language and culture in nationalist politics gives it immediate relevance to struggles over communication policies and structures. Anticapitalist Third World nationalism was a driving force behind the movement for a New World Information and Communication Order (NWICO) in the 1970s and 1980s. A landmark for this movement was the UNESCO-commissioned report *Many Voices, One World*, authored by a commission headed by Sean MacBride.[4] While a sympathetic

---

[1] The CPBF deserves much more attention than space permits here. For background on it, I am indebted to interview respondents, and to an index of the twenty years of *Free Press*, prepared by Pablo Bose and Adam Schachhuber.

[2] Sara U. Douglas, *Labor's New Voice: Unions and the Mass Media* (Norwood, NJ: Ablex, 1986); Don Hazen, "Blurry Vision of Workers," in Hazen and Winokur (eds.), *We the Media*, pp. 115–116.

[3] Bernard Miege, *The Capitalization of Cultural Production* (New York: International General, 1989); cited in Mosco, *Political Economy*, p. 160.

[4] Sean MacBride et al., *Many Voices, One World: Towards a New More Just and More Efficient World Information and Communication Order* (London: Kogan Page/New York: Unipub/Paris: Unesco, 1980).

critic described the report as "ambiguous, contradictory, and deficient" in its efforts to straddle different positions, its commitment to the right to communicate and to a "balanced flow" of information between North and South—arguably the report's most important legacies—implied the structural reform of the dominant, western-based corporate media system.[1] Not surprisingly, these ideas were anathema to the corporate media and their political allies. NWICO's demise as an intergovernmental movement was ensured by the relentless hostility of the Reagan and Thatcher governments, the collapse of the Soviet bloc which had supported aspects of NWICO, the global hegemony of market liberalism, and the retreat from socialist and anti-imperialist versions of nationalism by Third World political elites. Those elites have abandoned NWICO "in favor of negotiating national and regional relationships with the global media powers."[2]

Nevertheless, the impetus behind NWICO has not altogether disappeared. Rather, given its appeal to the "communication imagination" of the Third World, it has arguably become a "people's movement" with "deep roots in a historic sociopolitical and cultural process" of decolonization, participatory development, and democratization. Since the 1980s, NGOs, social movements, local cultural producers, and some communication policy experts and institutes have been the main torchbearers for more equity and autonomy within global communication, and/or for more participatory communication institutions and stronger indigenous cultural expression within nations.[3]

Such developmental communication needs in the South have become the major focus of the ecumenical World Association for Christian Communication (WACC), which explicitly promotes media democratization and the right to communicate. Based in London and financed largely by development agencies and Protestant churches in the North, the WACC sponsors training programs and over 100 communication projects in the South, many of which give voice to marginalized people's criticisms of existing social injustices.[4]

---

[1]Carlos A. Valle, "Communication: International Debate and Community-Based Initiatives," in Philip Lee (ed.), *The Democratization of Communication* (Cardiff: University of Wales Press, 1995), p. 202.

[2]Mosco, *Political Economy*, pp. 208–209.

[3]Robert A. White, "NWICO has become a people's movement," *Media Development* 35/1 (1988), pp. 20-25.

[4]World Association for Christian Communication, *Statements on Communication* (London: WACC, 1997), pp. 2–3; WACC, Annual Report 1998.

Even in the North Atlantic geopolitical region, cultural nationalism in countries like France has helped put some brakes on global trade liberalization. Moreover, even such liberalization has a "silver lining," according to a leading Irish communications researcher: as the state deregulates and commercializes media, the ethic of public service (still strong in many liberal democracies other than the U.S.) can be used to lever state funding for democratic alternative and community media. The opportunity lies in the state's need for legitimacy, and in the widely perceived centrality of media to society's own image and sense of identity.

The defense of minority languages is a related wellspring of demands for media access and diversity. Economic and media globalization contributes to cultural homogenization, as a handful of dominant languages are expanding at the cost of others. Within the next century, 90 percent of the world's languages may die out. Control over language, crucial to cultural and personal identity, is a primary means of exerting power over other aspects of people's lives.[1] Millions of people are denied the right to use their own language (and may even be legally penalized for doing so) in state-supported education or public communication. Forced linguistic assimilation is not peculiar to authoritarian Third World regimes. Residential schools still haunt the living memories of aboriginal people in Canada, where dominant media still arguably contribute to their marginalization and misrepresentation.[2] A 1998 referendum in California, intended to deny Spanish-speaking children bilingual education, was one of five international cases selected by supporters of the People's Communication Charter (PCC) for the first public hearing on languages and human rights at the Hague in 1999.

Access and expression through public communication is the oxygen for such developmental and cultural needs. This point can be expanded: Media democratization is essential if human values in private and public life—values like friendship, citizenship, and the nurturing of children—are to be successfully defended against the corrosive logic of commercialization. Rejection of the idea that all aspects of human life can be bought and sold in the marketplace is developing. We now see resistance to the erosion of public broadcasting, the commodification of public information, the targeting by advertisers of children at home and in schools, and the intrusion of violent television programming in family life. Perceptions of commer-

---

[1] "First Public Hearing on Languages and Human Rights," *Media Development* 46/4 (1999), pp. 8–13.
[2] Bernie Harder, "Limitations of the Media in Representing Aboriginal Cultures in Canada," *Media Development* 42/3 (1995), pp. 21–23.

cial television's negative impact on the socialization of children have led parents and educators to media activism. Librarians have joined alliances to defend public access to information.

Religious commitments, too often ignored by the contemporary Left as a potential agent for progressive social change, have also inspired media activism. In one analysis, if religion is to survive in a modern world polarized between the strictly private sphere and the mass media, then it has no choice but to project itself through public communication and to challenge the dominance of commercial and political speech.[1] Does such religious intervention constitute media democratization? That depends. Patriarchal, monolithic and exclusionary forms of religious fundamentalism have fuelled efforts to censor and demonize gay people, for example. But the ecumenical, inclusive and dialogical vision of the WACC and other progressive religious organizations, committed to values of human dignity, love, and solidarity, has inspired critique and action against the materialistic, consumerist, and narcissistic individualist biases of commercial media.[2]

The communicative needs and practices of "new" social movements emerging since the 1960s have been another crucial springboard for challenges to the corporate media. The anti-Vietnam war protests and "counterculture" of the 1960s generated an upsurge of oppositional media forms, notably "underground" or alternative urban newspapers.[3] To be sure, most of these papers commercialized or disappeared as the youth counterculture re-integrated into the middle-class mainstream. According to one of its veteran editors, however, the alternative press enjoyed a revival during the Reagan–Bush era of the 1980s, in response to the mainstream media's political timidity and the emergence of a culturally progressive baby-boomer market.[4]

Other movements have had more staying power than the youth counterculture. Most notably, movements for civil rights—first for blacks, then Latinos, aboriginal peoples, and other ethnic minorities—have generally

---

[1]Stewart M. Hoover, "Mass Media and Religious Pluralism," in Lee, (ed.), *Democratization*, pp. 185–198.

[2]Carlos Valle, "Community and Dignity: From Manila to Mexico," *Media Development* 43/1 (1996), pp. 3–5; Joan Brown Campbell, "Diversity Within Unity in the Cultural Mainstream," in Duncan, (ed.), *Liberating Alternatives*, pp. 29–36.

[3]See John Downing, *Radical Media: The Political Experience of Alternative Communication* (Boston: South End Press, 1984); and David Armstrong, *A Trumpet to Arms: Alternative Media in America* (Boston: South End Press, 1981).

[4]Jay Walljasper, "Do We Still Need the Alternative Press?" in Don Hazen and Larry Smith (eds.), *Media & Democracy* (San Francisco: Institute for Alternative Journalism, 1996), p. 143; Hackett and Zhao, *Sustaining Democracy?*, p. 208.

sought not the revolutionary transformation of the social or media system, but rather fairer and greater representation within it. (The most militant such groups either politically marginalized themselves or, like the Black Panthers, were crushed by state repression.) Nevertheless, the reformist civil rights movement has generated significant demands for change in the dominant media — against exclusion or stereotyping of minorities in media content, and for more diversity in media employment and ownership.

Since the 1970s, movements for gender equality have engaged in similar kinds of media activism. According to the Gay and Lesbian Alliance against Defamation (GLAAD), "Great strides have been made toward more accurate and inclusive representation" of gays in the dominant U.S. news and entertainment media.[1] Arguably, the value to advertisers of the affluent gay male market has given the latter media leverage not enjoyed by many other minorities, like African Americans.

Likewise, feminism has unleashed energy for media transformation. At the national level, some elements of the feminist movement have long specialized in monitoring and advocacy work around media representation of women. Canada's MediaWatch and the Women's Desk at FAIR in New York are two examples. At the international level, no longer inhibited by the 1980s backlash against NWICO, women's rights conferences have increasingly placed the question of media power on their agenda. Women have expressed specific concerns about their commodification in advertising, their victimization in media violence, and their degradation in pornography. Definitions of communication rights, feminists argue, must take into account women's perspective before they can be considered genuinely "universal."[2] At the same time, many feminists argue that their struggle is not simply for their own power but rather for a more just, sustainable, people-centered (rather than capital-dominated) world order.[3] Because of the social construction of gender, women may be better placed than men to understand the need for, and to implement, more empowering and inclusive patterns of communication.[4]

---

[1] GLAAD, "Out of the Closet and into the Headlines," in Hazen and Winokur (eds.), *We the Media*, pp. 127–128.

[2] Margaret Gallagher, "Communication and Human Dignity: A Women's Rights Perspective," Media Development 42/3 (1995), pp. 6-9.

[3] "Women Call for Democratization of Media," *Media Development*, 41/2 (1994), p. 2.

[4] Riane Eisler, "From Domination to Partnership: Reclaiming our Future," in Duncan (ed.), *Liberating Alternatives*, pp. 121–132; Kamla Bhasin, "Women Empowering Communication: From Bangkok to Beijing," *Media Development* 43/1 (1996), pp. 13–17.

To be sure, there is no single feminist approach to media analysis or action; one must speak of feminisms. Michele Mattelart distinguishes between liberal feminists seeking equal participation in existing media structures dominated by patriarchal codes of professionalism and "objectivity," and a more radical questioning of the role of media structures and codes in constructing gender difference and colonizing women's definitions of themselves.[1]

Other critical social movements have also emerged in anglo–North America during the 1970s and 1980s—notably movements for environmental sustainability, for peace and nuclear disarmament, and against American military intervention in Central America and elsewhere. One example of media-oriented activism engendered by these movements was a 1986 campaign by peace groups and their allies against the ABC network production *Amerika*, a film depicting a UN-backed Soviet occupation of the U.S. One legacy of this campaign was the creation of America's leading progressive media watchdog group, FAIR.

By and large, however, while the peace and environmental movements sought to use the media to promote their primary political objectives, they have generated relatively few efforts to democratize the media themselves, by comparison with movements for gender and ethnic equality. Why would this be the case? One reason may be the relative self-satisfaction on the part of the environmental movement with its ability to convey its concerns through the existing media during the 1980s and early 1990s. Most notably, Greenpeace seemed to have spectacular success in building itself as the globe's leading environmental advocacy group precisely through staging media events. Greenpeace leaders apparently regarded the media, particularly television, as a politically neutral tool, available for exploitation by those who understood its technological logic.[2] A second reason for the relative absence of media challenges by environmental and peace movements was their focus on challenging state policies, and thus finding openings in the existing media to mobilize public opinion. By contrast, movements for gender and ethnic equality are comparatively more concerned about their cultural status and recognition. For these latter groups, the media loom more immediately as part of the landscape they wish to change.

---

[1] Michele Mattelart, "Women, Media and Power: A Time of Crisis," *Media Development* 41/2 (1994), pp. 8–11.

[2] Stephen Dale, *McLuhan's Children: The Greenpeace Message and the Media* (Toronto: Between the Lines, 1996), pp. 197–98.

As a hothouse for social movement media activism, the special case of the province of Quebec, a predominantly French-speaking enclave in North America, should be noted. It has a unique context of "cultural resistance to the centrifugal forces of the great North American melting pot." Rapid political and social modernization during the 1960s, growing working-class militancy, and a crystallizing polarization between the political options of preserving or leaving the Canadian federation in the 1970s all created "some unique examples of social and political uses of media," covering all kinds of activism.[1] Taken together, these elements have created "a distinctive media culture and a situation in which media are considered as part of the normal terrain of social struggle"—undoubtedly to a greater extent than elsewhere in North America, where national and class conflicts have not overlapped, and public media have not been used to forge and defend collective identities to the same degree.

The most recent emerging "new" social movement today is international rather than regional or national in scope. The growing opposition to corporate-driven trade liberalization—and conversely, the defense of democratic human rights—is bringing in a new generation of media-savvy activists. The communication needs of this movement are generating new forms of alternative international communication, most notably through the Internet and related new technology. As a partially successful effort to both influence and bypass the corporate news media, the Independent Media Center at the "battle of Seattle" World Trade Organization protests is being replicated elsewhere.[2] At the same time, the continued indifference or hostility of major corporate media to the progressive anti-WTO movement could help increase activists' awareness of the need for structural media reform, and the need to add the right to communicate to the emerging global human rights agenda.

There are indications of other new openings to gain hearings for communicative democracy. As the flipside of media commercialism and infotainment, public cynicism towards journalism, as measured in polls, has grown sharply in recent years, especially in the U.S.[3] Trade unionists, environmentalists, and

---

[1]Marc Raboy, "Communication, Politics, and Society: The Case of Popular Media in Quebec," in Wasko and Mosco, *Democratic Communication*, pp. 175–76. For a more detailed analysis, see Raboy's *Movements and Messages: Media and Radical Politics in Quebec* (Toronto: Between the Lines, 1984).

[2]Dorothy Kidd, "The Indymedia Centre," at www.presscampaign.org (*Free the Media* review).

[3]Danny Schechter, *The More You Watch, The Less You Know* (New York: Seven Stories Press, 1999), p. 462.

left-of-center parties and movements in Canada and the U.S. are becoming more aware that the rightward shift in the press, the elimination of social affairs and labor beats, media concentration, and the displacement of independent, public-interest journalism by commercially-driven infotainment, all mean that conventional media relations practices will have decreasing success in gaining media access for progressives. They will be forced to consider alternative strategies and coalitions to gain a public voice.[1]

CONCLUSION: HOW TO BUILD A MEDIA DEMOCRATIZATION MOVEMENT

I have argued that, notwithstanding formidable obstacles, there is an urgent need, a reasonably coherent paradigm, important social bases, and multiple forms of activism prefiguring a radical project of media democratization. The question remains: Can these factors really cohere into an effective new social movement? This question in turn raises others. Could media democratization be achieved simply as a byproduct of the political and communicative practices of existing movements? Or is a distinct new movement indeed necessary? If so, around what strategies, core program, and collective identities should such a movement mobilize? Should it be a movement of the Left, or a broader coalition? Should the Left put communicative democracy atop its own agenda, in hopes of finding new supporters for progressive social change, or would such a move further marginalize the Left? To what extent is media reform connected with and dependent upon broader social and political change?

Space does not permit adequate exploration of these questions here. Moreover, neither I nor most of the veteran media scholars and activists I interviewed could offer more than provisional and speculative answers. I conclude this essay with some of them.

Does media democratization require a movement? Robert White argues that new social movements are not only the main source of, but also a model for, democratic communication. Indeed, he virtually equates the two, for two reasons. First, movements need to practice horizontal, participatory communication internally, in order to attract loyal members, challenge hegemonic definitions of reality, enhance the movement's cultural status, and project its symbols into the public arena. Second, full-scale communica-

---

[1]See, e.g., Dale, *McLuhan's Children*, pp. 197–98; for a recent description of some of these trends in Canadian journalism, see David Taras, *Power and Betrayal in the Canadian Media* (Peterborough: Broadview Press, 1999).

tive democracy involves not only structural media reform, but also normative change, spreading participatory communication practices throughout society. For White, movements are the birthplace of such cultural transformation.[1]

Such a view perhaps romanticizes oppositional social movements. More importantly, it conflates democratization *through* the media (the use of media by groups seeking progressive change in other social spheres), and democratization *of* the media. These two processes are not identical.[2] They do overlap, however. In engaging in public communication for their primary objectives, progressive movements add to media diversity; conversely, structural media reform would create more public space for critical movements.

The latter, however, is unlikely to be achieved without a popular movement devoted specifically to this objective. Only sustained popular pressure is likely to persuade governments to challenge the power and earn the wrath of media conglomerates. Examples of socially progressive governments retreating from media reform in the face of virulent hostility from media capital abound, from Venezuela in 1974 and Mexico in 1977–1980 to Britain's New Labour government in the 1990s. In one case (Peru in the 1970s), a progressive nationalist military government expropriated major media outlets and turned them over to peasant and labor organizations, only to find that the latter were neither prepared nor very interested in managing the media.[3]

The communicative practices of various existing social movements are not on their own likely to put media reform on the political agenda. Industry structure and state policy institutions have created technologically-mediated public communication as a distinct sphere of economic and political activity. Coordinated popular action and the naming of a collective project—media democratization—is necessary to counter corporate power in this sphere. Such a project will likely be spearheaded by the groups with the most direct stake in media issues (independent journalists, communication researchers, etc.). It will need to draw from the energies and frustrations of other social movements prepared to devote at least a small portion of their resources to it. Clearly, the Left as a whole has a stake in the success of such a movement. It will have greater cultural and political resonance if it

[1] Robert A. White, "Democratization of Communication as a Social Movement Process," in Lee (ed.), *Democratization*, pp. 92–113.

[2] This distinction was made by Janet Wasko, "Introduction: Go Tell It to the Spartans," in Wasko and Mosco (eds.), *Democratic Communications*, p. 7.

[3] White, "NWICO," p. 23; Hackett and Zhao, p. 179.

can attract groups (such as parents, librarians, churches) which are critical of the corporate media but which do not currently identify with the Left. Is such a coalition possible, without sacrificing the progressive aspects of media reform? We do not yet know, but the 1996 founding convention of the Cultural Environment Movement in St. Louis offered encouraging evidence that it is. Founded by senior U.S. communications scholar George Gerbner and endorsed by 150 organizations, the CEM brought researchers, educators, policy-makers, cultural workers and producers together with religious, environmental, public health and children's rights groups. The CEM endorsed both the PCC and a "Viewer's Declaration of Independence" which called for change to a brutalizing and homogenized cultural environment dominated by media conglomerates with "nothing to tell but something to sell." Before it can fulfill its promise of becoming a genuine mass movement, the CEM or any similar grouping would need to attract organized labor, and to satisfy such organizational needs as long-term stable funding and staffing and representative collective decision-making. Still, the breadth of its vision and coalition indicates a potential, though embryonic, movement.

What should the strategic priorities of such a movement be? A 1998 survey of U.S. media activists found differences of opinion—for example, between building autonomous media and influencing or reforming the dominant media; between "insider" strategies of working with media professionals and policy elites, and the "outsider" strategy of mobilizing marginalized groups for an assault on the citadel; and between the inward-focused strategy of mending fences within the movement, and campaigns to spread the message outwards.[1]

Too often, activists disdain strategies for change which differ from their own. To be sure, one must often choose between the different forms of media activism; it is not simply a matter of allocating scarce resources, but also of choosing between constituencies which cannot simultaneously be attracted with the same language and tactics. For instance, San Francisco's Media Alliance, an impressive membership-based coalition which originated in the 1970s as an effort to reform and reinvigorate local journalism from within, may have alienated potential media supporters in the 1990s when it organized a protest against a local news outlet.

At the same time, media democratization is too big a project to be accomplished through any single strategy, and there are potential synergies between different approaches. For example, "those who focus directly on

---

[1]Hackett and Adam, "Is Media Democratization."

existing power structures and those who work to foster alternatives beyond them expand each other's social wiggle-room. The presence of oppositional movements can force dominant power structures to bow to opposing viewpoints, while activists who engage with mainstream media can push for practices and policies that offer more opportunities and resources for oppositional cultures to grow and thrive."[1]

Interviews with various activists suggest some of the guiding principles for any successful strategy. It must involve carefully building coalitions, which are broad enough to be politically effective but not so broad as to contain internal, potentially paralyzing divisions. Greater coordination or collaboration are essential, but it is neither possible nor necessary to fit all progressive media activism into the same tent. A movement needs a common and compelling focus, such as the right to communicate, but one which allows different groups to participate in different ways without sacrificing their autonomy. The Equal Rights Amendment, which energized the women's movement in the 1970s, has been suggested as a precedent in this respect.

Ideally, communicative democracy campaigns need to connect with deeply felt concerns of broad constituencies, find supporters within political and economic elites (or at least exploit divisions within them), and make possible links between local, national, and international action, as well as between "grassroots" and "tree-tops" (elite, policy-making) levels. Such campaigns need to use existing resources to reduce the costs of mobilization, give individuals psychological and material incentives to participate, and build networks which can respond quickly on different issues. Where possible, a campaign should not be simply reactive, but should create agenda-setting or springboard effects—for example, by participating in the institutional design and implementation of new technology, such as digital television. A media democracy movement needs to draw on the strengths rather than the potential divisiveness of its diversity. It should identify short-term, winnable objectives, building on the momentum of initial successes, and develop a "strategic capacity" that builds from individual initiatives to global organizations.[2]

Several candidates for such coalitions and campaigns present themselves. These include adding the right to communicate to the emerging international human rights agenda, building coalitions to defend media workers' rights and/or challenge media concentration, and reinvigorating public broadcasting. (The

[1] Stein, "Media and Democratic Action," p. 6.
[2] Sean O Siochru, "Strategies and Opportunities," pp. 5–6.

recently formed Citizens for Independent Public Broadcasting in the U.S. joins the older Friends of Canadian Broadcasting in the ranks of leading media reform groups in their respective countries.) The first step, though, is for progressive movements to place media democratization higher on their own agendas, as a precondition of their own political advance.

ROBERT A. HACKETT, professor of communication, co-directs NewsWatch Canada at Simon Fraser University near Vancouver. His recent publications include (with Richard Gruneau et al.) *The Missing News: Filters and Blind Spots in Canada's Press*, and (with Yuezhi Zhao) *Sustaining Democracy? Journalism and the Politics of Objectivity*. E-Mail: hackett@sfu.ca

THIS MODERN WORLD

by TOM TOMORROW

Panel 1:

NEXT ON THE AOL-TIME WARNER NETWORK--IT'S *LARRY KING LIVE!*

GOOD EVENING! MY GUESTS TONIGHT ARE STEVE CASE OF AOL AND GERALD LEVIN OF TIME WARNER! I UNDERSTAND YOU GENTLE-MEN HAVE AN *ANNOUNCEMENT* FOR US!

Panel 2:

THAT'S *RIGHT*, LARRY! AS PART OF THE AOL-TIME WARNER MERGER--

--GERALD AND I HAVE DECIDED TO HAVE BOTH OUR HEADS GRAFTED ONTO A *SINGLE BODY!*

Panel 3:

YOU SEE, LARRY, WE FELT THE WORLD'S LARGEST INTERNET-NEWS-AND-ENTER-TAINMENT CONGLOM-ERATE SHOULD HAVE A *SINGLE CHIEF EXECUTIVE OFFICER!*

WE'LL SAVE TIME SLEEP-ING, EATING, AND TAKING CARE OF OTHER ROUTINE BODILY FUNCTIONS--AND WE'LL PASS THE BENEFITS ALONG TO OUR *SHARE-HOLDERS!*

Panel 4:

THAT'S *GREAT*, GUYS! SO--DO YOU HAVE ANY PLANS FOR *FURTHER EXPANSION?*

WELL, WE CAN'T REALLY TALK ABOUT THAT RIGHT NOW, LARRY--

--BUT LET'S JUST SAY WE'VE STILL GOT PLENTY OF ROOM FOR *BILL GATES'* HEAD! HA, HA!

HA, HA!

CHAPTER 10

For the Record, an interview with Walter Cronkite

BY COREY HALE, PAT THURSTON,
AND THE PROJECT CENSORED RADIO TEAM

In spring 2000, Project Censored realized a long-standing dream—the regular radio broadcast of underreported stories. Called *For the Record* (FTR), each program in the series of 60-minute monthly radio documentaries focuses on a single pressing story, often from the yearbook. The broadcasts are then uplinked to the National Public Radio satellite system the last Tuesday of every month, and are available to all public and community stations across the country.

The first program, the two-part "American News: Democracy in Jeopardy," was released in fall 2000, and featured interviews with news notables Walter Cronkite and Peter Arnett, among others. Following is an excerpt from Part I of "American News: Democracy in Jeopardy," an interview with Walter Cronkite conducted by Corey Hale, as transcribed by program director and host, Pat Thurston.

FOR THE RECORD: Why have you become an advisor to the Media Channel and what role do you see the Internet taking in opening up news information?

WALTER CRONKITE: I think the Internet has taken a huge step in that direction, making it possible for people to get on the air without the huge backing of pre-established communication channels, that is, by publishing and broad-casting, obviously. And in that particular case, I think that the whistle-blower aspect of what they are doing is most important. It is a palliative for decisions that might be made on the larger communication media to suppress stories for one reason or another. That is particularly important today with the very thing that you are researching, which is the effect of mergers and the growth of single owner media. So that's why I'm there.

FTR: In your statement on the Media Channel you talked about consolidation as a crisis. Would you elaborate on that?

WC: Yes. Monopoly in journalism is, of course, a danger any way it shows its form. It's always been a danger and began to become a problem as the two-newspaper cities began to disappear from our national map. With the elimination of competition, with the single newspaper residing in the town or city, it creates a problem. And not just for the democracy but for the newspaper itself. If the newspaper is a well-meaning paper—as I think most of them are, and I want to make that point—I do not think they deliberately wish to exercise the prerogatives of monopoly, but they suffer from it because they have no way to check the accuracy of their own reporting. When there's newspaper competition in a city, each of the papers has an opportunity to check what the other is reporting and can test its own accuracy against that of the competition. Without a newspaper as competition, they have no way to do that. The reporting on radio and television is not as easily checked so it is not a reliable system to safeguard against errors in the newspaper. Small errors have a way of accumulating in the public's mind. They can be very simple errors like the misspelling of a name, the wrong address, or the wrong occupation or business to which an individual is connected. And while those things may not be terribly important in their own right, they build an attitude in the public of mistrust of the newspaper. Then when groups get together they'll say, "You know they spelled E's name wrong the other day." And the other person says, "Oh my God, did you see what they did with that story about my company?" And before they're through, they've built up quite a legend of bad reporting and bad editing on behalf of the surviving newspaper. A very dangerous attitude. Well, the main thing that the newspapers need is trust of the population in their reporting. And they lose that in that fashion. This is where monopoly journalism began to lose credibility with the community. Now we have gone further than that, and instead of simply having single-newspaper ownership in the cities, we have single-newspaper ownership through the giant group newspapers that control many cities in this fashion. So, the people, instead of saying that they don't believe necessarily their local paper, if they are smart and get around the country and understand, they might be inclined to say I don't believe anything in "X" group of newspapers. "X" would be obviously Knight-Ridder, Gannett, Hearst, whatever. And that begins to spread this concern about accuracy in media throughout the entire newspaper profession, the newspaper business. Now, you go further than that and you merge newspapers and broadcasting through these giant corporations that not only own the newspapers and broadcasting outlets, but they also own entertainment companies and cable outlets, and the danger proliferates rapidly through the entire community. And while it can be accidental that they make mistakes that are carried through their entire organization, it is even worse than that when they own competing operations, in entertainment, for instance—that they induce their journalistic properties to propagandize. That is a serious matter. And, of course, the ultimate danger is that in their vast organizations with vast investments all through the American economy, they will put pressure on their news outlets to subvert the news to ensure their profits elsewhere.

FTR: And how do they put this pressure on? How do they exert this pressure and how does it affect the journalists who are trying to do their jobs?

WC: Well, the journalist is affected as the journalist always has been affected, even in the most simple and smallest community when the publisher decides he wants to protect a friend or a business in which he has an investment. The journalist is seriously affected. The journalist's integrity is under attack but the journalist himself or herself, in having to protect an income for his or her family, is fairly helpless. This is why I like… organizations for professional journalists. I like the critical newspapers handling the journalistic profession, that is, the *Columbia Journalism Review* and so forth. And I have signed on to give whatever advice I can to an Internet operation, which permits these offended journalists to go public.

FTR: We've discussed the danger of consolidation and how limiting that can be for information and how hard it is for journalists to get their information out. What about the citizens in our country who aren't getting this information. What effect is that having on our democracy?

WC: Well, it's about as serious a danger to our democracy as the rogue states are. And we're not building any anti-missile defense, unfortunately, against it. I think that what we must do, in every way we can, taking every avenue that we journalists can, is keep the American people advised of the danger so that whenever this malappropriation of the journalistic field takes place, we can blow the whistle and people will respond to the alarm.

FTR: So, since you are known as the most trusted man in America, for good reason I believe...

WC: Well, I don't know about that...

FTR: Well, my question is, because you talked about how reporters have the pressure of having to go along, and the experience of an absence of encouragement, have you ever had either of those things happen in a story that you felt was important?

WC: You know, I perhaps have been as lucky as any person. I'm lucky along with a whole cadre of people who worked for CBS. I have never known an organization that was as free of any sort of pressure as CBS. In my 20 years running the *CBS Evening News,* I never had a single incident of pressure for economic reasons, for advertising reasons, and only one minor one for political reasons, and that was in 20 years there. And in my knowledge of all the other pieces I've done in the documentary area, none there either. It was absolutely a pressure-free organization in my day.

FTR: But that has changed... you see that as having changed?

WC: I don't know. I'm not that acquainted with the daily operation of the news.

FTR: And could you talk about the one time you did feel that pressure? Did the story eventually get out?

WC: Well, it's nothing secret at all. It's the time we did our long, two-parter on the Watergate scandal when the thing was beginning to disappear from the newspapers. There hadn't been any new revelations for a long time. We were coming up on the election and people had practically forgotten Watergate. Nothing had come of it really. And we did two long pieces reviewing the entire Watergate thing, doing the sort of A-B-Cs of what it was and what it amounted to, and the White House brought considerable pressure on CBS and Bill Paley. Our pieces were spread over the weekend... The two pieces bridged the weekend. We had the first piece on Friday. It was the longest piece we had ever done on the evening news, more than half the show. And Chuck Colson, representing President Nixon, put the pressure on Paley. Paley was resisting the pressure but he called and talked to the president of CBS news, Dick Salant, and said, "Is there any way we can relieve the pressure without violating the piece?" And he said, "My main problem is the time we gave to it." So, Dick Salant, very shrewdly, was able to call him back in a little while and say, "Well, we're going to cut the next piece. It's not going to be as long as they said it was going to be." And actually he'd come to us and said it was his problem that it was too long, never letting us know. And I didn't know for weeks that there was anybody other than Salant, whom I trusted entirely to not allow any pressure in the news department. He felt that he'd solved it, and he did very well because we could very well cut the second piece without affecting the impact of the story at all. But the only thing *that* did was cause me to have to say ever since then that, except for one exception, we never were interfered with.

FTR: I wonder if you could comment to the value that you see in projects like Project Censored.

WC: Well, specifically, this is what I'm talking about. There has to be a watch-dog organization, or many of them perhaps, that can ring the alarm bell when censorship is perceived and your organization can certainly do that.

FTR: You also speak of lively and provocative dissent. Can you also comment on that? What happens in the newsroom, what isn't happening in the newsroom that needs to be happening?

WC: You mean dissent within the newsroom as to the way the paper's edited?

FTR: The way the paper's edited, the way that the information is gotten out.... There doesn't seem to be a dialogue between the newsroom and the public because it seems...

WC: Well, that's a very difficult thing for the newsroom to do. They've got— the individuals in the newsroom have—to band together, or, operating singly, they have to sort of violate what is normally considered the relationship with their employer. That's why organizations are necessary. That's why this anonymous whistle-blowing—but with the facts of the case being investigated thoroughly before exposure to the public—that's why these things are so absolutely essential to us today. It's very difficult for a group or an individual working for a newspaper to stand up and tell the public, "My paper's wrong." You can't do that in any business.

FTR: Hasn't the newspaper business become one that's motivated as an entertainment business? And are the reporters having a hard time because of that?

WC: Well sure, it's got to be an annoyance. But I don't think that newspapers are so much an entertainment business.

FTR: No?

wc: No. I think that broadcasting is, obviously. That's its principle business. But the newspaper's principle business is still delivering the news.

FTR: How do you feel about the *Los Angeles Times* announcing last year that they were taking down the firewall between advertising and news?

wc: Well, you see that that fellow isn't there any longer.

FTR: Do you think that firewall is still in place in most newsrooms, or do you see that as coming down, that most marketing is driving the types of information?

wc: I think that the newspapers are more conscious of marketing perhaps than they ever were before. But I don't know. I don't know all the newspapers around the country. I don't know any of them really intimately anymore, about how they operate. So I really can't answer that.

TR: What would you say is the most important thing the American public can do in regard to getting this information that they need? What can the papers do... anything you think of that is really important that I haven't covered...

wc: Well, I think what is important is that the effort continues to be made and be redoubled among those organizations that are trying to advise the public as to the performance of their newspapers and their broadcasting outlets. That is about the only way it's going to work. And I think that can be effective. Your organization is essential to this job. I think that public radio and public television are great sources for this information. And they could do more. I can say that Project Censored is one of the organizations that we should listen to, to be assured that our newspapers and our broadcasting outlets are practicing thorough and ethical journalism.

CHAPTER 11

Building Indymedia

BY ERIC GALATAS

"By not having to answer to the monster media monopolies, the independent media has a life's work, a political project, and a purpose: to let the truth be known. This is increasingly important in the globalization process. Truth becomes a knot of resistance against the lie."

> —Subcomandante Insurgente Marcos
> La Realidad, Chiapas; January 31st, 1997
> from *Our Word is Our Weapon* (Seven Stories Press, 2000)

N30 stands for November 30, 1999. This was the day that thousands of activists from across the globe planned to shut down the "crown jewel" of corporate globalization, a Breton/Woods and GATT progeny known as the World Trade Organization (WTO). Labor, indigenous rights groups, environmentalists, organizations of faith, youth, anarchists, and more all made their way to Seattle to proclaim in a very loud voice that so-called free trade policies were costing the majority of people on the planet more than they could, or would, pay.

And the activists were creative. Ready to don turtle costumes, drop banners from high-rises and from expansion bridges, this unprecedented coalition intended to pull out every trick in the book to wow mainstream news outlets, to spread their message by becoming that day's media darlings on front pages the world over.

Independent media activists weren't convinced that corporate media would provide a platform for anti-corporate globalization critics. Conglomerate mergers had shrunk the number of corporate owned outlets from 50 in 1986, to fewer than 10 at the end of the millennium. PBS, NPR, and virtually every other supposedly public interest media organization had been successfully de-fanged by the time 85,000 activists put on costumes, carried signs of protest, and locked down in front of the Paramount Theater in the center of Seattle for the WTO opening ceremonies.

On N30, corporate coverage of the largest protests seen on U.S. soil since the 1960s turned out to be pretty much as the indy press had predicted. And from the point of view of the powerful, it almost worked.

Reporters bypassed the arguments of WTO critics, and instead gave focus to select images of mayhem and disaster. CNN reported that police were not using rubber bullets against window-smashing protestors—citing official police sources, of course. Everyone watching a screen across the planet saw virtually the same picture. Sure, the police in riot gear resembled Darth Vader storm troopers; but, as the respectable pundits were quick to point out, the troublemakers in the streets were the ones to blame. The activists bringing on the violence were, according to Milton Friedman's expansive arguments in the *New York Times*, "global village idiots" who didn't understand progress, and were standing in the way of the prosperity awaiting each and every one of us under the rule of a corporate controlled global economy.

But on November 30, 1999, something went wrong. Not only did official sources fail to predict the resolve and sheer number of people willing to put their bodies on the line to stop the WTO meetings, they failed to predict the emergence of a new media, a people's media, with just enough firepower to

THIS MODERN WORLD by TOM TOMORROW

effectively break through the corporate-owned media's information blockade.

More than 400 independent print, radio, photo, video, and Internet journalists worked nonstop during the weeks leading up to N30 to organize a new model for event-based, real-time news coverage. The experiment was called the Independent Media Center (IMC). Stringing together scrap-heap bound computers to high bandwidth internet connections (a revolutionary software that enables instantaneous publishing via the World Wide Web), along with overnight satellite television uplinks, a daily newspaper and several micro-radio transmitters, an ad hoc news room was created virtually overnight.

When CNN reported that no rubber bullets were being aimed at mothers and children, these independent journalists had an answer. The answer came in the form of a series of photos and video stills, taken directly in the line of fire, of the very same rubber bullets, concussion grenades, and chemical agents unleashed upon peacefully assembled global citizens. These images were posted on the Independent Media Center website, www.indymedia.org, alongside in-depth articles explaining *why* so many had taken to the streets to shut down the WTO. On N30, the IMC site registered over a million hits. CNN decided to change its story.

Since N30, the growing movement to disable corporate globalization has met the WTO and its ilk at every turn. In Washington, D.C., activists did not manage to shut down the International Monetary Fund and World Bank meetings. Instead, they shut down the entire U.S. federal government, as D.C. police sealed off some 90 square blocks to keep concerned citizens from disturbing anti-democratic and unaccountable globalization power brokers.

During the U.S. Presidential conventions in Philadelphia and Los Angeles, and the globalization resistance demonstrations in Davos, Windsor, Melbourne, Prague, and The Hague, the movement to challenge unbridled

corporate power stalled what was at one time considered to be a monolithic inevitability. A crisis of confidence among elite global powers became visible. In one example, Stephen Byers, Secretary of Trade and Industry for the United Kingdom, announced, "The WTO will not be able to continue in its present form. There has to be fundamental and radical change in order for it to meet the needs and aspirations of all 134 of its members."

And at every antiglobalization turn, Independent Media Centers have formed to ensure that activist voices are not silenced by a media system bought and paid for by the direct beneficiaries of global corporate power.

Since Seattle, live satellite television feeds reaching some 30 million households via Free Speech TV, community radio, and cable access have been added to the IMC information arsenal. Add to that multiple language publications, real-time webcasts, improved server capacity, increased bandwidth and advanced web-publishing software. The IMC experiment—one of purpose, collaboration, and collective effort—is expanding. There are now some 43 IMCs, spreading out from Seattle to international hubs in Quebec, Sydney, Italy, Israel, Mexico, Brazil, Colombia, the Congo, and more.

To get involved in, or help build, an IMC near you, follow these links:

AUSTRALIA
Melbourne
melbourne.indymedia.org

Sydney
sydney.indymedia.org

EUROPE
Finland
kulma.net/vaikuttava

Belgium
belgium.indymedia.org

Czech Republic
prague.indymedia.org

United Kingdom
uk.indymedia.org

France
france.indymedia.org

Italy
italy.indymedia.org

Switzerland
switzerland.indymedia.org

CANADA
Calgary
calgary.indymedia.org

Hamilton
hamilton.indymedia.org

Montreal
montreal.indymedia.org

Ontario
ontario.indymedia.org

Quebec
cmaq.net

Vancouver
vancouver.indymedia.org

Windsor
windsor.indymedia.org

OTHER COUNTRIES

Brazil
brasil.indymedia.org

Colombia
columbia.indymedia.org

Congo
congo.indymedia.org

Israel
indymedia.org.il

Mexico
mexico.indymedia.org

UNITED STATES

Albany
nycap.indymedia.org

Arizona
arizona.indymedia.org

Atlanta
atlanta.indymedia.org

Austin
austin.indymedia.org

Boston
boston.indymedia.org

Buffalo
buffalo.indymedia.org

Chicago
chicago.indymedia.org

Cleveland
cleveland.indymedia.org

Los Angeles
la.indymedia.org

Madison
madison.indymedia.org

Minneapolis
minneapolis.indymedia.org

New York City
nyc.indymedia.org

Ohio Valley
ohiovalleyimc.org

Philadelphia
phillyimc.org

Portland
portland.indymedia.org

Richmond
richmond.indymedia.org

Rocky Mountains
rockymountain.indymedia.org

Salt Lake City
saltlake.indymedia.org

San Francisco/Bay Area
sf.indymedia.org

Seattle
seattle.indymedia.org

Urbana-Champaign
urbana.indymedia.org

Washington, D.C.
dc.indymedia.org

ERIC GALATAS helped organize IMCs in Seattle and Washington, D.C., and was project coordinator for Free Speech TV's live satellite broadcasts of collaborative IMC programming from the Republican and Democratic Presidential Convention protests in Philadelphia and Los Angeles. Eric is Program Manager for Free Speech TV, now available 24 hours a day, 7 days a week on DISH Network Channel 9415, on community cable stations across the U.S. and on the net at www.freespeech.org.

THIS MODERN WORLD

by TOM TOMORROW

Panel 1: WHILE VISITING NEW YORK, BETSY CONSALLIS OF FAYETTEVILLE, ARKANSAS GETS LOST ON THE SUBWAY SYSTEM AND IS NEVER SEEN AGAIN--LEAVING HER SIX YEAR OLD SON ALLEN IN THE CARE OF *RELATIVES*...

--AND WE'VE DECIDED TO *KEEP* THE BOY!

AFTER ALL, NEW YORK HAS *MUCH* MORE TO OFFER HIM THAN *ARKANSAS!* I MEAN, GET *REAL!*

?

Panel 2: ALLEN'S FATHER, SPEAKING THROUGH AN INTERPRETER, MAKES A PASSIONATE PLEA FOR THE BOY'S RETURN TO ARKANSAS.

AH'M ORN'RIER THAN A RAZORBACK HAWG WITH A STICK UP HIS BEE-HIND! AH MAHT JEST COME UP THERE TO NEW YORK WITH MAH THIRTY-OUGHT-SIX, AH TELL YEW WHUT!

MR. CONSALLIS IS USING A COLORFUL METAPHOR TO EXPRESS HIS FRUSTRATION, AND SUGGESTS HE MIGHT TRAVEL TO NEW YORK WITH--UM--I BELIEVE IT'S SOME SORT OF FIREARM.

Panel 3: THE LITTLE BOY'S PLIGHT QUICKLY BECOMES THE *TALK* OF THE *TOWN!*

WELL, I SUPPOSE A BOY *SHOULD* BE WITH HIS FATHER--

--BUT NOW THAT HE'S TASTED *SOPHISTICATION*, CAN WE REALLY CONDEMN HIM TO A LIFE IN *ARKANSAS?*

I DON'T THINK THEY EVEN HAVE *MUSEUMS* THERE!

Panel 4: THE TUG OF WAR OVER LITTLE ALLEN'S FUTURE CONTINUES--BUT MEANWHILE, HE'S LIVING THE LIFE OF AN *AVERAGE NEW YORK CITY YOUNGSTER!*

LOOK, ALLEN! RUDY GIULIANI AND MICKEY MOUSE ARE HERE TO GIVE YOU A GUIDED TOUR OF THE *DISNEY STORE!*

YOU CAN HAVE *ANYTHING* IN THERE YOU WANT--*FREE!*

SO--DO YOU *REALLY* WANT TO GO BACK TO ARKANSAS?

UM--AON'T KNOW...

Most Censored News Stories for 2000 Publication Source List

Subscription Information for publications that produced the Top 25 stories (* indicates more than one article in the Top 25)

THE A-INFOS NEWS SERVICE
E-mail: a-infos@ainfos.ca
Website: www.ainfos.ca
or www.ainfos.ca/org

An online news service from around the world. Subscribe free at their website.

ALTERNET*
Institute for Alternative Journalism
77 Federal Street
San Francisco, CA 94107
Tel: (415) 284-1420
Fax: (415) 284-1414
E-mail: info@alternet.org
Website: www.alternet.org/

An online news service from around the country. Subscribe free at their website.

ARMS SALES MONITOR
Federation of American Scientists
307 Massachusetts Avenue NE
Washington, D.C. 20002
Tel: (202) 675-1018
Fax: (202) 675-1010
E-mail: llumpe@fas.org
Website: www.fas.org/asmp/
No data found.

CANADIAN DIMENSION
2B-91 Albert Street
Winnipeg, Manitoba
Canada R3B IG5
Tel: (800) 737-7051
Fax: (204) 943-4617
E-mail:
info@canadiandimension.mb.ca

Website: www.canadiandimension.mb.
ca/
$24.50/1 year (6 issues)
$18.50/1 year
(Students and unemployed)
$35.00/1 year (Organizations)
Postage outside Canada:
United States add $10.00
International add $15.00

COVERTACTION QUARTERLY
1500 Massachusetts Avenue NW #732
Washington, D.C. 20005
Tel: (202) 331-9763
Fax: (202) 331-9751
E-mail: info@caq.org
Website: www.caq.com
$22.00/1 year (4 issues)
$38.00/2 years (8 issues)

COUNTERPUNCH*
P.O. Box 18675
Washington, D.C. 20036
Tel: (202) 986-3665
Fax: (202) 986-0974
E-mail: counterpunch@
counterpunch.org
Website: www.counterpunch.org
$40.00/1 year (23 issues)
$30.00/1 year (low-income discount)

DENDRON MAGAZINE
Support Coalition
P.O. Box 11284
Eugene, OR 97440-3484
Toll Free Number:
1-877-MAD-PRIDE
Tel: (541) 345-9106
Fax: (541) 345-3737
E-mail: office@mindfreedom.org
Website: www.MindFreedom.org/
DENDRON/dendron_node.html
$20.00 to $50.00/1 year (sliding scale)

DESIGNER/BUILDER
2405 Maclovia Lane
Santa Fe, NM 87505
Tel/Fax: (505) 471-4549
$28.00/1 year, $48.00/2 years

DOLLARS AND SENSE:
WHAT'S LEFT IN ECONOMICS*
1 Summer Street
Somerville, MA 02143
Tel: (617) 628-4118
Fax: (617) 628-2025
E-mail: dollars@igc.epc.org
Website: www.igc.org/dollars
$18.95/1 year (6 issues)
$29.95/2 years (12 issues)

THE EMPEROR'S
NEW CLOTHES*
E-mail: emperors1000@aol.com
Website: www.tenc.net

An online news service from around the
world. Subscribe free at their website.

EXTRA! (ACTION ALERT)*
(Published by: Fairness
and Accuracy in Reporting)
130 West 25th Street
New York, NY 10001
Tel: (212) 633-6700
Fax: (212) 727-7668
E-mail: info@fair.org
Website: www.fair.org
$19.00/1 year
(6 issues + 6 *Extra! Updates*)
$29.00/2 years
(12 issues + 12 *Extra! Updates*)

FAMILY THERAPY NETWORKER*
7705 13th Street NW
Washington, D.C. 20012
Tel: (301) 589 6536
E-mail: ServiceFTN@aol.com

Website: www.familytherapynet-
worker.com
$18.00/year (six issues)
$24/year (outside the USA)

FREE SPEECH TV*
P.O. Box 6060
Boulder, CA 80306
Tel: (303) 442-8445
Fax: (303) 442-6472
E-mail: Programming@sftv.org
Website: www. freespeech.org/

An online news service from around the
country. Subscribe free at their website.

GENEWATCH*
Council for Responsible Genetics
5 Upland Road Suite #3
Cambridge, MA 02140
Tel: (617) 868-0870
Fax: (617) 491-5344
E-mail: crg@gene-watch.org
Website: www.gene-
watch.org/genewatch/

Become a CRG Associate, and receive
the newsletter GeneWatch, updates, and
other CRG literature for $35.00/1 year
for an individual or $100/1 year for
organizations. Subscribe to GeneWatch,
for $24.00/1 year for an individual,
$30.00/1 year for organizations or
libraries and $15/1 year for low income
or students. Send E-mail to receive a
free issue.

GUARDIAN WEEKLY*
75 Farringdon Road
London EC1M 3HQ
U.K.
Tel: (+44) (0) 20 7713-4441
Fax: (+44) (0) 20 7242-0985
E-mail: weekly@guardian.co.uk

Website: www.guardianweekly.com/
USA Expedited: $56/6 months,
$99/1 year, $177/2 years
USA Premium: $67/6 months,
$120/1 year, $215/2 years

HEALTH LETTER
Circulation Department
Public Citizen Health Research Group
1600 20th Street NW
Washington, D.C. 20009
Tel: (202) 588-1000
Fax: (202) 588-7796
E-mail: member@citizen.org
Website: www.citizen.org/hrg/
NEWSLETTERS/ hletter.htm
$18.00/year (12 issues)

IN THESE TIMES*
2040 North Milwaukee Avenue, 2nd
Floor
Chicago, IL 60647-4002
Tel: (773) 772-0100
Fax: (773) 772-4180
E-mail: itt@inthesetimes.com
Website: www.inthesetimes.com
$19.95/1 year (24 issues)
$34.95/2 years (48 issues)

INTERNATIONAL FORUM
ON GLOBALIZATION
Building 1062, Fort Cronkhite
Sausalito, CA 94965
Tel: (415) 229-9350
Fax: (415) 229-9340
E-mail: ifg@ifg.org
Website: www.ifg.org
$25/year (Basic Membership)

THE KONFORMIST
P.O. Box 24825
Los Angeles, CA 90024-0825
Tel: (310) 737-1081

Fax: (310) 737-1081
E-mail: robalini@aol.com
Website: www.konformist.com

For a free subscription to The Konformist Newswire, visit www.eGroups.com/list/konformist/ and sign up. Or e-mail konformist subscribe@egroups.com.

LABOR NOTES
7435 Michigan Avenue
Detroit, MI 48210
(313) 842-6262
Fax: (313) 842-0227
E-mail: labornotes@labornotes.org
Website: www.labornotes.org/
Subscription rates:
Individual $20/1 Year,
$35/2 Year
Supporting $30/1 Year,
$55/2 Year
Institutions $30/1 Year,
$55/2 Year
Individual outside US
$25/1 Year, $45/2 Year
Institution outside US
$35/1 Year, $65/2 Year
First class and airmail costs
an extra $10 per year.
Free sample copy.

LONDON OBSERVER
Website: www.londonobserver.com/

LOS ANGELES ALTERNATIVE
MEDIA NETWORK*
8124 West Third Street, Suite 208
Los Angeles, CA 90048
E-mail: laamn-announce-owner@egroups.com

For free e-mail subscription send message to address above and type in "Subscribe."

MOTHER JONES*
731 Market Street, Suite 600
San Francisco, CA 94103
Tel: (415) 665-6637
Fax: (415) 665-6696
E-mail: query@motherjones.com
Website: www.motherjones.com
$18.00/1 year (6 issues)
$31.00/2 years (12 issues)

MULTINATIONAL MONITOR*
P.O. Box 19405
Washington, D.C. 20036
Tel: (202) 387-8034
Fax: (202) 234-5176
E-mail: monitor@essential.org
Website: www.essential.org/monitor/subscribe.html
U.S. Individual: $25.00,
U.S. Individual Renewal: $25.00,
U.S. Nonprofit: $30.00,
U.S. Business: $40.00,
U.S. 2-yr. Individual: $45.00
Canada/Mexico Individual: $35.00,
Canada/Mexico Individual Renewal: $35.00,
Canada/Mexico Nonprofit: $40.00,
Canada/Mexico Business: $50.00,
Canada/Mexico 2-yr. Individual: $55.00
Other Foreign Individual: $40.00,
Other Foreign Nonprofit: $45.00,
Other Foreign Business: $55.00,
Other Foreign 2-yr. Individual: $60.00

NEW SCIENTIST
(Published in England)
201 Spear Street, Suite 400
San Francisco, CA 94105
Tel: (888) 800-8077
Fax: (202) 331-2082
E-mail: newscientist@lexis-nexis
Website: www.newscientist.com
$69.99/1 year (51 issues)

NORTH COAST XPRESS
P.O. Box 1226
Occidental, CA 95465
Tel: (707) 874-3104
Fax: (707) 874-1453
E-mail: doretk@sonic.net
Website: www.sonic.net/~doretk/
$20/1 Year, $36/2 Year, $45/1 Year
Institutional, $35/1 Year Foreign,
$10/1 Year for Prisoners
(Stamps/Embossed envelopes O.K.)

PACIFIC NEWS SERVICE
450 Mission Street, Room #204
San Francisco, CA 94105
Tel: (415) 438-4755 or 243-4364
Fax: (415) 438-4935
E-mail: pacificnews@pacificnews.org
Website: www.pacificnews.org/

An online news service from around the
country. Subscribe free at their website.

PR WATCH (Published by Center
for Media and Democracy)
3318 Gregory Street
Madison, WI 53711
Tel: (608) 233-3346
Fax: (608) 238-2236
E-mail: stauber@compuserve.com
Website: www.prwatch.org
Businesses: $200/year, Nonprofit
Groups: $60/year,
Journalists and Individuals: $35/year

THE PROGRESSIVE*
409 East Main Street
Madison, WI 53703
Tel: (608) 257-4626
Fax: (608) 257-3373
E-mail: progressive@peacenet.org
Website: www.progressive.org
$12.00/1 year (12 issues)
Free sample copy

RACHEL'S ENVIRONMENT
& HEALTH WEEKLY*
Environmental Research Foundation
P.O. Box 5036
Annapolis, MD 21403-7036
Tel: (410) 263-1584
Fax: (410) 263-8944
E-mail: erf@rachel.org
Website:
www.rachel.org/home_eng.htm
Free e-mail subscription:
listserv@rachel.org
Paper subscriptions are also available.

RANDOM LENGTHS NEWS
1300 South Pacific Avenue
San Pedro, CA 90731
Tel: (310) 519-1442
Fax: (310) 832-1000
E-mail: 71632.201@compuserve.com
$23.00/year (26 issues)

THE SAN FRANCISCO BAY
GUARDIAN*
520 Hampshire
San Francisco, CA 94110-1417
Tel: (415) 255-3100
Fax: (415) 255-8762
E-mail: sfguardian@aol.com
Website: www.sfbg.com
$17.00/6 months (26 issues)
$32.00/1 year (52 issues)

SCIENCE FEATURE
Center for Health,
Environment and Justice
P.O. Box 6806
Falls Church, VA 22040
Tel: (703) 237-2249
Fax: (703) 237-8389
E-mail: chej@chej.org
Website: www.chej.org
$10.00/year.

SPIRIT OF CRAZY HORSE
(Published by Leonard Peltier
Defense Committee)
P.O. Box 583
Lawrence, KS 66044
Tel: (785) 842-5774
Fax: (785) 842-5796
E-mail: questions@freepeltier.org
Website: www.freepeltier.org/
newspaper.htm#top
In the United States:
$15.00/year (6 issues)
Senior Citizens: $8.00/year
Internationally: $25.00/year
Prisoners: Free

THE SUSTAINABLE TIMES
1657 Barrington Street, Suite 508
Halifax, Nova Scotia
Canada BJ3 2A1
Tel: (902) 423-6852
Fax: (902) 423-9736
E-mail: times@web.net
Website: www.chebucto.ns.ca/
CommunitySupport/CUSO/home2.html
$8.00 for 4 issues. (Subscriptions
outside of Canada, please remit in
U.S. funds)

TASH NEWSLETTER
29 W. Susquehanna Avenue
Suite 210
Baltimore, MD 21204
Tel: (410) 828-8274
Fax: (410) 828-6706
E-mail: info@tash.org
Website: www.tash.org/
Individual: $33/year
Reduced Fee: $20/year
Family: $66/year
Organizational: $200/year

TERRAIN
The Ecology Center
2530 San Pablo Avenue
Berkeley, CA 94702
Tel: (510) 548-2235
Fax: (510) 548-2240
E-mail: terrain@ecologycenter.org
Website: www.ecologycenter.org/
terrain/terrain.html
No subscription data

THIRD WORLD RESURGENCE
Third World Network
228 Macalister Road
Penang, Malaysia
Tel: (+60) 4 226-6728 or -6159
Fax: (+60) 4 226-4505
E-mail: twn@igc.apc.org
Website: www.twnside.org.sg
Surface mail:
Developed Countries
(Institutions): $45/year
Developed Countries
(Individuals): $30/year
Air mail:
Developed Countries
(Institutions): $60/year
Developed Countries
(Individuals): $45/year

THIS MAGAZINE
35 Rivera Drive #17
Markham, Ontario
Canada M5V 3A8
Tel: (416) 979-8400
Fax: (416) 979-1143
E-mail: thismag@web.net
Website: www.thismag.org
$34.00/1 year
$57.00/2 years
$77.00/3 years

TOWARD FREEDOM
Box 468
Burlington, VT 05402-0468
Tel: (802) 658-2523
Fax: (802) 658-3738
E-mail: TFmag@aol.com
Website: www.towardfreedom.com
$22.50/1 year (8 issues)

THE WASHINGTON FREE PRESS
1463 E. Republican Street, #178
Seattle, WA 98112
Tel: (206) 860-5290
E-mail: freepress@scn.org
Website: www.speakeasy.org/wfp
$16.00/year (6 issues)

WASHINGTON MONTHLY
1611 Connecticut Avenue NW
Washington, D.C. 20009
Tel: (202) 462-0128
Fax: (202) 332-8413
E-mail:
letters@washingtonmonthly.com
Website: www.washingtonmonthly.com
$29.95/1 year (10 issues), $52/2
years, $72/3 years

THE WORKBOOK
(Published by Southwest Research
and Information Center)
P.O. Box 4524
105 Stanford SE
Albuquerque, NM 87106
Tel: (505) 262-1862
Fax: (505) 262-1864
E-mail: TheWorkbook@sric.org
Website:
www.sric.org/Workbook/index.html
No subscription data

THIS MODERN WORLD

by TOM TOMORROW

MORE PROPOSED DEBATE OPTIONS FROM THE BUSH CAMPAIGN

AS LEAKED TO TOM TOMORROW

WE'RE NOT WORRIED-- RIGHT, KARL?

UH--SURE, GEORGE.

---

1. ALL THREE DEBATES TO BE MODERATED BY A TRAINED CHIMPANZEE AND SHOWN ONLY ON CABLE ACCESS IN *BILLINGS, MONTANA*.

WHAT'S THAT, CHUCKLES? YOU THINK AL GORE SMELLS LIKE A MONKEY *TOO*?

HEY! POINT OF ORDER!

EEE! EEE! OOOH! OOH!

---

2. AL GORE NOT ALLOWED TO ATTEND IN PERSON--INSTEAD TO BE REPRESENTED BY A LIFE-SIZED *CARDBOARD CUTOUT*.

SO WHAT DO YOU SAY TO *THAT*, MISTER CARDBOARD MAN? WHAT'S THE MATTER--CAT GOT YOUR TONGUE?

---

3. GORE ATTENDS, BUT IS REQUIRED TO WEAR THAT SCARY FACE RESTRAINT FROM "SILENCE OF THE LAMBS."

MMMPH! MMMPH!

I THINK MY OPPONENT IS SAYING HE MIGHT AS WELL CONCEDE DEFEAT RIGHT NOW.

---

4. INSTEAD OF DEBATING, CANDIDATES SPEND NINETY MINUTES PLAYING A GAME OF *"PICTIONARY."*

UM--LOOKS LIKE...A TAX INCREASE?

YOU THINK *EVERYTHING* LOOKS LIKE A TAX INCREASE, MR. GORE!

---

5. AL GORE MUST UNDERGO ROOT CANAL SURGERY DURING THE DEBATES.

MORE NITROUSH OXSHIDE PLEASHE.

BOY--THAT LOOKS AS PAINFUL AS ANOTHER *DEMOCRATIC ADMINISTRATION*!

GEORGE W. BUSH--CONDITIONALLY WILLING TO DEBATE ANYTIME, ANYWHERE!

TOM TOMORROW© 9-13-00... tomorrow@well... www.thismodernworld.com

APPENDIX B

Media Activist Resource Guide

50 YEARS IS ENOUGH
U.S. Network For Global
Economic Justice
1025 Vermont Avenue NW, Suite 300
Washington, D.C. 20005
Tel: (202) 879-3187
Fax: (202) 879-3186
E-mail: wb50years@igc.apc.org

A network of 200 social and economic justice organizations working to bring about radical reform of the World Bank and the International Monetary Fund. 50 Years is working with domestic groups to strengthen public understanding of the domestic impacts of global economic policy, and to mobilizeAmericans around these issues.

ABORIGINAL MULTI-MEDIA
SOCIETY
15001-112 Avenue
Edmonton, Alberta T5M 2V6
Tel: (780) 455-2700
Fax: (780) 455-7639

E-mail: markety@ammsa.com
Website: www.ammsa.com/ammsa.html

Provides a forum through print and electronic media for the exchange of information about issues in Native communites and cultural issue and events.

AFRICA NEWS SERVICE
P.O. Box 3851
Durham, NC 27702
Tel: (919) 286-0747
Fax: (919) 286-2614
E-mail: newsdesk@afnews.org
Website: www.africanews.org

Disseminates stories from African news organizations.

ALTERNATIVE MEDIA, INC.
P.O. Box 21308
Washington, D.C. 20009
Tel: (202) 588-9807
Fax: (202) 588-9809

E-mail: mpaulsen@aminc.com
Website: www.washingtonwire.com

Alternative Media, Inc. publishes *Detroit Metro Times*, *Orlando Weekly*, and *San Antonio Current*. AMI also publishes *Washington Wire*, a syndicated national report for alternative media.

ALTERNATIVE PRESS INDEX
P.O. Box 33109
1443 Gorsuch Avenue
Baltimore, MD 21218-0401
Tel: (410) 243-2471
Fax: (410) 235-5325
E-mail: altpress@igc.apc.org
Website: www.altpress.org/

Alternative Press Center publishes the Alternative Press Index and Annotations. A guide to independent critical press (with the IPA). Also maintains a library.

ALTERNET (INSTITUTE FOR ALTERNATIVE JOURNALISM)
77 Federal Street
San Francisco, CA 94107
Tel: (415) 284-1420
Fax: (415) 284-1414
Website: www.alternet.org/

A news service for the alternative press, IAJ supports independent and alternative journalism and is best known for sponsoring the Media & Democracy Congress.

AMERICAN LIBRARY ASSOCIATION OFFICE FOR INTELLECTUAL FREEDOM
50 East Huron Street
Chicago, IL 60611
Tel: (312) 280-4223
or (800) 545-2433

Fax: (312) 280-4227
E-mail: oif@ala.org
Website: www.ala.org/oif.html

Organized to educate librarians and the general public about the nature and importance of intellectual freedom in libraries.

AMNESTY INTERNATIONAL
304 Pennsylvania Avenue SE
Washington, D.C. 20003
Tel: (800) 266-3789 or (202) 544-0200
Fax: (202) 546-7142
E-mail: admin-us@aiusa.org (to become a member: aimember@aiusa.org)
Website: www.amnesty.org

An international organization which works to ensure human rights throughout the world and opposes human rights abuses.

ARMS SALES MONITORING PROJECT
Publishes the *Arms Sales Monitor*
307 Massachusetts Avenue NE
Washington, CA 20002
Tel: (202) 675-1018
Fax: (202) 675-1010
E-mail: tamarg@fas.org
Website: www.fas.org/asmp/

Organized to promote accountability, transparency, and reduction in tranfers of US conventional arms. Has recently published "The Arms Trade Revealed: A Guide for Investigators and activists" by Laura Lumpe.

ASIAN AMERICAN
JOURNALISTS ASSOCIATION
1765 Sutter Street, Suite 1000
San Francisco, CA 94115
Tel: (415) 346-2051
Fax: (415) 931-4671
E-mail: aajal@aol.com
Website: www.aaja.org/

Committed to insuring diversity in
American journalism and expressing the
Asian-American perspective

ASSOCIATION FOR EDUCATION
JOURNALISM AND MASS
COMMUNICATION
University of South Carolina
1621 College Street
Columbia, SC 29208
Tel: (803) 777-2005

ASSOCIATION OF
ALTERNATIVE
NEWSWEEKLIES
1660 L Street NW, Suite 316
Washington, D.C. 20036
Tel: (202) 822-1955
Fax: (202) 822-0929
E-mail: ann@intr.net
Website: www.aan.org

A coordinating and administrative organization for 113 alternative newsweeklies
in the U.S. and Canada.

ASSOCIATION
OF AMERICAN
PUBLISHERS
71 Fifth Avenue
New York, NY 10003
Tel: (212) 255-0200
Fax: (212) 255-7007
Website: www.publishers.org/

BERKELEY MEDIA
STUDIES GROUP
2140 Shattuck Avenue
Suite 804
Berkeley, CA 94704
Tel: (510) 204-9700
Fax: (510) 204-9710
E-mail: bmsg@bmsg.org

BEYOND MEDIA
1629 Asbury Avenue
Evanston, IL 60201
Tel: (847) 869-6888

BLACK PRESS INSTITUTE
2711 East 75th Place
Chicago, IL 60649
Tel: (312) 375-8200
Fax: (312) 375-8262

BLACK WOMEN
IN PUBLISHING
P.O. Box 6275, FDR Station
New York, NY 10150
Tel: (212) 772-5951

CALIFORNIA FIRST
AMENDMENT COALITION
926 J Street, Suite 1406
Sacramento, CA 95814-2708
Tel: (916) 447-2322
Fax: (916) 447-2328
Website: cfac.org

CAMPUS ALTERNATIVE
JOURNALISM PROJECT
Center for Campus Organizing
P.O. Box 425748
Cambridge, MA 02142
Tel: (617) 725-2886
Fax: (617) 547-5067
E-mail: cco@igc.apc.org
Website: www.cco.org

CAPJ supports the work of campus progressive activists who make their own print ed media. We provide resource guides, trainings, and consultation, and organize a 100+ network of publications.

THE CENTER FOR
COMMERCIAL-FREE
PUBLIC EDUCATION
Home of the Unplug Campaign
360 Grand Avenue
P.O. Box 385
Oakland, CA 94610
Tel: (510) 268-1100
Fax: (510) 268-1277
E-mail: unplug@igc.apc.org

CENTER FOR INTEGRATION AND
IMPROVEMENT OF JOURNALISM
San Francisco State University
San Francisco, CA 94610
Tel: (415) 243-4364
Website: www.journalism.sfsu.edu/
www/ciij/ciij.html

CENTER FOR INVESTIGATIVE
REPORTING
500 Howard Street, Suite 206
San Francisco, CA 94105-3000
Tel: (415) 543-1200
Fax: (415) 543-8311
E-mail: CIR@igc.org
Website: www.muckraker.org/pubs/
papertrails/index.html

CENTER FOR MEDIA
AND DEMOCRACY
Publication: *PR Watch*
3318 Gregory Street
Madison, WI 53711
Tel: (608) 233-3346
Fax: (608) 238-2236
E-mail: stauber@compuserve.com

Website: www.prwatch.org

Editors John Stauber and Sheldon Rampton wrote *Toxic Sludge is Good for You: Lies, Damn Lies, and the Public Relations Industry.*

CENTER FOR MEDIA
AND PUBLIC AFFAIRS
2100 L Street NW, Suite 300
Washington, D.C., 20037-1526
Tel: (202) 223-2942
Fax: (202) 872-4014
Website:
www.cmpa.com/html/2100.html

CENTER FOR MEDIA EDUCATION
Publication: *InfoActive Kids*
1511 K Street NW, Suite 518
Washington, D.C. 20005
Tel: (202) 628-2620
Fax: (202) 628-2554
E-mail: cme@cme.org
Website: www.cme.org/cme

InfoActive Kids is a quarterly print publication for the child advocacy, consumer, health, and educational communities as well as a resource for journalists covering children and media topics.

CENTER FOR MEDIA LITERACY
4727 Wilshire Boulevard, Suite #403
Los Angeles, CA 90010
Tel: (213) 931-4177
Fax: (213) 931-4474
E-mail: cml@medialit.org
Website: www.medialit.org

CENTER FOR PUBLIC INTEGRITY
Publication: *The Public I*
1634 I Street NW, Suite 902
Washington, D.C. 20006
Tel: (202) 783-3900

Fax: (202)783-3906
E-mail: contact@publicintegrity.org
Website: www.publicintegrity.org

The CPI provides a mechanism through which important national issues can be analyzed by responsible journalists over time and the results can be published in full form without the traditional time and space limitations.

CENTER FOR
THIRD WORLD
ORGANIZING (CTWO)
Publication: *ColorLines*
1218 East 21st Street
Oakland, CA 94606-9950
Tel: (510) 533-7583
Fax: (510) 533-0923
E-mail: ctwo@igc.org
Website: www.igc.org/ctwo

Since 1980, CTWO has been on the cutting edge of social organizing, becoming nationally recognized for its innovative organizer training and leadership programs in communities of color.

CENTER FOR
WAR, PEACE AND
THE NEWS MEDIA
New York University
10 Washington Place, 4th Floor
New York, NY 10003
Tel: (212) 998-7960
Fax: (212) 995-4143
Website: www.nyu.edu/globalbeat

CHICAGO MEDIA WATCH
P.O. Box 268737
Chicago, IL 60626
Tel: (773) 604-1910
E-mail: cmw@mediawatch.org

CITIZENS FOR INDEPENDENT
PUBLIC BROADCASTING
1029 Vermont Avenue NW, Suite 800
Washington , D.C. 20005
Tel: (202) 638-6880
Fax: (202) 638-6885
E-mail: jmstarr@cais.com

Coordinates a national education campaign to reform public broadcasting as a public trust, independent of government and ccorporate control, and to organize community groups to democratize their local public broadcasting stations.

CITIZENS FOR MEDIA LITERACY
34 Wall Street, Suite 407
Asheville, NC 28801
Tel: (704) 255-0182
Fax: (704) 254-2286
E-mail: cml@main.nc.us
Website: www.main.nc.us/cml

CITIZENS' MEDIA CORPS
c/o Steve Provizer
23 Winslow Road
Brookline, MA 02446
Tel: (617) 232-3174
Website: www.radfrall.org

Seeks out the most politically and culturally disenfranchised citizens and community groups and provides them with the tools necessary to both access mainstream media and to create alternative media outlets.

THE CIVIC MEDIA CENTER
& LIBRARY, INC.
1021 W. University Avenue
Gainsville, FL 32601
Tel: (352) 373-0010
Website: www.gator.net

A nonprofit library and reading room of alternative press publications. Contains books, periodicals, reference materials (including the Alternative Press Index), E-zine library, and an audio & video collection.

COLLISION COURSE
VIDEO PRODUCTIONS
Contact: Doug Norgerg
P.O. Box 347383
San Francisco, CA 94134-7383
Tel: (415) 587-0818
Fax: (415) 587-0818
E-mail: video@collissioncourse.com
Website: www.collisioncourse.com

Creates and distributes activist videos on anti-interventionism, police abuse, abortion rights, and indigenous issues; also the educational video "Viva La Casa! 500 years of Chicano History." Produces two your-oriented cable TV shows each month in San Francisco.

COMMITTEE TO PROTECT
JOURNALISTS
330 Seventh Avenue, 12th Floor
New York, NY 10001
Tel: (212) 465-1004
Fax: (212) 465-9568
E-mail: Info@cpj.org
Website: www.cpj.org

The Committe to Protect Journalists is dedicated to safeguarding journalists and freedom of expression worldwide is a nonprofit, nonpartisan organization that monitors abuses of the press and promotes press freedom internationally.

COMMON DREAMS
611 Pennsylvania Avenue SE
Suite 2000
Washington, D.C. 20003
Tel: (800) 584-2730
Website: www.commondreams.org

A national nonprofit, grassroots organization whose mission is to organize an open, honest, and nonpartisan national discussion leading up to Election Day 2000. The website is one of the best-organized on national and international topics.

COMMUNICATIONS C
ONSORTIUM AND
MEDIA CENTER
1333 H Street NW, Suite 700
Washington, D.C., 20005
Tel: (202) 682-1270
Fax: (202) 682-2154
Website: www.womenofcolor.org/about.html

COMMUNITY MEDIA
WORKSHOP
Columbia College
600 South Michigan Avenue
Chicago, IL 60605-1996
Tel: (312) 344-6400
Fax: (312) 344-6404
E-mail: Cmw@newstips.org
Website: www.newstips.org

Trains community organizations and civic groups to use media more effectively and helps journalists learn of their stories. Publishers of *Getting on the Air & Into Print*, a 200-page citizen's guide to media in the Chicago-area.

CULTURAL ENVIRONMENT
MOVEMENT (CEM)
Publishes the *Cultural
Environment Monitor*
3508 Market Street, Suite 3-030
Phildelphia, PA 19104
Tel: (215) 204-6434
Fax: (215) 387-1560
E-mail: ggerbner@nimbus.Temple.edu

A broad-based international coalition of citizens, scholars, activists, and media professionals who promote democratic principles in the cultural environment.

DEMOCRACY NOW!
Website: www.webactive.com/pacifica/demnow.html

Launched by Pacifica Radio in 1996 to open the airwaves on a daily basis to alternative voices traditionally excluded from the political proces. Programs with Amy Goodman are now available online.

DIRECT ACTION MEDIA
NETWORK (DAMN)
Website: www.damn.tao.ca

An online multimedia news service that covers direct actions that progressive organizations and individuals toake to attain a peaceful, open enlightened society.

DISABILITY MEDIA PROJECT
Contact: Suzanne Levine
P.O. Box 22115
San Francisco, CA 94122-0115
Tel: (415) 387-0617
Fax: (415) 387-0583
Website: www.dmedia.org

Disability Media Project was founded to challenge and assist media educators, the news media and creative media in fostering fair representation of people with disabilities.

DOWNTOWN
COMMUNITY CENTER
87 Lafayette Street
New York, NY 10013
Tel: (212) 966-4510
Fax: (212) 219-0248
E-mail: Wed@dctvny.org
Website: www.dctvny.org

Founded in 1972, DCTV believes that expanding public access to the electronic media arts invigorates our democracy. DCTV pursus a grasroots mission to teach people, particularly members of low-income and minority communites, how to use media.

EARTH FIRST!
P.O. Box 1415
Eugene, OR
Tel: (541) 344-8004
Fax: (541) 344-7688
E-mail: earthfirst@igc.apc.org
Website: envirolink.org/orgs/es

The voice of the radical environmental movement

ECONOMIC POLICY INSTITUTE
1660 L Street NW
Washington, D.C. 20036
Tel: (202) 331-5549
Fax: (202) 775-0819
Website: epinet.org

Its mission is to broaden public debate over economic policy to better serve the needs of America's working people. It also seeks to expose the myths behind the supposed success of the neoliberal economic paradigm.

ELECTRONIC FRONTIER
FOUNDATION
1550 Bryant Street, Suite 725
San Francisco, CA 94103
Tel: (415) 436-9333
Fax: (415) 436-9993
E-mail: Eff@eff.org
Website: www.eff.org

A leading civil liberites organization devoted to maintaining the Internet as a global vehicle for free speech.

FAIRNESS AND ACCURACY
IN REPORTING (FAIR)
130 West 25th Street
New York, NY 10001
Tel: (212) 633-6700
Fax: (212) 727-7668
E-mail: Fair@fair.org
Website: www.fair.org

A national media watchdog group that focuses public awareness on "the narrow corporate ownership of the press," FAIR seeks to invigorate the First Amendment by advocating for greater media pluralism and the inclusion of public interest voices in national debate.

FEMINISTS FOR
FREE EXPRESSION
2525 Times Square Station
New York, NY 10108
Tel: (212) 702-6292
Fax: (212) 702-6277
E-mail: Freedom@well.com
Website: www.well.com/user/freedom

A national nonprofit organization of feminist women and men who share a commitment both to gender equality and to preserving the individual's right to read, view, rent, or purchace media materials of their choice, free from government intervention.

FOOD NOT BOMBS
P.O. Box 40485
San Francisco, CA 94140
Tel: (650) 985-7087
E-mail: sffnb@iww.org
Website: webcom.com/peace/

An organization that focuses on peaceful cooperation and eliminating hunger.

FREE SPEECH TV
P.O. Box 6060
Boulder, CA 80306
Tel: (303) 442-8445
Fax: (303) 442-6472
E-mail: Programming@sftv.org
Website: www. freespeech.org

Progressive voice in the media revolution bringing activist& alternative mdia into seven million homes each week.

FREEDOM FORUM WORLD CENTER
1101 Wilson Boulevard
Arlington, VA 22209
Tel: (703) 528-0800
Fax: (703) 522-4831
E-mail: News@freedomforumu.org
Website: www.freedomforum.org

A nonpartisan, international foundation dedicated to free press, free speech and free spirit for all people.

FREEDOM OF EXPRESSION
FOUNDATION
171-B Claremont Avenue
Long Beach, CA 90803
Tel: (562) 434-2284

E-mail: crsmith@csulb.edu
Website: www.csulb.edu/~research/
Cent/lamend.html

FREEDOM OF
INFORMATION CENTER
University of Missouri at Columbia
127 Neff Annex
Columbia, MO 65211
Tel: (573) 882-4856
Fax: (573) 884-4963
E-mail:
Kathleen_Edwards@jmail.jour.
missouri.edu
Website: www.missouri.edu/~foiwww

The Freedom of Information Center collects and indexes materials relating to controls on the flow and content of information to research free-press issues.

FREEDOM OF INFORMATION
CLEARINGHOUSE
P.O. Box 19367
Washington, D.C. 20036
Tel: (202) 588-7790
E-mail: foia@citizen.org
Website: www.citizen.org/public_
citizen/litigation/foic/foic.html

FREEDOM TO READ FOUNDATION
Judith Krug, Executive Director
and Secretary
50 East Huron Street
Chicago, IL 60611
Tel: (312) 280-4226
Fax: (312) 280-4227
E-mail: Ftrf@ala.org
Website: www.ftrf.org

Promotes and protects freedom of spech and freedom of the press; protects the public's right to access to librariees, supplies, legal counsel, and otherwise supports libraries and librarians suffering injustices due to their defense of freedom of speech and of the press (run by ALA, but a separate organization does First Amendment litigation).

FRIENDS OF FREE SPEECH RADIO
905 Parker Street
Berkeley, CA 94710
Tel: (510) 548-0542
E-mail: savepacifica@peacenet.org
Website: www.savepacifica.net

Founded in April 1999, working to preserve community radio stations owned by Pacifica, and to institute democratic practice in their governance.

FUND FOR INVESTIGATIVE
JOURNALISM
5120 Kenwood Drive
Annandale, VA 22003
Tel: (703) 750-3849
Website: www.fij.org

GLOBAL EXCHANGE
An active participant in the
"50 Years Is Enough" campaign
2017 Mission Street, Suite 303
San Francisco, CA 94110
Tel: (415) 255-7296
Fax: (415) 255-7498
E-mail: info@globalexchange.org
Website: www.globalexchange.org

Global Exchange publishes books and pamphlets on various social and economic topics; promotes alternative trade for the benefit of low-income producers; helps build public awareness about human rights abuses; and sponsors Reality Tours to foreign lands, giving participants a feel for the people of a country.

GLOBALVISION, INC.
1600 Broadway, Suite 700
New york, NY 10019
Tel: (212) 246-0202
Fax: (212) 246-2677
Website: www.globalvision.org &
mediachannel.org

An independent international media
company specializing in an "inside-out"
style of journalism. It has produced
"Rights & Wrongs: Human Rights
Television" and "South Africa Now,"
along with many highly acclaimed
investigative documentaries; and has
recently launched an Internet supersite
focusing on global media issues.

THE GRASSROOTS
MEDIA NETWORK
1602 Chatham
Austin, TX 78723
Tel: (512) 459-1619
E-mail: gnn@grassrootsnews.org
Website: www.onr.com/user/gnn

Grassroots News Network, Queer News
Network, Pueblos-Unidos. Grassroots
film and video collective.

GREENPEACE USA
1436 U Street NW
Washington, D.C. 20009
Tel: (202) 462-1177
Fax: (202) 462-4507
Website: www.greenpeaceusa.org

Its purpose is to create a green and
peaceful world. Greenpeace embraces
the principle of nonviolence, rejecting
attacks on people and property. It allies
itself with no political party and takes
no political stance.

HISPANIC EDUCATION

AND MEDIA GROUP, INC.
P.O. Box 221
Sausalito, CA 94966
Tel: (415) 331-8560
Fax: (415) 331-2636
E-mail: margotsegura@yahoo.com

Dedicated to improving the quality of
life in the Latino community with main
focus on high school dropout prevention
and health issues.

HUCK BOYD NATIONAL CENTER
FOR COMMUNITY MEDIA
Kansas State University
105 Kedzie Hall
Manhattan, KS 66506
Tel: (913) 532-6890
Fax: (913) 532-5484
E-mail: Huckboyd@ksu.edu
Website: www.jnc.ksu.edu/~hbnc/
hbnc.html

The mission of HBNC is to strenghten
local media in order to help create better, stronger communites in America.

INDEPENDENT PRESS
ASSOCIATION
2390 Mission Street #201
San Francisco, CA 94110
Tel: (415) 643-4401
E-mail: indypress@indypress.org
Website: www.indypress.org

A membership-based association providing nuts-and-bolts technical assistance, loans. and networking to over 175
independent, progressive magazines
and newspapers. Formed during the first
Media & Democracy Congress in San
Francisco (1996), the IPA promotes a
diversity of voices of the newstand.

INSTITUTE FOR
PUBLIC ACCURACY
65 Ninth Street, Suite 3
San Francisco, CA 94103
Tel: (415) 552-5378
Fax: (415) 552-6787
E-mail: Institute@igc.org
Website: www.accuracy.org

Serves as a nationwide consortium of progressive policy researchers, scholars, and activists providing the media with timley information and perspectives on a wide range of issues.

INSTITUTE FOR
ALTERNATIVE JOURNALISM
77 Federal Street
San Francisco, CA 94107
Tel: (415) 284-1420
Fax: (415) 284-1414
E-mail: alternet@alternet.org
Website: www.mediademocracy.org

INSTITUTE FOR MEDIA ANALYSIS
145 4th Street
New York, NY 10012
Tel: (212) 254-1061
Fax: (212) 254-9598

INSTITUTE FOR MEDIA POLICY
AND CIVIL SOCIETY
207 W. Hastings Street, Suite 910
Vancouver, British Columbia V6B 1H6
Tel: (604) 682-1953
Fax: (604) 683-4353
E-mail: Media@impacs.org
Website: www.impacs.bc.ca

The society's mission is to build strong communites by training and educating Canadian civil society organizations.

INSTITUTE FOR POLICY STUDIES
733 15th Street NW, Suite 1020
Washington, D.C. 20005
Tel: (202) 234-9382
Fax: (202) 387-7915
E-mail: Ipsps@igc.apc.org
Website: www.ips.dc.org

Since 1963, IPS has been the nation's leading center of progressive research link to activism.

INTERNATIONAL ACTION CENTER
39 West 14th Street, # 206
New York, NY 10011
Tel: (212) 633-6646
Fax: (212) 633-2889
E-mail: Iacenter@iacenter.org
Website: www.iacenter.org

Initiated in 1992 by former Attorney General Ramsey Clark and other antiwar activists, IAC coordinates international meetings, teach-ins, massive demonstrations, publishes news releases, and produces video documentaries.

INTERNATIONAL CONSORTIUM
OF INVESTIGATIVE JOURNALISTS
(ICIJ)
Center for Public Integrity
1634 I Street NW, Suite 902
Washington, D.C. 20006
Tel: (202) 783-3900
Fax: (202) 783-3906
E-mail: info@icij.org
Website: www.icij.org

ICIJ is a working consortium of leading investigative reporters from around the world that sponsors investigations into pressing issues which transcend national borders.

INVESTIGATIVE JOURNALISM
PROJECT
Fund for Constitutional Government
122 Maryland Avenue NE, Suite 300
Washington, D.C. 20002
Tel: (202) 546-3732
Fax: (202) 543-3156

THE INVESTIGATIVE
REPORTING FUND (FIRE)
2 Wall Street, Suite 203
Asheville, NC 28801-2710
Tel: (704) 259-9179
Fax: (704) 251-1311
E-mail: calvina@main.nc.us
Website: www.main.nc.us/fire

JUST THINK FOUNDATION
80 Liberty Ship Way, Suite 1
Sausalito, CA 94965
Tel: (415) 289-0122
Fax: (415) 289-0123
E-mail: think@justthink.org
Website: www.justthink.org

KLANWATCH AND
MILITIA TASKFORCE
Southern Poverty Law Center
400 Washington Avenue
Montgomery, AL 36104
Tel: (334) 264-0286
Fax: (334) 264-8891
Website: www.splcenter.org/splc.html

LONG ISLAND
ALTERNATIVE MEDIA
120 Orleans Lane
Jericho, NY 11753
Tel: (516) 822-2582
E-mail: robmgold@sec.net

Focuses on the production and distribution of progressive educational material. Members have participated in a

number of radio and public access cable
projects.

LOOMPANICS UNLIMITED
P.O. Box 1197
Port Townsend, WA 98368
Tel: (360) 385-2230
Fax: (360) 385-7785
E-mail: loompanix@olympus.net
Website: www.loompanics.com

Champions of the First Amenment, LU
publishes and sells publications covering a variety of controversial topics. Has
an online catalogue.

LOS ANGELES ALTERNATIVE
MEDIA NETWORK
8124 West Third Street, Suite 208
Los Angeles, CA 90048
E-mail: laamn-announce@egroups.com

A network of journalists in print, radio,
video, and on the Internet, dedicated to
creating a democratic media by increasing the coverage of those whom the
media would otherwise ignore. Through
media outlets, they provide a voice for
the voiceless, and produce the stories
that remain untold.

MEDIA ACCESS PROJECT
1707 L Street NW
Washington, D.C. 20036
Tel: (202) 232-4300
Fax: (202) 223-5302
E-mail: www.mediaaccess.org/

MEDIA ACTION RESEARCH
CENTER (MARC)
475 Riverside Drive #1948
New York, NY 10115
Tel: (212) 870-3802
Fax: (212) 870-2171

MEDIA ALLIANCE
Publication: *Mediafile*
814 Mission Street, Suite 205
San Francisco, CA 94103
Tel: (415) 546-6334
Fax: (415) 546-6218
E-mail: ma@igc.org
Website: www.media-alliance.org

Review and analysis of San Francisco
Bay Area media isues.

MEDIA COALITION/AMERICANS
FOR CONSTITUTIONAL FREEDOM
139 Fulton Street, Suite 302
New York, NY 10038
Tel: (212) 587-4025
Fax: (212) 587-2436
E-mail: mediacoalition@mediacoalition.
org
Website: www.mediacoalition.org

An organization that defends the American public's First Amendment right to
have access to the broadest possible
range of opinion and entertainment.

THE MEDIA CONSORTIUM
2200 Wilson Boulevard, Suite 102–231
Arlington, VA 22201
Tel: (703) 920—1580
Fax: (703) 920-0946
E-mail: Rparry@ix.netcom.com
Website: www.consortiumnews.com

An independent investigative news
company.

THE MEDIA & DEMOCRACY INSTI-
TUTE
77 Federal Street
San Francisco, CA 94107
Tel: (415) 284-1420
Fax: (415) 284-1414
E-mail: congress@igc.org

Website: www.alternet.org/an/Congress.
html

THE MEDIA EDUCATION
FOUNDATION
26 Center Street
Northampton, MA 01060
Tel: (800) 897-0089
or (413) 584-8500
Fax: (800) 659-6882
or (413) 586-8398
E-mail: mediaed@mediaed.org
Website: www.mediaed.org

MEF provides media research and
production fostering analytical media
literacy. It has produced and distributed
a number of educational videos including "The Myth of the Liberal Media"
(with Noam Chomsky and Ed Herman),
"Killing Us Softly III" (with Jean Kil-
bourne), and "Tough Guise: Violence,
Media & the Crisis of Masculinity" (with
Jackson Katz).

MEDIA ISLAND INTERNATIONAL
P.O. Box 7204
Olumpia, WA 98507
Tel: (360) 352-8526
E-mail: mii@olywa.net
Website: www.mediaisland.org

MII works to popularize social, political
justice and environmental frontline
issues by helping coordinate issue-
focused organizations with media organizations and mapping allies for change
internationally.

MEDIA NETWORK
Alternative Media Information Center
2565 Broadway, #101
New York, NY 10025
Tel: (212) 501-3841

MEDIACHANNEL
Website produced by
Globalvision New Media
1600 Broadway #700
New York, NY 10019
Website: www.mediachannel.org

An online global media supersite.

MEDIAVISION
P.O. Box 1045
Boston, MA 02130
Tel: (617) 522-2923
Fax: (617) 522-1872
E-mail: mediavi@aol.com

Working for wider exposure of progressive views through mass media,
MediaVision provides strategic media
consulting, training, and other services
for organizations and individuals.

MOSAIC TV
P.O. Box 7740
Chicago, IL 60680
Tel: (888) 667-2423 or (773) 933-9776
Website: www.mosaictv.com

Provides the global truth perspective for
black people, featuring video lectures,
research and coverage of news that is
ignored or purposefully hidden by
mainstream media.

NATIONAL ASIAN AMERICAN
TELECOMMUNICATION
ASSOCIATION
346 9th Street, 2nd Floor
San Francisco, CA 94103
Tel: (415) 863-0814
Fax: (415) 863-7428
Website: www.naatanet.org

An organization seeking to increase
Asian and Pacific Islanders' participation
in the media and the promotion of fair and
accurate coverage of these communities.

NATIONAL ASSOCIATION
OF BLACK JOURNALISTS
8701A Adelphi Road
Adelphi, MD 20783-1716
Tel: (301) 445-7100
Fax: (301) 445-7101
E-mail: nabj@nabj.org
Website: www.nabj.org

Its mission is to strengthen ties among
African-American journalists, promote
diversity in newsrooms, and expand job
opportunities and recruiting activities
for established African-American journalists and students.

NATIONAL ASSOCIATION
OF HISPANIC JOURNALISTS
National Press Building, Suite 1193
Washington, D.C. 20045
Tel: (888) 346-NAHJ or (202) 662-7145
Fax: (202) 662-7144
E-mail: nahj@nahj.org
Website: www.nahj.org

NAHJ is dedicated to the recognition
and professional advancement of Hispanics in the news industry.

NATIONAL ASSOCIATION OF
MINORITY MEDIA EXECUTIVES
5746 Union Mill Road, Box 310
Clifton , VA 20124
Tel: (703) 830-4743

NATIONAL ASSOCIATION
OF RADIO TALK SHOW HOSTS
Trade Association for
Radio Talk Industry
1030 15th Street NW, Suite 700
Washington, D.C. 20005

Tel: (202) 408-8255
Fax: (202) 408-5788
E-mail: nashe@priority1.net
Website: www.talkshowhosts.com

Provides a resource guide to talk radio worldwide.

NATIONAL CAMPAIGN
FOR FREEDOM OF EXPRESSION
918 F Street NW, #609
Washington, D.C. 20004
Tel: (202) 393-2787
Fax: (202) 347-7376
E-mail: ncfe@artswire.org
Website: www.artswire.org/~ncfe/

The NCFE is an educational and advocacy network of artists, arts organizations, audience members and concerned citizens formed to protect and extend freedom of artistic expression and fight censorship throughout the United States.

NATIONAL COALITION
AGAINST CENSORSHIP
275 7th Avenue, 20th Floor
New York, NY 10001
Tel: (212) 807-6222
Fax: (212) 807-6245
E-mail: ncac@ncac.org
Website: www.ncac.org

Founded in 1974, NCAC is an alliance of over 40 national nonprofit organizations. It works to educate members and the public at large about the dangers of censorship and how to oppose it.

NATIONAL CONFERENCE
OF EDITORIAL WRITERS
6223 Executive Boulevard
Rockville, MD 20852
Tel: (301) 984-3015

NATIONAL EDUCATIONAL
MEDIA NETWORK
655 13th Street, Suite 1
Oakland, CA 94612
Tel: (510) 465-6885
Fax: (510) 465-2835
E-mail: nemn@nemn.org
Website: www.nemn.org

NATIONAL FORUM
ON INFORMATION LITERACY
American Library Association
50 East Huron Street
Chicago, IL 60611

NATIONAL LESBIAN
AND GAY JOURNALISTS
ASSOCIATION
1718 M Street NW, #245
Washington, D.C. 20036
Tel: (202) 588-9888
Fax: (202) 588-1818
E-mail: nlgja@aol.com
Website: www.n/gja.org

NATIONAL TELEMEDIA
COUNCIL
Publication: *Telemedium*,
the journal of media literacy
120 East Wilson Street
Madison, WI 53703
Tel: (608) 257-7712
Fax: (608) 257-7714
E-mail: NTelemedia@aol.com
Website: danenet.widip.org./ntc

NTC is a national nonprofit educational organization that promotes media literacy education with a positive, nonjudgmental philosophy. The oldest national media literacy organization in the U.S., it is in its forty-fifth year.

NATIONAL WOMEN'S
HEALTH NETWORK
Publication: *The Network News*
1325 G Street NW
Washington, D.C. 20005
Tel: (202) 347-1140
Fax: (202) 347-1168

National center focusing on women's health and related issues. Publishes a bimonthly newsletter for members.

NATIONAL WRITERS UNION
113 University Place, 6th floor
New York, NY 10003
Tel: (212) 254-0279
Fax: (212) 254-0673
E-mail: nwu@nwu.org
Website: www.nwu.org/nwu/

NWU's national quarterly, *American Writer*, tracks developments in the media/information industry and the labor movement that concern working writers, and reports on union activities.

NEW MEXICO MEDIA
LITERACY PROJECT
6400 Wyoming Boulevard, NE
Albuquerque, NM 87109
Tel: (505) 828-3129
Fax: (505) 828-3320
Website: www.nmmlp.org

NEWSWATCH CANADA
School of Communication
Simon Fraser University
8888 University Drive
Burnaby, British Columbia V5A 1S6
Tel: (604) 291-4905
Fax: (604) 291-4024
E-mail: censored@sfu.ca
Website:
newswatch.cprost.sfu.ca/newswatch

NICAR: NATIONAL
INSTITUTE FOR
COMPUTER-ASSISTED
REPORTING
University of Missouri
138 Neff Annex
Columbia, MO 65211
Tel: (573) 882-2042
Fax: (573) 882-5431
E-mail: ourire@muccmail.missouri.edu
Website: www.nicar.org

PACIFIC NEWS SERVICE
Publications:
The Beat Within, Yo!,
and *New California*
450 Mission Street, Room #204
San Francisco,, CA 94105
Tel: (415) 438-4755 or 243-4364
Fax: (415) 438-4935
E-mail: pacificnews@pacificnews.org
Website: www.pacificnews.org/ncm

Produces an article per day for reprint in a variety of newspapers worldwide.

THE PAUL ROBESON FUND
FOR INDEPENDENT MEDIA
THE FUNDING EXCHANGE
Publication: *Funding Exchange*
666 Broadway, #500
New York, NY 10012
Tel: (212) 529-5300
E-mail: jan.strout@fex.org
Website: www.fex.org\robeson

The PR Fund supports media activism and grassroots organizing by local, state, national or international organizations and individual media producers by funding radio, film and video productions.

PEACE ACTION
1819 H Street NW, Suite 420
Washington, D.C. 20006-3606
Tel: (202) 862-9740
Fax: (202) 862-9762
Website: www.webcom.com/peaceact/

PRISON NEWS SERVICE
P.O. Box 5052 Station A
Toronto, Ontario M5W 1W4

PROGRESSIVE MEDIA PROJECT
409 East Main Street
Madison, WI 53703
Tel: (608) 257-4626
Fax: (608) 257-3373
E-mail: pmproj@itis.com
Website: www.progressive.org/media-aproject.html

It provides opinion pieces from a progressive perspective to daily and weekly newspapers all over the country.

PROJECT CENSORED
Sociology Department
Sonoma State University
1801 East Cotati Avenue
Rohnert Park, CA 94928-3609
Tel: (707) 664-2500
Fax: (707) 664-2108
E-mail: project.censored@sonoma.edu
Website: www.sonoma.edu/Project-Censored

PUBLIC CITIZEN
Global Trade Watch
215 Pennsylvania Avenue SE
Washington, D.C. 20003
Tel: (202) 546-4996
Fax: (202) 547-7392
Website: www.citizen.org

PUBLIC CITIZEN
Litigation Group
1600 20th Street NW
Washington, D.C. 20009-1001
Tel: (202) 588-1000
Website: www.citizen.org

PUBLIC MEDIA CENTER
446 Green Street
San Francisco, CA 94133
Tel: (415) 434-1403
Fax: (415) 986-6779

REPORTER'S COMMITTEE
FOR FREEDOM OF THE PRESS
Publications: *News Media Update*
and *News Media and The Law*
1101 Wilson Boulevard, Suite 1910
Arlington, VA 22209
Tel: (703) 807-2100
Fax: (703) 807-2109

SOCIETY OF ENVIRONMENTAL
JOURNALISTS
Publication: *SEJournal*
P.O. Box 27280
Philadelphia, PA 19118-0280
Tel: (215) 836-9970
Fax: (215) 836-9972
E-mail: SEJoffice@aol.com
Website: www.sej.com

Dedicated to supporting environmental journalists and furthering environmental journalism.

SOUTHWEST ALTERNATIVE
MEDIA PROJECT
1519 West Main Street
Houston, TX 77006
Tel: (713) 522-8592
Fax: (713) 522-0953
E-mail: cyberia@swamp.org
Website: www.swamp.org

THE TELEVISION PROJECT
2311 Kimball Place
Silver Springs, MD 20910
Tel: (301) 588-4001
Fax: (301) 588-4001
E-mail: mapluhar@tvp.org
Website: www.tvp.org

THIRD WORLD NETWORK
228 Macalister Road
Penang, Malaysia
Tel: (+60) 4 373-511
Fax: (+60) 4 368-106

UNION PRODUCERS AND
PROGRAMMERS NETWORK
Labor Education Services
437 Management
& Economics Building
University of Minnesota
271 18th Avenue South
Minneapolis, MN 55455
Tel: (612) 624-4326
E-mail: jsee@csom.umn.edu
or uppnet@labornet.org
Website:
www.mtn.org/jsee/uppnet.html

Organized to promote production and
use of TV and radio shows pertinent to
the cause of organized labor and working people. Publishes *UPPNET News*.

WE INTERRUPT
THIS MESSAGE
965 Mission Street
Suite 220
San Francisco, CA 94103
Tel: (415) 537-9437
Fax: (415) 537-9439
E-mail: interrupt@igc.org

Interrupt builds capacity in public
interest groups to do traditional media

and publicity work as well as to reframe
public debate and interrupt media
stereotypes.

WHISPERED MEDIA
P.O. Box 40130
San Francisco, CA 94140
Tel: (415) 626-4942 or 789-8484
Website: www.whisperedmedia.org

Produces activist videos; is a member of
Video Activist Network.

WOMEN FOR MUTUAL SECURITY
Women's Peace Movement
and MEDIA
5110 West Penfield Road
Columbia, MD 21045
Tel: (410) 730-7483
Fax: (410) 964-9248
E-mail: foerstel@aol.com
Website: www.iacenter.org/wms/

WMS is a network of women's organizations and individuals committed to
making a paradigm shift in the world
from a heirarchical and violent mode of
society to a new cooperative and peaceful model.

WOMEN'S INSTITUTE
FOR FREEDOM OF THE PRESS
3306 Ross Place NW
Washington, D.C. 20008-3332
Tel: (202) 966-7783
Fax: (202) 966-7783
E-mail: wifponline@igc.apc.org
Website: www.igc.org/wifp/

Explores ways to assure that everyone
has equal access to the public, speaking for themselves, so everyone's information can be taken into account in
decision-making.

WORLD PRESS FREEDOM
COMMITTEE
The Newspaper Center
11600 Sunrise Valley Drive
Reston, VA 22091
Tel: (703) 715-9811
Fax: (703) 620-6790
E-mail: freepress@wpfc.org

A coordination group of national and
international news media organizations,
WPFC is an umbrella organization that
includes 44 journalistic organizations
united in the defense and promotion of
freedom.

About the Editor/Director

Peter Phillips is an Associate Professor of Sociology at Sonoma State University and Director of Project Censored. He teaches classes in Media Censorship, Power, Class Stratification, and Social Welfare. This is his fifth edition of *Censored: The News That Didn't Make the News* from Seven Stories Press. Also from Seven Stories Press is Project Censored's *Progressive Guide to Alternative Media and Activism* 1999.

Phillips writes op-ed pieces in the alternative press and independent newspapers nationwide having published in *Z* magazine, *Social Policy* and numerous independents. He frequently speaks on media censorship, and various sociopolitical issues on radio and TV talks shows including *Talk of the Nation*, *Public Interest*, *Talk America*, *World Radio Network*, *Democracy Now!*, and the *Jim Hightower Show*.

Phillips had a long career in human service administration. His experiences include two and half decades of community service and social activism, including serving as a War on Poverty administrator, Head Start director, and refugee assistance consultant.

Phillips earned a B.A. degree in Social Science in 1970 from Santa Clara University, and an M.A. degree in Social Science from California State University at Sacramento in 1974. He earned a second M.A. in Sociology in 1991 and a Ph.D. in Sociology in 1994. His doctoral dissertation was entitled A Relative Advantage: Sociology of the San Francisco Bohemian Club.

Phillips is a fifth generation Californian, who grew up on a family-owned farm west of the Central Valley town of Lodi. Phillips lives today in rural Sonoma County with his wife Mary Lia-Phillips and their two cats moon and gray and four pet chickens: Millie, Lilly, Dilly, and Booster.

Index

New Guinea, 43
New World Information and
Communication Order (NWICO),
312-313, 316, 320
NAFTA, 11, 40-41, 172, 244, 248
Nike, 70, 287, 298
Nixon, Richard, 92, 143, 167, 217,
242, 244, 254, 328
Nuclear Information and Resource
Service, 52
Oaks, David, 59, 61, 63
Occidental Oil, 11
Occupational Safety and Health
Administration (OSHA), 7, 44-45,
114, 149-150, 202, 208, 222
Office of Solid Waste, 75
Ogata, Sadako, 69
Organization for African Unity (OAU),
52, 54
Orwell, George, 281
Oswald, Donald, 45
Pacifica Radio, 19, 71, 170, 212, 250,
351, 353
Palestinian situation, 31-33, 117
Palestinian Authority, 117
Parenti, Christian, 84
Parenti, Michael, 8, 13, 16, 19, 135,
184, 190
PCBs, 100, 230, 248
People's Communication Charter
(PCC), 307, 314, 321
Perot, Ross, 111
Physicians Committee for Responsible
Medicine (PCRM), 109-110
Pitt, Brad, 252, 255, 258
Pomper, Stephen, 59, 61
Posada, Eduardo, 92
Pot, Pol, 266-268, 270, 273
Powell, Colin, 190, 263, 282-283
President's Council on Sustainable
Development, 75
Princess Diana, 252

Program of Assertive Community
Treatment (PACT), 60, 137, 226,
243
Prostate cancer, 142
Psychological operations (Psyops),
7, 46-47, 106
Public Citizen, 46, 61, 78, 239, 242,
339, 361
Pulitzer, Joseph, 255
Ramsey, JonBenet, 252, 255, 263-264
Reagan, Ronald, 28, 97, 108-109,
125, 214-216, 218-223, 225-226,
228, 234, 240, 259-261, 313
Reagan administration, 214-215, 219,
221-223, 225-226, 228, 240
Reform Party, 111
Reno, Janet, 130
Residents Against McDonald's, 104
Rio Tinto, 70
Risch, Peggy, 117
Rockwell International, 63, 218
Rockwell, Rick, 257
Rosset, Peter, 71
Rwanda, 7, 52-55
Rwandan Patriotic Army (RPA), 53
Sack, Steven, 124
Safer Guns Now, 111
Sanger, Margaret, 80
Scharf, Adria, 126
Schiller, Herbert, 221, 280
Schneider, Alison, 115
Seaman, Barbara, 8, 13, 16, 20, 135,
146, 148
Seattle, 11, 70, 73-74, 78, 88, 91,
114, 160, 172-175, 198, 287,
291-298, 300-302, 318, 331-332,
334-335, 343
Shaw, Larry, 8, 13, 16, 135, 173, 175
Shell, 70, 136-138, 244
Shimatsu, Yoichi, 48
Shiva, Vandana, 39
Shultz, Jim, 39, 42-43

United Nations (UN), 8, 40, 52-54, 68-71, 74, 77, 92, 101, 108, 158, 164, 166, 183-184, 186, 188, 191, 194-196, 204-205, 212, 215, 228, 237, 241, 267-268, 272, 275, 293

United Nations Children's Fund (UNCF), 77

United States Department of Agriculture (USDA), 109-110, 150, 231

United Steelworkers of America (USWA), 45-46, 124

Universal Declaration of Human Rights, 74

Unocal, 69-70, 136, 156

Urbina, Ian, 50-52

USAID, 13, 179-180, 182

USDA *see* United States Department of Agriculture

Vanishing Voter Project, 27, 29

Viacom, 107, 288

Vieques, Puerto Rico, 96

Violence against people with disabilities, 94-95

Voting Rights Act, 129-130, 132

Vujovic, Dusan, 85

Vukotic, Veselin, 85

Vulliamy, Ed, 91

Walters, Barbara, 258

Warwick, Hugh, 71

Waste Management, 63

West Timor, 274-275

Westinghouse, 50-51

Whittelsey, Frances Cerra, 99-101

Who Want's to Marry a Multimillionaire?, 252, 255

Who Wants to Be a Millionaire?, 252, 255, 257

Wilson, Bill, 63

Wilson, Kimberly, 87, 89-90

Wilson, Woodrow, 30

World Association for Christian Communication (WACC), 313, 315

World Bank, 30, 39-41, 70, 84-85, 113, 156, 178-179, 181-182, 190, 195, 198, 246, 270-271, 294, 298, 333, 345

World Water Forum, 41

World Trade Organization (WTO), 8, 11, 13, 40-41, 70, 73-74, 76-78, 87-88, 139-140, 160, 172-176, 195, 198, 291, 294, 301, 331-334

Zapatistas, 299

Zenger, John Peter, 281

Zoll, Daniel, 39

Zunes, Stephen, 71

How to Nominate a Censored Story

Some of the most interesting stories Project Censored evaluates are sent to us as nominations from people all over the world. These stories are clipped from small-circulation magazines or the back pages of local newspapers. If you see a story and wonder why it hasn't been covered in the mainstream media, we encourage you to send it to us as a Project Censored nomination. To nominate a *Censored* story send us a copy of the article and include the name of the source publication, the date that the article appeared, and the page number. If you see internet published news stories of which we should be aware please forward the URL to Censored@sonoma.edu.

CRITERIA FOR PROJECT CENSORED NEWS STORIES NOMINATIONS

1. A censored news story is one which contains information that the general United States population has a right and need to know, but to which it has had limited access.
2. The news story is timely, ongoing, and has implications for a significant number of residents of the United States.
3. The story has clearly defined concepts and is backed up with solid, verifiable documentation.
4. The news story has been publicly published, either electronically or in print, in a circulated newspaper, journal, magazine, newsletter, or similar publication from either a foreign or domestic source.
5. The news story has direct connections to and implications for people in the United States, which can include activities that U.S. citizens are engaged in abroad.

We evaluate stories year-round and each week post important underpublished stories on our World Wide Web at www.sonoma.edu/projectcensored. The final deadline for nominating a Most Censored Story of the year is announced on our website at www.projectcensored.org. Please send regular mail nominations to the address below or e-mail nominations to: censored@sonoma.edu. Our phone number for more information on Project Censored is (707) 664-2500.

> Project Censored Nominations
> Sonoma State University
> 1801 East Cotati Avenue
> Rohnert Park, CA 94928

Thank you for your support.

Peter Phillips
Director, Project Censored